The Beauty of the Lord is a t
thetics. Dr. Jonathan King
in a brilliant way but also

qualitatively expands and ̲_̲_̲_̲_̲_̲_̲_̲ ̲_̲_̲_̲_̲_̲_̲_̲_̲_̲_̲_̲ ̲a̲n̲d̲ ̲v̲i̲s̲i̲o̲n̲ ̲o̲f̲
the God of the Bible. Captivated by his arguments, attention to detail,
and logical and theological acuity, I found myself worshiping God as I
turned each page. Thank you, Dr. King!

Paul Shockley, Professor of Philosophy, Theology, and
Bible at the College of Biblical Studies-Houston and
Lecturer of Philosophy, Multidisciplinary Programs,
Stephen F. Austin State University

This is the kind of theology that edifies the church. While many theoretical discussions about certain far-flung doctrines may be hard to relate
to the everyday life of the Christian, this discussion of God's beauty
is different. Sound doctrine is always salutary, but it does not always
stir the heart. By way of contrast, this study of the beauty of the Lord
aims not only to give the reader right understanding, but also right
heartedness: a right perspective on and a passion for the fittingness of
God's plan of redemption.

Kevin J. Vanhoozer, Research Professor of Systematic Theology,
Trinity Evangelical Divinity School, Deerfield, Illinois

Truth and goodness are essential, but—in contrast with our forebears—
beauty seems to have been marginalized in modern Reformed and evangelical theology. This volume is therefore a serious contribution, filling
a lacuna in our systematic theology. Grounded in the triune Beauty,
revealed consummately in Christ, and informed by Balthasar and other
major interpreters of the catholic tradition, *The Beauty of the Lord* carves
out its own unique place in reflection on theological aesthetics. A feast
for the soul, this book will transform the way we think about God and
his works.

Michael Horton, J. Gresham Machen Professor of
Systematic Theology and Apologetics,
Westminster Seminary California

How can one not like a book that praises the beauty and glory of God and Christ? Even more, Professor King's thoroughgoing engagement of scriptural beauty—understood as the supreme fittingness of the scriptural "theodrama" for revealing Trinitarian beauty—unites the insights of classic Reformed theologians such as Jonathan Edwards and Herman Bavinck, along with the insights of a wide array of Reformed exegetes and theologians, with classical Catholic voices such as Anselm and Aquinas and contemporary Catholic theologians such as Hans Urs von Balthasar. The result is a display of ecumenical goodwill that, in praising divine beauty as manifested in the works of God, is itself beautiful!

Matthew Levering, James N. and Mary D. Perry Jr.
Chair of Theology, Mundelein Seminary,
University of Saint Mary of the Lake

The beauty of God is an area of theological reflection that has been ignored by theologians for much of the past two hundred and fifty years. It was probably in the mid-eighteenth century when this discussion was last a topic of significant reflection with Jonathan Edwards. In the past twenty years or so, though, the subject has been cropping up in various places, and I was thrilled to read this new work by Jonathan King on God's beauty. It is cogently argued from both Scripture and Church History, and will hopefully become a touchstone for future reflection and thought on this vital subject. Highly recommended.

Michael A. G. Haykin, Professor of Church History &
Director of The Andrew Fuller Center for Baptist Studies,
The Southern Baptist Theological Seminary,
Louisville, Kentucky

THE BEAUTY
of the LORD

Theology as Aesthetics

THE BEAUTY
of the LORD

Theology as Aesthetics

JONATHAN KING

STUDIES IN HISTORICAL AND SYSTEMATIC THEOLOGY

LEXHAM PRESS

The Beauty of the Lord: Theology as Aesthetics
Studies in Historical and Systematic Theology

Copyright © 2018 Jonathan King

Lexham Press, 1313 Commercial St., Bellingham, WA 98225
LexhamPress.com

Print ISBN 978-1-68-359058-3
Digital ISBN 978-1-68-359059-0

Lexham Editorial Team: Todd Hains, Jennifer Edwards, Michael Haykin
Typesetting: Beth Shagene

To my wife, Sharm—the Lord's precious gift to me.

You are my muse in all things beautiful, but more than that, the whole of my life with you is incomparably better than the sum of our lives individually, and that is a dimension of beauty I am so blessed to experience because of you.

Contents

Foreword

Of the three medieval "transcendentals," *beauty* typically takes third place in modern theology, behind *truth* and *goodness*. Many systematic theologies set forth the truth of Scripture; liberation theologies focus on the importance of doing what is good and right, especially pursuing justice, but few have taken up the cause of beauty. Many Christians associate beauty with a concern for aesthetics. And yet, while they would not deny that art and music and perhaps even architecture enhance worship, when the budget gets tough, the arts get cut.

Jonathan King's book is not about the arts. It is not about the beautiful things humans create in a variety of media (i.e., a theology of the arts). It is not about the beauty of the natural world (i.e., a natural theology of beauty). It is not an exercise in theological correlation (i.e., theology and the arts). Rather, it is a dogmatic account of the beauty of the Lord (i.e., it is a proposal about the doctrine of God). Beauty is not merely in the eye of the beholder (this way modern subjectivism lies); rather, beauty is in the being and activity of God, rooted in the divine attributes. Accordingly, King focuses on the beauty of the plan of God, the unified history of redemption recounted in the Scriptures and enacted in the history of Jesus Christ.

The main strength of this book—indeed, its peculiar beauty—lies in the way King unpacks the objective beauty of God in a threefold manner, namely, in terms of (1) God's own immanent triune life, (2) the display of God's own beauty in his external work, the economy of redemption that encompasses creation, salvation, and consummation, and (3) the person, work, and benefits of Jesus Christ, as the climax and coherence of the whole economy.

This work appeals above all to the person and work of Christ as the objective anchor to our understanding of beauty. In particular, King suggests that "fittingness with the history of Jesus Christ" is the biblical criterion for discerning the beauty of the Triune Lord (Eph 1:10). We know that the cross of Christ defines God's love and wisdom, and the fittingness of Jesus' death suggests that the cross, like everything God does, has its own peculiar beauty as well.

What I most appreciate and admire in this book is the way it unfolds the beauty of the Lord from Genesis (creation) to Revelation (consummation). Indeed, King is most persuasive in showing how protology anticipates eschatology and how eschatology recalls protology. This is a biblical theology of divine beauty that provides a beautiful frame for the portrait of beauty incarnate: the gospel of Jesus Christ. To put it in terms of the Gospel of Luke: "And beginning with Moses and all the Prophets, he interpreted to them in all the Scriptures the things concerning the beauty of the Lord."

I also appreciate and admire the way in which King keeps his eye on disciple-making. Though the present book may have started out as a doctoral dissertation, its significance goes far beyond the academic. This is the kind of theology that edifies the church. While many theoretical discussions about certain far-flung doctrines may be hard to relate to the everyday life of the Christian, this discussion of God's beauty is different. Sound doctrine is always salutary, but it does not always stir the heart. By way of contrast, this study of the beauty of the Lord aims not only to give the reader right understanding but also right heartedness: a right perspective on and a passion for the fittingness of God's plan of redemption.

If the church is the temple of God, then edification is not unrelated to beautification. King sees that disciples are called to become little Christs, that is, to embody the truth, goodness, and beauty of Jesus Christ as they conform their spirits to his. The point of focusing on the beauty of the Lord is to inspire readers to live fittingly at all times and places as followers of Jesus Christ, to the glory of God. That is beautiful indeed.

—Kevin J. Vanhoozer

Acknowledgments

My initial inspiration to explore the area of theological aesthetics really started as an initial curiosity during my final year and a half at Westminster Seminary California to try to understand how beauty pertains theologically to the core doctrines of the Christian faith. I am grateful to my professors at Westminster, Michael Horton and David VanDrunen, for granting me the latitude to explore the theology of Hans Urs von Balthasar in the research papers for my systematic theology courses. My curiosity to better understand beauty from a biblical and theological perspective became the key driving motivation for my pursuing this as the area of my doctoral research.

I am in debt to numerous persons who were so vital to my improving upon this project. I wish to express my deepest thanks to my doctoral advisor and mentor, Kevin Vanhoozer, whose insight, feedback, guidance, and modeling of Christian character and scholarship has been invaluable to me. I am likewise grateful to Graham Cole; I have learned and benefitted from his Christian wisdom. A number of friends deserve special mention as well. In particular I am grateful to Scott Harrower, Paul Manata, Hans Madueme, Brannon Ellis, and Jared Compton who served as trustworthy and tremendously helpful discussion and sparring partners for me. Their criticism, advice, and encouragement during the stage of my doctoral research remains imprinted on the substance and quality of this revised and expanded work. Beyond these, I also want to express my appreciation to Geoff Fulkerson, Jason Stanghelle, and Chris Donato whose camaraderie was a regular staple of intellectual sharpening and refreshment while I was completing my research and teaching at Trinity Evangelical Divinity School. The editorial process went exceptionally smooth in readying this book for publication. My sincere thanks to the editorial team at Lexham Press, and most especially Todd Hains, for not making my life harder than it otherwise might have gone, and for turning my work into such a beautiful book. Last but not least, I want to express my deepest love and gratitude to my wife Sharm, my precious companion and greatest encourager.

Abbreviations

AB	Anchor Bible
AH	Irenaeus of Lyons, *Against Heresies*, in *The Ante-Nicene Fathers*, vol. 1, eds. Alexander Roberts and James Donaldson (Buffalo, NY: Christian Literature, 1885; reprint, South Bend, IN: Ex Fontibus, 2010)
BDAG	W. Bauer, F. W. Danker, W. F. Arndt, and F. W. Gingrich, *A Greek-English Lexicon of the New Testament and Other Early Christian Literature*, 3rd ed. (Chicago/London: University of Chicago Press, 2000)
BSac	*Bibliotheca Sacra*
CBQ	*The Catholic Biblical Quarterly*
CD	Karl Barth, *Church Dogmatics*, ed. G. W. Bromiley and T. F. Torrance. trans. G. W. Bromiley (Edinburgh: T&T Clark, 1956–)
DBI	*Dictionary of Biblical Imagery*, ed. L. Ryken, J. C. Wilhoit and Tremper Longman III (Downers Grove, IL/Leicester, England: InterVarsity Press, 1998)
EBC	Expositor's Bible Commentary
ESV	English Standard Version
GL	Hans Urs von Balthasar, *The Glory of the Lord: A Theological Aesthetics*, Volumes I–VII (San Francisco: Ignatius Press, 1982–1991)
ICC	International Critical Commentary
IET	Francis Turretin, *Institutes of Elenctic Theology*, 3 vols., ed. James T. Dennison Jr., trans. George Musgrave Giger (Phillipsburg, NJ: P&R Publishing, 1992–1997)

IJST	*International Journal of Systematic Theology*
JBL	*Journal of Biblical Literature*
JETS	*Journal of the Evangelical Theological Society*
JSNT	*Journal for the Study of the New Testament*
JSNTSup	Journal for the Study of the New Testament: Supplement Series
JSOTSup	Journal for the Study of the Old Testament: Supplement Series
JSPL	*Journal for the Study of Paul and His Letters*
JTC	*Journal for Theology and the Church*
JTI	*Journal of Theological Interpretation*
L&N	Johannes P. Louw, and Eugene A. Nida, ed., *Greek-English Lexicon of the New Testament: Based on Semantic Domains*, 2nd ed. (New York: United Bible Societies, 1989), 2 vols.
LCC	The Library of Christian Classics
LXX	Septuagint
NDBT	*New Dictionary of Biblical Theology*
NEB	New English Bible
NET	New English Translation, 1st ed. (Biblical Studies Press, 2005)
NICNT	New International Commentary of the New Testament
NICOT	The New International Commentary on the Old Testament
NIDNTT	*The New International Dictionary of New Testament Theology*
NIDOTTE	*New International Dictionary of Old Testament Theology and Exegesis*
NIGTC	The New International Greek Testament Commentary
NIVAC	NIV Application Commentary
NovT	*Novum Testamentum*
NTS	*New Testament Studies*
PNTC	Pillar New Testament Commentary

PRRD	Richard Muller, *Post-Reformation Reformed Dogmatics: The Rise and Development of Reformed Orthodoxy, ca. 1520-1725*, 4 vols. (Grand Rapids: Baker Academic, 2003)
RD	Herman Bavinck, *Reformed Dogmatics*, 4 vols., ed. John Bolt, trans. John Vriend (Grand Rapids: Baker Academic, 2003-2008)
SBJT	*Southern Baptist Journal of Theology*
SBTS	*Sources for Biblical and Theological Study*
ST	Saint Thomas Aquinas, *Summa Theologica*, 5 vols., trans. Fathers of the English Dominican Province (Westminster, MD: Christian Classics, 1981 [1947])
TD	Hans Urs von Balthasar, *Theo-Drama: Theological Dramatic Theory*, Volumes I-V (San Francisco: Ignatius Press, 1988-1998)
TDNT	*Theological Dictionary of the New Testament*
THNTC	The Two Horizons New Testament Commentary
TL	Hans Urs von Balthasar, *Theo-Logic: Theological Logical Theory*, Volumes I-III (San Francisco: Ignatius Press, 2000-2005)
TynBul	*Tyndale Bulletin*
WBC	Word Biblical Commentary
WJE	Jonathan Edwards, *The Works of Jonathan Edwards*, 26 vols. (New Haven, CT: Yale University Press, 1957-2008)
WTJ	*Westminster Theological Journal*
WUNT	Wissenschaftliche Untersuchungen zum Neuen Testament
ZAW	*Zeitschrift für die alttestamentliche Wissenschaft*

Introduction

The intent of this work is to explore and develop a theology of beauty based on God's plan in Christ. Thus the nature of beauty, as defined by the divine economy of redemption, which sums all things up in Jesus Christ (Eph 1:10), is pursued in a specifically biblical and systematic way from beginning to end. The aesthetic dimension more broadly considered is a further motivating interest.[1] Karl Barth (1886–1968) poses a cogent rationale for this agenda, namely, that all concepts of universal significance need to be interrogated in terms of the name and the narrative of Jesus Christ.[2] Beauty counts here as one such concept. This project's agenda neither proposes nor advocates a critical "turn to aesthetics" for doing biblical and systematic theology. The lacuna that exists requires a recovery of and reinvigorated attention to theological aesthetics, but it does not require a methodological "turn" as such. What is advocated, however, is that the locus of beauty and the subject of theological aesthetics be given wider recognition and inclusion in the work and pedagogy of systematic theology within a broadly evangelical perspective. Why? At a minimum, so that we may gain a fuller appreciation of the sublimity of God's eternal plan, which reveals a consistent outworking of the beauty intrinsic to the Trinity. The Son incarnate is manifestly key to this outworking, for the economic Trinity "displays" in time the eternal beauty/fittingness of the immanent Trinity. With

---

1. The phrase "theology of beauty" in this work is used interchangeably with "theological aesthetics." As with the definitional distinction between metaphysic and metaphysics, a theological aesthetic denotes a system of theological aesthetics.

2. See Karl Barth, *CD*, IV/1, 16–17. I am indebted to Graham Cole for drawing this reference to my attention.

this appreciation we come to apprehend better the aesthetic entailment of how the whole of God's plan is incomparably greater than the sum of its parts.

THEOLOGIES OF AESTHETICS

"Theological aesthetics" does not imply there is homogeneity in the kind of theological scholarship on aesthetics that has been/is being done. On the contrary, the diversity of distinct theological approaches to the subject of aesthetics can only rightly be described as heterogeneous. Effectively there are four basic categories in terms of respective concerns and the ways theology applies and is integrated: (1) natural theology of beauty, (2) theology of the arts, (3) religious aesthetics, and (4) theological aesthetics. As employed here, these categories apply as pedagogical distinctions, if not formal ones, for distinguishing and describing the basic (even if in certain respects overlapping) differences. What is not subsumed or entailed in these categories is philosophical aesthetics since its focus and substance do not necessarily address specifically theological concerns.[3] It is not any of our interest, however, to provide a comparative evaluation of these theologies of aesthetics, nor explicate any of them except the last one that we are describing as theological aesthetics. For our purposes I wish only to provide a clear, though brief, description here of these four distinct categories so the reader will not mistakenly assume that all theological scholarship on aesthetics

---

3. Philosophical aesthetics certainly *may* address theological concerns, of course, but such scholarship can also be done under a fully secular or atheistic set of assumptions. Few would dispute that Immanuel Kant's *Critique of Judgment*, published in 1790, is the foundational treatise in modern philosophical aesthetics, setting the stage for the different schools of idealist aesthetic philosophies that followed in its wake (e.g., Hegel, Fichte, Schopenhauer, Schiller, and Schelling). Around the middle of the twentieth century, though, philosophical aesthetics began to be used in the wide sense of philosophy of art, where art nowadays is taken broadly to include literature, music, painting, sculpture, architecture, dance, theater, photography, and film. The aesthetics of nature and the environment, and the religious dimensions of art are sometimes treated too. Many topics of more general philosophical interest, such as the nature of representation, imagination, emotion, and expression are addressed in respect of their roles in the arts and artistic appreciation. For a recommended treatment of the development of the philosophy of art, see Noël Carroll, *Art in Three Dimensions* (Oxford: Oxford University Press, 2010).

pursues the same common concern or applies and integrates theology using a common approach. What I am putting forward is a properly dogmatic (i.e., Trinitarian) account of aesthetics.

Our first category, *natural theology of beauty*, seeks to give an account from the perceivable beauty of the natural world in attestation of the God that Christianity upholds and proclaims. The aim here is to provide evidential value in the cause of understanding-seeking-faith and/or apologetic value in the cause of faith-seeking-understanding. The affective power of beauty to elicit such visceral responses as "awe," "fear," and "wonder" is generally seen as substantiating the universal search for meaning and spiritual insight within human aesthetic experience. Natural theology of beauty often concerns the aesthetic dimension in relation to the natural and mathematical sciences as well. A common thrust concerning the perceivable order of nature is to emphasize a clear resonance with the transcendentals of truth, goodness, and beauty, along with the teleological character of creation.[4]

The second category, *theology of the arts*, seeks to understand the place of the arts in the life of faith and in the religious community. It is distinguished typically in terms of exploring the relationship between art and theology from the perspective of artistic technique, that is, the manner in which artwork or artistry is executed. It aims to arrive at conclusions about the capacity of genuine works of art; specifically, how all genuine art can function in its own way as a source of theology and spirituality. A Christian perspective informs one's artistic expression and endeavors in ways both creative and redemptive. According to theology of the arts, by the creative act the artist participates in the highest excellence of God, and this involvement is a basic fact of aesthetic expression for every instance of art.[5] The spiritual dimension in

---

4. Representative works concerning natural theology of beauty include: Alister E. McGrath, *The Open Secret: A New Vision for Natural Theology* (Malden, MA: Blackwell Publishing, 2008); Thomas Dubay, *The Evidential Power of Beauty: Science and Theology Meet* (San Francisco: Ignatius Press, 1999). For a recommended article addressing this category, see Ryan West and Adam C. Pelser, "Perceiving God through Natural Beauty," *Faith and Philosophy* 32 no. 3 (July 2015): 293–312.

5. The description used here is appropriated loosely from Christopher Evan Longhurst, "Discovering the Sacred in Secular Art: An Aesthetic Modality That 'Speaks of God,'" *American Theological Inquiry* 4 no. 1 (2011): 13–14.

all art is thus presumed to be salutary to one's spiritual formation as part of God's creative and redemptive purposes.[6]

Our next category, *religious aesthetics*, attempts to understand the nature of aesthetic phenomena in art and the natural world, but especially in relation to one's participation in religious traditions and expression. Such understanding is predicated chiefly on aesthetic perception and experience. Here, insight from Scripture may indeed inspire a greater sense of spirituality or worship, but aesthetically rich works of culture also serve as essential sources for enhancing and attuning our spiritual sensibilities. Thus, our growth in spiritual maturity is understood to be conditioned in some measure through appreciating such sources of culture. Religious aesthetics, then, seeks to understand and apply a subjective evaluation of the aesthetic dimension to enhance one's overall religious perspective, practice, and experience, as well as one's aesthetic appreciation of art and nature. There is a vital connection seen between our spiritual growth and reflection on the aesthetic best that culture has to offer. Indeed, in a post-Kantian context, religious aesthetics serves to repudiate a purely intellectualist approach to the world, interpenetrating as it were the spiritual dimension of the natural world, works of culture and art, and cultivating spirituality via aesthetic perception and experience.[7]

And lastly, our fourth category, *theological aesthetics,* is premised on the canon of Scripture being the norm that norms other norms (*norma normans*) over all matters pertaining to Christian doctrine and practice. Scripture's authority as such holds preeminence in how we interpret theologically everything considered general/natural revelation as well as expressions of culture.[8] By extension, biblical authority presides over the domain of aesthetics in its understanding of the whole

---

6. Representative works concerning theology of the arts include: Richard Viladesau, *Theology and the Arts: Encountering God through Music, Art, and Rhetoric* (New York: Paulist Press, 2000); Jeremy Begbie, ed., *Sounding the Depths: Theology Through the Arts* (London: SCM Press, 2002).

7. Representative works concerning religious aesthetics include: Frank Burch Brown, *Religious Aesthetics: A Theological Study of Making and Meaning* (New York: Oxford University Press, 1999); Aidan Nichols, *Redeeming Beauty: Soundings in Sacral Aesthetics* (Aldershot, Hants, England: Ashgate, 2007).

8. In short, general or natural revelation (in contrast to special revelation whose formal principle is the canon of Scripture) pertains to that available and

of creation—the *theatrum gloriae Dei*, as John Calvin (1509–1564) puts it.[9] The basic position of theological aesthetics, argued by reasonable inference from Scripture, is that beauty corresponds in some way to the attributes of God, and as such is a communicated property or phenomenon of the *opera Dei ad extra*. Inferred from the previous point is that the objective reality of beauty comes from its correspondence to the attributes of God; it is this correspondence that grounds a metaphysically realist view of beauty. In general terms, theological aesthetics derives from biblical- and systematic-theological work concerning or pertaining to the aesthetic dimension as integral to and as apprehended throughout the canon of Scripture. The fruit of theological aesthetics for theology more broadly is its consequent interpretation and implications for doctrine and practice. In this work, theological aesthetics is directed primarily on the objective beauty of the person of Christ, the beauty of the work of Christ (redemption accomplished), and the beauty of Christ's work ongoing through the Holy Spirit (redemption applied). The constructive development of this project involves a biblical-theological characterization of God's beauty—notably in and through God the Son—as reflected economically in the phases of creation, redemption, and consummation.[10] We want to be especially clear, however, that because the eternal beauty/fittingness of the immanent Trinity is manifest in the divine economy, the standard and substance of a theological aesthetic is the economic Trinity itself, with Scripture attesting to, and being itself an ingredient in, the economies of

apprehensible knowledge of God and the created order, evidenced in and through all creation, which God communicates in a universal fashion to all humanity.

9. See John Calvin, *Institutes of the Christian Religion* 1.5.1–2, 8, 10; 1.6.2; 1.14.20; 2.6.1, ed. John T. McNeill, trans. Ford Lewis Battles (LCC; Louisville: Westminster John Knox, 2006).

10. The definition of biblical theology this work assumes reflects that of B. S. Rosner, "Biblical Theology," in *NDBT*, ed. T. D. Alexander and B. S. Rosner (Downers Grove, IL: InterVarsity, 2000), 3–11, here 10: "What is biblical theology? To sum up, *biblical theology may be defined as theological interpretation of Scripture in and for the church. It proceeds with historical and literary sensitivity and seeks to analyze and synthesize the Bible's teaching about God and his relations to the world on its own terms, maintaining sight of the Bible's overarching narrative and Christocentric focus*" (emphasis in the original). As a single summary treatment, Geerhardus Vos, *Biblical Theology: Old and New Testaments* (Edinburgh: Banner of Truth Trust, 1975), 3–18, remains one of the most helpful discussions on the biblical theological method.

revelation and redemption. For theological aesthetics, then, the *sine qua non* of what makes our aesthetic reflection/perception "theological" is not, in the first place, Scripture but the divine economy.

These categorial distinctions also connote important differences concerning the authoritative norm applied in service of discovering theological/spiritual meaning in pursuit of their respective interests. The authoritative norms applied in the first three categories amount to natural revelation, artistic/creative expression, and aesthetic perception and experience respectively. These norms are not necessarily taken to be authoritative in the ultimate sense, but they are the norms applied to get at the meaning and apprehension of what each category is seeking to understand. For theological aesthetics, on the other hand, the canon of Scripture *is* the authoritative norm in the ultimate sense — norming all other norms — for its part in the economies of revelation and redemption. Scripture itself is thus the final court of appeal in any dispute between authorities, including tradition or reason or experience. This idea of an authoritative norm also bears upon the issue of hermeneutics, understood here in terms of methodological approaches for interpretation that seek to get at the best meaning and apprehension of something. In line with the canon of Scripture being the *norma normans* for theological aesthetics, the present work commends the canonical-linguistic approach. At the heart of the canonical-linguistic approach, explains Kevin Vanhoozer, "is the suggestion that the norm of Christian theology is a function of the way language is used in the biblical canon rather than ecclesial culture. The relationship between Scripture and church theology is asymmetrical: the wisdom embodied in the canon must govern the church's speech, thinking, and action today rather than vice versa."[11]

A brief word here about the general witness of Scripture to the aesthetic dimension is in order before we move on. The assertion above that theological aesthetics derives from biblical- and systematic-theological

---

11. Kevin J. Vanhoozer, *Faith Speaking Understanding: Performing the Drama of Doctrine* (Louisville: Westminster John Knox Press, 2014), 65, n40. For a thorough presentation of the canonical-linguistic approach, see Vanhoozer's earlier work, *The Drama of Doctrine: A Canonical-Linguistic Approach to Christian Theology* (Louisville: Westminster John Knox Press, 2005).

work concerning or pertaining to the aesthetic dimension in evidence throughout the canon of Scripture properly sets the stage to consider the following statement: "That the Bible is an ethical book is evident. Righteousness in all the relations of man as a moral being is the key to its inspiration, the guiding light to correct understanding of its utterance. But it is everywhere inspired and writ in an atmosphere of aesthetics."[12] At a minimum we may affirm that claim in the following sense: the Scriptures attest quite clearly to the beauty of the created order and describe throughout the biblical canon all manner of things in language denoting or connoting an aesthetic sense, not least "the beauty (נֹעַם) of the Lord" (Ps 27:4).[13] At the lexical level both the Old Testament and the New Testament reveal a rich vocabulary of terms that convey a sense of beauty or aesthetics. An abbreviated summary of such terms, along with a selection of examples in support of the general witness of Scripture to the aesthetic dimension, is given in Appendix 1.

THE PATH FORWARD IN ACADEMICS AND SCHOLARSHIP FOR THEOLOGICAL AESTHETICS

It is true that the Scriptures, for their part, nowhere either explicitly justify beauty or explain the principles of beauty. It is primarily if not precisely for that reason that constructive engagement in the area of theological aesthetics among biblical and theological scholars exists today at the margins. A quick search of theological and philosophical works on aesthetics shows that published books and doctoral dissertations alike abound. On the other hand, specifically biblical- and systematic-theological treatments do not. The core weakness of theological aesthetics throughout the history of its various developments has been the primary neglect of a specifically biblical- and systematic-theological treatment.

The reasons behind the aforementioned state of affairs in contemporary scholarship are manifold, but a prominent one clearly would be the lack of consensus that exists on the validity of beauty as a proper locus

---

12. C. Caverno, "Beauty" in *The International Standard Bible Encyclopaedia*, vol. 1, ed. James Orr (Chicago: The Howard-Severance Company, 1915), 420.

13. Unless otherwise noted, all Scripture translation and verse references provided throughout are from the ESV.

of theology, or if it is affirmed, to which locus it belongs. Sensibilities and commitments on that question run the gamut from the antagonistic to the ambivalent to the occasionally ecstatic. Another reason why beauty and aesthetics are treated in relative isolation from biblical and systematic theology is that theological scholarship on aesthetics is done overwhelmingly in the way of religious aesthetics or theology of the arts, and often esoterically at that. In Christian scholarship today, the scandal of contemporary theological aesthetics is that there is not much of a theological aesthetic.[14] For the work and pedagogy of systematic theology within a broadly evangelical perspective, this is not so much a sin of commission but of omission. This state of affairs translates over to the way systematic-theological treatment of aesthetics is virtually if not altogether absent in the teaching of theology and doctrinal courses taught in Christian higher education, seminaries, and such. A theological view of beauty plays no part, with rare exception, in any of the traditional loci of theology and doctrinal courses that are offered in Christian higher education. The academic state of affairs as such is that the traditional loci of theology and doctrinal courses—for example, the doctrine of God, of Christ, of the Holy Spirit, of man (anthropology), of the church, of the Christian life/ethics, just to name some basic ones—find no place (or rarely so) to include and engage theologically the subject of beauty. And if that were asking too much of Christian academies in the pedagogy of traditional doctrines, efforts toward providing a secondary or elective theology course concerning a theology of beauty in the way of theological aesthetics could no doubt address this lacuna appreciatively. The constructive argumentation I set forth in this project will help serve as a corrective to this neglect. It is my hope that any progress in the recovery of and reinvigorated attention to theological aesthetics at the level of the academy will translate into offering theological and spiritual benefit at the pastoral level for the upbuilding of the church, and for gospel outreach to a world that is hungering to know the ultimate source of all that is true, good, and beautiful.

---

14. Cf. Mark Noll, *The Scandal of the Evangelical Mind* (Grand Rapids: Eerdmans, 1994), 3.

A CLASSICIST THEORY OF BEAUTY

In this introductory section it is necessary to set out key definitions and concepts concerning beauty and theological aesthetics in the development of a biblical and systematic theology of beauty.[15] I shall start with setting out a formal but more generic answer to the age-old question about the nature of beauty ostensibly posed in conversation between Socrates and the sophist Hippias: "How, if you please, do you know, Socrates, what sort of things are beautiful and ugly? For, come now, could you tell me what the beautiful is?"[16] The following will serve as our definition stemming out of the classical tradition. Beauty is an intrinsic quality of things which, when perceived, pleases the mind by displaying a certain kind of fittingness. That is to say, beauty is discerned via objective properties such as proportion, unity, variety, symmetry, harmony, intricacy, delicacy, simplicity, or suggestiveness.[17] As a quality distinguishable in a thing, therefore, beauty has objective criteria, yet the apperception of the quality of beauty depends on the percipience of the mind (the mental faculty of perceiving), since it is the mind that renders relation of aesthetic properties as something perceived.[18] As I am applying the term in this work, then, fittingness functions as an overarching term expressive of the full range of aesthetic properties

---

15. For a helpful treatment of how biblical theology and systematic theology relate as disciplines to enable the theological interpretation of Scripture, see Graham A. Cole, *The God Who Became Human: A Biblical Theology of Incarnation* (Downers Grove, IL: InterVarsity Press, 2013), 171–74.

16. Plato, *Greater Hippias* 286cd. The Greek word here translated "beautiful" is from καλός, a widely applicable term denoting that which is aesthetically beautiful, morally excellent, noble, organically sound, desirable, praiseworthy, and the like. The Platonic authenticity of this dialogue is debated, but its philosophical content is generally accepted by scholars as genuinely Platonic, even if not actually penned by him.

17. For an excellent discussion on objective aesthetic properties and criteria, see Nicholas Wolterstorff, *Art in Action: Toward a Christian Aesthetic* (Grand Rapids: Eerdmans, 1980), 156–74.

18. This is not to say that we only perceive and appreciate the beauty of something if we know or have knowledge that it is beautiful. Epistemically, a percipient may not have "knowledge" that a thing has certain aesthetic properties, but her mind may nonetheless perceive and appreciate something as beautiful without necessarily *knowing* that it is beautiful. More formally, it is the mind that renders the positive epistemic status our aesthetic beliefs have, even if there is insufficient warrant to have *knowledge* about it.

that identify any and all objective characteristics of beauty. The idea of "fittingness-intensity" advanced by Nicholas Wolterstorff (1932–) develops the point here further:

> Now I suggest that when works are praised for their vitality, their delicacy, their tenderness, their gracefulness, and so forth, they are being praised for a particular fittingness-intensity of their characters. And if that is correct, then what can be said is that among the fittingness-intensities of things we find a great many of the aspects that function for people as aesthetic merits of those things.[19]

Fittingness has been recognized by old (Anselm [1033–1109]) and new (Wolterstorff) theologians as a measure of aesthetic merit. A judgment of fittingness implies a judgment about the degree to which a thing exhibits beauty, and vice versa. And beauty broadly conceived will be expressed throughout this work often by the term "aesthetics" or "aesthetic dimension."

The question may be fairly asked, why appropriate *fittingness* to God's beauty rather than to some other perfection? In other words, can fittingness be characteristic not only of the beautiful but of other perfections such as God's righteousness or his wisdom? In answer to this question we begin in recognition of the fact that the concept of fittingness can apply to one realm of discourse or another. So, for example, there is a fittingness that we associate more with wisdom which is seen as correlated more pronouncedly to truth, and a fittingness that has righteousness/justice in plain view which is seen as correlated more pronouncedly to goodness. With an understanding that there is indeed something to the idea of the non-coincidence of truth, goodness, and beauty in the order of reality (more on this below), there is warrant to say that the fittingness that characterizes something beautiful is not an uncorrelated reality from the fittingness that characterizes something that is wise (or some other perfection). Herman Bavinck's (1854–1921) contention that "beauty always derives its content from the true and the good, and it is their revelation and appearance" goes along with this and is making essentially the same point.[20] In other words we need

---

19. Wolterstorff, *Art in Action*, 167.
20. Herman Bavinck, "Of Beauty and Aesthetics," in *Essays on Religion, Science,*

not accept that categories or discourses of fittingness are uncorrelated with each other. Rather, on the view I am presenting the transcendental relation between the true, the good, and the beautiful informs all Christian theology (more on this below). Nicholas Healy captures this idea in regard to the actions of God as follows:

> [T]he theologian should attempt to explain why these means to salvation are the best by displaying the appropriateness of God's actions as they are described in Scripture. The argument for fittingness is therefore something like an aesthetic argument because it searches for structure and proportion. The French Dominican, Gilbert Narcisse, gives this definition: "Theological fittingness displays the significance of the chosen means among alternative possibilities, and the reasons according to which God, in his wisdom, has effectively realized and revealed, gratuitously and through his love, the mystery of the salvation and glorification of humanity."[21]

As it relates to human actions, wisdom as a certain species of truth can be proximately understood as lived out knowledge and understanding, involving the ability to make sound judgments in the exercise of our Christian freedom. So wisdom is manifest in its fittingness to know what to do or to say in a given context. And because contexts change wisdom is lived out improvisationally. Its fittingness is seen in discerning the propriety of what to say or do in contextually appropriate ways. Vanhoozer puts it like this: "Disciples improvise each time they exercise Christian freedom fittingly, in obedient response to the gracious word of God that set it in motion. Improvising to the glory of God is ultimately a matter simply of being who one has been created to be in Christ, so that one responds freely and fittingly as if by reflex or second nature."[22] Wisdom as such is lived-out knowledge and understanding that conforms to the truth and understanding as it is found in Christ. In this sense, then, the fittingness that we associate with wisdom correlates to truth more pronouncedly than it does to beauty. With all this

---

and Society, ed. John Bolt, trans. Harry Boonstra and Gerrit Sheeres (Grand Rapids: Baker Academic, 2008), 256.

21. Nicholas M. Healy, Thomas Aquinas: Theologian of the Christian Life (Burlington, VT: Ashgate Publishing, 2003), 38.

22. Vanhoozer, Faith Speaking Understanding, 191.

in mind I will comment at points throughout the theological aesthetic I am putting forward how the fittingness identified in a given context may be characteristic not only of the beautiful but manifestly also of other perfections such as God's righteousness or his wisdom.

Integral to our theory is that the beauty of something evokes from the percipient (the perceiving subject) an affective response of delight—that is, a kind of aesthetic pleasure. The lapidary statement by Etienne Gilson provides a critical insight that applies here: "The pleasure experienced in knowing the beautiful does not constitute beauty itself, but it betrays its presence."[23] Indeed, what uniquely characterizes the quality of beauty is its effect of evoking pleasure or delight in the act of perceiving it. Given the fluidity of language, however, Roger Scruton rightly notes the need for aesthetic common sense: "Delight is more important than the terms used to express it, and the terms themselves are in a certain measure anchorless, used more to suggest an effect than to pinpoint the qualities that give rise to it."[24] Since beauty is perceived through our senses and mind—seeing and hearing, notably, but overall in the synthetic operation of the senses with the mind—such delight is effected in us in countless ways and immeasurable degrees. At times that delight is more through a sensory presentation and other times more through an intellectual presentation—it depends on the nature of the thing perceived. With visual art or music, for example, the pleasure evoked in perceiving its aesthetic quality is effected more through a sensory presentation. With a work of literature, on the other hand, the pleasure evoked in perceiving its aesthetics is effected more through an imaginational presentation.[25] Empirically or experientially speaking, one may understand objective properties identified as objective criteria for beauty as simply being attempts to say what evokes pleasure in the act of perceiving the beauty of something. The criteria are always *a posteriori* gestures to the *qualia* of beauty as universal.[26]

---

23. Etienne Gilson, *Elements of Christian Philosophy* (Garden City, NY: Doubleday, Catholic Textbook Division, 1960), 162.

24. Roger Scruton, *Beauty* (Oxford: Oxford University Press, 2009), 15.

25. See Scruton, *Beauty*, 22–26.

26. In this sense beauty is identifiable as a subjective universal, serving as our access to a thing's aesthetic properties. To note, technically there is a distinction between identifying something as being "objective" and identifying something as

In any case, this is not to say that the subjective response of pleasure or delight evoked in perceiving the beauty of something would be identical—whether in quality or degree—for every person. The variable factors that influence the subjective response affected in the act of perceiving a given thing's beauty are manifold. Factors external to a person such as one's inculturation, background, and acquired aesthetic sophistication bear influence in conjunction with all the factors internal to a person that make up one's individuality and personality, and even one's preconceptions of something. Within the variation and differences among people in the way beauty is subjectively experienced are both the mystery and complexity of what I will argue is the dichotomous unity of body and soul that constitutes every human person. It is sufficient for our purposes to affirm only that, when perceived, beauty is experienced in a subjective response of pleasure or delight. I will not seek to explicate further the mystery and complexity of the variable dimensions that influence the subjective response affected in the act of perceiving a thing's beauty.

To be clear, however, a realist view of beauty is premised here.[27] On this view, the quality of beauty inherent in any given thing exists independent of any creaturely percipient, that is, whether or not it is perceived. In my judgment Augustine's certain reply to the age-old question concerning whether beauty is an objective reality or only a subjective reality still speaks truth: "If I were to ask first whether things are beautiful because they give pleasure, or give pleasure because they are beautiful, I have no doubt that I will be given the answer that they give pleasure because they are beautiful."[28] We can thus affirm that

---

being "universal." The former implies mind-independence, while the latter implies a metaphysical realism. The idea of "qualia" denotes the internal and subjective component of sense perceptions, what philosophers loosely refer to as the *raw feels*.

27. Phenomenalism is all about the study of the way things appear to us. It is often assumed to entail that beauty has no independent reality outside the experience of human perception. Against the idea of phenomenalism entailing an antirealist view about beauty, aesthetic objectivism strongly affirms that beauty does have an independent reality outside the experience of human perception. For a recommended defense on aesthetic objectivism, see Eddy M. Zemach, *Real Beauty* (University Park, PA: Pennsylvania State University Press, 2004).

28. Augustine, *De Vera Religione*, cited in Umberto Eco, *The Aesthetics of Thomas Aquinas*, trans. Hugh Bredin (Cambridge, MA: Harvard University Press, 1988), 49.

beauty is indeed in the eye of the beholder, though it is not reduced to that. In other words an objectivist view of beauty affirms that a given thing appears to a person *as beautiful*, but without that being reduced in meaning to simply as beautiful *to them*.[29] The classicist theory of beauty I am presenting, therefore, is that beauty is objectively real and thus affective response-independent—that is, the affective response does not act as a trigger to constitute some x as beautiful. The response comes into play for a subject in the act of that subject perceiving the beauty of some thing. So its beauty does trigger an affective response of aesthetic pleasure or delight, but this response is evoked in the act of perceiving it. Thus there does not have to be some perceiver that judges some x as having a certain quality of beauty for it to have that quality of beauty. Rather, the nature of beauty is such that to human percipients at least, an aesthetic pleasure of some form and degree is elicited in the act of perceiving some x. In sum, I am postulating a realist view of beauty, and the unique nature of beauty involves the effect it has of eliciting a subjective response of aesthetic pleasure as we perceive it.

It follows, moreover, that the degree to which the quality of beauty is present in a particular thing determines the degree to which that thing is beautiful. Since the degree to which a thing is beautiful implies the degree of its fittingness in a certain dimension, the idea of "fittingness-intensity," which functions as an evaluative measure of the aesthetic merit of some work or thing, can be adopted and applied here. Considered in negative terms, the degree to which a thing is perceived as "ugly" implies the degree of its ill-fittingness in a certain dimension. Assuming a realist view of beauty, then, "ugliness" represents the degree of something's negative objective beauty, its

---

29. Cf. N. T. Wright, *Simply Christian: Why Christianity Makes Sense* (San Francisco: HarperSanFrancisco, 2006), 44: "On the one hand, we must acknowledge that beauty, whether in the natural order or within human creation, is sometimes so powerful that it evokes our very deepest feelings of awe, wonder, gratitude, and reverence. Almost all humans sense this some of the time at least, even though they disagree wildly about which things evoke which feelings and why. On the other hand, we must acknowledge that these disagreements and puzzles are enough to press some, without an obvious desire to be cynical or destructive, to say that beauty is all in the mind, or the imagination, or the genes. ... It seems we have to hold the two together: beauty is *both* something that calls us out of ourselves *and* something which appeals to feelings deep within us."

deformity/malformity of form, as it were. Scruton sums up the larger
point this way:

> Beauty can be consoling, disturbing, sacred, profane; it can be exhil-
> arating, appealing, inspiring, chilling. It can affect us in an unlim-
> ited variety of ways. Yet it is never viewed with indifference: beauty
> demands to be noticed; it speaks to us directly like the voice of an
> intimate friend. If there are people who are indifferent to beauty,
> then it is surely because they do not perceive it.[30]

In short, the nature of beauty implies objective properties—with
such properties themselves able to serve as objective aesthetic criteria—and involves a complex, affective response from the percipient,
whether positively or negatively.

The basic position of theological aesthetics that beauty is a communicated property or phenomenon of the *opera Dei ad extra* means
that the existence of beautiful things requires, if you will, the existence of a Beautifier. The question posed by Hans Urs von Balthasar
(1905–1988) is germane to our interest: "may it not be that we have a
real and inescapable obligation to probe the possibility of there being
a genuine relationship between theological beauty and the beauty of
the world?"[31] While a justification for aesthetics and an explanation
of aesthetic criteria are under-determined by Scripture, there are
numerous examples of things in Scripture, material and immaterial
in nature, that are described in regard to their beauty or in aesthetic
terms.[32] The following point Kevin Vanhoozer advances is axiomatic

---

30. Scruton, *Beauty*, xi.

31. Hans Urs von Balthasar, *GL*, I, 80.

32. Cf. Paul Helm, "The Impossibility of Divine Passibility" in *The Power and
Weakness of God: Impassibility and Orthodoxy*, ed. Nigel M. de S. Cameron (Edinburgh:
Rutherford House, 1990), 135: "Biblical language and metaphysical concepts
(whether these concepts are derived from Greek sources or from elsewhere) are not
strict rivals. This is because of the fact that from the point of view of metaphysics
the Bible is an underdeveloped book; there are few, if any, passages which are theoretical and reflective, or which make general claims and which rebut alternatives,
of the sort typically advanced in metaphysical discussion. So the Bible does not
repudiate developed metaphysics; rather, for the most part it obliquely sidesteps
it, for its interests are for the most part elsewhere. But this does not mean that its
first-order statements do not have metaphysical implications, only that they are
not themselves metaphysical claims."

to our efforts: "The vocation of the theological interpreter of Scripture is to render judgments—ethical, epistemological, and yes, metaphysical—concerning what is 'meet and right' for Christians to affirm of God on the basis of the various modes of divine self-showing, self-giving, and self-saying."[33] The task going forward involves answering how theological beauty relates to the beauty of the world, and conceptually to elaborate just what God's "beautiful self-showing" consists in.[34] As will be shown integral to my argumentation, the objective beauty of the person of Christ, the beauty of the work of Christ (redemption accomplished), and the beauty of Christ's work ongoing through the Holy Spirit (redemption applied) are the preeminent aspects of God's "beautiful self-showing" according to the redemptive-eschatological fulfillment of his original creational purposes.

A biblical and systematic theology of beauty, moreover, needs to give full recognition to aesthetics both narrowly and broadly conceived. Aesthetics *narrowly conceived* denotes any real thing that is perceivable by human beings as patently or conspicuously beautiful. One is consciously attracted to such a thing for its outright aesthetic quality, perhaps a particular quality that stands out—for example, x has perfect proportion; y has lovely harmony. An instance of explicitly recognized beauty is at the same time an instance of that thing being fitting, reflecting in its form and features aesthetic qualities of God's manifest glory. The aesthetic dimension *broadly conceived*, however, understands fittingness to involve more than that which one is consciously attracted to or recognizes for its outright and particular aesthetic quality. While something that exhibits fittingness in a given context may be perceived for a particular aesthetic quality that stands out, it may also be recognized

---

33. Kevin J. Vanhoozer, *Remythologizing Theology: Divine Action, Passion, and Authorship* (Cambridge: Cambridge University Press, 2010), 198.

34. A recommended treatment on issues pertinent here is found in William Edgar, "Aesthetics: Beauty Avenged, Apologetics Enriched," *WTJ* 63 no. 1 (Spring 2001): 107–22. Worth noting as well is the implication for aesthetics more generally considered. If beauty is a divine attribute or a phenomenological quality corresponding to the revelation of God's attributes in the divine economy, the ontological ground exists to posit a full-orbed realist view of aesthetics. The scope of this project does not entail treating this broader point, however, as our concern is fundamentally in regard to a theological, and more particularly, christological treatment of beauty.

in much more subtle terms regarding its propriety or its overall sense of order or harmony and such like. Pythagoras' classical theory of the "music of the spheres," albeit an obsolete metaphysic, represents an ancient example of aesthetics broadly conceived.[35] Thus, aesthetics broadly conceived is simply a formal distinction that acknowledges the less conspicuous or less perceptible subtle aesthetic aspects that God's glory takes in the design and outworking of his eternal plan in all its diversely splendored forms. We could therefore think of the aesthetic dimension conceived in a narrow sense and the aesthetic dimension conceived in a broad sense as the recognition of a focal/particular perception of beauty versus a subsidiary/synthetic perception of it. Thus, visual art or music might serve as an example of aesthetic qualities perceivable in a narrow sense, and a certain crafting of narrative or work of literature as an example perhaps of aesthetic qualities perceivable in a broad sense. The aesthetic dimension conceived both narrowly or broadly, then, entails the full compass of characteristics betraying God's beauty, all of which are expressions of the aesthetic quality of his manifest glory (more on this below).

BEAUTY AMONG THE TRANSCENDENTALS OF BEING

The notion of "transcendental properties of being" played a foundational role in the metaphysical worldview originating during the Classical Greek period. It remained a key notion in the thinking of the ancient and medieval church Fathers and Schoolmen, and figures prominently in the development of their theological aesthetics. My purposes here are

---

35. Discovering that harmonic music is expressed in exact numerical ratios of whole numbers, Pythagoras reasoned that music was the ordering principle of the world. For Pythagoras, this fact demonstrated the intelligibility of reality and the existence of a reasoning intelligence behind it. As he pondered the harmonious wonder of music as delivered through singing and through musical instrumentation, Pythagoras concluded that musical harmony was a reflection of a more majestic harmony in the universe—"the music of the spheres." That is to say, music at its best reflected the harmonious sound (itself expressible by numbers) that the heavenly spheres produced together in their rotations through space. In this sense music was number reflected in aural harmony. This harmony of the universe was thought to be composed of various levels of musical tones that humanly produced music could proximate. What music represented, then, was nothing less than human participation in the harmony of the universe, which was able to effect spiritual harmony in one's soul.

limited to describing in brief the following: first, a classical Thomistic view of the transcendental property of being; and second, the transcendental relation concerning truth, goodness, and beauty. Clarifying these transcendentals prepares the way for understanding how beauty relates to the divine attributes.

"Being" is the most general and comprehensive concept we have to describe everything that exists. In Thomistic metaphysics (and late medieval generally) "being" is called a "transcendental" because the act of existing ("to be") is a property common to all real beings, and as such it transcends all distinctions made at the level of genus, category, or individual in the order of reality.[36] Which other properties qualify as transcendentals has been variously argued throughout the history of classical and scholastic metaphysics. Nonetheless, late medieval theories were in basic agreement that a transcendental property of being is "a positive attribute that can be predicated of every real being, so that it is convertible with being itself."[37] For such an attribute to be convertible

---

36. The idea of "being" as the most general property common to all real beings is suggested in *ST* Ia, q.65, a.3, in which Aquinas states, "Now the underlying principle in things is always more universal than that which informs and restricts it; thus, being is more universal than living, living than understanding, matter than form."

37. W. Norris Clarke, *The One and the Many: A Contemporary Thomistic Metaphysics* (Notre Dame, IN: University of Notre Dame Press, 2001), 290–91. This definition begs the question, however, on what is meant here by "real being" and "being itself." The nature of "being" is a fundament of Thomistic metaphysics, of course, but we need not unpack all that for our purposes. Clarke, 25–34, includes a helpful treatment on the Thomistic meaning of "being," which I give here in summary form: "a being" is *that which is*, i.e., actually exists in the real order. A distinction is made between *real* being (*ens realis*) and *mental* being (*ens rationis*). Real being is what exists, in the strong sense of the term, independent or outside of the mind, and is the primary existential meaning of being. Unless otherwise specified, real being is the ordinary meaning of being and has two main modes: (1) a *complete* being, or substance, which exists on its own and not as part of any other being; and (2) any *part* or attribute of a real being which cannot be said to exist on its own, but only to be in another, e.g., "He is a *kind* man." Mental being, on the other hand, is what exists exclusively in the mind, i.e., as being-thought-about by a real mind. Thus, a horse is a real being, whereas a unicorn is only a mental being. Since mental being can only be understood by reference to the mind thinking it, it is radically secondary, dependent, or parasitic on real being, which is primary. All mental beings thus in some way derive from and refer back to the order of real being. Transcendental properties of being are thus predicated, in the proper sense, of every real being, and are not predicated of any mental being since such are strictly eidetic, i.e., these do not exist independent of the mind.

with being itself (i.e., every being) means that it marks a conceptual distinction within the nature of being but it does not mark any real (i.e., ontological) distinction within that nature. In other words the respective concepts that apply to the different transcendental properties "are distinct from each other in what they explicitly affirm about being, but they refer to the identical reality as it exists in itself."[38] Each transcendental property makes explicit some aspect of being that is not made explicit by the term "being," and does so without adding anything ontologically to being.[39] Transcendental properties as such are different attributes of being that are coextensive with being itself, revealing themselves to be universal attributes of the real order. A transcendental property is thus an attribute by which all existing things are predicated in some degree or other as a necessary condition of their very existence.

From the patristic era through to the Middle Ages we find that beauty was on the whole considered a transcendental quality of being, along with truth, goodness, and oneness—*unus et verum et bonum et pulchrum convertuntur*.[40] This presupposition was commonly held by the ancient and medieval church Fathers and Schoolmen, both Eastern and Western, which they found to be consistent with the Scriptures. Although doing theology in the Middle Ages involved straining Neoplatonism and/or Aristotelianism through a Christianizing sieve, the theological synthesis that was produced to the time of Aquinas provided an invaluable legacy of theological aesthetics for all future theological development of its kind. In the course of this work the theological aesthetics of Irenaeus of Lyons (c.130–c.200), Anselm of Canterbury and Thomas Aquinas (1225–1274) are representative of the best of the

---

38. Clarke, *The One and the Many*, 291.

39. Clarke, *The One and the Many*, 291.

40. The following treatments on the long history and development of theological aesthetics are recommended: Hans Urs von Balthasar, *The Glory of the Lord*, vols. II–V (San Francisco: Ignatius Press, 1984–1991); Umberto Eco, ed., *History of Beauty*, trans. Alistair McEwen (New York: Rizzoli, 2004); Francis J. Kovach, *Philosophy of Beauty* (Norman, OK: University of Oklahoma Press, 1974); Wladyslaw Tatarkiewicz, *History of Aesthetics*, vols. 1–3 (New York: Continuum, 2005); David Konstan, *Beauty: The Fortunes of an Ancient Greek Idea* (Oxford: Oxford University Press, 2015). For a concise patristic/medieval survey of the positions held on beauty as a transcendental, see Francis J. Kovach, "Beauty," in *New Catholic Encyclopedia*, vol. 2, 2nd ed. (Washington, DC: Gale Group, 2003), 184–86.

patristic/medieval tradition, with Aquinas' contribution generally considered the acme of its development. To a fair extent this project's overall thesis is a constructive engagement with their ideas.[41]

Since beauty was considered a transcendental property of being, it was considered to belong to the divine essence itself, qualifying it as a divine attribute. In this regard the transcendental properties have long been considered "perfections" that exist in their most perfect form in God. However, given the infinite ontological divide between Creator and creature, the divine perfections are taken to be analogical extensions of being (*analogia entis*) from God to the created world. This points up the idea affirmed in Thomistic metaphysics that a thing is perfected by becoming what by its very nature it is meant to be.[42] The transcendentals of truth, goodness, and beauty correspond respectively to being as true, good, and beautiful.[43] What is meant regarding "being as true" is ontological truth—that is, being as intrinsically intelligible to the mind. In this sense truth is the relation of being to the mind, or simply, *being as knowable*. So the more fullness of truth a thing has, the greater one's apprehension will be towards that truth. And the more perfectly you know that thing, the more you realize its truth. Likewise, "being as good" denotes ontological goodness—that is, being as intrinsically desirable to the will, corresponding to its perfection (i.e., what by its very nature a thing is meant to be). In this sense goodness is the relation of being to the will, or simply, *being as desirable*. So the more fullness of goodness a thing has, the greater one's desire will be towards that goodness. And the more perfectly you desire that thing, the more you realize its goodness. In the same way, "being as beautiful" denotes ontological

---

41. Scholarship in the last forty years has produced notable works on the theological aesthetics of these church Fathers, including the following: Eric Osborn, *Irenaeus of Lyons* (Cambridge: Cambridge University Press, 2001); David S. Hogg, *Anselm of Canterbury: The Beauty of Theology* (Burlington, VT: Ashgate Publishing, 2004); Umberto Eco, *The Aesthetics of Thomas Aquinas*, trans. Hugh Bredin (Cambridge, MA: Harvard University Press, 1988); Brendan Thomas Sammon, *The God Who Is Beauty: Beauty as a Divine Name in Thomas Aquinas and Dionysius the Areopagite* (Eugene, OR: Pickwick Publications, 2013).

42. Francesca Aran Murphy, *Christ the Form of Beauty: A Study in Theology and Literature* (Edinburgh: T&T Clark, 1995), 216–17.

43. See Clarke, *The One and the Many*, 294–302, for a helpful treatment on this topic.

beauty—that is, being as intrinsically delightable to both the mind and will in the perception of it, or simply, *being as delightable*. So the more fullness of beauty a thing has, the greater one's pleasure or delight will be towards that beauty. And the more perfectly you delight in that thing, the more you realize its beauty. The distinctive characteristic of beauty, then, over against that of truth and goodness, is that beauty as *beauty* is not desired as a means to another end but communicates to the perceiver of it an associated pleasure or delight *as* that end.

A classical way the transcendentals of truth, goodness, and beauty are characterized is that in the true the intellect is at rest, and in the good the will is at rest, but in the beautiful both intellect and will together are at rest. We might put it less formally this way: knowledge is about approaching the true in the way that the will is about approaching the good, and delight is about approaching the beautiful. It was from this perspective that the medieval church Fathers and Schoolmen believed that what is true and good is likewise beautiful in form and content, and vice versa. Although British philosopher Roger Scruton demurs on the status of beauty as an ultimate value, his comments offered from a philosophical perspective are nonetheless germane: "Why believe *p*? Because it is true. Why want *x*? Because it is good. Why look at *y*? Because it is beautiful. In some way, philosophers have argued, those answers are on a par: each brings a state of mind into the ambit of reason, by connecting it to something that it is in our nature, as rational beings, to pursue."[44] This is the non-coincidence of the "true," the "good," and the "beautiful," as it has been called. We also note that the concept of transcendental beauty is fully consistent, mutatis mutandis, with the theory of beauty we sketched out earlier—that is, that beauty is objectively real, subjectively experienced. I will assume with regard to our theory of beauty the premise that the ontological grounding of beauty is a transcendental reality.[45] It was just this intuition that led

---

44. Scruton, *Beauty*, 2.

45. Granting that the ontological grounding of beauty is a transcendental reality, it makes a great deal of sense for the pleasure experienced in perceiving the beautiful to elicit along with that some sort of eschatological longing in us. Wright, *Simply Christian*, 40–41, describes just this sort of longing: "Beauty, like justice, slips through our fingers. We photograph the sunset, but all we get is the memory of the moment, not the moment itself. We buy the recording, but the symphony

C. S. Lewis (1898–1963) to remark, "The sweetest thing in all my life has been the longing ... to find the place where all the beauty came from."[46] This premise comports with our theological premise that beauty corresponds in some way to the attributes of God (more on this below). As I will argue, the transcendentals of truth, goodness, and beauty in God's work of creation, redemption, and consummation are strongly correlated because these attributes—coordinate with God's knowledge, will, and beatitude—are communicable perfections of God's essential nature and thus are expressed inherently in all his outward works. As a final point here, since the canon of Scripture is the *norma normans* for the theological aesthetics with which our biblical and systematic theology of beauty as defined by the divine economy of redemption is developed, the theory of beauty stemming out of the classical tradition that has served to fund this will be more properly qualified as needed in the Conclusion.

SUMMARY OF OVERALL ARGUMENT

Granting the postulation premised earlier that the Bible is "everywhere inspired and writ in an atmosphere of aesthetics," what should a sound theology of beauty about the plan of God in Christ look like? Let me pose the grand concern here in Pauline fashion: what ways does a theological aesthetic highlight certain aspects of the plan and purposes of God, promised before the ages began, that he has realized in Christ Jesus? My aim overall is to put forward the christological contours of a biblically-based theology of beauty in answer to that question. The term "contours" here pertains to the principal phases of God's eternal plan in salvation history—the drama of redemption or *theodrama*, if you will—in its outworking of creation, redemption, and consummation. What is at issue in all this is the doctrine of God in the first instance and, following from this, a greater appreciation of an aspect of God's self-revelation that has been generally overlooked when we speak about

---

says something different when we listen to it at home. We climb the mountain, and though the view from the summit is indeed magnificent, it leaves us wanting more; even if we could build a house there and gaze all day at the scene, the itch wouldn't go away. Indeed, the beauty sometimes seems to be in the itching itself, the sense of longing, the kind of pleasure which is exquisite and yet leaves us unsatisfied."

46. C. S. Lewis, *Till We Have Faces: A Myth Retold* (Orlando: Harcourt, 1980), 75.

the doctrines of creation, fall, incarnation, redemption, and consummation, namely, the aesthetic dimension.[47] Our focus on perceiving the beauty of the theodrama, moreover, invites a kind of heuristic approach through applying aesthetic criticism to aid our viewing of that beauty.

My working hypothesis is twofold: first, beauty corresponds in some way to the attributes of God; second, the theodrama of God's eternal plan in creation, redemption, and consummation entails a consistent and fitting expression and outworking of this divine beauty. The way undertaken in this work involves giving up-front theological reflection on beauty in relation to both the Trinity relating essentially (ad intra) and the Trinity operating economically (ad extra). My thesis is that the Son's fittingness as incarnate Redeemer, and in the divine economy in general, is the critical lens for seeing God's beauty, serving as well to display the Son's glory in every stage of the theodrama. The properly dogmatic (i.e., Trinitarian) ground of the Son's fittingness is God's beauty which, in conjunction with divine simplicity, entails that everything God does is, by definition, beautiful (i.e., God-glorifying). I trace this theological aesthetic across the principal phases of the theodrama (creation, redemption, and consummation) through the lens of Christology and the related theme of the imago Dei. In the order of my presentation I have chosen first to set out the concept of fittingness and then examine the plan of God in Christ as it is reflected economically in the phases of creation, redemption, and consummation. To be crystal clear, however, the order of reality is the divine economy, and any conceptual proposals I offer for consideration must follow as these relate to the divine economy.

A constructive development in argument of this thesis is put forward, involving a biblical- and systematic-theological characterization of God's beauty—notably in and through the Son as incarnate Redeemer

---

47. On this point, Millard J. Erickson, *Christian Theology*, 3rd ed. (Grand Rapids: Baker Academic, 2013), 1144, writes, "Beyond the logical or rational character of theology, there is also its aesthetic character. There is the potential, as we survey the whole of God's truth, of grasping its artistic nature. There is a beauty to the great compass and the interrelatedness of the doctrines. The organic character of theology, its balanced depiction of the whole of reality and of human nature, should bring a sense of satisfaction to the human capacity to appreciate beauty in the form of symmetry, comprehensiveness, and coherence."

and with respect to humans as divine image-bearers—in relation to the principal phases of the theodrama: creation, redemption, and consummation. I refer to this constructive development as the christological contours of beauty. The christological contours of beauty will demonstrate the following points:

1. The beauty of the divine plan is a function of the fittingness of the Son as incarnate Redeemer being foundational to its design and outworking.

2. The beauty of our formation as Christian disciples is that vital part of God's work in this present age of forming and making beautiful his children, which is all about their being conformed to the image of his Son. The work of spiritual formation involves Christians living out fittingly their identity in Christ, which is part and parcel of the progressive work of spiritual transformation that God through Christ by the Spirit does in us. That central purpose of spiritual transformation in the plan of salvation is integral to the church of God—the Bride of Christ—being formed and "adorned" in preparation for her nuptial union with Christ.

An important element of my argument is that the beauty of God manifested economically is expressed and perceivable *as a quality of* the glory of God inherent in his work of creation, redemption, and consummation. The display of God's glory is thus always beautiful, always fitting, always entails an aesthetic dimension to it. Furthermore, the motif of God's glory is the primary material point in Scripture that I develop in reference to the christological contours of beauty.[48] A core focus of my argument, moreover, concerns the outworking of the divine plan centrally in the fate of the creature made in God's image. Within my development of the christological contours of beauty the image of God serves as a major theological motif, which I also develop in relation

---

48. Christopher W. Morgan, "Toward a Theology of the Glory of God," in *The Glory of God*, ed. Christopher W. Morgan and Robert A. Peterson (Wheaton, IL: Crossway, 2010), 159, encapsulates nicely the idea of God's glory and glorification *ad extra* this way: "[T]he triune God who is glorious displays his glory, largely through his creation, image-bearers, providence, and redemptive acts. God's people respond by glorifying him. God receives glory and, through uniting his people to Christ, shares his glory with them—all to his glory."

to the glory motif. The symmetry of the divine plan, which entails the symmetrical nature of the Son's agency in it, is an integral part of the aesthetics inherent in the structure (i.e., form) that God's glory takes in his work of creation, redemption, and consummation. That symmetry is revealed in the following basic ways:

1. That the work of creation is through the Son, so likewise the work of redemption (re-creation or the renewal of creation) also is accomplished through the Son.

2. That the Son is the preexistent image of God through whom humanity is imaged protologically, so likewise through the Son as the last Adam the redeemed are imaged eschatologically.

3. That as an analogue of the only-begotten Son's relationship to the Father, the Son of God as incarnate Redeemer procures adoptive sonship for all those he redeems, so that these may become beloved sons of God the Father.

The christological contours of beauty also entail that our formation as Christian disciples is that vital part of God's work in this present age of forming and making beautiful his children, which is all about their being conformed to the image of his Son.[49] That complete work of spiritual formation encompasses the church of God being prepared so that Christ as Bridegroom can present her to himself as his glorified Bride. Theological aesthetics performed in this key resounds to the true beauty reflected in the glory of God's work in the economy of salvation, which contrasts with and shows as altogether bankrupt the pretender cultural ideals of beauty represented by all with which the world is enthralled and that she idolizes.

On a final note, an entailment of our thesis is that the outward manifestation of God's beauty is expressive of that perfection of beatitude and sense of delight that belongs to the Trinity *ad intra*. It is God's own beatitude, I suggest, that, in this present age, correlates with a properly aesthetic dimension to our faith seeking understanding, the fruit and expression of which is a knowing pleasure and heartfelt delight

---

49. In addition, theological aesthetics presents an untapped lode for thinking about the correlation between the aesthetic domain and the ethical domain.

in God and in his gospel of grace through Jesus Christ. Such delight suggests itself as being a faint reflection of that aesthetic delight—that beatitude—in God's own being, and is the doxological component of divine beauty's effect on us that provides a foretaste in this life of our enjoying God forever in the next. For it is of the highest spiritual caliber in our sojourn with God to not only grow in sound knowledge of God and the revelation of his plan—that is, growing in "truth"; and not only to perform more faithfully and reflect in our lives the revelation of his ways and character—that is, growing in "goodness"; but equally vital, to *delight* increasingly in God for who he is and for making us partakers through the person and work of Christ of his eternal Triune life—that is, growing in "beauty." In this way the spiritual growth of each believer becomes more in step with and partakes more fully in the truth, goodness, and beauty that is coordinate with God's knowledge, will, and beatitude.

SYNOPSIS

The following chapter previews adumbrate the christological contours of beauty that I present in this work. The previews serve only to sketch out the bare contours of each chapter, highlighting important theological and aesthetic areas addressed. In addition, for Chapters 3, 4, and 6 I include a featured theologian who has contributed valuably to the subject of divine beauty or to theological aesthetics more generally, and set out in summary form their view on that. In Chapter 2, which concerns the doctrine of God, I set out the respective view on divine beauty of four featured theologians. The theologians all featured vary from the medieval period up to the recent modern, and I chose them based on their theology of beauty being especially relevant to the primary chapter in which each is contributing. Pertinent aspects of their theology are cited or engaged with throughout the chapter as well. Featuring and appropriating the work of such theologians in this way represents a mode of retrieval that "commends a more celebratory style of theological portrayal ... [that] rehabilitates classical sources of Christian theology and draws together their potential in furthering the theological task."[50] What this does is constructively braid into the development of my overall argumentation a variety of theological aesthetic perspectives from different church traditions and various periods of church history—in conjunction with the diverse work of other theologians and scholars I engage with throughout. Given the fundamentally constructive nature of this work, these featured theologians serve primarily as theological protagonists in its development, and theologically antagonistic points of issue are referenced against my argumentation but I do not focus on these. In the Conclusion I will compare and contrast the key aspects of their theological aesthetics with the theological aesthetics for which I have argued in the christological contours of beauty.

Chapter 2, "Beauty Triune," begins with the doctrine of God, which is the foundation for our theology of beauty. Our featured theologians on divine beauty are Anselm of Canterbury, Thomas Aquinas, Herman Bavinck, and Karl Barth. In broad strokes, the focus is all about God's beauty and glory, explicated with regard to Trinitarian doctrine and the divine attributes. Theological reflection on beauty is developed in relation to both the Trinity operating economically (ad extra)—that is, God's saving activity in history, centered on the work of the Son and the Spirit—and the Trinity relating essentially (ad intra)—that is, God's own eternal, internal, life as Father, Son, and Spirit. The larger effort here concerns the theodramatic fittingness of the Son as incarnate Redeemer, taken to be fundamental to the design and outworking of God's eternal plan. That central idea drives the christological contours of beauty.

Chapter 3, "Creation: Beauty's Debut," considers the divine work of creation, focusing primarily on Genesis 1-2 as our base text. Our featured theologian is Irenaeus. From Genesis 1-2 the idea of the "proto-eschaton" is developed, understood as prototypical themes of creation that anticipate consummative themes of the eschaton; these themes are integral to the design and consummative fulfillment of God's eternal plan. A theological interpretation of the image of God is given, arguing that everything constitutive of the image of God is comprehended

---

50. John Webster, "Theologies of Retrieval" in *The Oxford Handbook of Systematic Theology*, ed. John Webster, Kathryn Tanner, and Iain Torrance (Oxford: Oxford University Press, 2009), 596.

in three principal aspects—the official (royal priest), constitutional (whole person, i.e., body-soul), and ethical-relational. The fall of Adam and Eve in Genesis 3 and God's consequent curse on the created order is in turn briefly addressed. In view of the narrative prominence of divine justice, the largely ignored notion of fittingness in reference to retributive justice is presented.

Chapter 4, "The Incarnation: Beauty Condescending," addresses how God's eternal plan plays out climactically in the person and work of Christ. Hans Urs von Balthasar is our featured theologian. The christological contours of beauty are developed here in regard to four key aspects of Christ's identity, followed by an excursus. First, *Christ the Image of God*. Attention here is on Christ as the image of God whose glory is made visible in and expressed through the form of his humanity. Second, *Christ the Form of a Slave*. A theological interpretation of Philippians 2:6–8 is given, arguing that the beauty of Christ is qualified by the theodramatic fittingness of his identity revealed in the form of a slave. Third, *Christ the Last Adam and the True Israel*. The theodramatic fittingness of Christ is argued in how he recapitulates in his life the history of the first Adam and God's covenant people Israel. Fourth, *Christ the Transfigured*. A theological interpretation is given in reference to Christ's identity as revealed at the event of his transfiguration. The aesthetic dimension argued here pertains to the redemptive-historical fittingness of the event, and the theodramatic fittingness of the Son with respect to his transfigured form. And fifth, *Excursus: Theological Aesthetic of Isaiah 53:2*. A theological aesthetic of Isaiah 53:2b is given, addressing Isaiah's Servant of the Lord as identified with the person of Christ, described here by the prophet as having "no form or majesty that we should look at him, and no beauty that we should desire him."

Chapter 5, "The Cross: Beauty Redeeming," develops the christological contours of beauty in reference to the accomplishment of Christ's work on the cross and the already but not-yet accomplished work of Christ in the state of his heavenly exaltation. A theological interpretation of Hebrews 2:10 and 7:26 is given concerning the notion of fittingness that the author of Hebrews takes up in direct reference to Christ's high priestly mediatorship. Following this, Christ's kingly glory is argued as being epitomized in his death on the cross. The christological contours of beauty then shift in reference to the already but not-yet order of reality governed under the preeminence of Christ's heavenly rule. Argued here is how the facets of God's will being done on earth as it is in heaven are defining of Christ's reconciling rule, which operates in various ways (and to varying degrees) in the spheres of human-divine relations and human-human relations in an already but not-yet consummate unity and harmony.

Chapter 6, "Re-creation: Beauty's Denouement," shows how the prototypical themes from Genesis 1–2 of the proto-eschaton come at last to rest and have their eschatological fulfillment. Our featured theologian to conclude with is Jonathan Edwards (1703–1758). The theological aesthetics here initially concern the unitive and unifying work of God given from two perspectives: first, how every believer is called to be conformed to the image of Christ; and second, the pattern after which the church universal images Christ in and to the world. Presented in the first instance is how everything constitutive of the protological image of God as comprehended in its three principal aspects—the official, constitutional, and ethical-relational—undergoes now through the Spirit for sons and daughters of God the progressive work of being transformed into the image of Christ from glory to glory. Presented in the second instance is how this present age is the already but not-yet order of reality in which God is doing that preparation of making his church beautiful for her end-time glorification as the wife of the Lamb. With respect to the damned in hell, it is proposed that these do not in any way participate in God's creational intention, which is revealed in its eternal fullness in the consummation when all things become summed up ultimately in Christ. The fittingness of God's retributive justice carries through in how the profound dignity conferred by God on man and woman alike by virtue of being created in his image becomes, for the damned, their being and bearing the utmost indignity. Lastly, shown here is how the eschatologically realized beauty of God in the economy of consummation becomes especially distinguished in its gloriousness against that of the economies of creation and redemption. The concluding note considers how the eschatological end of creation will be incomparably and everlastingly more glorious than its protological beginning for the redeemed in Christ.

2

Beauty Triune

The foundation for our christological contours of beauty begins with the doctrine of God. To recall from the Introduction, the constructive development of this project involves a biblical-theological characterization of God's beauty—notably in and through God the Son—as it is reflected economically in the phases of creation, redemption, and consummation. The distinct conceptual content of beauty that applies to the beauty of God manifested economically is what I had set out in our classicist theory of beauty in the Introduction. Our theological aesthetic of the doctrine of God and christological contours of beauty overall will therefore be concordant with our theory of beauty. Since the focus of my argumentation here is trained on the relation of beauty to God, it is necessarily limited in its scope and more in the way of a proposed theological aesthetic model. I am assuming upfront a doctrine of God fully consistent with Nicene Trinitarianism, and thus the development of our theological aesthetic will be in ways fully consistent with that. Additionally, the featured theologians in this chapter are Anselm of Canterbury, Thomas Aquinas, Herman Bavinck, and Karl Barth. The contributions of all four theologians to the subject of divine beauty are especially relevant to the theological aesthetic of the doctrine of God that I am putting forward, and to a fair extent this chapter constructively appropriates and engages their ideas. As a first order of business, then, I will summarize their respective positions on divine beauty, and will engage with various aspects of their theology accordingly throughout the rest of this chapter, and to lesser degrees in succeeding chapters.

The interest of this chapter is to put forward a theological aesthetic model of the doctrine of God, and notably with respect to God the Son, that will serve as the properly dogmatic (i.e., Trinitarian) ground for the constructive argument set forth in the subsequent chapters. My argumentation here in regard to the doctrine of God is developed in five main sections as follows:

1. *Beauty—A Divine Attribute?* First, I present how the beauty of God is most basically associated in Scripture with God's glory. In consideration of beauty as a divine perfection, the doctrine of divine simplicity, I argue, provides a systematic theological way to disambiguate how beauty relates to the other attributes.

2. *The Relation between Beauty and God's Glory.* I define the theological relation between God's glory and beauty. First, I set out what is meant or entailed by the glory of God expressed in his outward works (*ad extra*) and the glory of God in himself (*ad intra*). Following that I define the relation of God's glory to the objectively real aspect of God's extrinsic beauty.

3. *The Relation between Beauty and God's Beatitude.* I address the subjectively experienced aspect of God's extrinsic beauty, arguing that a theological aesthetic relation exists between beauty and God's beatitude. First, I set out what is meant or entailed by God's beatitude. Following that I clarify the relation of God's beatitude to beauty. Based on that relation, I draw together the fuller connection of transcendental truth, goodness, and beauty to the working of the Trinity *ad extra*.

4. *The Immanent Form of the Godhead's Beauty.* I define the immanent form of the Godhead's beauty, which is developed from our preceding argumentation for divine beauty and God's fullness of being as the Trinity of persons.

5. *The Fittingness of God the Son as Incarnate Redeemer.* Our Trinitarian account of aesthetics centers on the theological claim at the heart of this project's overall constructive argument, namely, that the Son's fittingness as incarnate Redeemer is displayed in Scripture as being fundamental to the design and outworking of God's eternal plan. The aesthetic notion of fittingness plays a critical role in my argumentation. First, I argue that all Trinitarian action in the divine economy is fittingly performed from the Father, through the Son, and in the Holy Spirit. Following that I lay out three theologically significant ways

the Scriptures attest to how the theodramatic fittingness of the Son has correspondence to the symmetrical nature of his agency in the work of the divine economy. Lastly, using Anselm and Aquinas as my guides, I consider the concept of fittingness in regard to the persons of the immanent Trinity, focusing in on the immanent fittingness of the Son.

THEOLOGIANS' POSITIONS ON DIVINE BEAUTY

ANSELM OF CANTERBURY ON DIVINE BEAUTY

Anselm works out his doctrine of God from metaphysical principles influenced largely by and consonant with Augustine's: God is what he possesses in all the highest perfections. Each positive good on the creaturely plane of reality, beauty included, is carried to its highest perfection in God.[1] For Anselm, these divine perfections are neither constituent qualities or quantities of God's being, nor is there any contradiction internal to God between coextensive "supremes." The supreme nature just *is* all of them. An entailment of this is that the full compass of redemptive-history in which God's plan and purposes are fully realized involves an aesthetic expression of God's own nature, for God and his ways are wholly beautiful. Anselm gives expression to this basic idea in *Proslogion* chapter 17, affirming the harmony and beauty integral to God's nature: "For you have these qualities in you, O Lord God, in your own ineffable way; and you have given them in their own perceptible way to the things you created."[2] Moreover, the aesthetic nature of God provides the proper "optics" through which to describe sin and evil, while vindicating God from being its author. The harmony of the cosmos itself is served by the principle of contrariety.

---

1. Anselm, *Monologion* in *Basic Writings*, ed. and trans. Thomas Williams (Indianapolis: Hackett, 2007), 24, gives clear expression to this (chap. 16): "Now it is clear that whatever good things the supreme nature is, he is that supremely. And so he is the supreme essence, supreme life, supreme reason, supreme salvation, supreme justice, supreme wisdom, supreme truth, supreme goodness, supreme greatness, supreme beauty, supreme immortality, supreme incorruptibility, supreme immutability, supreme beatitude, supreme eternity, supreme power, supreme unity, which is none other than supremely being, supremely living, and other similar things." See also Augustine, *Confessions* 1.4.4, trans. Henry Chadwick (Oxford: Oxford University Press, 2008).

2. Anselm, *Proslogion* in *Basic Writings*, ed. and trans. Williams, 91.

As Frank Burch Brown points out in regard to the disorder, disharmony and ugliness brought about by evil, "Anselm says only that any
ugliness in the order of things would ultimately be intolerable to God;
and because hell is designed to remedy [i.e., rectify] the ugliness of sin,
he implies—without stating it outright—that hell should be seen as in
some way beautiful."[3] The underlying premise is that hell is designed to
rectify the ugliness of sin by way of divine justice being fully vindicated.

Basic to Anselm's understanding of the divine nature is the concept
of fittingness. In *Cur Deus Homo* 1.3, for example, fittingness is a defining
characteristic of the aesthetic aspect of redemption, seen in the evident
symmetry entailed in its outworking:

> And it was fitting that the devil, who through the tasting of a tree
> defeated the human being whom he persuaded, should be defeated
> by a human being through the suffering on a tree that he inflicted.
> And there are many other things that, if carefully considered,
> demonstrate the indescribable beauty that belongs to our redemp-
> tion, accomplished in this way.[4]

The redemptive-eschatological structure of the divine plan will be
perfected in unity and symmetry, for only in this way will God's ultimate purposes in creation and redemption be perfectly fitting. This is
demonstrated in the aesthetic unity in which all things are governed
and brought to their ultimate completion. Even the exact number of
angels who fell irreparably through sin will be replaced in corresponding proportion from the redeemed lot of humanity, since "it was God's
plan to replace the fallen angels from out of the human race" for that
heavenly city that awaits.[5]

---

3. Frank Burch Brown, "The Beauty of Hell: Anselm on God's Eternal Design,"
Journal of Religion 73 (Jul 1993): 329–56, here 340. Along similar lines, David Hogg,
Anselm of Canterbury, 151, explains: "The challenge of disorder, disharmony and
ugliness brought about by evil is countered by Anselm when he places evil within
the larger context of aesthetic concerns, thereby showing the paradox of evil: it
can only exist within a world marked by beauty."

4. Anselm, *Cur Deus Homo* in *Basic Writings*, ed. and trans. Williams, 248. In the
full context, Anselm cites other examples of such symmetry. *Cur Deus Homo* 2.11
(*Basic Writings*, ed. and trans. Williams, 303–4), discusses fittingness in the plan of
redemption further.

5. *Cur Deus Homo* 1.19 (*Basic Writings*, ed. and trans. Williams, 300).

Thomas Aquinas on Divine Beauty

Like Anselm, Aquinas considered beauty a divine perfection as well, though his formulations to a considerable extent are the fruit of having worked out the Pseudo-Dionysian conceptions of beauty in a scholastic climate now warmed up to Aristotelianism.[6] For Aquinas, beauty is an attribute of God's being, which itself is the primal cause of the created order of all things.[7] And flowing from the fullness of God's being—i.e., the plenitude of his perfections—is the free participation of all created beings in the fullness of God's beauty (*supersubstantiale pulchrum*), which is the fount of all the beautiful. Aquinas thus writes in his commentary on the *Divine Names* of Dionysius, "The beauty of the creature is nothing else than the likeness of the divine beauty participated in things."[8] Although Aquinas' system begins with God as the first cause of being and the fullness of being, "it is clear," Francis Kovach explains, "that the basis of Thomas' theory of the essence of beauty rests on observations of an impressively broad scope and on the employment of the principle of the analogy of being."[9] From this Aquinas posits three formal criteria of beauty: proportion or consonance (*proportio sive consonatia*), integrity or wholeness (*integritas sive perfectio*), and clarity or splendor (*claritas sive splendor*).[10]

---

6. It was under the teaching authority of Albertus Magnus (c.1200–1280) that Aquinas received the ideas of aesthetics that influenced him the most, namely, the Dionysian conceptions of beauty. In actuality, Albertus' influence on Aquinas regarding aesthetics can be thought of foremost as mediating Dionysius in a scholastic climate that had embraced the Aristotelianism of its day. See Umberto Eco, *The Aesthetics of Thomas Aquinas*, trans. Hugh Bredin (Cambridge, MA: Harvard University Press, 1988), 25–26.

7. Scholarly opinion varies as to whether or not Aquinas considered beauty a transcendental quality of being, and hence of the divine essence itself. The opinion here agrees with such Thomistic scholars as Jacques Maritain, Etienne Gilson, G. B. Phelan, Armand A. Maurer, Umberto Eco, and W. Norris Clarke.

8. Aquinas, *In Divinis Nominibus*, c.4, lect. 5, n337, quoted in Armand A. Maurer, *About Beauty: A Thomistic Interpretation* (Houston: Center for Thomistic Studies, 1983), 116.

9. Francis J. Kovach, *Scholastic Challenges to Some Medieval and Modern Ideas* (Stillwater, OK: Western Publications, 1987), 248.

10. In *ST* Ia, q.39, a.8, Aquinas provides a systematic formulation of these three criteria. The question posed in this *Summa* article, and thus the context of Aquinas' formulation is "Whether the Essential Attributes Are Appropriated to the Persons [of the Trinity] in a Fitting Manner by the Holy Doctors?" A recommended

For Aquinas, *proportion* as an essential quality in beauty is synonymous with harmony and symmetry; proportion as such is "an analogous term, having many meanings, each determined by its context."[11] All meanings of proportion, moreover, are a function of being's "form," because for all being, whether sensible or intelligible, form provides the proximate ground of its beauty—"to be" is thus to be beautiful.[12] *Integrity*, although related to proportion, expresses the realized perfection of a thing—that is, what by its very nature a thing is meant to be. A thing is integral or whole that lacks nothing both in its existence and in whatever its form requires it to be in its telic wholeness. To be whole, as such, is what by its very nature a thing is meant to be perfectly and completely. "In a second sense," states Armand Maurer, "a thing is integral when it is perfect in its operation [or function]. Wholeness, in short, demands perfection in being and action. Lacking any of the parts required for the perfection of its form, or failing in its perfect operation, it falls short of the wholeness due to it, and to that extent it is ugly."[13] *Clarity* likewise is a function of being's form, just as we saw with proportion. For Aquinas, clarity is the distinctive "light" or splendor that each form imparts in its act of being. Since clarity is an analogous term as well, the kind of thing something is—sensible or intelligible, corporeal or spiritual—determines the kind of radiance perceivable by the percipient. Aquinas also attributes to *claritas* an expressive or communicative quality in itself, which signifies a "manifestation"—that is, expression—of a state of internal beauty.[14]

---

treatment regarding this is found in Eco, *The Aesthetics of Thomas Aquinas*, chapter IV: The Formal Criteria of Beauty.

11. Maurer, *About Beauty*, 11.

12. In the Thomistic perspective, "form" is the natural basis ontologically for why everything is the kind of thing that it is, and serves as the principle for why matter has the particular structure that it has. In virtue of a thing's form, the conditions that are constitutive of aesthetic value are given for its own distinctive beauty. A thing is beautiful in proportion to its own form, according to the level of perfection it has in its form.

13. Maurer, *About Beauty*, 12. In n21, Maurer explains, "What is ugly is less than it should be; it falls short of the actuality due to it. It may be wanting in wholeness, like a person without an arm or a leg, or in order or proportion, like the discordant notes in a musical composition or a badly balanced mathematical equation."

14. Aquinas, *ST* IIa IIae, q.132, a.1, cited in Eco, *Thomas Aquinas*, 251, n129.

Since God is the fullness of being, then, fullness of perfect proportion and integrity must be present in his immanent form. At the same time, since the immanent form of God's beauty has to do with Triune beauty, it cannot be considered strictly in terms of the unchangeable essence *de Deo uno*.[15] The divine essence is whatever the three persons are together, whose essential qualities are represented in the Unity-in-Trinity that is God. Armand Maurer puts it this way: "Now God is absolutely one by nature; from this point of view He exhibits no order or proportion. Here there is only pure unity. But He is three in Persons. In His personal life there is harmony and proportion and consequently beauty."[16] In the same way, perfect clarity is represented in that communicative quality in God that manifests and expresses his internal Triune beauty.

Herman Bavinck on Divine Beauty

The late nineteenth/early twentieth century Dutch Reformed theologian Herman Bavinck treats the topic of beauty in his *Reformed Dogmatics* in connection with God's attributes, blessedness, and glory.[17] Although articulating his theology of beauty from a distinctly Reformed perspective, Bavinck does base his view, at least in part, on certain premises common to the theological aesthetics of Anselm and Aquinas. Especially noteworthy here is the analogical predication of creaturely attributes to divine attributes: "Just as contemplation of God's creatures directs our attention upward and prompts us to speak of God's eternity and omnipresence, his righteousness and grace, so it also gives us a glimpse of God's glory. What we have here, however, is analogy, not identity."[18] Thus, for Bavinck, in the *ordo cognoscendi* an aesthetics from below precedes an aesthetics from above. He also speaks approvingly of the

---

15. In his treatment of the divine persons, Aquinas, *ST* Ia, q.42, a.4, ad 3, echoes as much: "all the relations together are not greater than only one; nor are all the persons something greater than only one; because the whole perfection of the divine nature [*tota perfectio divinae naturae*] exists in each person."

16. Maurer, *About Beauty*, 114.

17. For Bavinck's overall treatment pertaining to divine beauty, see *RD*, 2:249–55. Although beauty is treated there but briefly, it is the first modern work of dogmatics proper to recognize it in relation to the divine attributes.

18. Bavinck, *RD*, 2:254.

classical triad of truth, goodness, and beauty as transcendental qualities of God's being: "The pinnacle of beauty, the beauty toward which all creatures point, is God. He is supreme being, supreme truth, supreme goodness, and also the apex of unchanging beauty."[19] But Bavinck recognized the Neoplatonic association such language carries, and thus with respect to divine beauty makes clear his preference "to speak of God's majesty and glory" instead. Be that as it may, for Bavinck God's beauty is synonymous with his glory.[20]

KARL BARTH ON DIVINE BEAUTY

Like Bavinck, Barth treats beauty in his *Church Dogmatics* under the doctrine of God in connection with the divine perfections, though he is clear that beauty itself is not included "with the divine perfections which are the divine essence itself."[21] For Barth, the idea of beauty is invoked as an explanatory concept of God's glory. To say that God is beautiful is "to say how he enlightens and convinces and persuades us" in his revelation.[22] That is to say, God's glory is beautiful in how it evokes response from human beings by that which it gives. And exactly what God's glory gives that elicits response is "his overflowing self-communicating joy," a joy that has the "peculiar power and characteristic of

---

19. Bavinck, *RD*, 2:254. In a separate article, Bavinck's description of the features of beauty bears noticeable similarities to that of Aquinas: "Beauty always derives its content from the true and the good, and it is their revelation and appearance. Beauty thus consists in the agreement with content and form, with essence (idea) and appearance; it exists in harmony, proportion, unity in diversity, organization, glow, glory, shining, fullness, perfection revealed or whatever one wants to name it. But beauty always is in relation to form, revelation, and appearance." Herman Bavinck, "Of Beauty and Aesthetics," in *Essays on Religion, Science, and Society*, ed. John Bolt, trans. Harry Boonstra and Gerrit Sheeres (Grand Rapids: Baker Academic, 2008), 256.

20. Bavinck *RD*, 2:256, explains, "Speaking of creatures, we call them pretty, beautiful, or splendid; but for the beauty of God Scripture has a special word: glory. For that reason it is not advisable to speak—with the church fathers, scholastics, and Catholic theologians—of God's beauty." Previously, Bavinck, *RD*, 2.252, defines God's glory as "the splendor and brilliance that is inseparably associated with all of God's attributes and his self-revelation in nature and grace, the glorious form in which he everywhere appears to his creatures."

21. Karl Barth, *CD*, II/1, 652. For Barth's overall treatment pertaining to divine beauty, see *CD* II/1, §31.3 (608–677).

22. Barth, *CD*, II/1, 650.

giving pleasure, awakening desire, and creating enjoyment."[23] Barth identifies the objective basis of God's glory as something in God's perfections "which justifies us in having joy, desire and pleasure towards him." As he relates,

> We shall not presume to try to interpret God's glory from the point of view of His beauty, as if it were the essence of His glory. But we cannot overlook the fact that God is glorious in such a way that He radiates joy, so that He is all He is with and not without beauty. Otherwise His glory might well be joyless. ... We are dealing here solely with the question of the form of revelation.[24]

This "something" that obliges, summons, and attracts us to God is the "form" of God's glory, and is concomitant with the form of the revelation of God. Barth offers three central examples as to how the form of God's glory is known. First, God's attributes are revealed in the form of his self-revelation as the Lord, the Creator, Reconciler, and Redeemer. Second, the Trinity of God: it is only as the one being of the Father, the Son and the Holy Spirit that God is the perfections that he is. The Triunity of God is thus seen as the secret of his beauty. The third example is the incarnation—"the center and goal of all of God's works and therefore the hidden beginning of them all." What is reflected in the relationship between the divine and human nature in Christ is thus the beautiful form of the divine being.[25]

The beauty of God is best conceptualized, then, as that persuasive and convincing element in God's revelation, manifest in the form of his glory. The dynamic of God's beauty is thus interrelated with Barth's view of the *analogia fidei*, and his foundational thesis of the being of God may be adapted to describe his view of divine beauty as follows: *God's beauty is what it is in the glory of his revelation, and thus, God's beauty is Triune glory in act.*[26]

---

23. Barth, *CD*, II/1, 653. In all this Barth seems to be attempting to hold together God's beauty *in se* and *pro nobis*, so that neither is conceptualized apart from the other. I am indebted to Brannon Ellis for this insight.

24. Barth, *CD*, II/1, 655.

25. See Barth, *CD*, II/1, 657–65.

26. Emphasis added. The mature conception of Barth's christocentric theology in relation to the particular question of the being of God is captured in his thesis:

BEAUTY—A DIVINE ATTRIBUTE?

The names by which God identifies himself or by which God is referred to in Scripture have been recognized throughout church history as making known, explicitly or implicitly, various attributes of God, that is, ascriptions that are intrinsically true of him.[27] The names are "telling," but they are not "definitive" or directly ascriptive. Although explicit biblical references to the "beauty" of God (or otherwise identifying God specifically in terms of his beauty) are few, verses such as Psalm 27:4; 96:6; 145:5,12 and Isaiah 28:5 and 33:17 link directly images of a crown, a diadem, kingdom, and the sanctuary of the Lord to God's beauty. From these texts a connection is evident between divine beauty and the majesty and glory, the kingship and sovereignty of God (cf. Job 40:10; Zech 9:16–17). In many instances the imagery describing theophanies and prophetic visions conveys the same kind of association in language charged with aesthetic overtones. Isaiah's vision of the Lord enthroned in majestic glory (Isa 6:1–4; John 12:41), Ezekiel's vision of God's glory (Ezek 1), and John's apocalyptic vision of Christ (Rev 1:13–18; 4:2–3) are striking examples.[28] Terms in Scripture expressive of "beauty," moreover, are also used in a parallel relationship with "glory" (e.g., Exod 28:2). In short, the beauty and sublimity of God is most basically associated in Scripture with God's glory.[29] Indeed, we saw already the deep

---

"God is who He is in the act of His revelation," and thus, God's being is Triune "being in act." See Barth, *CD*, II/1, 257 and 262.

27. Herman Bavinck, *RD*, 2:96, 111, summarizes the point here thus: "All that we can say about God must be based on his self-revelation. ... As God reveals himself, so is he; in his names he himself becomes knowable to us. Though he is indeed infinitely superior to all his creatures—so that we can possess only an analogical knowledge of him not an exhaustive (adequated) knowledge—yet his several attributes, attributes that come through in his revelation, bring to our mind, each time from a special perspective, the fullness of his being." What God has revealed to us about himself in the Holy Scriptures is our paramount source and authority for this, although this is not at all to preclude making use of insights from general revelation/natural theology enlisted as an *ancilla theologiae*. Note, because divine attributes are understood to be intrinsic to God's essence or nature, the term divine "perfections" is sometimes stated as being preferable. In this work the terms "attributes" and "perfections" are used synonymously. See Bavinck, *RD*, 2:96–112 and 2:137–47.

28. "Beauty" in *DBI*, 84.

29. In John-Mark Hart, "Triune Beauty and the Ugly Cross: Towards a Theological Aesthetic," *TynBul* 66 no.2 (2015): 295–96, Hart expounds on the

connection between beauty and the glory of God reflected explicitly in the positions on divine beauty of Herman Bavinck and Karl Barth. I will further elaborate on that connection in the next section.

BEAUTY AND DIVINE SIMPLICITY

We are trying to answer whether beauty is of the divine nature itself, qualifying it as a divine perfection, or if not, how beauty should be qualified with respect to the divine nature. Among the featured theologians engaged with in this chapter, Anselm of Canterbury, Thomas Aquinas, Herman Bavinck, and Karl Barth have argued theological positions on beauty in relation to the divine perfections in two basic ways: beauty

---

above-noted connection in Scripture between beauty and God's splendor, majesty and glory: "Because Aaron has been set apart as high priest of the holy God, he is to wear holy garments, which represent the sacredness of his vocation 'for glory and for beauty'. The text goes on to describe in some detail the appearance of these clothes. As J. A. Motyer notes, 'the same colours, fabrics and gold were used for [Aaron's] garments as for the tabernacle,' with the effect that Aaron's clothes visually represent his consecration as God's 'heavenly man'. The high priest has been set apart to serve a transcendent God whose heavenly reign is gloriously manifest among his people at the site of the tabernacle. To put this a different way, the tabernacle and priesthood of Israel are the channels that God has chosen for his presence to break into the fallen world, and the aesthetic beauty of the tabernacle and priestly garments are meant to signify the sacredness of God's in-breaking glory. Thus, in this text, the concepts of glory and beauty are closely parallel, and they are both related to the perceptible manifestation of God's transcendent presence. Similar dynamics are at work in the interplay of the words glory (kabod) and beauty (tipharah) in Psalm 96. The Psalm repeatedly speaks of God's glory and beauty alongside other closely related terms such as splendour (hod), majesty (hadar), and strength (oz). These first two terms each have a semantic range that overlaps considerably with kabod and tipharah, while 'strength' is repeated in this context to emphasize the manifestation of God's transcendent power through his 'wonderful deeds among all the peoples' (verse 3). These wonderful deeds are also described as God's works of salvation as well as his righteous and faithful judgements among the peoples of the world (verses 2, 13). Thus the terms glory, beauty, splendour, majesty, and strength all signify the manifestation of God's transcendent goodness as it becomes apparent in his works of love, justice, and faithfulness. In response to these manifestations of divine goodness, the psalm invites 'all the earth' and the 'families of the peoples' to tremble before him, worship him with exuberant songs of praise, and proclaim his 'salvation from day to day'. The psalm also contrasts God's glory and beauty with the worthlessness of idols, in which none of God's righteousness, grace, faithfulness, and power are apparent (verses 4–5). Thus the concepts of glory and beauty in Psalm 96 involve the manifestation of God's transcendent greatness through his mighty acts, and this manifest greatness calls for exuberant worship and witness from humanity."

either is a divine perfection or corresponds in some way to the divine perfections. The mysterious and theologically slippery nature of beauty again presents itself. Nuancing the question at issue even further, is beauty a divine attribute itself, or a quality of every attribute, or the sum of them? Should we perhaps say instead that the way all the attributes comport in God—that is, the way they coexist in perfect harmony and sublime agreement—is beautiful and is what we mean by divine beauty? Scripture does not exactly parse out these subtleties. In consideration of beauty as an attribute, the doctrine of divine simplicity (DDS) provides a systematic-theological approach to disambiguate how beauty relates to the other attributes. Without exception, our featured theologians—Anselm, Aquinas, Bavinck, and Barth—are all proponents of divine simplicity.[30] A defense of the DDS will not be mounted here; I am stipulating, however, that I accept the DDS as valid.[31]

Our interest here is limited to describing in brief four basic claims of the DDS. Following that, I will put forward a biblically consistent construal on beauty in relation to God's attributes. It is important to note that the DDS is not so much a notion read explicitly or implicitly from the biblical data as it is the theological rationale seen to underlie the divine perfections that *are* readable from the biblical data.[32] According to Eleonore Stump the doctrine can be thought of as comprising the following claims:[33]

---

30. On the topic in hand, Richard Muller, *PRRD*, III, 39, states: "The doctrine of divine simplicity is among the normative assumptions of theology from the time of the church fathers, to the age of the great medieval scholastic systems, to the era of Reformation and post-Reformation theology, and indeed, on into the succeeding era of late orthodoxy and rationalism."

31. For a recommended defense of the DDS, see James E. Dolezal, *God without Parts: Divine Simplicity and the Metaphysics of God's Absoluteness* (Eugene, OR: Pickwick Publications, 2011); also, Thomas H. McCall, "Trinity Doctrine, Plain and Simple" in *Advancing Trinitarian Doctrine: Explorations in Constructive Dogmatics*, ed. Oliver D. Crisp and Fred Sanders (Grand Rapids: Zondervan, 2014), 42–59. The DDS has mixed scholarly support, and in more recent times has become noticeably more controverted in both systematic and philosophical theology. For a helpful discussion and exposition, see Dolezal, *God without Parts*, Chapter 1: Friends and Foes of the Classical Doctrine of Divine Simplicity.

32. Dolezal, *God without Parts*, 67.

33. Eleonore Stump, "Simplicity" in *A Companion to Philosophy of Religion*, 2nd ed., ed. Charles Taliaferro et al. (Malden, MA: Wiley-Blackwell, 2010), 270. Stump's use of the term "property" here is synonymous with attribute.

1. God cannot have any spatial or temporal parts.

2. God cannot have any intrinsic accidental properties.

3. There cannot be any real distinction between one essential property and another in God's nature.

4. There cannot be a real distinction between essence and existence in God.

Implicitly affirmed in the first claim are God's incorporeality and eternality.[34] Both these ascriptions lay claim to the "unboundedness" of God such that his complete, undivided, and unchanging life is ontologically unconditioned by space or time. The notion of divine simplicity, then, offers a useful way to explain conceptually/metaphysically how God can "be simultaneously present to all moments of time [and places of space] in the completeness of his being and essence."[35] Thus, God is not only unconditioned by space and time, but in virtue of this, he is wholly "present" to all spaces and times. According to claim two, a change in God's extrinsic (accidental) properties can occur without a change in God, while a change in God's intrinsic (essential) properties *would be* a change in God.[36] At stake in this claim is God's immutability. The basic idea of claim three is that the distinctions between divine attributes mark a conceptual distinction within God's nature but do not mark any real (i.e., ontological) distinction within it. In line with how we defined transcendental properties of being in the Introduction, what we thus distinguish conceptually as the various divine attributes "is the single thing that is God but recognized by us under differing

---

34. Stump, "Simplicity," 270. Stump adds, "On the doctrine of simplicity, the life of a simple God is not spread out over time, any more than God is spread out over space."

35. See Dolezal, *God without Parts*, 88–92, here 91–92.

36. Along the same lines Thomas H. McCall, *Forsaken: The Trinity and the Cross, and Why It Matters* (Downers Grove, IL: IVP Academic, 2012), 78, explains, "Attributes that are essential to God on the one hand are those that make God who he is—they are characteristics or perfections of God's own life. Attributes that God has only in relation to the world, on the other hand, are not essential to him but instead are contingent. After perceiving this distinction between essential and contingent attributes, it is important to note that within the unity of God's being and act the attributes that are contingent are grounded in and flow from what is essential to him."

descriptions or in different manifestations."[37] And lastly, according to claim four, "God is so radically one that there is no composition in him even of essence and existence. Consequently, God does not have an essence; instead, he is identical with his essence, and even his existence cannot be distinguished from that essence."[38] Put another way, there is no difference between *what* God is and *that* God is.[39]

Accepting as valid the supposition that God's nature is "pure act," postulating God in himself (*in se*) as being all his attributes comports in Thomistic terms with saying that there is no unrealized metaphysical potentiality in God. He is *actus purus*, pure undivided (and never passive) act.[40] "With God we do not hypothesize any unity underlying the diversity because there is no diversity" with respect to nature, explains Katherin Rogers. "There is just the one, perfect act which is God."[41] With respect to our consideration of beauty as an attribute, then, the DDS account of God's identity suggests that beauty be considered a divine

37. Stump, "Simplicity," 271.

38. Stump, "Simplicity," 271. James Ross, "Religious Language" in *Philosophy of Religion: A Guide to the Subject*, ed. Brian Davies (Washington, DC: Georgetown University Press, 1998), 113, elaborates the point in terms of the act-potency relation: "God's essence is said to be identical with his existence ... in the sense that, unlike all other real things, there is no real distinction (no real difference) between God's being and what God is, while with all other things, *what* they are is related to their *being* as a *capacity* to its *realization* (a potency that limits act). So, for any other thing, *what-it-is* limits its being: a dog can only be a dog, not a lion."

39. For a helpful discussion of the different models that proponents of the DDS use to defend it, see Dolezal, *God without Parts*, chapter 5: Simplicity and God's Absolute Attributes.

40. Elaborating on this same point, Eleonore Stump, "Dante's Hell, Aquinas's Moral Theory, and the Love of God," *Canadian Journal of Philosophy* 16 no. 2 (June 1986), 186, writes, "So on the doctrine of simplicity there are in reality no distinctions within the divine nature, and God is in some sense identical with whatever can be really attributed to him. But the respect in which God is devoid of real distinctions does not preclude our distinguishing God's actions in the world from one another and does not require our taking the terms for divine attributes as synonymous. On the doctrine of simplicity, then, there is something inaccurate in saying that God is omnipotent. It is more nearly correct to say that he is identical with omnipotence, but even that statement is misleading. Perhaps the best available formulation is that God is identical with the single indivisible act which he is, one of whose manifestations or partial descriptions is omnipotence." See Aquinas, *ST* Ia, q.3, a.7; *ST* Ia, q.4, a.2, ad 1.

41. Katherin A. Rogers, *The Anselmian Approach to God and Creation* (Lewiston, NY: Edwin Mellen Press, 1997), 39.

perfection in its own right without other qualifications necessary. In sum, the ontological basis for predicating beauty of God is identical with the ontological basis for predicating all of the perfections of God—God simply *is* all his perfections in pure act. It would be inconsistent theologically, therefore, to consider beauty to be a "special case" relative to all of God's other perfections. Thus, beauty is neither a separate portmanteau quality correlated in some way to the divine attributes, or the sum of the attributes, or just the way all the attributes comport in God. In other words, beauty is not itself the ultimate integrative harmony, another way of talking about divine simplicity. Rather, the DDS leads us to say that God ontologically is all his perfections, one of which we have biblical witness and support to say is beauty.[42] This still does not address just what God's beauty consists in; we will attend to that question in short order, however.

THE RELATION BETWEEN BEAUTY AND GOD'S GLORY

At the beginning of this chapter, we saw the deep connection between beauty and the glory of God reflected explicitly in the positions on divine beauty of Herman Bavinck and Karl Barth. The same connection is reflected in the positions of Hans Urs von Balthasar and Jonathan Edwards, which I present in Chapters 3 and 5 respectively. Here, I will define the theological relation between God's glory and beauty. First, I will set out what is meant or entailed by God's glory *ad extra* and *ad intra*, and then I will clarify the relation of God's glory to beauty.

DEFINING GOD'S GLORY

The referent "glory" in Scripture normally pertains to the Trinity operating economically, but it is arguably used of the Trinity relating essentially as well. The former is considered properly God's extrinsic glory (*ad extra*) and the latter his intrinsic glory (*ad intra*). Bavinck touches on both stating, "When Scripture speaks of God's face, glory, and majesty, it uses figurative language. Like all God's perfections, so also that of God's glory is reflected in his creatures. It is communicable. In the created world there is a faint reflection of the inexpressible glory

---

42. See the sub-section of Chapter 2, Beauty—A Divine Attribute? and Appendix 1: The General Witness of Scripture to the Aesthetic Dimension.

and majesty that God possesses."[43] As we shall see, the glory of God functions in Scripture in a way parallel to the revealed names of God, namely, both bring to our mind, each time from a special perspective, the plenitude of his perfections.

By far the predominant Hebrew word used for "glory" in the OT (some 200 times) is כָּבוֹד, and it is employed most often in reference to God, his sanctuary, his city, or other sacred objects. The constellation of meanings of כָּבוֹד (e.g., weight, gravity, honor, fame, dignity, splendor, etc.) attain a certain fixation of meaning, and in the process an overall enrichment of meaning, with the advent of the Septuagint, which uses δόξα to translate virtually all the Hebrew words for glory. As well, the more pedestrian meanings of δόξα similarly came to be replaced by the rich Hebrew concept of the glory of God.[44] The concept of God's glory *ad extra* pervades the sweep of Scripture in creation, redemption, and consummation.

Between the biblical narrative of paradisal creation and eschatological consummation we have the great unfolding of revelation of God's manifest glory-presence in redemption. It is sufficient for our present purposes just to highlight some key examples. The visible and active presence of God in the midst of his covenant people is manifest in sundry ways throughout much of the OT as a theophanic glory-presence. In the Exodus account, God's glory-presence involves both deliverance from and destruction of Israel's enemies (Exod 13:21–22; 14:24–25; 16:10; 24:17).[45] Subsequently, God's dwelling among his people is signified in more focal terms by the dwelling of his glory in the tabernacle (the tabernacle functioning as a mobile temple of sorts), as it was in Israel's later temple in Jerusalem (Exod 29:43; 40:34–38; 1 Kgs 8:10–11; 2 Chr 5:13–14; 7:1–3).[46] By the time of Judah's Babylonian exile,

---

43. Bavinck, *RD*, 2:254.

44. Bernard Ramm, *Them He Glorified: A Systematic Study of the Doctrine of Glorification* (Grand Rapids: Eerdmans, 1963), 10–11.

45. See James M. Hamilton Jr., *God's Glory in Salvation through Judgment: A Biblical Theology* (Wheaton, IL: Crossway, 2010) for a thorough treatment on the connection between glory and judgment.

46. In the unique case of Moses, his vis-à-vis with the glory-presence of the Lord was enough to cause *his* face to radiate luminously (Exod 34:29–35). Ramm, *Them He Glorified*, 13–14, points out that "the apostle Paul affirmed that this manifestation of the divine presence was one of Israel's greatest benefits, for he wrote

however, the glory of the Lord departs from the temple altogether (Ezek 9–11). In the fullness of time it reappears with the advent of the Son of God incarnate, who as the Redeemer of the world is the definitive expression of the glory-presence of God (John 1:14; 1 Tim 4:10; Heb 1:1–3). The reference to Jesus in John 1:14, notes Andreas Köstenberger, "also harks back to OT references to the manifestation of the presence and glory (*kābôd*) of God, be it theophanies, the tabernacle, or the temple."[47]

In the eschatological consummation, the incarnate presence of God in the person of Jesus Christ glorified will dwell eternally with his people—the Bride of Christ, the church of God glorified (Rev 21:1–22:5). This marks the new heavens and earth, the full realization of what Isaiah foresaw: "The glory of the Lord shall be revealed, and all flesh shall see it together" (Isa 40:5; ch. 60, especially verses 1–2, 13, 19; cf. Num 14:21; Hab 2:14). On the apostle John's vision of Christ in Revelation 21–22, Köstenberger writes, "Most importantly, in this final vision it is made clear that God shares his glory with his people in fulfillment of Jesus' vision and desire that his followers be allowed to see his preexistent glory (John 17:24; cf. 17:5)."[48] Indeed, Isaiah prophesied of this shared glory in regal and aesthetic language, stating that God's people will be "a crown of beauty in the hand of the LORD, and a royal diadem in the hand of your God" (62:2–3; cf. Zech 9:16–17). The apostle Peter simply describes this as being "a partaker in the glory that is going to be revealed," although still noting its regal aspect (1 Pet 5:1, 4; cf. Rom 9:23; 1 Cor 15:43; Col 1:27; 3:4). It thus awaits until the consummation of all things for the redeemed in Christ to fully realize the "glory and

---

that to them belonged the *glory* (Rom 9:4). Similarly, the cherubim of the mercy seat are called (in Heb 9:5) 'cherubim of glory' because of the glory that glowed between them. The dwelling of the glory of God in the tabernacle not only gives a visible sign of the presence of the Lord but it also makes the entire structure holy." See also the treatment by Tremper Longman III, "The Glory of God in the Old Testament" in *The Glory of God*, ed. Christopher W. Morgan and Robert A. Peterson (Wheaton, IL: Crossway, 2010), 47–78.

47. Andreas J. Köstenberger, "John" in *Commentary on the New Testament Use of the Old Testament*, ed. G. K. Beale and D. A. Carson (Grand Rapids: Baker Academic, 2007), 422. The treatment in Ramm, *Them He Glorified*, chapter III: The Glory of Jesus Christ, is recommended as well.

48. Andreas J. Köstenberger, "The Glory of God in John's Gospel and Revelation," in *The Glory of God*, ed. Christopher W. Morgan and Robert A. Peterson (Wheaton, IL: Crossway, 2010), 125.

honor" with which they have been crowned, for only then will they fully partake in the glory and honor with which Jesus himself has been crowned on their behalf (Heb 2:9; cf. Ps 8:5).[49]

In a variety of ways, and with cumulative effect, the intrinsic glory of God is also attested to in Scripture. To begin with, it is perhaps telling how "the word glory (*kābôd*) serves as a synonym for God himself: 'Has a nation changed its gods, even though they are no gods? But my people have changed their glory [i.e., their God] for that which does not profit' (Jer 2:11)." Along with this, in Isaiah 42:8 the Lord identifies himself in terms of his name and his own *kābôd*, which cannot belong to any other.[50] Similarly, in the New Testament God the Father is referred to by Peter as the "Majestic Glory" (2 Pet 1:17), an unusual expression that is likely used here to avoid naming God directly; likewise Paul speaks of "the Father of glory" (Eph 1:17; cf. Acts 7:2). As Ramm observes, these designations are fulsome, implying "that he is a glorious God, that he gives glory, and that he is a being to whom glory belongs."[51] With regard to Jesus, one of the most telling statements is given in John 17:5 in which he refers directly to the glory *ad intra* that he too had with the Father "before the world existed." And just like with the Father, the same fulsomeness of glory is implied in the designations of Jesus as "the Lord of glory" and "the radiance of the glory of God and the exact imprint of his nature" (2 Cor 2:8; Jas 2:1; and Heb 1:3).[52]

Furthermore, it is in Romans 1:18–23 where we find attributes of God's nature described as being "clearly perceived" in creation, revealing "the glory of the immortal God" to humanity (cf. Ps 106:19–20). What is more, the word "glory" frequently serves in Scripture in tandem with or as a proxy for specific attributes of God. In such instances, of

---

49. See also the relevant treatments in Ramm, *Them He Glorified,* chapter VII: The Glorification and the New Jerusalem, and Morgan, "Toward a Theology of the Glory of God."

50. Ramm, *Them He Glorified,* 18–19. For a helpful discussion on the complementary relation between God's name and his glory, see J. Gordon McConville, "God's 'Name' and God's 'Glory'," *TynBul* 30 (1979): 149–63.

51. Ramm, *Them He Glorified,* 25.

52. Morgan, "Toward a Theology of the Glory of God," 157, rounds this out, stating, "The Spirit, too, is identified with glory (1 Pet 4:14; cf. John 16:14; Eph 1:13–14), especially through the language of presence, indwelling, and temple (John 14-16; Rom 8:9–11; 1 Cor 3:16; 6:19–20; 14:24–25; 2 Cor 6:16; Eph 2:11–22; 5:18; 1 Thess 4:8)."

course, the specific attribute(s) has to be determined from the context. Examples here include the following: goodness in the aspects of mercy and grace (Exod 33:18–19; Eph 1:6, 12, 14); truthfulness (1 Sam 15:29); holiness (Isa 6:3); majesty (Isa 35:2); righteousness (Rom 3:23); and power (John 11:40; Rom 6:4; 2 Thess 1:8–9). Indeed, in Scripture glory does seem to connote the publication or external manifestation/realization of God's perfections. "Such biblical data suggests that God's intrinsic glory is broader than a single attribute," observes Christopher Morgan. "It corresponds with his very being and sometimes functions as a sort of summation of his attributes."[53] The associative effect of linking glory so directly with (or as a substitute for) a variety of divine attributes suggests the nature of glory being intrinsic to God in se.[54]

Although the above explication of the biblical concept of glory does not account for all its aspects and constellation of meanings, overall it more than suggests that glory "refers not so much to an attribute of God, unlike [e.g.,] 'omnipotence', but is the term that when theologically considered encapsulates the eminence of all God's attributes viewed together in the light of the tota Scriptura (the whole biblical testimony)."[55] On this view the immanent glory of God comprehends all of God's attributes. And thus the immanent glory of God means the same as the altogether perfection of God. Consonant with the notion of divine simplicity offered earlier, then, and with a nod towards Aquinas, a perfectly proper way to characterize God's fullness of being would be as supersubstantiale gloriosum, his fullness of glory. The relation of white light to the full color spectrum may be figuratively illustrative here. As Isaac Newton demonstrated in the late seventeenth century, an optical prism can be used to separate white light into its constituent spectral colors. The prism does not create colors but simply reveals that all the colors already exist in the light (more technically, it evidences the existence of a spectrum of wavelengths present in visible light).[56]

---

53. Morgan, "Toward a Theology of the Glory of God," 165. See also Ramm, Them He Glorified, 19.

54. Cf. Kittel, δόξα, TDNT, 2:244: δόξα denotes the "divine nature or essence either in its invisible or its perceptible form."

55. Graham A. Cole, God the Peacemaker: How Atonement Brings Shalom (Downers Grove, IL: InterVarsity Press, 2009), 225.

56. In a closely related vein of thinking, Gregory of Nyssa applied the

Newton proved this by using a second prism to recompose the spectrum back into white light. So let us say that the white light represents God's glory *ad intra*, then all the spectral colors revealed by the prism represent the revelation of God's extrinsic glory in all its manifestations. And most amazingly, this fullness of glory is fully composed in the person of Christ Jesus.

DEFINING THE RELATION BETWEEN
BEAUTY AND GOD'S GLORY

We are in position now to define the theological relation between God's glory and beauty. I have argued so far that the immanent glory of God means the same as the altogether perfection of God. God's glory as such "encapsulates the eminence of all God's attributes," including beauty as being one of those attributes. God's extrinsic beauty is thus one facet of the innumerable facets of his extrinsic glory, all of which is fully consistent with saying that God's extrinsic beauty is a communicable perfection expressed in his outward works. The distinct conceptual content of beauty that applies to the beauty expressed in God's outward

---

illustration of the rainbow in grappling with the difficulty that the human mind encounters in reconciling the oneness and threeness of God: "You have before now, in springtime, beheld the brilliance of the bow in the clouds—I mean the bow which is commonly called the 'rainbow'. ... Now, the brightness [of the rainbow] is both continuous with itself and divided. It has many diverse colors; and yet the various bright tints of its dye are imperceptibly intermingled, hiding from our eyes the point of contact of the different colors with each other. As a result, between the blue and the flame-color, or the flame-color and the purple, or the purple and the amber, the space which both mingles and separates the two colors cannot be discerned. For when the rays of all the colors are seen they are seen to be distinct, and yet at the same time ... it is impossible to find out how far the red or the green color of the radiance extends, and at what point it begins to be no longer perceived as it is when it is distinct. Just as in this example we both clearly distinguish the different colors and yet cannot detect by observation the separation of one from the other, so, please consider that it is also possible to draw [similar] inferences with regard to the divine doctrines. In particular, one can both conclude that the specific characteristics of [each of] the Persons [of the Godhead], like any one of the brilliant colors which appear in the rainbow, reflect their brightness in each of the [other] Persons we believe to be in the Holy Trinity, but that no difference can be observed in the ... nature of the one as compared with the others." Gregory of Nyssa in a document that has been titled *On the Difference between* ousia [being] *and* hypostasis [person], quoted in Michael A. G. Haykin, "Defending the Holy Spirit's Deity: Basil of Caesarea, Gregory of Nyssa, and the Pneumatomachian Controversy of the 4th Century," *SBJT* 7 no.3 (Fall 2003), 78.

works is what I set out in our classicist theory of beauty in the Introduction, summarized in abbreviated form as follows: Beauty is an intrinsic quality of things that, when perceived, pleases the mind by displaying a certain kind of fittingness. That is to say, beauty is discerned via objective properties such as proportion, unity, variety, symmetry, harmony, intricacy, delicacy, simplicity, or suggestiveness. As I am applying the term, then, fittingness functions as an overarching term expressive of the full range of aesthetic properties that identify any and all objective characteristics of beauty. What uniquely characterizes the quality of beauty is its effect of evoking pleasure or delight in the act of perceiving it. Thus, a realist view of beauty is postulated in which the unique nature of beauty implies objective properties—with such properties themselves able to serve as objective aesthetic criteria—and involves the effect beauty has of eliciting a subjective response of aesthetic pleasure as we perceive it.[57]

In accordance with our received theory of beauty, therefore, the beauty expressed in God's outward works is objectively real and subjectively experienced. Here, we are only addressing the objectively real aspect of God's extrinsic beauty in relation to his glory. The subjectively experienced aspect of God's extrinsic beauty will be addressed in the next section in our discussion of the relation between beauty and God's beatitude.

Inasmuch as an objectivist view is premised in our theory of beauty, this implies that the quality of beauty has no real being in the abstract (i.e., not purely nominal) but must have existence in an objective form.[58] That is to say, beauty in the order of reality pertains only to something that has form, for something that has no form is sheer abstraction.[59]

---

57. As I had noted in the Introduction, since the canon of Scripture is the *norma normans* for the theological aesthetics with which our biblical and systematic theology of beauty as defined by the divine economy of redemption is developed, the theory of beauty stemming out of the classical tradition that has served to fund this will be more properly qualified as needed in the Conclusion.

58. The basic universalized meaning of "form" serving here is the given mode, structure, pattern, or essential nature in which any real thing (material or immaterial) exists, occurs or is experienced, expressed, or done. In regard to theological aesthetics in particular, it is important to note that acts as well as things (entities) can be beautiful.

59. What is meant here by "abstraction" is any notional entity or general

And all the countless forms that God's glory takes in creation, redemption, and consummation are themselves objective forms entailing an aesthetic quality of whatever degree. To be clear, beauty is not identical or does not simply equate to glory or the objective forms that God's glory takes—beauty is *not* a synonym for glory, in other words. The distinction here is a subtle one but important to grasp. The theological relation between God's glory and beauty translates as follows: the beauty of God manifested economically (*pulchritudo Dei ad extra*) is expressed and perceivable *as a quality of* the glory of God inherent in his work of creation, redemption, and consummation.[60] The display of God's glory is thus always beautiful, always fitting, always entails an aesthetic dimension to it. The universal scope of this means that an aesthetic dimension—in illimitable expressions and degree—is inherent in the structure (i.e., form) of God's extrinsic glory.[61] Reminiscent here is Anselm's affirmation of the harmony and beauty integral to God's nature: "For you have these qualities in you, O Lord God, in your own ineffable way; and you have given them in their own perceptible way to the things you created."[62] What I am proposing, then, is that the countless forms of the glory of God *ad extra*, down to their most infinitesimal features, are inherently imbued with the full compass of his communicable attributes, one of which is beauty with the untold array of aesthetic characteristics it entails.

Lastly, there is a critical caveat I must register. The ramifications of a creational order radically affected by sin and laboring under the

---

concept considered apart from an actual instance of a real being. Since sheer abstraction does not have an objective form, it is impossible that an abstraction could have the quality of beauty. Indeed, it is arguable that no attribute has "real being in the abstract."

60. To illustrate the point here in simple fashion, we could say that "wetness" is a particular quality of water in liquid form. We would not want to say, however, that "wetness" is liquid water. The "is" in the latter case is simply an "is" of predication.

61. The view I set forth here affirms the ontological ground of the objective forms glory takes in creation, redemption, and consummation as being God's own fullness of glory. Barth, in contrast, views the "form" of God's glory as the specifically persuasive and convincing element in God's revelation. Barth, *CD*, II/1, 659, wants nevertheless to distinguish but not separate God's form from his being, stating that the form is made perfect by the content, i.e., God himself, since the form is necessary to the content and belongs to it.

62. Anselm, *Proslogion* in *Basic Writings*, 91.

judgment curse of God from the fall of our primal parents in Genesis 3, compromise and affect the integrity of all dimensions of the creational order, including the aesthetic. The extrinsic glory of God now pertains to a creation under his judgment curse; a creation groaning to be set free from its bondage to corruption (Rom 8:21–22), and a humanity who by their unrighteousness suppress the truth of what can be perceived and known of God's nature in the things that have been made (Rom 1:18–20). The beauty of God manifested economically does not change from being a quality of his glory inherent in his work of creation. But such glory is reflected now in a created order and a humanity operating under the effects of God's judgment curse, and thus in indeterminable ways the created order itself is tainted/corrupted, and humanity's ability to rightly perceive the attributes of God reflected in creation is obscured/distorted. I will address the undoing of the effects of the judgment curse and the ultimate renewal of creation as I work through the christological contours of beauty in respect of the redemptive-eschatological outworking of the divine plan in the economy of salvation.

THE RELATION BETWEEN BEAUTY AND GOD'S BEATITUDE

In the previous section I defined the theological relation between God's glory and beauty, addressing only the objectively real aspect of God's extrinsic beauty in relation to his glory. In this section I address the subjectively experienced aspect of God's extrinsic beauty, making a theological connection to God's beatitude. Why God's beatitude? In what way does God's beatitude figure in to our theological aesthetic? In the properly dogmatic account of aesthetics that I am putting forward, a theological aesthetic relation exists between beauty and God's beatitude. In defining that theological relation, I will first set out what is meant or entailed by God's beatitude, and then I will clarify the relation of this to beauty. Based on the relation between God's beatitude and beauty, I will draw together the fuller connection of transcendental truth, goodness, and beauty to the working of the Trinity *ad extra*.

God's beatitude refers to his intrinsic or *ad intra* "blessedness." Just as with beauty, however, explicit biblical references identifying God specifically in terms of his beatitude are few. The clearest verses to do so are 1 Timothy 1:11 and 6:15 in which μακάριος ("blessed") is used as an epithet for the only God (6:15), pointing up blessedness as being intrinsic to the very identity of who God is.[63] The idea of God's own beatitude or blessedness denotes the eternal condition in himself of absolute felicity, delight, satisfaction, and repose.[64] It is worth noting how closely the language Paul uses in 1 Timothy 6:15–16, albeit doxologically driven, resonates with the pronounced aspects in Scripture concerning the beauty of God and his manifest glory, namely, the majesty, kingship, and splendor of God.[65] The Greek word normally used for "blessed" in the sense of God being "worthy of praise" is εὐλογητός.[66] However, while many scholars regard Paul's use of "blessed" in 2 Corinthians 1:3 and

63. As an adjective "blessed" could apply to mean the "praised" God in the sense that he receives the praise or blessing of which he is worthy, but the common consensus among commentators is that "blessed" here means God is blessed in himself, i.e., blessedness is intrinsic to who God is.

64. That various idioms Paul uses in 1 Timothy (and the Pastoral Epistles generally) point to the Hellenistic milieu to which he is writing is well attested. In his commentary on 1 Timothy, Raymond F. Collins, *1 and 2 Timothy and Titus: A Commentary* (Louisville: Westminster John Knox, 2002), 34–35, states that in using "blessed" as an epithet for God, "[Paul] speaks as did Hellenistic Jews who use the language of Hellenism to express their Jewish faith. Thus, Philo wrote, 'God alone is happy and blessed, exempt from all evil, filled with perfect forms of good, or rather, if the real truth be told, himself the good, who showers the particular goods on heaven and earth' (*Special Laws* 2.53) and that God is the 'Imperishable Blessed One' (*Unchangeableness of God* 26). Hellenistic Judaism's use of 'blessed' to describe God is derived from the Greeks. Aristotle, for example, affirmed that the gods enjoy 'supreme felicity [μακάριος] and happiness' and that the activity of the gods is transcendent in blessedness (*Nicomachean Ethics* 10.8.7). He went on to affirm that 'the whole of the life of the gods is blessed, and that of humans insofar as it contains some likeness to the divine activity' (10.8.8). Philo shared the notion that it is only in relationship to God that other things can be called blessed: 'The good and beautiful things in the world could never have been what they are, save that they were made in the image of the archetype, which is truly good and beautiful, even the uncreated, the blessed, the imperishable' (*Cherubim* 86; see *Gaius* 5)."

65. William D. Mounce, *Pastoral Epistles* (WBC 46; Waco, TX: Word, 2000), 361, offers the following commentary on 1 Timothy 6:15: "The language, drawn from the OT, the Hellenistic synagogue, and Hellenism, describes a mighty and transcendent God who deserves Timothy's loyalty. Some of the language is directed against emperor worship, which had a center in Ephesus, claiming that God and not the emperor possesses immortality, that God is the King over all kings and Lord over all lords, and that God alone possesses might."

66. Examples in both the LXX and the New Testament include the following: 1 Kgs 1:48; 2 Chr 2:11; 6:4; Pss 40:14; 71:18; 88:53; Luke 1:68; Rom 1:25; 9:5; 2 Cor 11:31; 1 Pet 1:3. Cf. Rev 4:11; 5:12–13.

Ephesians 1:3 to be extolling God as "worthy of praise," others suggest the best interpretation of these texts is not the optative sense but the indicative—that is, Paul is referring to God's intrinsic blessedness.[67]

The creaturely experience of blessedness naturally expresses itself in the experience of "happiness" or "delight." Although the full dimension of blessedness surely involves more than possessing a certain sense of felicity, we should not think it involves less than this either. In *ST* Ia, q.62, a.4, Aquinas posits this same idea of God having absolute blessedness in himself: "Perfect beatitude is natural only to God, because existence and beatitude are one and the same thing in Him."[68] As Katherin Rogers succinctly (if over-simplistically) puts it, "The medieval position is simply that it is better to be happy than sad, so God must be infinitely happy."[69] For Aquinas (and the medievals generally) the issue was not whether God is utterly impassive—that is, that he experiences no emotions at all—for "there is no question that in the classical tradition God enjoys complete love and happiness, while 'negative' emotions,

---

67. For example, the translator's note on Ephesians 1:3 in the NET states: "There is no verb in the Greek text; either the optative ("be") or the indicative ("is") can be supplied. The meaning of the term εὐλογητός, the author's intention at this point in the epistle, and the literary genre of this material must all come into play to determine which is the preferred nuance. Εὐλογητός as an adjective can mean either that one is praised or that one is blessed, that is, in a place of favor and benefit. The meaning "blessed" would be more naturally paired with an indicative verb here and would suggest that blessedness is an intrinsic part of God's character. The meaning "praised" would be more naturally paired with an optative verb here and would suggest that God ought to be praised. Pauline style in the epistles generally moves from statements to obligations, expressing the reality first and then the believer's necessary response, which would favor the indicative. ... When considered as a whole, although a decision is difficult, the indicative seems to fit all the factors better. The author seems to be pointing to who God is and what he has done for believers in this section; the indicative more naturally fits that emphasis. Cf. also 2 Cor 1:3; 1 Pet 1:3." Lending perhaps indirect support is the substantival use of εὐλογητός in Mark 14:61 in which the high priest Caiaphas, interrogating Jesus, asks, "Are you the Christ—the son of the Blessed [i.e., God]?" (ὁ υἱὸς τοῦ εὐλογητοῦ). This reference to God as "the Blessed One" is properly seen as a Jewish circumlocution for God's name, similar to the periphrastic way Peter refers to God as the "Majestic Glory" (2 Pet 1:17).

68. Continuing, Aquinas adds, "Beatitude, however, is not of the nature of the creature, but is its end." E.g., also *ST* Ia, q.26; Ia IIae, q.3, a.1, ad 1; Ia IIae, q.3, a.2, ad 1, 4.

69. Katherin A. Rogers, *Perfect Being Theology* (Edinburgh: Edinburgh University Press, 2000), 51.

like hate and sorrow, which are the falling away from love and joy, are impossible for a perfect being to experience (*ST* Ia, q.20)."[70] To affirm such "positive" emotions of God is to analogically predicate at least well-ordered creaturely emotions to him. What is assumed here is not an anthropomorphic projection of our image upon God, but rather a theomorphic projection of God's image upon us.[71] The anthropomorphous God, in other words, corresponds to the theomorphous human being. "We are usually quite content to speak of the divine mind," points out Graham Cole, "Why balk at speaking of God's feelings?"[72] It is, in other words, to take as *illegitimate* the premise that God's nature is simply impassive and as *legitimate* the ascription to God of an intrinsic emotional life, not in the merely metaphorical sense, but analogical to our own emotional life if this were not infected by and without the effects of sin. On this view an emotional life that is labile or entails real imperfection, impropriety, or disquietude must not be predicated of God. Yet at the same time the attribute of impassivity is likewise to be considered its own kind of imperfection. A proper distinction is to be made, however, between divine impassivity and divine impassibility—these concerns are not identical ones. The core concern of divine impassibility is whether God can be affected by something outside himself. Discussions on this oftentimes have to do with whether and/or how God is subject to the so-called "negative" emotions, often distinguished as "passions."[73] For obvious reasons the matter of Christ's suffering is

---

70. Rogers, *Perfect Being Theology*, 51.

71. Brian G. Mattson, *Restored to Our Destiny: Eschatology and the Image of God in Herman Bavinck's Reformed Dogmatics* (Boston: Brill, 2012), 120, notes the significance of the *imago Dei* to our point: "The theologian is authorized to analogically apply human attributes of God (as scripture does) precisely because God already created human beings as an analogical image of himself."

72. Graham A. Cole, "The Living God: Anthropomorphic or Anthropopathic?," *The Reformed Theological Review* 59 no.1 (April 2000): 24. Bavinck, *RD*, 2:50, makes the obverse point on our capacity to know as well as *feel* God: "If God cannot be known, then neither can he be felt and, in that feeling, enjoyed."

73. There is an important difference to mark here between God being passionate and his having passions—the former being proper to affirm but not the latter (*the passion* in reference to Christ Jesus suffering death is altogether something different, however, from what we mean here by God having passions). Cole, "The Living God," n23, is instructive on this point, noting, "there is an old theological distinction going back to Tertullian (c.160–c.225CE) that distinguishes between God having emotion and feeling (*'motus'* and *'sensus'*) as we do and God having passions

an inescapable part of these discussions as well. Issues pertaining to divine impassibility are adjacent but not central to our present interest, though, which is the beatitude of God in himself.

A key question is whether or not God's beatitude is subject to any essential change. A partial answer at this point can be given. According to divine simplicity, the Triune God as Father, Son, and Spirit is his attributes—his fullness of glory—and since God himself is not subject to any essential change, neither are his attributes. God's beatitude does not "suffer change." God is not impassive, in other words, but can be understood as being impassible in this sense—the *infinite quality and integrity* of God's intrinsic emotional life does not suffer change.[74] And because the essence of who God is cannot suffer change, he cannot become more beatified than he is or less beatified than he is.

This is fully consistent with our view that God simply is all his perfections. As Stephen Holmes relates, "If God is simple, then God's existence is necessarily dependent only on a single basis, which is (by supposition) his own good pleasure in his existence. ... This means, necessarily, that God is possessed of the perfection of aseity: his life is consequent on nothing other than himself."[75] Indeed, whatever else the I AM revealed to Moses in Exodus 3:14 may denote about God's identity, it does seem to connote with it the ontological notion of divine aseity.[76]

('*passiones*') which subvert His character as they do our own. According to Tertullian, God has emotions and feelings but not passions." Cf. Augustine, *Confessions*, 1.4: "You love without burning, you are jealous in a way that is free of anxiety, you 'repent' (Gen 6:6) without the pain of regret, you are wrathful and remain tranquil."

74. Cf. Rob Lister, *God Is Impassible and Impassioned: Toward a Theology of Divine Emotion* (Wheaton, IL: Crossway, 2013), 175: "[I]t is in fact Scripture that leads us to the conclusion that God is *both* invulnerable to *involuntarily* precipitated emotional vicissitude *and* supremely passionate about his creatures' practice of obedience and rebellion, as well as their experience of joy and affliction."

75. Stephen R. Holmes, "A Simple Salvation? Soteriology and the Perfections of God" in *God of Salvation: Soteriology in Theological Perspective*, ed. Ivor J. Davidson and Murray A. Rae (Farnham, Surrey, England: Ashgate, 2011), 39. Holmes, 39–40, further states, "Aseity also has consequences, however: if God is *a se*, then God is also necessarily immutable and impassible, if both these perfections are properly understood. Both are essentially claims that God's life is not changed or damaged by anything beyond himself."

76. Concerning theological interpretation of Exodus 3:14, Kevin J. Vanhoozer, *Remythologizing Theology: Divine Action, Passion, and Authorship* (Cambridge: Cambridge University Press, 2010), 42, states: "The ontological 'I am' does not

The apostle Paul's words to the Athenians seem to connote as much: "The God who made the world and everything in it, being Lord of heaven and earth, does not live in temples made by man, nor is he served by human hands, as though he needed anything, since he himself gives to all mankind life and breath and everything" (Acts 17:24–25). In this light the perfection of divine aseity may be seen as cousin to the perfection of divine beatitude. Bavinck captures this idea nicely: "[God] does not have to become anything, but is what he is eternally. He has no goal outside himself but is self-sufficient, all-sufficient (Ps 50:8ff; Isa 40:28ff; Hab 2:20). He receives nothing, but only gives. All things need him; he needs nothing or nobody. He always aims at himself because he cannot rest in anything other than himself."[77] The relation of the *ad intra* blessedness of God to his altogether perfection begins to come into more integrated focus now. John Webster characterizes the latter thus:

> God's perfection is not first and foremost a negative concept, denoting the absence of restriction or fulfillment in the being of God; these entailments may follow, but perfection chiefly refers to the sheer positive plenitude of God's being. Further, like the closely parallel concepts of God as *a se* or *causa sui*, the concept of divine perfection is not primarily a formal concept but a material one. "We call that perfect which lacks nothing of the mode of its perfection," says Aquinas [*ST* Ia, q.4, a.1].[78]

Consonant with this depiction of God's perfection as "the sheer positive plenitude of his being," the apostle Paul, after surveying God's purposes in salvation history, concludes, "For from him and through him and to him are all things. To him be glory forever" (Rom 11:36).

---

exhaust all possible readings of God's name. There is another tradition of interpretation that focuses more on the biblical *mythos* itself. Here, the spotlight shines on the narrative context, where God's naming is part of a longer dialogue between God and Moses, which in turn is an episode in the story of Moses' call and, beyond that, a key scene in the even larger story of God's covenant with Abraham. This covenanted 'I am' gives rise to a different 'metaphysics of the Exodus' where what is at issue is not simply God's existence but covenant faithfulness." See Vanhoozer, *Remythologizing Theology*, 40–44, for the fuller discussion.

77. Bavinck, *RD*, 2:211.

78. John Webster, "God's Perfect Life," in *God's Life in Trinity*, ed. Miroslav Volf and Michael Welker (Minneapolis: Fortress Press, 2006), 143.

Christopher Morgan expands on this nicely: "God's self-sufficiency and glory are intricately linked: God is the creator ("from him"), sustainer ("through him"), and goal ("to him") of all things. The self-sufficient and independent God creates out of fullness, guides out of fullness, and receives back according to his communicated fullness."[79]

The theological synthesis of God's beatitude and beauty that obtains at this point is along these lines: the beatitude of God represents the eternal condition in himself of absolute satisfaction and delight, which is bound up with the sheer positive plenitude of his being—that is, the altogether perfection of who God is as Father, Son, and Spirit. This "plenitude" of God is synonymous with his fullness of glory. Bavinck encapsulates the point likewise: "The perfection of God, which is inwardly the ground of his blessedness, outwardly as it were carries his glory with it."[80] As I argued earlier, God's beauty is also bound up with the altogether perfection of who God is as Father, Son, and Spirit. Manifested economically, the beauty of God (*pulchritudo Dei ad extra*) is expressed and perceivable as an aesthetic quality of his glory inherent in his work of creation, redemption, and consummation. The universal scope of this means that an aesthetic dimension—in illimitable expressions and degree—is inherent in the structure (i.e., form) of God's extrinsic glory. What uniquely characterizes the subjectively experienced aspect of the beauty expressed in God's outward works is its effect of evoking pleasure or delight in the act of perceiving it. The distinctive characteristic of beauty, moreover, is that beauty as *beauty* is not desired as a means to another end but communicates to the perceiver of it an associated pleasure or delight *as* that end. That characteristic to communicate delight as its own end is correlative to

---

79. Morgan, "Toward a Theology of the Glory of God," 163. Cf. Aquinas, *ST* Ia, q.26, a.4.

80. Bavinck, *RD*, 2:252. In consistent terms, *The Westminster Confession of Faith* 2.2 affirms as much: "God hath all life, glory, goodness, blessedness, in and of himself; and is alone in and unto himself all-sufficient, not standing in need of any creatures which he hath made, nor deriving any glory from them, but only manifesting his own glory in, by, unto, and upon them. He is the alone fountain of all being, of whom, through whom, and to whom are all things; and hath most sovereign dominion over them, to do by them, for them, or upon them whatsoever himself pleaseth."

that absolute self-delight that characterizes God's own eternal, internal, life as Father, Son, and Spirit.

Drawing this altogether, I propose the following postulate on the theological aesthetic relation between beauty and God's beatitude: *the beauty of God ad extra as it is perceived and experienced by human beings is what most clearly evinces that perfection of beatitude and sense of delight that belongs to the Trinity ad intra.* From this perspective, the subjectively experienced aspect of beauty points beyond itself to that absolute self-delight that characterizes God in himself. "In the beautiful," writes David Bentley Hart, "God's glory is revealed as something communicable and intrinsically delightful, as including the creature in its ends, and as completely worthy of love."[81] As I suggest below, it is God's beatitude in himself that correlates with a properly aesthetic dimension to our faith seeking understanding, the fruit and expression of which is a knowing pleasure and heartfelt delight in the Lord.

One subtlety to call out here is that the economic forms of God's glory have an aesthetic dimension to them, however narrowly or broadly conceived their aesthetic qualities may be. Aesthetics *narrowly conceived* denotes any real thing that is perceivable by human beings as patently or conspicuously beautiful. One is consciously attracted to such a thing for its outright aesthetic quality, perhaps a particular quality that stands out. An instance of explicitly recognized beauty is at the same time an instance of that thing being fitting, reflecting in its form and features aesthetic qualities of God's manifest glory. The aesthetic dimension *broadly conceived*, however, understands fittingness to involve more than that which one is consciously attracted to or recognizes for its outright and particular aesthetic quality. While something that exhibits fittingness may be perceived for a particular aesthetic quality that stands out, it may also be recognized in much more subtle terms regarding its propriety or its overall sense of order or harmony and such like. Thus, aesthetics broadly conceived is simply a formal distinction that acknowledges the less conspicuous or less perceptible subtle aesthetic aspects that God's glory takes in the design

---

81. David Bentley Hart, *The Beauty of the Infinite: The Aesthetics of Christian Truth* (Grand Rapids: Eerdmans, 2003), 17.

and outworking of his eternal plan in all its diversely splendored forms. We could therefore think of the aesthetic dimension conceived in a narrow sense and the aesthetic dimension conceived in a broad sense as the recognition of a focal/particular perception of beauty versus a subsidiary/synthetic perception of it. The aesthetic dimension both narrowly or broadly conceived, then, entails the full compass of characteristics betraying God's beauty, all of which are expressions of the aesthetic quality of his manifest glory.

Lastly, the same critical caveat I registered in the previous section bears repeating regarding the ramifications of a creational order radically affected by sin and laboring under the judgment curse of God from the fall of our primal parents in Genesis 3. What uniquely characterizes the subjectively experienced aspect of the beauty expressed in God's outward works is still its effect of evoking pleasure or delight in the act of perceiving it. But the consequent condition of human fallenness now means that humanity's ability to subjectively experience that pleasure or delight involves, in indeterminable ways and degree, a spoiling or diminishing of that experience.

The Relation of Divine Beatitude to Transcendental Truth, Goodness, and Beauty

The theological aesthetic relation between beauty and God's beatitude discussed above has a direct bearing on what I referred to in the Introduction as "the non-coincidence of the true, the good, and the beautiful." I will argue here that the transcendentals of truth, goodness, and beauty in God's work of creation, redemption, and consummation are strongly correlated because these attributes are communicable perfections of God's essential nature that are coordinate with God's knowledge, will, and beatitude.

God's fullness of being, which is the glorious life of God *ad intra*, "does not mean that God's perfection is simple stasis," writes Webster, "God *enacts* his perfection."[82] As Scripture amply indicates, it is according to God's perfect knowledge and will that all things from him and through him and to him are so enacted (e.g., Rom 11:33; Col 2:2–3; Eph

---

82. Webster, "God's Perfect Life," 147.

1:11; Rev 4:11). Aquinas puts it concisely: "The knowledge of God, joined to His will, is the cause of all things."[83] If the notion of divine simplicity is to apply here, however, then the perfection of God's knowing and willing are perfections of his infinite act.[84] The analogical predication of these activities to God thus requires proper qualification, as Matthew Levering relates: "When we speak about the supremely simple God using words taken from the perfections of creatures, we distinguish God's intellect and will, even though in him they are the same."[85] There is thus no differentiation between what God in himself knows and wills and his act of knowing and willing.[86] "If we say, 'God is omniscient,'" explains Rogers, "we should not understand this to mean that God possesses some quality, omniscience, which enables Him to know everything. Rather 'God is omniscient,' means just that God knows everything. Strictly speaking, God does not *have* the power to do things. God does things."[87] Accepting this picture, and given as I argued earlier that blessedness is also a perfection of God's fullness of being, we may round out our concept of God's beatitude as follows: *God's beatitude is bound up with his knowledge and will of which the very knowing and willing is his absolute satisfaction and delight.* God enacts his

---

83. *ST* Ia, q.14, a.9, ad 3; see also *ST* Ia, q.14, a.1, ad 1–3; Ia, q.19, a.1.

84. The Reformed orthodox understanding of "the *vita* and *aseitas Dei*," as Muller, *PRRD*, III, 377, notes, maintained this basic view: "It is not merely the case that the divine life is related to and understood in terms of the other divine attributes; the divine life is the actualization of all the other attributes—and, as the actuosity of an essentially spiritual and rational being, it is characterized by intellect and will or knowing and willing."

85. Matthew Levering, *Scripture and Metaphysics: Aquinas and the Renewal of Trinitarian Theology* (Malden, MA: Blackwell Publishing, 2004), 97.

86. In service here are the classical definitions of divine knowledge and will common to the medieval and the Protestant scholastics. In basic terms the intellect is that which knows objects, and the will is that which has an appetite or desire for them. The *veritas Dei* is the correspondence of the *intellectus Dei* and *voluntas Dei* with the essence of God. For its part, the *voluntas Dei* operates to bring about the good known to and desired by God as the highest end or greatest good (*summum bonum*) of all things. See respective terms in Richard A. Muller, *Dictionary of Latin and Greek Theological Terms: Drawn Principally from Protestant Scholastic Theology* (Grand Rapids: Baker Book House, 1985).

87. Rogers, *The Anselmian Approach to God and Creation*, 37–38. Cf. Aquinas, *ST* Ia, q.8, a.3, ad 3.

perfection, we may thus better say, according to his perfect knowledge, will, and beatitude.[88]

To speak in terms of God enacting his perfection, of course, is to mean that his perfect knowledge, will, and beatitude extend to other than himself, that is, from his glory *ad intra* to his glory *ad extra* in his work of creation, redemption, and consummation. Respecting here the infinite ontological divide between Creator and creature, God *in se* must be distinguished from the work that he does. The question Levering poses speaks to a seeming tension at the heart of the matter: "But why does [God's] will extend to anything beyond himself? If he wills the other things that we see around us, moreover, it would seem that these other things might either frustrate God's will or be unfitting things for God to will."[89] Considering the overall scheme of things, why would God even *want* to enact the theodrama? It is a fair question, after all, in view of our argument above regarding the aseity and *ad intra* blessedness of God. As far as what has been revealed to us, it all concerns God's eternal plan and purposes according to the Scriptures, of which cardinal points will be explored in the succeeding chapters of this work. That said, Levering's engagement with Aquinas is instructive here. Quoting Aquinas,

> If natural things, in so far as they are perfect, communicate their good to others, much more does it appertain to the divine will to communicate by likeness its own good to others as much as possible. Thus, then, He wills both Himself to be, and other things to be; but Himself as the end, and other things as ordained to that end; inasmuch as it befits the divine goodness that other things should be partakers therein.[90]

---

88. Addressing the topic of "The Decrees of God in General and Predestination in Particular," Francis Turretin, *IET*, vol. 1, Topic IV, Quest. III, Sec. III, states along related lines, "God's decrees depend on his good pleasure (*eudokia*) (Matt 11:26; Eph 1:5; Rom 9:11). Therefore they are not suspended upon any condition outside of God." (page 316). Turretin (1623–1687) was a Swiss-Italian Reformed theologian among the Genevan Reformers. Cf. also Muller, *PRRD*, III, 456–69.

89. Levering, *Scripture and Metaphysics*, 99.

90. *ST* Ia, q.19, a.2 quoted in Levering, *Scripture and Metaphysics*, 99 (the *Summa* quote here extends beyond Levering's).

Aquinas thus argues that since a self-giving inclination is a natural aspect of a well-ordered human will to share the good it possesses with others, such a perfection would naturally and accordingly belong to God. Levering's follow-up commentary is helpful: "Our question—why would God will other things, when he is delighting in his own infinite goodness—is thus turned on its head: embracing his own infinite goodness does not in fact trap God in his own self, but rather constitutes precisely the reason why God wills to share his being in finite ways, that is, why God wills other things."[91] But lest we be guilty of "fill[ing] the content of God's inner life with images drawn from what someone happens to regard as humanity's 'best practice,'" a theologically sound answer requires further filling in according to the Scriptures.[92] We will simply mark for now the idea that, in virtue of his self-giving nature, God communicates himself so that we might be partakers "in the glory that is going to be revealed" (1 Pet 5:1).

With God, as I have presented the case, his knowledge, will, and beatitude are all of a piece. But as a formal distinction at least, we may understand the transcendentals of truth, goodness, and beauty to function in coordinated relation to God's knowledge, will, and beatitude, respectively. By extension it follows that the transcendentals of truth, goodness, and beauty are coordinate with the performative enactment of God's thought, will, and beatitude for his eternal plan. The knowability, desirability, and delightability of the created order are thus "transcendental" aspects of reality—*per prius et posterius*—inasmuch as: (a) their ultimate grounding is in God as the Creator, Redeemer, and Consummator of all things; and (b) the givenness of the truth, goodness, and beauty of the world is a precondition of all subjective personal engagement with the world.[93]

---

91. Levering, *Scripture and Metaphysics*, 99. Along the same lines, Bavinck, *RD*, 2:233, states: "[God's] love for himself incorporates into itself the love he has for his creatures and through them returns to himself. Therefore, his willing, also in relation to creatures, is never a striving for some as yet unpossessed good and hence no sign of imperfection and infelicity. On the contrary: his willing is always— also in and through his creatures—absolute self-enjoyment, perfect blessedness, divine rest. In God rest and labor are one; his self-sufficiency coincides with absolute actuality."

92. Vanhoozer, *Remythologizing Theology*, 160.

93. In the order of knowing (*ordo cognoscendi*), the truth, goodness, and beauty

We are in position now to propose a modest reframing of the classical way that the transcendentals of truth, goodness, and beauty have been characterized: *in the true the intellect (knowledge) is at rest, in the good the will is at rest, and in the beautiful the beatitude is at rest.*[94] In this qualified sense the metaphysical ground of all truth is coordinate with God's knowledge, of all goodness is coordinate with God's will, and of all beauty is coordinate with God's beatitude. Qualified in this way, then, I suggest that it is God's own beatitude that, in this present age, correlates with a properly aesthetic dimension to our faith seeking understanding, the fruit and expression of which is a knowing pleasure and heartfelt delight in the Lord. Such delight suggests itself as being a faint reflection of that aesthetic delight, that beatitude in God's own being, and is the doxological component of divine beauty's effect on us that provides a foretaste in this life of our enjoying God forever in the next. With respect to the effect of God's beauty on us, it is worth noting the striking affinity here with Barth's view: "The glory of God, to share in which is the intention and purpose of his love for the creature, is the overflowing of the inner perfection and joy of God."[95] While Barth held that beauty itself is not a divine perfection, he nonetheless grasped the significance of the correlation that exists between the experience of perceiving beauty and the overflowing delight identified with it. In the chapters ahead, we will see the same striking affinity regarding the

---

of the world in the prima facie sense (i.e., from below) precede the transcendentals of truth, goodness, and beauty in the ultima facie sense (i.e., from above). I accept a metaphysic of analogical extensions of being from God to the created world. In this way I am affirming an extramental realism by affirming God as the divine subject who is absolutely necessary/non-contingent to that realism. Human subjects, on the other hand, are contingent in a basic sense but necessary in the sense that their engagement with the world is a conditional necessity for perceiving the knowability, desirability, and delightability of the world.

94. The idea of "at rest" here implies the idea of being "fully satisfied." Striking in part a similar chord is Aquinas' treatment "Of the Cause of Love" in *ST* Ia IIae, q.27, a.1. In the first article he addresses "Whether Good Is the Only Cause of Love?" In ad 3 he begins by stating, "The beautiful is the same as the good, and they differ in aspect only. For since good is what all seek, the notion of good is that which calms the desire; while the notion of the beautiful is that which calms the desire, by being seen or known."

95. Barth, *CD*, II/1, 671.

effect of God's beauty on us reflected in the positions of Hans Urs von Balthasar and Jonathan Edwards.

THE IMMANENT FORM OF THE GODHEAD'S BEAUTY

In the interest of filling out a properly dogmatic account of aesthetics with respect to the doctrine of the immanent Trinity, my aim here is to define the immanent form of the Godhead's beauty. The focus of our discussions has been on the perfections of God's essential nature with respect to beauty, the God who out of his fullness of glory enacts his eternal plan according to his perfect knowledge, will, and beatitude. In cumulative argument so far I have presented the case for understanding beauty theologically in a threefold way. Specifically, beauty as being (a) an attribute of God; (b) a quality of the glory of God *ad extra* inherent in his work of creation, redemption, and consummation; and (c) the divine perfection *ad extra* as it is perceived and experienced by human beings that most clearly evinces that perfection of beatitude and sense of delight that belongs to the Trinity *ad intra*. Admittedly, I have so far only referenced the Trinity in my argumentation in more or less passing fashion. Our attention here on the Triunity of God keeps in mind our objectivist premise that beauty in the order of reality (not just *created* reality) pertains only to something that has form. In defining the immanent form of the Godhead's beauty, I will first set out God's fullness of being in terms of the Trinity of persons. The theological groundwork laid here all pays forward in the subsequent section as we address the fittingness of the eternal Son as incarnate Redeemer.

As there is no real distinction between essence and existence (being) in God, so there is no real distinction between the essence of God and the Trinity of persons. For the being and nature of God who enacts his eternal plan is the selfsame Trinity—"the one who is himself as he executes his own being in his acts as Father, Son and Holy Spirit."[96]

---

96. John Webster, *Confessing God: Essays in Christian Dogmatics II* (London: T&T Clark, 2005), 112. Brannon Ellis, *Calvin, Classical Trinitarianism, and the Aseity of the Son* (Oxford: Oxford University Press, 2012), 206, captures the point here well in summary: "Consistent with the classical practice of locating the distinctions in God between the persons and not 'in' the essence, then, we should affirm unqualifiedly that Father, Son, and Spirit are *this* God in all respects and unqualifiedly. Every attribute of God is equally an attribute of each person of the Triune God."

On these terms there is no reason at all to view the doctrine of the one God (*de Deo uno*) to be at variance with that of the Trinity (*de Deo trino*), nor should either one be considered of first importance over the other. Whereas the latter is concerned with the distinct persons of the Trinity, the focus of the former is more on the divine nature and attributes that are common to all three persons of the Godhead and as such are understood to be integrally essential to Trinitarian doctrine.[97] The twofold use of "God" in John 1:1 is a traditional prooftext that refers to both the *person* of the Father and the *divine nature* shared by the Father and the Son. The person of the Spirit shares the same. As Brannon Ellis notes, "The God who is from himself is the Trinity, so that the persons are no more separable with respect to deity as they are identical with respect to one another."[98] The tri-personal God, therefore, has *one nature*, that is, one divine essence that is *one life*. The Godhead, in other words, does not simply have "a life" held in common or united as one by some sort of confederation between the persons of the Trinity, but rather numerically one life *ad intra* that is indivisibly tri-personal.[99] Indeed,

---

97. In regard to developments in theology proper after the Reformation, Richard Muller, *PRRD*, III, 156, states: "The *locus* [doctrine of God] does not segment Trinity off from the discussion of essence and attributes: the issue addressed by this order is not a movement from an extended philosophical or speculative discussion of 'what' God is to a biblicistic, Trinitarian definition of 'who' God is, but the movement from a statement of 'what' (or 'who') the existent One is, namely, God, to a lengthy discussion in terms of attributes and Trinity, of precisely 'what sort' of God has been revealed, namely, a triune God who is simple, infinite, omnipotent, gracious, merciful, and so forth." For a helpful discussion on issues as relates to classical theism, see Vanhoozer, *Remythologizing Theology*, 82–93; also James E. Dolezal, "Trinity, Simplicity and the Status of God's Personal Relations," *IJST* 16 no. 1 (Jan 2014): 79–98.

98. Ellis, *Calvin*, 209.

99. Cf. Calvin, *Institutes* 1.13.5, ed. McNeill, trans. Battles: "Say that in the one essence of God there is a trinity of persons; you will say in one word what Scripture states, and cut short empty talkativeness. Indeed, if anxious superstition so constrains anyone that he cannot bear these terms, yet no one could now deny, even if he were to burst, that when we hear 'one' we ought to understand 'unity of substance'; when we hear 'three in one essence,' the persons in this trinity are meant. When this is confessed without guile, we need not dally over words." See also the helpful discussion in Brannon Ellis, "The Spirit from the Father, of Himself God: A Calvinian Approach to the Filioque Debate," in *Ecumenical Perspectives on the Filioque for the 21st Century*, ed. Myk Habets (London and New York: Bloomsbury T&T Clark, 2014), 87–106.

the God who enacts his eternal plan according to his perfect knowledge, will, and beatitude is the Trinity of persons who subsist in an order of relations of mutual love and eternal delight with and in one another (i.e., perichoretically), and whose perfections are together shared in full equality in every respect.

Like all attributes of the divine nature, beauty is properly taken to be common to all three persons of the Godhead. We have no clear reasons from Scripture to think that beauty is to be identified with only one or two persons of the Trinity. The concept of the immanent form of the Godhead's beauty is developed from our overall argumentation for divine beauty and God's fullness of being as the Trinity of persons. The ordered Triunity of God the Father, God the Son, and God the Holy Spirit is already a theologically basic description of the "form" of the Godhead. However, there are a few further points that bear mentioning here.

To begin with, we may affirm that the infinitude of God in his perfections in no way denotes any sort of "formlessness" in God. "[B]eauty and the infinite entirely coincide," postulates David Bentley Hart, "for the very life of God is one of—to phrase it strangely—infinite form."[100] On this view, God's "infinite form" does not equate to God's "formlessness of being" (cf. John 5:37) but rather, to "the sheer positive plenitude of his being," that is, to God's fullness of glory. God is as such *Forma Formarum*. To be sure, since the immanent form of God's beauty has to do with Triune beauty, it cannot be considered strictly in terms of the unchangeable essence *de Deo uno*. Unity in a monadic sense, moreover, does not comport with beauty as understood to entail the aspect of fittingness, for beauty as such involves a context of plurality or diversity to "be fitting." That idea is reminiscent of Aquinas' view of divine beauty given earlier, which says that perfect proportion and integrity in God are present in virtue of the Triunity of the persons. From another perspective, the infinitely perfect God "who dwells in unapproachable light, whom no one has ever seen or can see" (1 Tim 6:16) is the selfsame Trinity of persons who dwell in mutual love and eternal delight with and in one another. Here, the notion of God dwelling in

---

100. Hart, *The Beauty of the Infinite*, 131.

"unapproachable light" is reminiscent of Aquinas' aesthetic criterion of *claritas*, which as regards God signifies his internal beauty.[101]

The concept of divine simplicity informs us that the divine essence is whatever the three persons are together, whose essential qualities are represented in the Unity-in-Trinity that is God. As Stephen Wright explains, "If the divine essence is whatever the three are together, then a doctrine of simplicity is not incompatible with a theology that prefers to make constant reference to the mutual activity of the Father, Son, and Spirit—which is simply the revealed name for the singular divine essence. The grammar of simplicity is a subset of a Trinitarian grammar."[102] In the most basic terms, then, *the immanent form of the Godhead's beauty is God's Triunity—his three-in-oneness—consisting of all its absolute perfections in triadic divine simplicity, or better, Triune simplicity*. Worth noting here is Karl Barth's view of divine beauty given earlier, which includes his point that the Triunity of God is the secret of God's beauty.

The only form of the Godhead revealed to us, however, is the economic form, which "has its origin from the Father, proceeds through the Son, and is perfected in the Holy Spirit."[103] For since the eternal beauty/fittingness of the immanent Trinity is manifest in the divine economy, the standard and substance of a theological aesthetic is the economic Trinity itself, with Scripture attesting to, and being itself an ingredient in, the economies of revelation and redemption. Christopher Holmes captures nicely the relation between God's Triunity and his perfections manifest in the divine economy this way:

> The one God who is himself a multiplicity of attributes communicates himself in history: his history is a genuine bestowal or

---

101. Suggestively, Nicholas Wolterstorff, *Art in Action: Toward a Christian Aesthetic* (Grand Rapids: Eerdmans, 1980), 167, poses the following questions with respect to his idea of "fittingness-intensity," which is taken as a measure of aesthetic merit: "Could it be that when Aquinas spoke of the 'brightness' [*claritas*] of a work he had in mind the very same thing that I have called the work's *intensity*? And could it be that when our contemporary critics speak of a work's 'expressiveness' they also mean the very same thing?"

102. Stephen John Wright, *Dogmatic Aesthetics: A Theology of Beauty in Dialogue with Robert W. Jenson* (Minneapolis: Fortress Press, 2014), 81.

103. Gregory of Nyssa, *To Ablabius, on "Not Three Gods"* Nicene and Post-Nicene Fathers, 2nd ser., 5:334 cited in Vanhoozer, *Remythologizing Theology*, 247.

disclosure of the holy fellowship that God is. Thus, attributes are always understood to be attributes of the triune God, attributes peculiar to the persons' relations and their perichoresis which overflows in their creating, reconciling, and perfecting action in the world.[104]

And that brings us now to the central idea informing the christological contours of beauty for which this project argues—the fittingness of God the Son as incarnate Redeemer.

THE FITTINGNESS OF GOD THE SON AS INCARNATE REDEEMER

Our Trinitarian account of aesthetics subsumes the idea of the Son's fittingness as incarnate Redeemer. The theological claim at the heart of this project's overall constructive argument is that the Son's fittingness as incarnate Redeemer is foundational to the design and outworking of God's eternal plan. The christological contours of beauty developed in the chapters following take their basic shape from the overarching design of the divine plan, which can be characterized in terms of a fundamental *symmetry* between creation and re-creation.[105] The symmetry of that design, along with the symmetrical nature of the Son's agency in it, are an integral part of the aesthetics inherent in the structure (i.e., form) that God's glory takes in his work of creation, redemption, and consummation. This creational-re-creational symmetry is identifiable by the symmetrical nature of the Son's agency in the work of the divine economy, which I will unpack below. The section is divided into three parts: (1) the fittingness of the Trinity operating economically; (2) the theodramatic fittingness of the Son as incarnate Redeemer; and (3) the immanent fittingness of the Son in the ordered Triunity of God.

---

104. Christopher R. J. Holmes, *Revisiting the Doctrine of the Divine Attributes: In Dialogue with Karl Barth, Eberhard Jüngel and Wolf Krötke* (New York: Peter Lang, 2007), 3.

105. I set out my argument for the basic shape of the divine plan in Chapter 3; see in particular my discussion of the Sublime Comedy: The Theodramatic Form of the Divine Plan.

The Fittingness of the Trinity
Operating Economically

The Trinity, as John Webster states in traditional Nicene language, is that "life in the processions or personal relations that constitute [God's] absolute vitality *in se*. God is perfect as the Father who begets the Son. ... Further, God is perfect as the Father and the Son who together breathe the Spirit, and so as the Spirit who proceeds from them."[106] The language of "begotten" and "proceeding" (or "spirating"), used respectively with regard to the Son and the Spirit, refers traditionally to their eternal relations—that is, their respective processions within the Godhead. From the revelation of the Son and the Spirit in their economic missions is discerned the irreducibly real distinctions of the persons of the Trinity. On this point, Robert Reymond provides a helpful gloss:

> The distinguishing property of the Father is paternity (*paternitas*) from which flow "economical" activities which are unique to his paternity; the Son's is filiation (*filiatio*) from which flow "economical" activities which are unique to his filiation; and the Holy Spirit's is spiration (*spiratio*) from which flow "economical" activities which are unique to his spiration.[107]

The fittingness of the economical activities of the Father, Son, and Holy Spirit, respectively, is basic, I submit, to what characterizes the aesthetic dimension (i.e., beauty) of the Trinity operating economically.[108] Unpacking that a bit, the economical activities of the persons in the economies of creation, redemption, and consummation reflect with

---

106. Webster, "God's Perfect Life," 149.

107. Robert L. Reymond, *A New Systematic Theology of the Christian Faith*, 2nd ed. (Nashville: Thomas Nelson, 1998), 340.

108. Nicholas M. Healy, *Thomas Aquinas: Theologian of the Christian Life* (Burlington, VT: Ashgate Publishing, 2003), 38, offers the following insight: "[T]he theologian should attempt to explain why these means to salvation are the best by displaying the appropriateness of God's actions as they are described in Scripture. The argument for fittingness is therefore something like an aesthetic argument because it searches for structure and proportion. The French Dominican, Gilbert Narcisse, gives this definition: 'Theological fittingness displays the significance of the chosen means among alternative possibilities, and the reasons according to which God, in his wisdom, has effectively realized and revealed, gratuitously and through his love, the mystery of the salvation and glorification of humanity.'" See also Aquinas, *ST* IIIa, q.1.

perfect fittingness the paternity of the Father (the working of all things is *from the Father*), the filiation of the Son (the working of all things is *through the Son*), and the spiration of the Holy Spirit (the working of all things is *in the Spirit*).[109] Here, there is perfect unity in perfect freedom and personal distinction. Since I characterize that relation of the persons in terms of "perfect fittingness," I should clarify what is entailed in the idea of the fittingness being "perfect." For this I am adopting and adapting the principle advanced by Oliver Crisp that *"for any given created theatre, God's glory must be exercised in such a manner as to display all his divine attributes."*[110] What I submit is that not only do the respective economical activities of the persons reflect a proper fittingness in relation to the real distinctions of the persons, but their economical activities reflect a *perfect* fittingness because through their extratrinitarian works, God's fullness of glory is brought to a consummative expression that is all-dimensional in scope, cosmic in scale. According to the biblical theodrama, that consummative expression entails a glorified new creation with all those who would become partakers of the divine nature becoming themselves consummately glorified.[111]

Relating the above principle to our primary interest—the Son's fittingness as incarnate Redeemer—obtains in the following proposition: *it is in Christ and through Christ that God's glory is manifested in dramatic, or better, theodramatic fashion so that all God's perfections might be wondrously displayed* (cf. Col 2:9). Stephen Holmes articulates essentially the same point in relation to God's work of salvation through the Son:

---

109. We will have more to say as relates to the real distinctions of the persons of the Trinity in the discussion below under The Immanent Fittingness of the Son in the Ordered Triunity of God.

110. Oliver D. Crisp, *Retrieving Doctrine: Essays in Reformed Theology* (Downers Grove, IL: IVP Academic, 2010), 91 (emphasis in the original). For the full discussion, see chapter 4: Francis Turretin on the Necessity of the Incarnation. With regard to the last part of Crisp's statement, it perhaps better should say "all his *communicable* attributes" if the idea here is that they are to be displayable (so, perceivable/experienceable).

111. Granted, the mystery of theodicy and perdition are also part of God's revealed plan. These are factors that cannot be simply marginalized or glossed over. We can only confess the inscrutability of God's wisdom on such things (Deut 29:29). The theodrama can thus in no wise be simplistically considered.

An adequate soteriology will not accept any setting aside or opposing of God's perfections. God's life is a single, glorious and unending stream of joy and love; we speak of our differing experiences of this single act using diverse language, but all that language must be referred to the one origin. In acting in Christ to save, every possible aspect of God's perfection is necessarily fully and completely expressed; if our accounts of salvation do less, they remain inadequate.[112]

The christological contours of beauty developed in the chapters following seek to show how the outworking of God's eternal plan through the Son brings to consummative expression the fullness of God's glory; this outworking involves how all things that God redeems through Christ play a role sharing in and perhaps in some sense magnifying the glory that is to be revealed.

Although Christ alone is the incarnate Redeemer, it is only ever the Triune God who orchestrates redemption and ultimately consummates it. In this way, God has revealed and interpreted himself through the person and work of Christ and by the personal work of the Holy Spirit. As to the economy of redemption, "The Father redeems, but always through the Son in the Spirit; the Son redeems, but always from the Father in the Spirit; the Spirit redeems, but always from the Father through the Son, so that the Father together with the Son and the Spirit pursue and accomplish the redemption that belongs to God alone (Isa 45:21–25; Rom 14:11; Phil 2:10)."[113] The indivisible and intra-essential unity in the relation of the persons of the Trinity is identified, then, in the unsubstitutable distinctions of the Father, Son, and Holy Spirit, which are revealed in their extratrinitarian works.

A critical point I need to clarify concerns how we understand the respective fittingness of the persons for our doctrine of God. To position this in negative terms first, the respective fittingness of the economical activities of the persons do not play out in the divine economy on account of the *absolute necessity* of the case. If something is absolutely necessary, it cannot be any other way no matter what else was the

---

112. Holmes, "A Simple Salvation?," 46.
113. Ellis, *Calvin*, 224.

case. In short, the way things are is the way they must be. So for the economical activities of the persons to be fitting because these activities are absolutely necessary means that it is not possible that these play out any other way, regardless of any prior (temporal or logical) contingent fact that was the case. Such a conception of fittingness is problematic because, at a minimum, it violates God's freedom to create or not create.[114] Rather, on the view I am positing, the respective fittingness of the economical activities of the persons play out in the divine economy on account of the *conditional necessity* of the case. So for the economical activities of the persons to be fitting because these activities are conditionally necessary means that these play out as they do given (conditional on) the prior contingent fact of God's free decision to create as he did. The eternal plan God sovereignly and freely willed and delighted to enact is the created condition established, and thus the economical activities of the persons reflect with perfect fittingness the paternity of the Father, the filiation of the Son, and the spiration of the Holy Spirit in relation to *this* plan.[115] Nonetheless, it seems theologically sound to accept that, in principle, God's freedom could have entailed his free decision either to not create at all or to enact a plan(s) different from the one that he did. In the latter case, it seems fair to presume that, in relation to *that* hypothetical plan(s), the economical activities of the persons would likewise reflect with perfect fittingness the paternity of the Father, the filiation of the Son, and the spiration of the Holy Spirit.

114. On this point I affirm John Webster's statement as being axiomatic: "The triune God could be without the world; no perfection of God would be lost, no triune bliss compromised, were the world not to exist; no enhancement of God is achieved by the world's existence." "Trinity and Creation," *IJST* 12 no. 1 (Jan 2010): 12.

115. What Augustine is keen to emphasize is that the divine actions in relation to the plan of redemption were most fitting. See, e.g., Augustine, *The Trinity* 13.4, 2nd ed., ed. John E. Rotelle, trans. Edmund Hill (Hyde Park, NY: New City Press, 2012): "Now there are people who say, 'Was there no other way available to God of setting men free from the unhappiness of this mortality, that he should want his only begotten Son, God coeternal with himself, to become man by putting on a human soul and flesh, and, having become mortal, to suffer death?' And it is not enough to rebut them by maintaining that this way God chose of setting us free through *the mediator between God and men the man Christ Jesus* (1 Tim 2:5) is good and befitting the divine dignity; we must also show, not indeed that no other possible way was available to God, since all things are equally within his power, but that there neither was nor should have been a more suitable way of curing our unhappy state" (page 355). See also Aquinas, *ST* IIIa, q.1, a.2.

THE THEODRAMATIC FITTINGNESS OF THE SON AS INCARNATE REDEEMER

The principal aim of this section is to lay out three theologically significant ways the Scriptures attest to how the theodramatic fittingness of the Son has correspondence to the symmetrical nature of his agency in the work of the divine economy.[116] All of this sets up and anticipates the christological contours of beauty developed in the succeeding chapters and serves to highlight certain important structural aspects of the contours. The contours *in nuce* unfold in God's redemptive love toward his covenant people, and climactically so in the person and work of Christ. The symmetrical nature of the Son's agency in the work of the divine economy that I will be fleshing out below is summarized as follows:

1. That the work of creation is through the Son, so likewise the work of redemption (re-creation or the renewal of creation) also is accomplished through the Son.

2. That the Son is the preexistent image of God through whom humanity is imaged protologically, so likewise through the Son as the last Adam the redeemed are imaged eschatologically.

3. That as an analogue of the only-begotten Son's relationship to the Father, the Son of God as incarnate Redeemer procures adoptive sonship for all those he redeems, so that these may become beloved sons of God the Father.

These primary symmetries of the Son's agency in the divine economy are bound up with his fittingness as incarnate Redeemer, which itself is foundational to the design and outworking of God's eternal plan. That is the theological claim at the heart of this project's overall argument. As a basic point, the beauty of redemptive-history is recognized as a function of the fittingness involved in its design and outworking. Moreover, the beauty of redemptive-history is theodramatic, which

---

116. Cf. Healy, *Thomas Aquinas*, 38: "Fittingness arguments are found throughout Scripture where analogies are drawn, connections between things, events and people are noted, and references made back and forward. One of the most obvious examples of such arguments is figurative exegesis, such as Paul's contention that Christ is the second Adam, or the implication in Luke that the Twelve are to be linked with the people of Israel. Such connections do not depend upon deductive logic; they must appeal to one's sense of proportion or fittingness."

pertains to the person/role of Christ. I refer to the beauty of Christ's identity in terms of theodramatic fittingness, that is, his being and doing as displayed predominantly in his obedient relationship to the Father demonstrated through the experiences of his earthly life.

Primary Symmetry 1

That the work of creation is through the Son, so likewise the work of redemption (re-creation or the renewal of creation) also is accomplished through the Son. The Son's role as creator is writ large in the opening verses of John's Gospel. Plainly echoing the opening declaration of Genesis, John 1:1 states, "In the beginning was the Word, and the Word was with God, and the Word was God." As the prologue reveals, the Word, the divine Logos, is none other than the "only Son" (μονογενὴς, John 1:14, 18) of the Father, who "became flesh" (John 1:14) as Jesus Christ (John 1:17). The particular nature of the Son's role as creator is given in verse 3: "All things ἐγένετο through him." As Craig Koester points out, "This too echoes the biblical creation story. The main verb is ἐγένετο, which is used repeatedly in the Greek translation of Genesis: "God said, 'Let there be light,' and there was (ἐγένετο) light" (Gen 1:3)."[117] God's performative word thus brought into being out of nothingness all of creation *through* his own Word, the only Son of the Father (cf. Heb 11:3; 2 Pet 3:5). Orchestrated in Trinitarian terms, of course, the Holy Spirit was agent in creation as well (Gen 1:2; cf. Pss 33:6–9; 104:30). In *The Demonstration of the Apostolic Preaching*, Irenaeus expresses the Trinitarian pattern of creation this way:

> Since God is rational, therefore by [the] Spirit he adorned all things: as also the prophet says: *By the word of the Lord were the heavens established, and by his spirit all their power* [Ps 33:6]. Since then the Word establishes, that is to say, gives body and grants the reality of being, and the Spirit gives order and form to the diversity of the powers; rightly and fittingly is the Word called the Son, and the Spirit the Wisdom of God. Well also does Paul His apostle say: *one God, the Father, who is over all and through all and in us all* [Eph 4:6].

---

117. Craig R. Koester, *The Word of Life: A Theology of John's Gospel* (Grand Rapids: Eerdmans, 2008), 30. In the LXX translation of Genesis 1, ἐγένετο is scattered throughout no less than twenty times.

For *over all* is the Father: and *through all* is the Son, for through Him all things were made by the Father; and *in us all* is the Spirit, who cries *Abba Father*, and fashions man into the likeness of God.[118]

In consistent terms, then, the working of the Trinity in the economy of creation is the same, mutatis mutandis, as I described above with respect to the economy of redemption: the Father creates, but always through the Son in the Spirit; the Son creates, but always from the Father in the Spirit; the Spirit creates, but always from the Father through the Son, so that the Father together with the Son and the Spirit pursue and accomplish the creational work that belongs to God alone.[119]

The author of Hebrews likewise describes the Son as the agent "through whom also [God] created the world" (Heb 1:2).[120] In verse 10 of the same chapter, he ascribes to the Son what was said there of the Lord (Yahweh) in Psalm 102:25: "You, Lord, laid the foundation of the earth in the beginning, and the heavens are the work of your hands." Consonant with both the Johannine prologue and the epistle to the Hebrews, Pauline teaching links similarly the creational and redemptive work of the Son. A *locus classicus* is 1 Corinthians 8:6, a christianized reformulation of the *Shema'* (Deut 6:4) whose wording is divided between God the Father and Jesus Christ the Son: "yet for us there is one God, the Father, from whom are all things and for whom we exist, and one Lord, Jesus Christ, through whom are all things and through whom we exist." Paul's formulation encompasses the whole of reality

---

118. Iain M. MacKenzie, *Irenaeus's Demonstration of the Apostolic Preaching: A Theological Commentary and Translation*, trans. J. Armitage Robinson (Aldershot, Hants, England: Ashgate, 2002), 2. This is found in section 5 of Irenaeus's *The Demonstration of the Apostolic Preaching*.

119. Bavinck, *RD*, 2:423, rounds this out, stating, "While there is cooperation, there is not division of labor. All things originate simultaneously from the Father through the Son in the Spirit. The Father is the first cause; the initiative for creation proceeds from him. Accordingly, in an administrative sense, creation is specifically attributed to him. The Son is not an instrument but the personal wisdom, the Logos, by whom everything is created. ... And the Holy Spirit is the personal immanent cause by which all things live and move and have their being, receive their own form and configuration, and are led to their destination, in God."

120. The Greek term translated "world" here, τοὺς αἰῶνας, denotes "ages" or "worlds," and is similarly used for the whole universe of space and time in Hebrews 11:3.

created by God—both creation and redemption—in God's bringing "all things" to ultimate fulfillment in himself, in new creation (cf. 2 Cor 5:17).

In the Christ-hymn of Colossians 1:15-20, the apostle expands on what he had previously accredited to Christ in 1 Corinthians 8:6 by attributing the totality of God's creational and redemptive work and purposes all to the Son: "For by him all things were created ... all things were created through him and for him" (1:16). The repeated emphasis on Christ's relation to "all things" (Col 1:16, 17, 20) highlights his role as the only mediator of creation and new creation. Thus, through him for whom all things were made, all things shall be made new (Rev 21:5). Commenting on these two thematic divisions of the hymn, Marianne Thompson writes: "In its structure, it sets creation and redemption parallel to each other. Each has its focal point in Christ, who is the firstborn, agent, and goal of both creation and new creation. Because Christ is the agent of creation, he is also the agent of the re-creation of the world."[121]

Primary Symmetry 2

That the Son is the preexistent image of God through whom humanity is imaged protologically (image of their Creator), so likewise through the Son as the last Adam the redeemed are imaged eschatologically (image of their Redeemer). With reference once again to the Colossians Christ-hymn, Paul declares the Son *to be* "the image of the invisible God, the firstborn of all creation" (Col 1:15). The repetition of πρωτότοκος unites the two thematic divisions of the hymn—the "*firstborn* of all creation" (Col 1:15) and the "*firstborn* from the dead" (Col 1:18). Given how the hymn depicts the Son as agent of both creation and redemption (re-creation), the following distinction can be drawn from Paul's character-ization of the Son in verse 15: "The image of God language clarifies the Son's consubstantial relation to the Father (cf. Col 1:19 and 2:9), and the firstborn language clarifies the Son's fundamental relation to creation."[122]

---

121. Marianne Meye Thompson, *Colossians and Philemon* (Grand Rapids: Eerdmans, 2005), 28.

122. Lane G. Tipton, "Christology in Colossians 1:15-20 and Hebrews 1:1-4: An Exercise in Biblico-Systematic Theology," in *Resurrection and Eschatology: Essays in Honor of Richard B. Gaffin Jr.*, ed. Lane G. Tipton and Jeffrey C. Waddington (Phillipsburg, NJ: P&R Publishing, 2008), 188.

Hebrews 1:3a expresses in a parallel way the Pauline idea of the Son as
the image of God, applying in context here to the Son incarnate: "He is
the radiance of the glory of God and the exact imprint (χαρακτήρ) of his
nature" (cf. John 1:14; 2 Cor 4:6). The author of Hebrews, notes William
Lane, "used the word χαρακτήρ to convey as emphatically as he could
his conviction that in Jesus Christ there has been provided a perfect,
visible expression of the reality of God."[123]

The allusion in Colossians 1:15 to Genesis 1:26–27 is patent, with Paul
employing εἰκών, the Septuagint's rendering of צֶלֶם ("image"). Furthermore, the emphasis of the Colossians hymn on Christ's preeminence
over all things (Col 1:18) is reminiscent of the theme of dominion in
Genesis 1:26–28. The force of the allusions together recommends understanding the creation of humankind through a christological lens. Two
basic points pertaining to protology and eschatology are derivative here
and concern Paul's language elsewhere of the "two Adams." First, the
preexistent Son not only is the image of God, but is himself the image
archetype in which Adam was formed at creation, and indeed in whose
image all human beings are constituted. In other words, human beings
are created in the image of God, and the image of God is God the Son.[124]
Second, the Son incarnate is the image of God in the person of Jesus
Christ whom Paul calls the second or last Adam (1 Cor 15:45–46). And
"as the last, or eschatological, Adam, whose life is as decisive for the
nature and possibilities of human life as the first, or protological, Adam,"
Christ embodies the divine purpose for humanity in accordance with
which the first Adam was created (cf. Rom 5:14b).[125] That purpose, as

---

123. William L. Lane, *Hebrews 1–8* (WBC 47A; Waco, TX: Word, 1991), 13.

124. While it is fair to say that Genesis 1 is ambiguous as to whether it gives a
God-the-Son or a Trinitarian content to the *imago Dei*, the New Testament itself
relates the content of the *imago Dei* exclusively to Christ. Concerning Genesis 1:26–
27, Philip Edgcumbe Hughes, *The True Image: The Origin and Destiny of Man in Christ*
(Grand Rapids: Eerdmans, 1989), 17, writes: "True enough, it is the triune God who
said, 'Let us make man in our image,' but the pronoun 'our' does not necessarily
imply plurality in that image. That this in fact is not the implication is made plain
by the designation of the Son as the image of the invisible God (Col 1:15; 2 Cor 4:4).
That is why the image in which man was made and to which he must conform is
specifically the eternal Son, the Second Person of the Holy Trinity."

125. Stephen R. Holmes, "Image of God" in *Dictionary for Theological
Interpretation of the Bible*, ed. Kevin J. Vanhoozer (Grand Rapids: Baker Academic,
2005), 319.

the New Testament makes clear, involves becoming the glorified new humanity conformed to the image of Christ.

While taking the Son to be the preexistent image of God through whom every human bears the divine image protologically, Scripture witnesses also to the reality that, because of the fall, humans are malformed by sin and can no longer properly image God. In other words, humans are unable to be-like-God as we were created to be. The further witness of Scripture, of course, is that through Christ as the last Adam, all those who are in his fellowship bear Christ's image eschatologically (cf. 1 Cor 15:49). The aspect of our redemption lying in between the eschatological "already" and the "not-yet" is that divine work Paul describes as our "being transformed ($\mu\epsilon\tau\alpha\mu\rho\rho\phi\sigma\acute{\nu}\mu\epsilon\theta\alpha$) into the same image [as Christ] from one degree of glory to another" (2 Cor 3:18). Likewise, our new nature in Christ "is being renewed in knowledge after the image of its creator" (Col 3:10). The capstone of this divine work is to have Christ fully "formed" in us (Gal 4:19) in accordance with the design of the divine plan (Rom 8:29–30).[126] The symmetry of the Son's role is perhaps best summarized by Philip Hughes: "The divine purpose of creation is grounded in the Son, and what was begun in the Son is also completed in the Son."[127]

Primary Symmetry 3

That as an analogue of the only-begotten Son's relationship to the Father, the Son of God as incarnate Redeemer procures adoptive sonship for all those he redeems, so that these may become beloved sons of God the Father.[128] In the first place, the idea of adoptive sonship in the Old

---

126. In reference to the Romans text, Gordon D. Fee, *Pauline Christology: An Exegetical-Theological Study* (Peabody, MA: Hendrickson Publishers, 2007), 184, adds, "This is what God's new people have been predestined for: to be conformed to the *image of his Son*, who himself has assumed the role of πρωτότοκος (*firstborn*) among many brothers and sisters."

127. Hughes, *The True Image*, ix.

128. Cf. Healy, *Thomas Aquinas*, 39: "It is because of the absolute fittingness of Christ's humanity that we are able to perceive the *convenientia* between the triune God and creation. ... A son is naturally like his father, which means that people are called sons and daughters of God in so far as they participate, by way of likeness, in him who is the Son of God by nature; and they know God in the measure that they resemble him, since all knowledge is brought about by assimilation to him."

Testament theologically informs that of the New Testament. Here too, the creation narrative provides the starting point. The record of the birth of Adam's son, Seth, in Genese 5:1-3 makes explicit that the relationship of Seth to Adam is analogous to Adam's relationship to God. As Beale explains, "For Seth to be 'in the likeness, according to the image' of Adam indicates that he has been born from Adam, reflects Adam's nature, and is Adam's son. This is 'sonship' language," and thus, the "language in Genesis 1:26 indicates that Adam is a son of God."[129] Meredith Kline likewise states, "To be the image of God is to be the son of God."[130] That Luke in his Gospel account concludes the genealogy of Jesus with "Seth, the son of Adam, the son of God" (3:38) shows that the filial connection here is hardly incidental.

The notion of divine sonship is conspicuous again where, even before the Exodus and establishment of the Sinai covenant, the Lord calls Israel his son: "Thus says the LORD, Israel is my firstborn son, and I say to you, 'Let my son go that he may serve me'" (Exod 4:22-23; cf. Ps 80:15; Hos 11:1). Scripture makes clear that it was in electing grace and according to his sovereign purposes that the Lord adopted Israel as his son. For where Israel as a whole is called Yahweh's son, or conversely, Yahweh is referred to as Israel's father,[131] is not explained by any other reason than that God had "set his love on" Israel and had chosen her for himself in keeping the oath that he swore to Abraham, Isaac, and Jacob (Deut 7:7-8; 9:5-6). Sonship in this light entails covenantal privilege. But where Israelites are addressed as "sons" (בָּנִים, often translated as "children") of Yahweh, this aspect of Israel's sonship "corresponds to the other side of the covenant relationship, namely the imperative demand for obedience—a demand which applied to all individual members of that nation."[132] It is especially in the Davidic covenant, prophesied in 2 Samuel 7:11-14 (cf. Pss 2:6-7; 89:26-27; 132), that we see both these aspects of sonship signified in a pronounced way. On this point

129. G. K. Beale, *A New Testament Biblical Theology: The Unfolding of the Old Testament in the New* (Grand Rapids: Baker Academic, 2011), 402.

130. Meredith G. Kline, *Images of the Spirit* (Eugene, OR: Wipf & Stock, 1999), 35.

131. E.g., Deuteronomy 32:6, 18; Hosea 11:1; Jeremiah 31:9; Isaiah 63:15-16; 64:8.

132. Christopher J. H. Wright, *Knowing Jesus through the Old Testament* (Downers Grove, IL: InterVarsity Press, 1992), 123. E.g., Deuteronomy 14:1; Isaiah 1:2; 30:1, 9; Jeremiah 3:22.

Christopher Wright observes, "Among other things, it points to the way the king in a sense 'embodied' Israel, since Israel was also designated Yahweh's 'firstborn son' (Exod 4:22). But in the context of the Davidic covenant it has a double purpose: to emphasize God's love (i.e., his unbreakable commitment) on the one hand, and the requirement of obedience (the primary duty of sonship) on the other."[133]

As to why Israel is called God's "son" and "firstborn," Beale takes a wide-lens approach and draws the following connection: "The likely reason ... is that the mantle of Adam had been passed on to Noah and then to the patriarchs and their 'seed,' Israel. ... [T]he OT constantly reiterates Adam's commission from Gen 1:28 and applies it to Israel."[134] Thus, Israel's sonship can be seen as a positional status she inherited from God in connection with the commission Adam was given as God's son.[135] It is this background that theologically informs and eschatologically points to the new covenant adoption of believers in Christ.

The New Testament uses language of "new birth" and "adoption" to describe believers' *filial* relationship to God through Christ. While both represent models of familial relationship, the former represents the Johannine model, characterized best as sonship by *regeneration* or *new birth*; the latter represents the Pauline model, characterized best as sonship by *adoption*.[136] Worth noting, the Greek term υἱοθεσία (adoption) occurs in the New Testament only in Paul and never in the Septuagint.[137] Moreover, as 2 Corinthians 6:18 makes plain (paraphrasing 2 Sam 7:14 and Isa 43:6), both males and females are included in Paul's concept of divine "sonship."

---

133. Wright, *Knowing Jesus through the Old Testament*, 91. For a helpful discussion on this point, see Gerald Cooke, "The Israelite King as Son of God," *ZAW* 73 no. 2 (1961): 202–25.

134. Beale, *A New Testament Biblical Theology*, 402.

135. For a recommended treatment on the relationship between Genesis 1–3 and Old Testament Israel's history, see Seth D. Postell, *Adam and Israel: Genesis 1–3 as the Introduction to the Torah and Tahakh* (Eugene, OR: Pickwick Publications, 2011).

136. The description given here draws from David B. Garner, "Adoption in Christ" (PhD diss., Westminster Theological Seminary, Philadelphia, PA, 2002), chapter 3: Adoption in Contemporary Context: John and Paul. It may well be that John's view of Christ's sonship as *sui generis* leads him to prefer calling believers "children of God" (τέκνα θεοῦ) rather than "sons of God" (υἱοὶ θεοῦ).

137. In reference to believers it is used in Romans 8:15, 23; Galatians 4:5; and Ephesians 1:5.

According to Ephesians 1:3–6, "he [God the Father] predestined us for adoption as sons through Jesus Christ, according to the purpose (εὐδοκία) of his will" (Eph 1:5).[138] Recognizable here is the consistent nature of the Son's agency, namely, that just as through Christ the redeemed are re-created in his image, so also through him the redeemed receive adoptive sonship. This would seem to follow from the correlation we saw above between the image of God and sonship. A further point here, εὐδοκία conveys a thicker meaning than indicated in our English translation, for it "signifies not simply the purpose of God but also the delight that he takes in his plans."[139] Although God delights perfectly in all of the divine plan, our adoption as sons through Christ seems to be at the heart of it. In the paean of Ephesians 1:3–14, Paul extols its christocentric as well as its Trinitarian dimensions.[140]

Beginning in Galatians 4:4, Paul again expresses the manifest purpose of God's will—that for which he sent forth his Son, the mission for which the Son became flesh—namely, "to redeem those who were under the law, so that we might receive adoption as sons." The context of Galatians 4:1–7 highlights the redemptive-historical development from old covenant sonship, belonging to Israel as a child minor (Gal 4:1–2), to the mature sonship of new covenant adoption (Gal 4:5–7), procured and realized through the messianic Sonship of Christ for all who are the spiritual descendants of Abraham through faith (Galatians 3). Lastly, in Romans 8, as in Galatians, the apostle again describes the

---

138. The study note on Ephesians 1:5 in the NET states: "*Adoption as his sons* is different from spiritual birth as children. All true believers have been born as children of God and will be adopted as sons of God. The adoption is both a future reality, and in some sense, already true. To be adopted as a son means to have the full rights of an heir. Thus, although in the ancient world, only boys could be adopted as sons, in God's family all children—both male and female—are adopted."

139. Peter T. O'Brien, *The Letter to the Ephesians* (PNTC; Grand Rapids: Eerdmans, 1999), 103. O'Brien continues, "The preposition 'according to' (*kata*) indicates the norm or standard, showing that his choosing many to come into a special relationship with himself was in keeping with what he delighted to do and with his saving plan. 'He enjoys imparting his riches to many children.' Consequently, as men and women break out in praise (vv. 3, 6, 12, 14), their pleasure in God is a response to his delight in doing good to them."

140. Garner, "Adoption," 60, summarizes this accordingly: "The Father lovingly ordains his eternal purpose (vv. 3–6), the Son willingly carries out these eternal purposes in *Heilsgeschichte* (vv. 7–12), and the Holy Spirit applies the eternal purposes of the Father on the basis of the work of the Son (vv. 13–14)."

believers' adoption in terms of freedom from bondage, filial intimacy with the Father, and redemptive transformation. "Summarily, in Rom 8:1–23," writes Garner, "Paul joins the juridical (justification) and renovative (sanctification) under *adoptive sonship* through the ministry of the eschatological Spirit, whereby through union with the Son of God, the sons of God participate in *all* that Jesus Christ, the eschatological Son, accomplished."[141]

The Immanent Fittingness of the Son in the Ordered Triunity of God

In our discussion earlier on the immanent form of the Godhead's beauty, I defined that as God's Triunity—his three-in-oneness—consisting of all its absolute perfections in Triune simplicity. In this section our interest again has to do with the immanent Trinity, but the focus is narrowed in on the immanent fittingness of the Son. Our efforts here will help round out the concept of fittingness in regard to the persons of the immanent Trinity, and the role of the Son as Redeemer in particular. To that end, we will revisit Aquinas' *Summa* article, *ST* Ia, q.39, a.8, in which he provides a systematic formulation of his three formal criteria of beauty in answer to the question, "Whether the Essential Attributes Are Appropriated to the Persons of the Trinity in a Fitting Manner by the Holy Doctors?" Aquinas' discussion in *ST* Ia, q.39, a.8, pertains directly to the notion of the immanent fittingness of the Son. While Aquinas understood beauty to be an attribute of the divine nature and thus common to all three persons of the Godhead, he also argues in this *Summa* article that *beauty* is the designation that applies best to the Son and therefore is specifically "appropriated" to him.[142] But on what basis does Aquinas see beauty as characterizing best the personal mode of being of the Son? His answer has to do with what are, in Aquinas' view, three identifying aspects of the Son's filial relation to the Father. Those three identifying aspects are characterized by the three essential

---

141. Garner, "Adoption," 117.

142. In this article, Aquinas also advances and explains that to the Father the name *eternity* is most proper, and to the Holy Spirit the name *use* is most proper.

qualities of beauty, namely, *proportion*, *integrity*, and *clarity*.[143] He reasons accordingly along the following lines. By virtue of the Son:

1. Being the express image of the Father, i.e., the perfect likeness of the original, the condition of perfect proportion is satisfied.

2. Having in himself "truly and perfectly the nature of the Father," the condition of perfect integrity or wholeness is satisfied.

3. Proceeding eternally from the Father as his Word, which is the perfectly communicated radiance of the Father, the condition of perfect clarity is satisfied.[144]

In my judgment, however, the idea here that essential attributes are appropriated to the personal modes of being of the Father, Son, and Holy Spirit lacks clear scriptural grounding. For our purposes it nonetheless serves illustratively, showing how, for Aquinas, the immanent fittingness of the Son is integrally connected to the filiation of the Son, whose identifying aspects exhibit perfectly all the hallmarks of beauty.

Assuming, as I have argued, that the economical activities of the Father, Son, and Holy Spirit are perfectly fitting according to God's eternal plan, a relevant question is whether or not the persons of the immanent Trinity could have substituted for the economical roles/activities of the other persons. For example, could the Father or the Holy Spirit have assumed the role of incarnate Redeemer instead of the Son? Both Anselm and Aquinas are instructive here, for both address this very question in terms of fittingness. Arguing from an *a posteriori* perspective, Anselm offers two main reasons for "why God assumed human being into a unity of person with the Son rather than into a unity with either of the other persons."[145] His first reason concerns our

---

143. It is not incidental, just to note, that Aquinas' fullest account of the three criteria of beauty occurs here in reference to God, specifically the beauty that characterizes the filiation of the Son.

144. Vanhoozer's comments, *Remythologizing Theology*, 51, are germane here: "The first word God spoke resulted in light (Gen 1:3). There is some debate among commentators as to whether the Son passively reflects or actively radiates light. In favor of the latter is a certain parallel with the Son as definitive word: both word and light are means of the Father's expressive presence. Just as the word expresses thought, so radiance expresses light."

145. Anselm, *On the Incarnation of the Word* in *Basic Writings*, ed. and trans. Thomas Williams (Indianapolis: Hackett, 2007), 228 (sect. 10).

finite human understanding. The most fitting choice by God was for the immanent Son to become the economic Son in order to not upset our capacity to make sense of the Trinitarian relations with regard to how God revealed himself economically.[146] His second reason concerns the way human thinking is naturally oriented. Because "the one who was to become flesh was to intercede for the human race," states Anselm, "the human mind more appropriately enough conceives a son pleading with his father than one individual pleading with another, although the human nature, not the divine nature, makes this supplication to the deity."[147] While Anselm offers a positive rationale for the propriety of the immanent Son assuming the role of the economic Son, it is unclear whether he actually denies the possibility (irrespective of fittingness) that the Father or the Holy Spirit could have assumed this role instead. It is Aquinas who gives the more definitive answer to this, at least as he sees it.

In *ST* IIIa, q.3, a.5, which addresses "Whether Each of the Divine Persons Could Have Assumed Human Nature?," Aquinas answers, "Whatever the Son can do, so can the Father and the Holy Spirit, otherwise the power of the three Persons would not be one. But the Son was able to become incarnate. Therefore the Father and the Holy Spirit were able to become incarnate." Aquinas' argument here rests on the fact that in divinity all three persons of the Godhead share full equality together in every respect. The Father or the Holy Spirit could therefore have assumed the role of the economic Son simply because of their common divine *ability*. To say in an absolute sense that *only* God the Son could have assumed the role of the economic Son, therefore, is to imply that the Son is different in essence from the Father and the Holy

---

146. Anselm argues thus: "If the Holy Spirit became flesh, as the Son became flesh, surely the Holy Spirit would be the son of a human being. Therefore, there would be two sons in the divine Trinity, namely, the Son of God and the son of the human being. And so some mixture of doubt would be generated when we were speaking of God the 'son.' For both would be God and son, although one would be the Son of God, the other the son of a human being. ... And if the Father were to have assumed a human being into the unity of his person, the multiplication of sons would result in the same improprieties in God." Anselm, *On the Incarnation of the Word* in *Basic Writings*, ed. and trans. Williams, 228 (sect. 10).

147. Anselm, *On the Incarnation of the Word* in *Basic Writings*, ed. and trans. Williams, 251. Anselm recapitulates this argument in *Cur Deus Homo* 2.9.

Spirit, not just in personal distinction from them. But this contravenes the intra-essential unity of the divine persons, for with respect to their common divinity the Father, Son, and Holy Spirit are equipollent. In my judgment Aquinas' argument here seems correct. Moreover, the distinct personal *suitability* (i.e., fittingness) of the divine persons comes into play as well. He writes in the same article, "It belongs to the Father to be innascible as to the eternal birth, and the temporal birth would not destroy this. But the Son of God is said to be sent in regard to the Incarnation, inasmuch as He is from another, without which the Incarnation would not suffice for the nature of mission" (ad 3).[148] Aquinas applies the idea of fittingness still further in *ST* IIIa, q.3, a.8, which addresses "Whether It Was More Fitting That the Person of the Son Rather Than Any Other Divine Person Should Assume Human Nature?" While Anselm's reasoning on this has mainly to do with how God accommodated human ways of thinking, Aquinas argues directly for the fittingness of the Son's role in the divine economy. "It was most fitting that the Person of the Son should become incarnate," states Aquinas. Represented in these extracts from the *Summa* article, the three reasons Aquinas gives are as follows:

1. *[ad 2] Creation/Re-creation through the Word:* "The first creation of things was made by the power of God the Father through the Word; hence the second creation ought to have been brought about through the Word, by the power of God the Father, in order that restoration should correspond to creation according to 2 Corinthians 5:19."

2. *The Word as Exemplar Likeness:* "Now the Person of the Son, Who is the Word of God, has a certain common agreement with all creatures, because the word of the craftsman, i.e., his concept, is an exemplar likeness of whatever is made by him. Hence the Word of God, Who is His eternal concept, is the exemplar likeness of all creatures."[149]

---

148. In *ST* Ia, q.43, a.4, which addresses "Whether the Father Can Be Fittingly Sent?," Aquinas answers, "The very idea of mission means procession from another, and in God it means procession according to origin, as above expounded. Hence, as the Father is not from another, in no way is it fitting for Him to be sent; but this can only belong to the Son and to the Holy Ghost, to Whom it belongs to be from another."

149. The idea Aquinas uses of "exemplar likeness" is understood in this way: the idea or image of a thing formed in the mind that serves as a model, original, or

3. Natural Sonship/Adoptive sonship: "Hence it was fitting that by Him Who is the natural Son, men should share this likeness of sonship by adoption, as the Apostle says in Romans 8:29."

What is noteworthy here is that the three reasons Aquinas offers for why it was most fitting that the Son should become incarnate are closely parallel to the three primary ways I presented above on how the theodramatic fittingness of the Son has correspondence to the symmetrical nature of his agency in the work of the divine economy. This gets back to the point that to a fair extent the christological contours of beauty that this project explores and develops, constructively appropriate and engage the theological aesthetics of our featured theologians, and fundamentally those of the medieval church Fathers in regard to the doctrine of God.

---

pattern to be copied or imitated; an archetype. See also Aquinas' answer in *ST* Ia, q.45, a.6, which addresses "Whether to Create Is Proper to Any Person?"

3

Creation: Beauty's Debut

The development of our theological aesthetic has its protological moorings in the biblical creation account. The symmetrical design of the divine plan, as we have said, is with respect to creation and re-creation, and the shape of the symmetry is according to the redemptive-eschatological fulfillment of God's original creational purposes. This chapter addresses the divine work of creation itself, centered primarily on Genesis 1-2 as our base text. The focus of my constructive argument here is on key themes that are integral to God's original creational purposes— the main one being the image of God, which figures in as a structural element of the christological contours of beauty and is developed in subsequent chapters. Theological aesthetic considerations relative to the fall of Adam and Eve in Genesis 3 are also presented. The featured theologian whose theological aesthetic contributes at places throughout this chapter is Irenaeus. I develop this in four main sections as follows:

1. *Sublime Comedy: The Theodramatic Form of the Divine Plan.* I argue that a consideration of the significance of literary form with respect to the Bible's overall story pattern helps elucidate an aspect of Scripture's aesthetic dimension, namely, its correspondence to the archetypal story pattern of dramatic comedy. I show how the story pattern of Scripture is unique, however, in its qualification as a theodramatic comedy. Following this, I present Irenaeus' account of the Bible's overall story pattern.

2. *The Proto-eschaton: The Beginning of the Telos of All Things.* Here, I develop the idea of the "proto-eschaton," which is the formalized notion that the opening chapters of Genesis lay out basic

pre-redemptive eschatological themes that serve to show the creational intention of the divine plan for humanity. The themes of the proto-eschaton—integral to God's original creational purposes—figure in as structural elements of the christological contours of beauty that are developed in subsequent chapters.

3. *Humans in the Image of God*. I offer a theological interpretation of the image of God, arguing that it is comprehended in three principal aspects—the official (royal priest), constitutional (whole person, i.e., body-soul), and ethical-relational. The tandem use in Scripture of image and glory plays a prominent role here. Relevant to our theological aesthetic, the characteristics of the three principal aspects are an integral part of the form in and through which humans bear the divine image. The beauty of human beings is expressed by reflecting most fittingly the ways that they bear all aspects of the divine image.

4. *Fittingness of Retributive Justice*. In view of the narrative prominence in Genesis 3 of the meting out of judgment by God against Adam and Eve, I consider the notion of fittingness in reference to retributive justice. The theological groundwork laid here figures in as part of the aesthetic dimension of redemptive-history, all of which pays forward in Chapter 5 as we address the judgment that God meted out upon Christ in the place of sinners.

SUBLIME COMEDY:
THE THEODRAMATIC FORM OF THE DIVINE PLAN

The design and outworking of the divine plan is reflected in the overall shape of its story pattern. All that we have said till now about that shape is just that it can be characterized in terms of a fundamental symmetry between creation and re-creation whose pivotal center is God's reconciling all things to himself through Christ in the redemptive-eschatological fulfillment of his original creational purposes. That characterization itself is fairly basic and generally recognized in biblical-theological glosses on the "big picture" of the Bible. For example, William Dumbrell describes "Creation—the Renewal of Creation (Redemption)—the New Creation, as the axis around which all biblical theology turns."[1] Beyond that, however,

---

1. William J. Dumbrell, *The End of the Beginning: Revelation 21–22 and the Old Testament* (Eugene, OR: Wipf & Stock, 2001), 196.

a consideration of the significance of literary form with respect to the Bible's story pattern from Genesis to Revelation helps elucidate an aspect of Scripture's aesthetic dimension, namely, its correspondence to the archetypal story pattern of dramatic comedy. In this case, I am not referring to Scripture strictly in terms of it being a work of literature in which the pleasure evoked in perceiving its aesthetics is effected through an imaginational presentation; I am referring to an aspect of its aesthetics conceived in a broad sense. As I argue here, the significance of the literary form of the biblical metanarrative (overarching story) is not its qualification as a dramatic comedy but rather as a theodramatic comedy. For the latter highlights the sublime conclusion to the christological contours of beauty in a theologically thicker way that simply calling attention to the creational-re-creational symmetry does not.

The question to which we will first turn, then, is what kind of story pattern does the Bible as a whole present? In the simplest of terms, the shape of the overall biblical plotline is given as follows: "It begins with the creation of all things, it takes a plunge into evil (Gen 3), it meanders through fallen human history, and it winds its way slowly and painfully back to the consummation of history, with the final defeat of evil and triumph of good."[2] More needs to be said, obviously, than that there is a unified thread of events having a beginning, a middle, and an end (what Aristotle called *mythos*, his definition of plot) that makes up the crude plotline just described. Scripture's overarching narrative unity is represented in the progression of the historical narrative in which the Bible's diverse literary forms and compositions are woven into a single coherent revelational whole—what is commonly called salvation history.[3] Yet, as Vanhoozer points out, it is *drama* that offers a better framework for interpreting God's speech and action on the stage of world history. And thus in literary terms, salvation history can be described as a drama—the drama of redemption—what is fittingly captured *in nuce* by the term "theodrama."[4]

---

2. "Bible" in *DBI*, 90–92, here 91.

3. For a helpful discussion on the Bible's grand metanarrative, see Christopher J. H. Wright, *The Mission of God: Unlocking the Bible's Grand Narrative* (Downers Grove, IL: IVP Academic, 2006), 62–65.

4. Kevin J. Vanhoozer, "Love's Wisdom: The Authority of Scripture's Form and

The concept of drama from the classic Greek period (5th–4th cent. BC) is instructive for our present discussion. Two distinct forms of drama developed in that context, pervading literary and artistic composition: comic drama (dramatic comedy) and tragic drama (dramatic tragedy). The Old Comedy plays of the ancient Greek theater, known through the works of Aristophanes (c.446–386 BC), developed first. The details of its literary structure are unimportant for our purposes. What is germane is its jubilant conclusion, characterized by *Komos* or *Komoidia*, meaning "a musical and dancing festivity" from which the English word "comedy" derives.[5] In subsequent periods dramatic comedy underwent phases of change in certain structural details or emphasis. Aristotle, for example, saw the essence of comedy as presenting protagonists of "humbler and meaner [inferior] types of character." The "happy ending," in his view, was certainly appropriate to comedy but not determined by it.[6] This notion is evident in Aristotle's *Poetics* where he writes,

> As for Comedy, it is an imitation of men worse than the average; worse, however, not as regards any and every sort of fault, but only as regards one particular kind, the Ridiculous, which is a species of the Ugly. The Ridiculous may be defined as a mistake or deformity not productive of pain or harm to others; the mask, for instance, that excites laughter, is something ugly and distorted without causing pain.[7]

Over time, however, both forms of drama (comic and tragic) became more generically established literary forms—what Leland Ryken describes respectively as archetypes of ideal experience and unideal experience.[8] And so what came to characterize the archetypal

---

Content for Faith's Understanding and Theological Judgment," *Journal of Reformed Theology* 5 no. 3 (January 2011): 257.

5. Francesca Aran Murphy, *The Comedy of Revelation: Paradise Lost and Regained in Biblical Narrative* (Edinburgh: T&T Clark, 2000), 16.

6. J. G. Warry, *Greek Aesthetic Theory: A Study of Callistic and Aesthetic Concepts in the Works of Plato and Aristotle* (New York: Barnes & Noble, 1962), 136.

7. Aristotle, *The Basic Works of Aristotle*, ed. Richard McKeon (New York: Modern Library, 2001), 1459 (*Poetics*, ch. 5).

8. Leland Ryken, *Words of Delight: A Literary Introduction to the Bible*, 2nd ed. (Grand Rapids: Baker Book House, 1992), 26–28. Ryken, 26, states further, "The two categories of archetypes ... are a vision of the world that people want and do not

story pattern of comedy is "a U-shaped story that begins in prosperity, descends into tragedy, but rises to a happy ending as obstacles to success are overcome."[9] Another key factor is that "drama manifests a combat between good and evil, because it is a moral category."[10] Moral conflict is thus an essential aspect of the comic drama, and figures critically in the comedy plot.

What all this corroborates is that the shape of Scripture's overall story pattern corresponds significantly to the archetypal story pattern of dramatic comedy. An important difference to mark between these two story patterns, however, is that a U-shaped story does not accurately reflect the overall story pattern of Scripture. For, strictly speaking, what "U-shaped" suggests is that the "happy ending" involves a reversal of fortune in which remediable evils are in some way overcome and parity with the "happy beginning" is regained. The meta-story the Bible presents likewise involves a reversal of fortune, with a happy-ever-after ending. But in this case the consummation ending is incomparably and everlastingly more glorious than the creation beginning, and is not simply restored to parity with it. The biblical meta-story is thus not simply a dramatic comedy as such, it is a *theo*dramatic comedy—or with the accent on the aesthetic, what we could call a *sublime comedy*.[11] In this sense, then, it is a sublime comedy whose christological contours we are developing in argument that everything God does is beautifully God-glorifying.[12]

---

want." Cf. Northrop Frye, "The Archetypes of Literature," in *The Myth and Ritual Theory: An Anthology*, ed. Robert A. Segal (Malden, MA: Blackwell, 1998), 218–30.

9. Ryken, *Words of Delight*, 49. The archetypal story pattern of tragedy, on the other hand, presents protagonists of relatively exalted and superior types of character, who, because of their own wrong choices, descend into tragedy and never reverse out of it. Their end is in utter calamity, suffering and abjection. Idem., 145–46.

10. Murphy, *The Comedy of Revelation*, 340.

11. My term "sublime comedy" carries the same meaning, except "sublime" serves to point up the aesthetic dimension of the theodrama—i.e., the creative elegance of its design, with its grandeur and beauty. This is all assumed in "theodrama." For a comparable presentation of seeing the shape of the Bible's overall story pattern as that of a theodramatic comedy, see Patrick Downey, *Serious Comedy: The Philosophical and Theological Significance of Tragic and Comic Writing in the Western Tradition* (Lanham, MD: Lexington Books, 2001), Part II: The Bible and Its Comic Narrator.

12. Peter Leithart, *Deep Comedy: Trinity, Tragedy, and Hope in Western Literature*

Given how the Bible's story pattern corresponds to the archetypal story pattern of comedy, let us walk through the movement of these elements in brief fashion. The comedy's beginning is characterized by a given state of prosperity for its protagonists. The creation account with Adam and Eve in the garden of Eden, in communion and right standing with God, represents that. God's command to not eat from the designated tree is the primal context of moral testing and conflict between good and evil. The dramatic movement that follows is the element of descent into tragedy. Adam's tragic choice in Genesis 3 and God's consequent curse on the created order defines the cause of the descent. But the protevangelium of Genesis 3:15—an intimation of the *Christus Victor* motif—guarantees an ultimate reversal out of tragedy into triumph. Throughout the unfolding history of the Old Testament, God's commitment to his covenant people advances the course of this reversal, even in the midst of egregious and inveterate sin and failure. At the theodrama's midpoint, God reconciles the world to himself through Christ's atoning sacrifice and subsequent resurrection and heavenly exaltation. That midpoint is the pivotal center of inversion in which the guaranteed reversal out of tragedy into triumph is accomplished. Christ's resurrection serves critically as the definitive anticipation of what will come at the end of the story for the redeemed people of God. In the final dramatic movement, the so-called happy-ever-after ending is fully realized. For the redeemed in Christ, a glorious new order is come. That gloss on the shape of the Bible's overall story is perfectly consonant with our gloss on the creational-re-creational symmetry of the divine plan, except even better, recognizing the literary form of the Bible as a theodramatic comedy serves to point up the surplus of the gloriousness of its consummation ending compared to its creation beginning.

(Moscow, ID: Canon Press, 2006), xii, proposes the term "deep comedy" along the same lines: "'Deep comedy' brings two additional nuances: First, in deep comedy the happy ending is uncontaminated by any fear of future tragedy, and, second, in deep comedy the characters do not simply end as well as they began, but progress beyond their beginning. Comedy may move from glory to glory restored, but deep comedy moves from glory to added glory. While the classical world did produce comedy, it did not produce 'deep comedy.'"

THE IRENAEAN FORM OF THE THEODRAMA

For Irenaeus, the Bible's story pattern unmistakably drove his theological interpretation of Scripture. Although idiosyncratic in certain ways, his account of the meta-story the Bible presents accords with the basic elements that characterize the dramatic comedy form—call it the Irenaean form of the theodrama. In keeping with our present discussion and throughout this chapter, Irenaeus's "big picture" understanding of Scripture serves as a theologically notable reference, figuring prominently also in our next chapter.[13]

According to Irenaeus, Adam and Eve's aboriginal state qualified as some kind of "infant" condition. In its own right it was a "happy beginning," but yet critically inferior to the state of perfected adulthood that God planned at the outset for humankind, and thus in this sense an imperfect condition. For Adam's initial condition of "infancy" was a protological reality, perfected adulthood an eschatological one. The idea of maturation is linked tightly to the goal of humanity's full perfection. "God thus determin[ed] all things beforehand for the bringing of man to perfection," states Irenaeus, "and that man may finally be brought to maturity at some future time, becoming ripe through such privileges to see and comprehend God."[14] Irenaeus refers regularly to Adam and Eve as infants/children (νήπιοι). That conception is integral to his theology of creation, and vitally informs the framework of his anthropology and soteriology.[15] That Adam started off in an imperfect condition effectively because he was νήπιος is clear enough from Irenaeus's discussions, but exactly what he meant by this term is highly disputed. According to Matthew Steenberg, "It is Adam's physicality, his material being, ... that is the root of his lack of full development and his relative 'distance' from the Creator."[16] In Thomas Holsinger-Friesen's view, on the other hand, Irenaeus associates the concept of infancy explicitly with "human

---

13. See my discussion in the Chapter 4 section, Christ the Last Adam and the True Israel.

14. Irenaeus of Lyons, *AH* 4.37.7 (page 540).

15. For the discussion in hand, I was helped by M. C. Steenberg, "Children in Paradise: Adam and Eve as 'Infants' in Irenaeus of Lyons," *Journal of Early Christian Studies* 12 no. 1 (2004): 1–22.

16. Steenberg, "Children in Paradise," 18.

moral growth."[17] However Irenaeus is to be best taken on this, the key point is that the human person *in virtue of being created in the image of God* betokens God's creational purposes for humanity and the process of development wherein humanity is brought to perfection. "Now God shall be glorified in His handiwork," writes Irenaeus, "fitting it so as to be conformable to, and modeled after, His own Son. For by the hands of the Father, that is, by the Son and the Holy Spirit, man, and not [merely] a part of man, was made in the likeness of God."[18]

The descent into tragedy that follows from Adam's infant beginning is all a part of the maturation of humanity in accordance with the divine plan.[19] The dramatic movement of the story as such has a twist added to the conventional description of going from an original state of perfection to a tragic fall in sin, which is then reversed in redemption. For Irenaeus, the drama advances from a state of infant imperfection, through a maturation process that involves the tragedy of sin and evil, which attains in redemption its goal of adult perfection. The observation by Holsinger-Friesen is well worth noting: "Irenaeus sees the fall as more of an interlude in the economy than a catastrophic disruption."[20] The *reversal* out of tragedy into triumph is the primary dramatic movement that follows, but the *traversal* action of being brought to perfection is a necessary secondary movement following from the primary one. The basis of the reversal is the "recapitulation" of all things in Christ. The concept of recapitulation is seen, with legitimate reason, as a virtual trope for Irenaeus' theology. We can glean a sense of its meaning from the following excerpt:

> [I]t was in the power of God Himself to grant perfection to man from the beginning; but the man, on the contrary, was unable to

---

17. Thomas Holsinger-Friesen, *Irenaeus and Genesis: A Study of Competition in Early Christian Hermeneutics* (Winona Lake, IN: Eisenbrauns, 2009), 133. Holsinger-Friesen takes *AH* 4.38.2 as the *locus classicus*. Here Irenaeus cites 1 Corinthians 3:3 in connection with "the infantile stage of man's existence."

18. Irenaeus of Lyons, *AH* 5.6.1 (page 566).

19. For example, in *AH* 3.20.1, Irenaeus writes, "From the beginning, did God permit man to be swallowed up by the great whale (Satan), who was the author of transgression, not that he should perish altogether when so engulphed; but, [He was] arranging and preparing the plan of salvation, which was accomplished by the Word" (page 363).

20. Holsinger-Friesen, *Irenaeus and Genesis*, 39.

receive it, since he was still an infant. And for this reason our Lord, recapitulating all things in Himself was able to come, but in such manner as we were able to behold Him. He could have come to us in His ineffable glory, but we were not able to receive the greatness of that glory. Therefore, as if to infants, He who was the perfect bread of the Father offered Himself to us as milk, since His coming was in keeping with a man.[21]

Adam thus stands at the head of the human race, created in a condition of infancy that is unable to behold God's glory, or participate in receiving it. The totality of human development in the divine economy, advancing from Adam on, is summed up and brought to perfection in the person and work of Christ. For in and through Christ all other human beings can become fully mature and thereby fully abled to participate in the life and glory of God.[22]

This maturation process means that human beings must become "habituated" or "accustomed" to the participatory life offered in the incarnate Son. Irenaeus thus states, "The Word of God who dwelt in man, and became the Son of man," did so "that He might accustom man to receive God, and God to dwell in man, according to the good pleasure of the Father."[23] This "accustomization," by which remediable evils are ultimately overcome, is perfected through the Holy Spirit's working in humanity: "But we do now receive a certain portion of His Spirit, tending towards perfection, and preparing us for incorruption, being little by little accustomed to receive and bear God."[24] In the final dramatic movement, everyone in Christ, "having received growth," "having been strengthened," "having abounded," "having recovered from the disease

---

21. Irenaeus of Lyons, *AH* 4.38.1 (page 541).

22. Summarizing Irenaeus' theology of recapitulation, Steenberg writes: "Christ enters into the race of humanity *as human*, as himself the personal reality of the whole race, since this reality has from its formation been defined as created in his image. What he accomplishes as human becomes universally recapitulative inasmuch as he accomplishes it in the person of the whole human family." Matthew C. Steenberg, *Of God and Man: Theology as Anthropology from Irenaeus to Athanasius* (London: T&T Clark, 2009), 48. See also the helpful treatment in Eric Osborn, *Irenaeus of Lyons* (Cambridge: Cambridge University Press, 2001).

23. Irenaeus of Lyons, *AH* 3.20.2III.XX.2 (page 367).

24. Irenaeus of Lyons, *AH* 5.8.1V.VIII.1 (page 570).

of sin," and ultimately "being glorified," receives at last the glorious privilege to "see his Lord."[25]

THE PROTO-ESCHATON:
THE BEGINNING OF THE TELOS OF ALL THINGS

"The origins of creation cannot properly be understood apart from their eschatological aim. If we understand creation (including ourselves) only in terms of an origin (protology) rather than also as a destiny (eschatology), we will miss the crucial point that creation—including humanity—is in an important sense unfinished."[26] From a canonical perspective, key features of the creation account can be seen as prototypical of their consummative fulfillment portrayed in the final chapters of Revelation.[27] Working from this idea, the proto-eschaton is the formalized notion that the opening chapters of Genesis lay out basic pre-redemptive eschatological themes that serve to show the creational intention of the divine plan for humanity.[28] The principal aim of this section is to mark out and characterize the basic pre-redemptive eschatological themes in Genesis 1–2 that clue us in about God's original

25. Irenaeus of Lyons, *AH* 4.38.3 (page 543).

26. Michael Horton, *The Christian Faith: A Systematic Theology for Pilgrims on the Way* (Grand Rapids: Zondervan, 2011), 379. Similarly, Graeme Goldsworthy, *The Son of God and the New Creation* (Wheaton IL: Crossway, 2015), states, "The Bible presents a picture of creation that was designed by God to contain the pattern of the structure of his future kingdom. The narratives of creation are much more than merely descriptive. They foreshadow the ultimate purposes of God. ... Essentially, we see from the outset of the biblical narrative the creation of a situation in which God rules over his people in fellowship with them in the place he has prepared for them. ... Every expression of the goal of God's redemptive action to save his people can be reduced to this basic creation paradigm: God, his people, and the place where the two parties meet and fellowship." (59–60)

27. Bernhard W. Anderson, *From Creation to New Creation: Old Testament Perspectives* (Minneapolis: Fortress Press, 1994), 38, sums it up this way: "The goal of history will be a return to the beginning, not in the sense of a historical cycle that repeats itself, but in the sense that the original intention of the Creator ... will be realized."

28. The concept of the proto-eschaton entails that the revelation of God's eternal plan and purposes unfolds from the seminal eschatological design of his creation project. In using the term "seminal" to describe the eschatological design of creation, I am not saying that the forward movement of creation is propelled by some kind of Hegelian necessity, nor that it unfolds in any kind of process theology sense or in any sense deistically. Rather, and only, creation is by the freedom of God's gracious (non-necessary) love.

creational purposes. The relevancy of this to our theological aesthetic relates to an element in our argument that the symmetrical shape of the divine plan is according to the redemptive-eschatological fulfillment of God's original creational purposes.

The central proto-eschaton theme is the image of God in which all humans are created. Two concomitant themes are (a) the notion of sacred time represented by God's Sabbath rest, and (b) the notion of sacred space represented by the garden of Eden, God's garden of delight. Since the image of God is a major theme in our theological aesthetic, I will address that separately in the next section. In this section I will briefly characterize the proto-eschaton themes of sacred time and sacred space, which themselves are contextually important for appreciating the creational intention of the divine plan for humanity and the beauty of its eschatological realization in the consummation. Before proceeding to those themes, however, I will set the backdrop of the creation narrative by giving attention to God's delight in his beautiful work of creation.

God's Delight in His Beautiful Work of Creation

One finds it scarcely possible to read the project of creation in the open-ing chapter of Genesis without seeing God as Master Artificer. Irenaeus declares as much in his magisterial work, *Against Heresies*: "[God] has fitted and arranged all things by His wisdom. ... He is the Former, He is the Builder, He is the Discoverer, He is the Creator, He is the Lord of all; and there is no one besides Him."[29] The processive structure of the days of creation exhibits a patent orderliness and a symmetry of com-plementarity. Evidenced by the explicit literary framing in Genesis 1,

---

29. Irenaeus of Lyons, *AH* 2.3.9 (page 257). Cf. *AH* 2.7.5. Marveling at the same, Calvin, *Institutes* 1.5.2, ed. McNeill, trans. Battles, writes: "There are innumerable evidences both in heaven and on earth that declare his wonderful wisdom; not only those more recondite matters for the closer observation of which astronomy, medicine, and all natural science are intended, but also those which thrust them-selves upon the sight of even the most untutored and ignorant persons, so that they cannot open their eyes without being compelled to witness them. Indeed, men who have either quaffed or even tasted the liberal arts penetrate with their aid far more deeply into the secrets of the divine wisdom. Yet ignorance of them prevents no one from seeing more than enough of God's workmanship in his creation to lead him to break forth in admiration of the Artificer."

the forming of habitations characterizes the first three days, while the filling of those habitations with inhabitants respectively fit for them characterizes days four to six. As the Master Artificer, God finished his creation project in six workdays, climaxing it with the Sabbath. While characterizing the whole project simply as a divine work of art seems reductionist on its face, it surely is not less than this, either. Indeed, the artistic patterning depicting the archetypal week of creation displays the aesthetic aspect entailed in God's expressed creational purposes.[30]

Throughout the narrative of the constructive process of creation, God looks upon what he made, "saw that it was good" (Gen 1:4, 10, 12, 18, 21, 25), and after completing his work of day six "saw everything that he had made, and behold, it was very good" (v. 31). The word for "good" in the Hebrew text (טוֹב) as well as in the Septuagint (καλός) have a broad semantic range that includes both ethical and aesthetic meanings. In some cases, commentators take "it was good" to mean something like "functioning properly," but while this view is certainly correct in affirming the purposeful design and proper operation of everything within creation, its description of the creation narrative is theologically thin in both ethical and aesthetic ways.[31] The fact that the Septuagint went with καλός instead of ἀγαθός only reinforces the sense that the created order in its altogether goodness is imbued altogether with beauty (cf. Gen 2:9; 1 Tim 4:4). Calvin put it this way: "Wherever you cast your eyes, there is no spot in the universe wherein you cannot discern at

---

30. As Leland Ryken, "In the Beginning, God Created" in *The Christian Imagination: Essays on Literature and the Arts*, ed. Leland Ryken (Grand Rapids: Baker Book House, 1981), 56, rightly argues, the form and content of Scripture together convey a theologically thicker sense of the biblical narrative: "All of this is to say that the imaginative form of Genesis 1 is itself part of the meaning, which is, of course, God's creation of the world. The meaning has been incarnated in the form. The artistry is not something added to the meaning, it is part of it. Nor does the writer step outside of his story to state his theme as a proposition. All of this, in turn, illustrates how the Bible contributes to aesthetic theory by its example, not simply by its doctrine. The most emphatic thing we can say along these lines is that the Bible does not distrust the imagination and artistic form as a means of expressing the truth." Cf. J. Richard Middleton, *The Liberating Image: The Imago Dei in Genesis 1* (Grand Rapids: Brazos Press, 2005), 74–77, 87–88.

31. Old Testament scholar, John H. Walton, for example, interprets "it was good" in this functionality sense in his book, *Genesis 1 as Ancient Cosmology* (Winona Lake, IN: Eisenbrauns, 2011).

least some sparks of his glory. You cannot in one glance survey this most vast and beautiful system of the universe, in its wide expanse, without being completely overwhelmed by the boundless force of its brightness."[32] A theologically thick description of the divine appraisal, "it was good," entails that what God sovereignly willed and delighted to enact is what he also expressed delight in (cf. Matt 3:17; 17:5). Genesis 1:31, it follows, gives expression to God's overall delight in the *fait accompli* of his creation. "It is important to recognize," writes Walter Brueggemann, "that along with this dimension of ethical demand in the ordering of this hidden God, there is also an aesthetic dimension that exults in the artistry of God, in the beauty of the created order, culminating in a response of amazement and astonishment." Rounding out his point—and consonant with my own—Brueggemann states:

> In Gen 1:31, at the conclusion of the sixth day of creation, Yahweh exclaimed, "It was very good." Most probably this is an aesthetic judgment and response to a brilliant act of creation. The sense of beauty, or loveliness evokes on Yahweh's part a doxological response to the created order, a sense of satisfaction on the part of the artist, a glad acknowledgment of success. Here and in some other places, a glad affirmation of creation is moved more by awe and delight than by ethical insistence or command. Thus Prov 8:30-31, in speaking of creation, culminates in a statement of "delight" and "rejoicing."[33]

Sacred Time: The Climactic Sabbath of the Creation Week

Following the six workdays of the creation week is God's Sabbath, the resting of the Master Artificer. C. John Collins, highlighting the verbs in this short account, offers the following commentary: "In Gen 2:1, the heavens and the earth *were finished*; in 2:2, God *finished* his work and

---

32. Calvin, *Institutes* 1.5.1, ed. McNeill, trans. Battles.

33. Walter Brueggemann, *Theology of the Old Testament: Testimony, Dispute, Advocacy* (Minneapolis: Fortress Press, 1997), 339. On a related note, David Bentley Hart posits, "For Christian thought, delight is the premise of any sound epistemology: it is delight that constitutes creation, so only delight can comprehend it, see it aright, understand its grammar. Only in loving creation's beauty—only in seeing that creation is beauty—does one apprehend what creation is." Hart, *The Beauty of the Infinite*, 253.

rested; and in 2:3 God *blessed* the seventh day and *made it holy*. These events do not involve strenuous activity; they do not involve work at all. Instead they convey the mental actions of enjoyment, approval, and delight."[34] Attendant upon God's completion of the creation project, then, is the idea of divine satisfaction and delight. That perfection of beatitude and sense of delight that belongs to the Trinity *ad intra* thus comes to its manifest satisfaction and repose in the Creator's Sabbath rest. The creation narrative leading up to the Sabbath already gives some indication of the special nature of the seventh day. In the processive structure of the narrative the seventh day, of course, *culminates* the archetypal week of creation; it stands apart from the parallel literary framing applied to the first six days as well. Moreover, God both "blessed" and "made holy" (i.e., set apart) only the seventh day, for on *that* day he "rested from all his work that he had done in creation" (Gen 2:3). That God *rested* from his work is twice stated, giving accent to this point.[35] And rounding it all off, it is the only day of the creation week with no evening component to it.

All of this together points up the eschatological orientation of the Sabbath. "The Sabbath finds its prototype in the life and works of God," writes Geerhardus Vos. "This rest of consummation was introduced into the life of man in order to show him his goal. Even in unfallen man the Sabbath was an eschatological sign because its meaning lies in the relation of man and God."[36] According to the divine schema, the telos of Sabbath follows the commission that God gave in Genesis 1:26–28. The latter serves as part of the grand work to be accomplished in history by humanity in fulfilling the divine purposes for which humans were

---

34. C. John Collins, *Genesis 1–4: A Linguistic, Literary, and Theological Commentary* (Phillipsburg, NJ: P&R Publishing, 2006), 70–71.

35. The Hebrew term שָׁבַת can be translated "to rest" ("and he rested") but it basically means "to cease."

36. Geerhardus Vos, *The Eschatology of the Old Testament*, ed. James T. Dennison Jr. (Phillipsburg, NJ: P&R Publishing, 2001), 75. Along the same lines, Bernard Anderson, *From Creation to New Creation*, 16, explains: "The week is governed not by an abstract principle of Time but by the will of God, which gives each day its meaningful content. In Israel's faith time does not move in a circle; it moves toward the culmination of the Creator's intention, just as the week of creation moves toward the Sabbath rest. Thus the creation faith is eschatological. The affirmation 'in the beginning' is incomplete without the related affirmation 'in the end.'"

created. Accepting Vos's point that the Sabbath has its prototype in God's own life and works, the nature of the Creator's Sabbath rest points toward a telos, at least in part, of God's creational intention for humanity, namely, beatific rest, or better, *consummation confirmed in beatitude*.[37] Corroborating that point from a canonical perspective, the telos of the Sabbath rest in its consummative fulfillment for redeemed humanity is portrayed in the final chapters of Revelation as a glorification confirmed in beatitude. Irenaeus understood God's creational design and Sabbath goal for human beings in much the same light: "These things ... were not unsymbolical, that is, neither unmeaning nor to no purpose, inasmuch as they were given by a wise Artist. ... Moreover, the Sabbath of God, that is, the kingdom, was, as it were, indicated by created things; in which [kingdom], the man who shall have persevered in serving God shall, in a state of rest, partake of God's table."[38]

Sacred Space: The Garden of Eden as the Archetypal Temple-Sanctuary

Just as the week of creation does not receive its meaningful content by an abstract principle of Time, neither does an abstract principle of Space govern the relation of humans and God. "Put more simply," explains philosopher Jeff Malpas, "one might say that things are never 'in' the world in some indeterminate fashion but are always oriented and located in relation to the other things around them. It is precisely the oriented and located character of any mode of being in the world that allows things to be in the world in the first place."[39] The garden of Eden, planted by God himself, was introduced into the life of humans likewise as part of God's creational intention for humanity (Gen 2:8-17).[40] The

---

37. Cf. Karl Barth, *CD*, III/4, §55.1 (374-85). Germane here is Barth's discussion of creation on the place of joy in human life.

38. Irenaeus of Lyons, *AH* 4.16.1 (page 440).

39. Jeffery Edward Malpas, "Putting Space in Place: Relational Geography and Philosophical Topography," *Planning and Environment D: Space and Society* 30 (2012): 238.

40. The study note on Genesis 2:8 in the NET states: "Nothing is said of how the creation of this orchard took place. A harmonization with chap. 1 might lead to the conclusion that it was by decree, prior to the creation of human life. But the narrative sequence here in chap. 2 suggests the creation of the garden followed the creation of the man."

garden's beauty is made explicit right at the outset. Its orchard of lush trees is described as "pleasant (Heb: טוֹב; LXX: ὡραῖος) to the sight and good for food" (Gen 2:9). Interestingly, the Hebrew name *Eden* (עֵדֶן) means "pleasure" or "delight." Thus, a proper connotation of the garden of Eden is *God's garden of delight*.[41] This is further reinforced in Genesis 3:23 LXX which says that the Lord sent Adam ἐκ τοῦ παραδείσου τῆς τρυφῆς ("from the orchard/garden of enjoyment/delight"). Later Old Testament prophetic texts use "Eden" in parallel with "garden of God" (Isa 51:3; Ezek 28:13; 31:8–9; cf. Gen 13:10), underscoring the point that, properly speaking, the garden of Eden was the garden *of God* (not unlike the seventh day of creation being *God's* Sabbath).

The garden was thus a sacred place where the presence of God was to be found. Meredith Kline captures nicely the setting's theological significance:

> At the first, then, man's native dwelling-place coincided with God's earthly dwelling. This focal sanctuary in Eden was designed to be a medium whereby man might experience the joy of the presence of God in a way and on a scale most suited to his nature and condition as an earthly creature during the first stage of his historical journey, walking with God.[42]

---

41. As well, the word for "garden" in the Septuagint is παράδεισος, a term that derives from the Old Persian word for "an enclosed park, a pleasure ground." With "paradise" then being associated in the New Testament with a heavenly domain/experience (Luke 23:43; 2 Cor 12:3; and Rev 2:7), the idea of paradise came to be identified more broadly with a pleasureful heavenly reality. In Luke 23:43 it refers to the abode of the righteous dead. In 2 Corinthians 12:3 it most likely refers to the "third heaven" (2 Cor 12:2) as the place where God dwells, while in Revelation 2:7 it refers to the restoration of Edenic paradise predicted in Isaiah 51:3 and Ezekiel 36:35. For a recommended discussion, see Jan N. Bremmer, "Paradise: From Persia, via Greece, into the Septuagint," *Paradise Interpreted: Representations of Biblical Paradise in Judaism and Christianity*, ed. Gerard P. Luttikhuizen (Leiden: Brill, 1999), 1–20.

42. Meredith G. Kline, *Kingdom Prologue: Genesis Foundations for a Covenantal Worldview* (Eugene, OR: Wipf & Stock, 2006), 49. Kline expounds on this point later, stating: "The original homeland of man might well have been named Immanuel. God was with man, man's dwelling-place was God's dwelling-place. That was the greatest glory of paradise and the supreme and ultimate blessedness of human life. The covenant servant had been created for friendship and fellowship with his Lord. He was qualified for this holy communion by the nature with which God's creating hand endowed him. And he found to his delight that his transcendent Maker was not a god far off, but the immanent Immanuel. Man did not have to

That the garden of Eden was an archetypal sanctuary where God's presence dwells "rests largely on the striking parallels that exist between the garden and later Israelite sanctuaries," namely, the desert tabernacle and Jerusalem temple.[43] Four main similarities between the garden and the tabernacle and/or Jerusalem temple are given below.[44]

1. Eden and the later sanctuaries were entered from the east and guarded by cherubim (Gen 3:24; Exod 25:18–22; 26:31; 36:35; 1 Kgs 6:23–29; 2 Chr 3:14).

2. The tabernacle menorah (or lampstand) possibly symbolizes the tree of life (Gen 2:9; 3:22; cf. Exod 25:31–35). Arboreal decorations adorned the temple.

3. The Hebrew verbs עָבַד, 'to serve, till', and שָׁמַר, 'to keep, observe, guard', used in God's command to the man 'to work it (the garden) and take care of it' (Gen 2:15), are found in combination elsewhere in the Pentateuch only in passages that describe the duties of the Levites in the sanctuary (cf. Num 3:7–8; 8:26; 18:5–6).

4. Gold and onyx, mentioned in Genesis 2:11–12, are used extensively to decorate the later sanctuaries and priestly garments (e.g., Exod 25:7, 11, 17, 31). Cf. Ezekiel 28:13.

The garden's sanctuary character in this light is best seen as a garden-temple, and thus the role given to Adam in Genesis 2:15 is not fundamentally about orchard-keeping. It is a priestly role of tending, cultivating, and keeping charge of God's garden-temple in Eden. Moreover, taken in conjunction with God's commission to humankind in

---

make a long pilgrimage to come to God's dwelling. There was no great wilderness to pass through, no perilous ascent on high or journey down into the depths was necessary to find God. For man was by creation's arrangement a house-guest at home in the house of God." (60)

43. T. Desmond Alexander, *From Eden to the New Jerusalem: An Introduction to Biblical Theology* (Grand Rapids: Kregel, 2008), 21.

44. The points offered here are drawn from Alexander, *From Eden to the New Jerusalem*, 21–23. See also the essay by Gordon J. Wenham, "Sanctuary Symbolism in the Garden of Eden Story," in *"I Studied Inscriptions from Before the Flood": Ancient Near Eastern, Literary, and Linguistic Approaches to Genesis 1–11*, ed. R. S. Hess and D. Tsumura (SBTS 4; Winona Lake, IN: Eisenbrauns, 1994), 399–404; and Jon D. Levenson, "The Temple and the World," *The Journal of Religion* 64 no. 3 (July 1984): 275–98.

Genesis 1:28, Adam's mandate can be seen to extend ultimately to fill the earth and transform it into a sacred place where all humanity might experience the pure enjoyment of God's presence. As Beale puts it, "The goal of the original Eden and Adam and Eve's covenantal order therein was that its beatitude was to be eschatologically perfected in greater blessedness."[45] All of this points up the eschatological orientation of the garden of Eden, with this focal sanctuary serving as a proteschatological garden-temple. In the same way that the creational Sabbath finds it prototype in the life and works of God to show human beings their telos, so also is the garden of Eden introduced into the life of human beings as a sacred place where God's presence dwells to show them another dimension of their telos. Tying this in to the narrative arc of the Bible—the sublime comedy as I call it—humanity's native dwelling place is to coincide with God's earthly dwelling presence in accordance with the commission that God gave in Genesis 1:26-28 in its eschatological realization in the consummation. Corroborating that point from a canonical perspective, the telos of the garden of Eden in its consummative fulfillment for redeemed humanity is depicted in terms of the Edenic imagery in Revelation 22:1-2, which, at the macro level, represents what the garden of Eden in Genesis 2:8-17 represents at the micro level as part of God's creational intention for humanity. In the age to come the eschatological garden of Eden will be eternally established in its consummative form according to what the apostle Peter describes as God's dwelling with his people in "new heavens and a new earth in which righteousness dwells" (2 Pet 3:13).

HUMANS IN THE IMAGE OF GOD

In our development of the christological contours of beauty, the image of God serves a major theological motif; thus, starting with the creation narrative, it is necessary to discern what it means for humans to bear the divine image. In line with our theory of beauty, the beauty of human beings is inherent in and expressed through the form that their

---

45. Beale, *A New Testament Biblical Theology*, 90. Expressing in essence the same point, Calvin states, "The natural order was that the frame of the universe should be the school in which we were to learn piety, and from it pass over to eternal life and perfect felicity." (*Institutes* 2.6.1, ed. McNeill, trans. Battles)

image-bearing takes. Human beauty, we may further say, is expressed by reflecting most fittingly the ways that humans were created to bear all aspects of the divine image. As the incarnate image of God, Christ is the full measure of that image-bearing. But this is getting ahead of ourselves. I put forward here a theological interpretation of the *imago Dei* in connection with the motif of glory. I argue that the attributes that properly characterize humans in the image of God are identifiable in terms of three principal aspects: official (royal priest), constitutional (whole person, i.e., body-soul), and ethical-relational.[46] I round things out with a brief discussion on the fall of Adam and Eve and its ramifications. The section is divided accordingly into five parts: (1) the glory of the image of God in humans; (2) the official aspect of the image of God; (3) the constitutional aspect of the image of God; and (4) the ethical-relational aspect of the image of God; and (5) the radical fall from Adam and Eve's original image-bearing glory.

The question that must first be addressed is the following: "What is it that constitutes the image of God in which our first parents were made?" Gerhard von Rad's statement on Genesis 1:26–28 highlights a key part of the difficulty in answer to it: "The declaration about God's image is indeed highly exalted, but it also remains intentionally in a certain state of suspense."[47] To be sure, the creation narrative does provide contextual clues that help fill in the answer. The correlation between the image of God and sonship evident in Genesis 5:1–3 is one such clue we noted previously. There are more to unpack, which we will do in short order. It is curious nonetheless that, besides Genesis 1:26–28 and 5:1–3, the exalted language describing humans in terms of being made in the divine "image" or "likeness" is mentioned explicitly only one additional time in the entire Old Testament—in Genesis 9:6. If God's declaration

---

46. The three principal aspects of the *imago Dei* that I advance are similar (though not identical) to those advanced by C. John Collins (i.e., resemblance; representative; and relational), and Meredith G. Kline (i.e., official; formal; and ethical). See respectively, Collins, *Genesis 1–4*, 62–67; and Kline, *Images of the Spirit*, 31. See also James R. Beck and Bruce Demarest, eds., *The Human in Theology and Psychology: A Biblical Anthropology for the Twenty-first Century* (Grand Rapids: Kregel, 2005), 141–47, who survey three similar theological perspectives: functional; relational; and substantive.

47. Gerhard von Rad, *Genesis: A Commentary*, rev. ed. (Philadelphia: Westminster Press, 1972), 59.

in Genesis 1:26-28 about making humans in his image, however, is an integral part of the seminal eschatological design of his creation project, then "a certain state of suspense" about what constitutes the image is precisely what we should expect at this beginning point of biblical revelation. The suspense of which von Rad remarks is thus best seen as a rhetorical implication of the proto-eschaton themes, the *imago Dei* being front and center. From a biblical-theological perspective, then, the progressive nature of divine revelation means that the theological concept of the *imago Dei* will be compositely or aggregately enriched in its synthetic development across the total biblical testimony (*tota scriptura*). "In other words," explains Graham Cole, "in theological use *imago Dei* acts as a master concept that catches up various elements in a biblical anthropology."[48] Suffice it to say for now that Genesis 1:26–28 serves as the creation prologue's theological nucleus, which plays out in salvation history in conjunction with other seminal themes of the proto-eschaton.[49]

THE GLORY OF THE IMAGE OF GOD IN HUMANS

Our theological interpretation of the *imago Dei* begins with recognizing its association in Scripture with glory. The idea of "glory" here is not meant in some general nondescript sense, but glory that is identifiable with various aspects of the divine nature.[50] For humans to bear the divine image is to reflect the image-bearing glory of that image.[51] As a case in point from the Old Testament, Psalm 8 is commonly taken as a *locus classicus*. By making humanity in his image, God crowned it "with

---

48. Graham A. Cole, *God the Peacemaker: How Atonement Brings Shalom* (Downers Grove, IL: InterVarsity Press, 2009), 55.

49. Old Testament scholar, Eugene H. Merrill, for example, calls attention to the significance of Genesis 1:26–28 in *Everlasting Dominion: A Theology of the Old Testament* (Nashville: Broadman & Holman, 2006). Specifically, he shows how its themes play out over the course of the Old Testament and are then fulfilled in the New Testament. Beale follows a similar course in *A New Testament Biblical Theology*.

50. Recall from Chapter 2 that glory frequently serves in Scripture in tandem with or as a proxy for specific attributes of God; see subsection, Divine Beauty and Divine Glory.

51. Corroboration of this point is developed well in Catherine L. McDowell, *The Image of God in the Garden of Eden: The Creation of Humankind in Genesis 2:5–3:24 in Light of the mīs pî pīt pî and wpt-r Rituals of Mesopotamia and Ancient Egypt* (Winona Lake, IN: Eisenbrauns, 2015), 158–68.

glory and honor" (Ps 8:5). Throughout the psalms, in fact, these excellencies are given as divine attributes (e.g., Pss 29:1, 4; 90:16; 104:1; 111:3; 145:5). With its clear allusion to Genesis 1:26–28, "Psalm 8 says that God's glory is to be spread throughout the earth by humanity 'ruling' over all 'the works of Your hands' (vv. 6–8)."[52] Our interest at the moment is simply to note the connection we find between glory and the image of God, as it is highly likely that Psalm 8's commentary on Genesis 1 influenced the apostle Paul to make this connection as well (more on this below).[53]

It was during the intertestamental period, however, that theological rumination about the image of God became most fertile, the fruit of which would likely have had some influence on the thinking of the New Testament writers. According to Gerald Bray, "It is a curious fact that almost all the ideas about the image which were later to be developed by the Christian Church appeared during this period, and are reflected in the speculations of the rabbis and others."[54] This included reflection on the link between God's image and glory.[55] As Bray relates, over the course of time the rabbis gradually came to prefer the term glory (δόξα) in place of image (εἰκών). A number of factors led to this shift in use, but key among them was the development in rabbinical tradition of the idea that "man was given a part in God's kābôd which he lost at the fall and as time went on, the belief grew that it would be restored by the Messiah."[56] The belief that Adam had lost the kābôd of God shows up

---

52. Beale, *A New Testament Biblical Theology*, 37.

53. Kenneth A. Mathews, *Genesis 1–11:26* (NAC 1A; Nashville: Broadman & Holman Publishers, 1996), 171.

54. Gerald Bray, "The Significance of God's Image in Man," *TynBul* 42 (1991): 203.

55. The Wisdom of Solomon 7:25–26 is representative of this: "Like a fine mist [wisdom] rises from the power of God, a pure effluence from the glory of the Almighty; ... She is the brightness that streams from everlasting light, the flawless mirror of the active power of God and the image of his goodness" (NEB).

56. Bray, "The Significance of God's Image in Man," 219. With reference to Adam's having lost his "glory" through sin (e.g., *Genesis Rabbah* 12:6; *Apocalypse of Moses* 20:1–3; 21:2, 6), see John R. Levison, "Adam and Eve in Romans 1.18–25 and the Greek *Life of Adam and Eve*," *NTS* 50 no. 4 (Oct 2004): 519–34. See also C. Marvin Pate, *The Glory of Adam and the Afflictions of the Righteous: Pauline Suffering in Context* (Lewiston, NY: Mellen Biblical Press, 1993), 67–89, in which he cites sundry Jewish sources holding forth this view; Steven E. Enderlein, "To Fall Short or Lack the Glory of God? The Translation and Implications of Romans 3:23," *JSPL* 1 no. 2 (Fall 2011): 213–24; Beale, *A New Testament Biblical Theology*, 442; and Kittel, εἰκών, *TDNT* 2:393.

prevalently as well in the claim that God would restore to the righteous the glory of Adam in the eschaton.[57] Until such restoration was brought by the Messiah, the *imago Dei* in fallen humanity was thus taken to be an image deprived of its original (i.e., pre-fall) glory—"a concept which Christians identified with His likeness, and the classical idea of a two-part image was born."[58] Although Adam had been created in the "image" of God, Irenaeus himself taught that Adam stood at the beginning of a long process of development to mature into the "likeness" of God. I will say more below about the condition of "glory" that characterized the *imago Dei* before the fall, as well as the post-fall ramifications to it.

Whatever theological rumination on image and glory blossomed during the intertestamental period, however, the relation between these concepts came to full flower in the New Testament, notably in the apostle Paul's writings.[59] I touched on this already in chapter 2 where I presented that Christ as the last Adam embodies the divine purpose for humanity in accordance with which the first Adam was created. That purpose involves becoming the glorified new humanity conformed to his image.[60] But, on this side of our eschatological glory— the penultimate side—believers are transformed into the image of Christ progressively "from one degree of glory to another" (2 Cor 3:18). Importantly here, it is not Christ's *image* that undergoes a progressive

---

57. Enderlein, "To Fall Short or Lack the Glory of God?," 217.

58. Enderlein, "To Fall Short or Lack the Glory of God?," 205. Irenaeus, in fact, held to a two-part image in which the "likeness" (or similitude) equates to the image of God bereft of glory, which through Christ is fully restored to its most glorious image: "For in times long past, it was said that man was created after the image of God, but it was not [actually] shown; for the Word was as yet invisible, after whose image man was created, Wherefore also he did easily lose the similitude. When, however, the Word of God became flesh, He confirmed both these: for He both showed forth the image truly, since He became Himself what was His image; and He re-established the similitude after a sure manner, by assimilating man to the invisible Father through means of the invisible Word." *AH* 5.16.2 (page 597).

59. The point here is not that any of the New Testament writings linking image and glory were based on the intertestamental writings, but simply that under the inspiration of the Holy Spirit, the theological connections between image and glory also figured into the revelation of the New Testament. Exactly how much and in what ways the thinking of the New Testament authors can be said to be influenced by intertestamental writings is not really determinable.

60. See chapter 2, subsection, The Theodramatic Fittingness of the Son as Incarnate Redeemer.

transformation in degrees, it is his *glory* in regenerated persons that progresses in degree as these are transformed into his image, being ultimately conformed to it (Rom 8:29). Paul links image and glory again in 2 Corinthians 4:4 where he identifies Christ as the image of God. Here, though, a different situation obtains. Because unbelievers are blind to the light of the gospel, they do not reflect Christ's glory, neither can they. Two verses later in 2 Corinthians 4:6, the situation is again reversed and we see that because God indeed *has* made the light of his gospel to shine in the hearts of believers, they can and do reflect the glory of Christ. Irenaeus captures the essence of this in his memorable remark, "For the glory of God is a living man; and the life of man consists in beholding God."[61]

Reminiscent of 2 Corinthians 4:4, Paul once again employs image and glory in tandem in Romans 1, describing there those who are spiritually unregenerate. In rejecting God, the unregenerate effectively reject his glory as well and replace it in the futility of their thinking with the glory of a false image, which is simply to say, a false and foolish glory (Rom 1:21–23; cf. Psalms 115 and 135).[62] Further on Paul states in unmistakably universal terms, "all have sinned and fall short of the glory of God" (Rom 3:23). The connection may be drawn here between the idea of glory and the ways in which humans are called to rightly image God. As Douglas Moo explains, "Paul, then, is indicating that all people fail to exhibit that 'being-like-God' for which they were created; and the present tense of the verb, in combination with Romans 8, shows that even Christians 'fall short' of that goal until they are transformed in the last day by God."[63] Although Scripture seems to suggest that the

---

61. Irenaeus of Lyons, *AH* 4.20.7 (page 462).

62. For a recommended treatment on a biblical understanding of idolatry, and how human beings take on the characteristics of what they worship, see G. K. Beale, *We Become What We Worship: A Biblical Theology of Idolatry* (Downers Grove, IL: IVP Academic, 2008).

63. Douglas J. Moo, *The Epistle to the Romans* (NICNT; Grand Rapids: Eerdmans, 1996), 226–27. On Romans 3:23, Bernard Ramm, *Them He Glorified: A Systematic Study of the Doctrine of Glorification* (Grand Rapids: Eerdmans, 1963), 28, states along compatible lines, "It is customary for commentators to take the *doxa* of God here to mean either the divine perfection or the divine approval. ... [However,] man was created sharing in the divine glory which he lost at the fall. Thus the passage means that man lacks his original created glory. *Doxa* in this passage does not, then, refer

glory of God in humans is indicative of how rightly they image him, which, again, means their reflection of God's glory can vary in degree, it does not seem to support the notion that the image of God proper in humans is itself something that varies in degree. In the context of humans in the post-fall state, for example, neither Genesis 9:6 or James 3:9 indicates that the *imago Dei* referenced there is anything other than the *imago Dei* referenced in the pre-fall state (the protological image of God in which all humanity is created). Nothing about the protological image of God in humanity being lost or somehow destroyed or erased is suggested.[64] The condition of falling short of the glory of God would not require the *imago Dei* itself to be vitiated, only that the image-bearing glory reflecting it is vitiated. Along these same lines of thought, Meredith Kline advances the following distinction between image and glory: "image is stative and expresses the fact of imageness, i.e., that man is secondary, not the original but different from it because of his createdness, while glory is active and expresses the content of the image, i.e., that man is similar to God in those features comprised by the concept of glory."[65]

In my judgment, the basic relation that Kline posits between the image of God and the glory of God in humans is valid. Following Kline's lead here, the image-bearing glory of humans in general terms is given along the following lines: "Though image-likeness is terminable, it is otherwise constant. The glory aspect of man's God-likeness, on the other hand, is variable; it is subject to degrees of reduction as well as to termination and it also may undergo intensification and expansion in the historical-eschatological process."[66] More specifically, in regard

---

to God's perfection nor to his approval, but to the original status of man." See also Kittel, δόξα, *TDNT* 2:250.

64. Henri Blocher, *In the Beginning: The Opening Chapters of Genesis*, trans. David G. Preston (Downers Grove, IL: InterVarsity Press, 1984), 94, makes the point thus: "All the indisputable references to the declaration of Gen 1:26f. appear to suppose the permanence of the-being-as-image-of-God (Gen 9:6; 1 Cor 11:7; Jas 3:9). If mankind no longer possessed this privilege, why would it be scandalous to take away his life, or to curse him at the same time as one is blessing the Lord?"

65. Kline, *Images of the Spirit*, 30–31.

66. Kline, *Images of the Spirit*, 31. Kline further adds, "Both image and glory mean likeness. Moreover, such is their equivalency that where all that constitutes the glory is gone, no vestige of the image remains."

to characterizing the image-bearing glory of: (a) Adam and Eve before the fall, (b) humans after the fall, (c) humans redeemed in Christ, and (d) humans ultimately damned, I propose the following:[67]

1. Adam and Eve were constituted with an original image-bearing glory encompassing their whole person that God appraised as "very good," though not yet a consummative glory.

2. Humans in the post-fall context are preserved with a measure of image-bearing glory by the common grace of God, though a glory vitiated in every way relative to Adam and Eve's original glory.

3. Humans redeemed in Christ are recreated in the image of Christ and transformed in the glory of the Spirit; in the eternal state these are constituted with a consummative image-bearing glory encompassing their whole person, body and soul.

4. Humans damned in the eternal state will no longer bear the image of God, and therefore will no longer reflect any image-bearing glory. The person himself/herself still remains a *human* being, but he/she will no longer be constituted in the image of God.

Given, as I argued in Chapter 2, that the beauty of God manifested economically is expressed and perceivable as a quality of the glory of God inherent in his work of creation, redemption, and consummation, the aesthetic dimension is an inherent aspect of the glory of God in humans. Image-bearing glory entails the quality of image-bearing beauty. Again, the beauty of human beings is inherent in and expressed through the form that their image bearing takes. It follows that the image-bearing beauty of (a) Adam and Eve before the fall, (b) humans after the fall, (c) humans redeemed in Christ, and (d) humans ultimately damned, are characterized precisely the same, mutatis mutandis, as I did above with respect to glory.

Moreover, of all God's works the privileged place of humanity is his special delight. As Bavinck puts it, "All creatures express some aspect of God's being, but of all of them human beings are at the top. They alone have the honor of being called 'image, son, child of God.' They alone are

---

67. The third and fourth of the proposed points will be developed further in Chapter 6.

called God's offspring."[68] Of all creatures, then, God delights most in humankind since it is these who are made in his image and dignified above all others to reflect and partake in God's own glory. In the absence of sin and evil, the most natural human response back to God is, as the traditional terminology puts it, a *connatural* one—an unalloyed reflection of God's own beatitude expressed as doxological delight. Entailed in such a connatural response is the subjectively experienced aspect of beauty, which points beyond itself to that absolute self-delight that characterizes God in himself. F. Duane Lindsey expands on this idea along similar lines:

> It appears that a biblical psychology would support the following statement: Along with (or perhaps somehow included in) man's intellectual response to the truth of God, his emotional response to the love of God, and his volitional response to the holiness of God, should be also his aesthetic response to the beauty of God. This aesthetic response would include, at the least, amazement, adoration, and joyful praise. Such amazement, adoration, and joyful praise combine in the voluntary, heart-felt, truth-claim and praise-exclamation: "God is beautiful!"[69]

Such was the original condition of Adam and Eve (albeit not eschatologically consummated), and such will be the eternal condition in the consummation for the redeemed in Christ.[70] In the balance of this section I will develop in further detail the principal aspects of the *imago Dei* whose features reflect the glory of God in humans.

THE OFFICIAL ASPECT OF THE IMAGE OF GOD

The official aspect of the *imago Dei* recognizes the royal (kingly) office and priestly office conferred by God on humankind—that is, it is

---

68. Herman Bavinck, *RD*, 2:103. Cf. Bavinck's statement, "God's delight in his creatures is part and parcel of his delight in himself" (251).

69. F. Duane Lindsey, "Essays Toward a Theology of Beauty," *BSac* 131 (April 1974): 136.

70. Cf. Arthur Michael Ramsey, *The Glory of God and the Transfiguration of Christ* (London: Darton, Longman & Todd, 1967), 151: "In Christ there is our human nature fulfilling both its true affinity to the creator and its true dependence upon Him in adoration; and the more we are brought to share in Christ's glory the more shall we share in that giving glory to the Father which was His mission and is our calling."

through this aspect that we image God in *office*. Relevant to our theological aesthetic, the characteristics of the royal-priestly office are an integral part of the form in and through which humans bear the divine image. The official aspect of the *imago Dei*, I contend, is one of three principal ways that the beauty of human beings is reflected in their image-bearing glory. I will present my argument for the official aspect, unpacking its characteristics primarily from the context of Genesis 1–2.

Writ large in Genesis 1:26–28 is the divine commission to humankind to have dominion or "to rule" (רָדָה) over all the earth, and "to subdue" (כבשׁ) it. These verbs in tandem "suggests that the characteristic human task or role vis-à-vis both the animal kingdom and the earth requires a significant exercise of communal power, and the primacy of *rādâ* paints the human vocation with a distinctly royal hue."[71] "In his own image" is how God created humankind.[72] "The expression," observes Christopher Wright, "is adverbial (it describes the way God made us), not adjectival (as if it simply described a quality we possess)." The *imago Dei* is what in essence qualifies humans to rule over creation. Exercising dominion is thus an implication or corollary of the image—*so that* humanity may exercise dominion. In Wright's words: "Or, to put it the other way round, because God intended this last-created species, the human species, to

---

71. Middleton, *The Liberating Image*, 52. Cf. Psalm 72:8 that illustrates kingliness with (רָדָה); 2 Samuel 8:11 does the same with (כבשׁ). The translator's note on Genesis 1:28 in the NET states: "Elsewhere the Hebrew verb translated 'subdue' means 'to enslave' (2 Chr 28:10; Neh 5:5; Jer 34:11, 16), 'to conquer,' (Num 32:22, 29; Josh 18:1; 2 Sam 8:11; 1 Chr 22:18; Zech 9:13; and probably Mic 7:19), and 'to assault sexually' (Esth 7:8). None of these nuances adequately meets the demands of this context, for humankind is not viewed as having an adversarial relationship with the world. The general meaning of the verb appears to be 'to bring under one's control for one's advantage.' In Gen 1:28 one might paraphrase it as follows: 'harness its potential and use its resources for your benefit.'"

72. The phrases "in our image" (בְּצַלְמֵנוּ) and "after our likeness" (כִּדְמוּתֵנוּ) denote the divine-human relationship, and while some ambiguity exists between their meanings, the best explanation is that these phrases are mutually reinforcing and refer to the same thing. See Collins, *Genesis 1–4*, 62; Gordon J. Wenham, *Genesis 1–15* (WBC 1; Waco, TX: Word, 1987), 28–29. Also worth noting is the view put forward by Peter J. Gentry and Stephen J. Wellum, *Kingdom Through Covenant: A Biblical-Theological Understanding of the Covenant* (Wheaton, IL: Crossway, 2012), 197–99, which argues that a proper distinction exists between the preposition "in" (בְּ), which emphasizes a way in which humans are closely like God, and "after" or "according to" (כְּ), which emphasizes a way in which humans are similar, but distinct.

exercise dominion over the rest of his creatures, for that express reason God purposefully created this species alone in his image."[73]

This "royal hue" in which humanity is divinely created simply reflects in a creaturely way God's own kingship. While the creation narrative does not explicitly use "royal" or "kingly" language in describing God's creational activities, such is unmistakably ascribed to him *implicitly*.[74] The threefold fiat pattern (Gen 1:3, 6, 14) may be the most salient: "God's first acts, his sovereign creating acts, are depicted as the initial edicts of the Great King by which he founded and ordered his kingdom."[75] The picture of God as the Great King is further highlighted in his assigning the sea, sky, and land creatures to their respective realms, and setting the sun and moon to govern the day/light and night/darkness (Gen 1:16–18). Perhaps what is most emblematic of God's kingship is the support that the whole order of creation, the entire cosmos (Gen 2:1), is God's cosmic palace-temple.[76] That is to say, just as the garden of Eden was sacred space, a focal sanctuary where the presence of God was to be found, so the heavens and the earth together represents the cosmic palace-temple from which God reigns.[77] Worth noting, God's enthronement

---

73. Christopher J. H. Wright, *Old Testament Ethics for the People of God* (Downers Grove, IL: InterVarsity Press, 2004), 119.

74. As Wright, *Old Testament Ethics*, 121, observes: "God's creating work exudes wisdom in planning, power in execution, and goodness in completion. These are the very qualities Psalm 145 exalts in 'my God the King', in relation to all his created works. There is a righteousness and benevolence inherent in God's kingly power that is exercised towards all he has made."

75. John H. Stek, "What Says the Scripture?," in *Portraits of Creation: Biblical and Scientific Perspectives on the World's Formation*, ed. Howard J. Van Till et al. (Grand Rapids: Eerdmans, 1990), 234, quoted in Middleton, *The Liberating Image*, 69. Moreover, however else we are to understand God's transforming the *tohu wabohu* (Gen 1:2) into created order, it clearly shows his sovereign power to order creation.

76. I am following here (somewhat loosely) the helpful discussion in Middleton, *The Liberating Image*, 77–87. See also the discussion in Walton, *Genesis 1 as Ancient Cosmology*, 178–86.

77. Cf. Rikki E. Watts, "On the Edge of the Millennium: Making Sense of Genesis 1," in *Living in the LambLight: Christianity and Contemporary Challenges to the Gospel*, ed. Hans Boersma (Vancouver: Regent College Publishing, 2001), 147–48: "Given the rather widespread Ancient Near Eastern notion linking creation, defeat-of-chaos, and temple-building, and the thorough-going architectural imagery which characterizes the biblical conceptualizing of creation, it would be very odd if Genesis 1 were not to be understood along the lines of cosmic palace-temple building. As the Great King, Elohim naturally creates realms for the lesser rulers

in heaven does not transcend creation. Rather, it is structurally part of the created cosmography (cf. Isa 66:1–2). "The heavens (or semantic equivalents) thus become a shorthand way of referring to the abode of God *within* the world" (cf. Pss 47:8; 103:19; Jer 23:23–24).[78] In this light the concept of the kingdom of God is identifiable right at the outset of the biblical story, introduced in Act 1 as it were of the theodrama.

According to J. Richard Middleton, "the description of ancient Near Eastern kings as the image of a god, when understood as an integral component of Egyptian and/or Mesopotamian royal ideology, provides the most plausible set of parallels for interpreting the *imago Dei* in Genesis 1."[79] Although the ancient Near Eastern context/worldview is not determinative for interpreting the biblical narrative, parallels between the two may provide corroborating insight for the task of the latter (the Scripture canon itself being always the *norma normans*). For example, understanding that cult images of the ancient Near Eastern deities were installed to mediate the deity's presence in pagan temples has been widely suggested by Old Testament scholars as a plausible parallel for understanding how God completes creation with humans to represent and mediate his presence on earth.[80] According to Ancient Near Eastern ideology, the king was a son of the god, and as such, he

---

(cf. Gen 1:16) as he forms his palace-temple out of the deep and gives order to and fills it. And as the Great King, having ordered his realm, he now rules over all in 'Sabbath' rest (see Exod 20), sitting in the great pavilion of his cosmos-palace-temple (cf. Psalm 93)."

78. Middleton, *The Liberating Image*, 87 (emphasis original), quoting Terence E. Fretheim, *The Suffering of God* (Overtures to Biblical Theology; Philadelphia: Fortress Press, 1984), 37. Middleton notes here also how the vision in Isaiah 6 provides a similar understanding of the cosmic sanctuary, complete with the royal metaphor.

79. Middleton, *The Liberating Image*, 121. Andreas Schüle, "Made in the 'Image of God': The Concepts of Divine Images in Gen 1–3," *ZAW* 117 (2005): 1–20, cites the exemplary case of an inscription (Aramaic and Akkadian) from northern Mesopotamia/Upper Syria found at the ninth-century-BC Tell Fekheriye that uses the same two words for image and likeness as Genesis 1:26–27. The inscription shows the terms used interchangeably in reference to the "statue" of the king on which it is inscribed.

80. Representative of this point is the discussion by David J. A. Clines, "Humanity as the Image of God," in *On the Way to the Postmodern: Old Testament Essays, 1967–1998* (JSOTSup 293; Sheffield, England: Sheffield Academic Press, 1998), II, 487: "The representational image in the ancient Near East is intended to portray the character of the god whose image it is; thus, for example, a fertility god may be represented by a bull. So in Genesis 1, humanity is not a mere cipher, chosen at

was the god's representative ruler of the world.[81] The biblical creation narrative informs us that humans as divine image-bearers are likewise "sons" of God and his royal representatives in the world.[82]

Furthermore, to reflect God's kingship is also to reflect his judgeship. Judgeship, in other words, is an essential feature of kingship (the latter entails former). Humans thus image God in their capacity to judge soundly—judgments of justice and equity as well as all manner of evaluative and discerning judgment. Adam's naming of the animals (Gen 2:19–20) and his calling "woman" she who is bone of his bones and flesh of his flesh (2:23) are the first examples of the latter and reflect God's naming of parts of creation in Genesis 1.[83] Even in the postlapsarian context the appeal to the *imago Dei* establishes not just the sanctity of human life but also human judicial authority, which is to be administered when such sanctity has been transgressed (Gen 9:6).

The nature of humanity's exercise of dominion also models God's creative activity and, as such, is inherently developmental and transformative.[84] Similarly, just as God artfully and artistically designed

random by God to be his representative, but to some extent also expresses, as the image, the character of God."

81. As Beale, *A New Testament Biblical Theology*, 36–37, relates, "Ancient Near Eastern kings were considered to be 'sons' of their god and to represent the image of their god in their rule, especially reflecting the god's glory and, accordingly, the manifestation of its presence." For a recommended article relevant to this point, see Shalom M. Paul, "Adoption Formulae: A Study of Cuneiform and Biblical Legal Clauses," *Maarav* 2 no. 2 (1979–1980): 173–85.

82. Corroboration of this point is developed well in Catherine L. McDowell, *The Image of God in the Garden of Eden: The Creation of Humankind in Genesis 2:5–3:24 in Light of the mīs pî pît pî and wpt-r Rituals of Mesopotamia and Ancient Egypt* (Winona Lake, IN: Eisenbrauns, 2015), 117–41.

83. On this point Henri Blocher, *In the Beginning*, 91, remarks, "What relationship does the man establish with the animals? He *names* them. Thus he indicates the right that he has over them. ... The names he gives summarizes his conclusion, and if the text adds, 'and whatever the man called every living creature, that was its name' (Gen 2:19), can that be only to confirm his authority? Does it not wish to praise his precision and his judgment? The picturesque, almost humorous, scene suggests a rudimentary kind of science, the means of man's dominion over nature."

84. Middleton, *The Liberating Image*, 89. To avoid any negative connotations associated with the concept of "dominion," humanity's kingship is often described instead as "stewardship." But properly speaking, the idea of stewardship as synonymous with kingship is incorrect. As Christopher Wright, *Old Testament Ethics*, 123, reminds us, the divine commission to humankind to have dominion "was not to be stewards of the earth, but to 'rule over' the other creatures. Our appropriate

and constructed all of creation, so humanity images God in its capacity for artful and creative development of all kind—call this the aesthetic aspect of ruling and subduing.[85] Humans image God's creative work as well in fulfilling the commission to create (i.e., "be fruitful and multiply and fill the earth with") other sons/daughters of God. As Beale notes, "The command for Adam to 'subdue, rule, and fill the earth' includes uppermost that of him as a king functionally filling the earth, not merely with progeny, but with image-bearing progeny who will reflect God's glory and special revelatory presence."[86]

In addition to the royal/kingly aspect of the *imago Dei*, Genesis 1–2 also presents us with humanity's priestly office. As argued earlier, the role given to Adam in Genesis 2:15 was a priestly one of tending, cultivating, and keeping charge of God's garden-temple in Eden. The divine commission to humankind appears to combine the function of king and priest: "Adam's commission to 'cultivate' (with connotations of 'serving') and 'guard' in Gen 2:15 as a priest-king is probably part of the commission given in 1:26–28. Hence, Gen 2:15 continues the theme of subduing and filling the earth by humans created in the divine image."[87] Humans as divine image-bearers are thus not only God's royal representatives in the world, but his priestly representatives as well. In short, then, the official aspect of the *imago Dei* means that all humans are created in a filial relationship with God to reflect his glory as his royal priests. The creational intention for humans to image God as priests was to transform the earth into a sacred place whereby humanity might experience the joy of the presence of God, and in so doing, mediate divine blessing throughout all the earth. From the standpoint of the proto-eschaton, writes Beale, Eden offered "a beginning establishment of a priest-king

---

and biblically authorized model, therefore, is that of kingship, providing we take seriously the full biblical teaching on what kings were supposed to be and do, as servants of those they ruled."

85. E.g., Middleton, *The Liberating Image*, 87: "Bezalel's Spirit-filled craftsmanship, which imitates God's primordial wise design and construction of the cosmos, is functionally equivalent to the *imago Dei*" (Exod 31:1–6; 35:30—36:1). David's musical compositions are another fine example.

86. Beale, *A New Testament Biblical Theology*, 36.

87. Beale, *A New Testament Biblical Theology*, 32.

in a sinless world order who was to be faithful and obedient to God *until that first creation was consummated.*"[88]

THE CONSTITUTIONAL ASPECT OF THE IMAGE OF GOD

The constitutional aspect of the *imago Dei* recognizes that being made "in the image of God" describes how God constituted humankind, not a quality or set of qualities (whether fully determinable or not) that humans have. I argue that the constitutional aspect comprises the whole human person, body and soul. As with the official aspect of the *imago Dei*, the characteristics of the constitutional aspect are an integral part of the form in and through which humans bear the divine image. The constitutional aspect is the second principal way that the beauty of human beings is reflected in their image-bearing glory. The beauty of human persons as such applies without qualification to the material/embodied dimension of their being as well as to its immaterial/spiritual dimension.

That the designator "image-bearer" denotes the whole person finds parallel support from the ancient Near Eastern royal ideology we discussed earlier in which kings, considered to be "sons" of their god, physically manifested the image of their god in their rule (reflecting the god's attributes in so doing). In this way the king was a physical representative of the god, not a representative of what the god physically looked like. Just as a statue of the king represented his presence in, say, a conquered land, or a statue of a god that was set up in a temple signified that god's real presence there, so too, analogously, humankind is set up within the physical realm of the earth as God's authorized and authoritative representatives—"in his image, after his likeness." Clines puts it thus: "That humanity is God's image means that it is the visible corporeal representative of the invisible, bodiless God; ... However, the term 'likeness' is an assurance that humanity is an adequate and faithful representative of God on earth. The whole person is the image of God, without distinction of spirit and body."[89] All of this points to the ontological nature of the image, which enables the human person

---

88. Beale, *A New Testament Biblical Theology*, 89 (emphasis original).
89. Clines, "Humanity as the Image of God," 495.

to exhibit the image-bearing glory of God in all their *being* and in all their *doing*.[90]

What I am definitely *not* affirming here is the view that the human body serves as the physical host of the *imago Dei* but is not itself considered part of the divine image. On that view the body operates strictly as the biological vehicle through which the *imago Dei* proper is functionally lived out and expressed. I accept and advocate the view, rather, that the whole human person is a dichotomous unity of body and soul (more on the soul below).[91] The nature of that unity, states Bavinck, "is so intimate that one nature, one person, one self is the subject of both and of all their activities. It is always the same soul that peers through the eyes, thinks through the brain, grasps with the hands, and walks with the feet."[92] And thus, it is not just by virtue of one's psychic or "soulish" faculties (whatever those may fully entail) that humans image God.[93] Since the only mode in which the image is expressed is the whole person, "it is the *homo*, not the *animus* or the *anima*, that is the *imago*

---

90. Along the same lines Cornelius Van Til states, "Man was created as an analogue of God; his thinking, his willing, and his doing is therefore properly conceived as at every point analogical to the thinking, willing, and doing of God." Van Til, "Nature of Scripture," in *The Infallible Word: A Symposium by the Members of the Faculty of Westminster Theological Seminary*, 3rd rev. ed., ed. N. B. Stonehouse and Paul Woolley (Phillipsburg, NJ: P&R Publishing, 2003), 273.

91. A proper defense of "dualism" (i.e., humanity constituted as a unity of body and soul) falls beyond the scope of this work. I take dualism as the most fitting and recommendable theological anthropology, though without specifying any one model over others among ones that have been proposed. The following works defending various or hybrid accounts of dualism are recommended: John W. Cooper, *Body, Soul, and Life Everlasting: Biblical Anthropology and the Monism-Dualism Debate* (Grand Rapids: Eerdmans, 2000); J. P. Moreland and Scott B. Rae, *Body and Soul: Human Nature and the Crisis in Ethics* (Downers Grove IL: InterVarsity Press, 2000); Stewart Goetz and Charles Taliaferro, *A Brief History of the Soul* (Malden, MA: Wiley-Blackwell, 2011); Michael Welke, ed., *The Depth of the Human Person: A Multidisciplinary Approach* (Grand Rapids: Eerdmans, 2014).

92. Bavinck, *RD*, 2:559.

93. The translator's note on Genesis 2:7 in the NET offers the following: "The Hebrew word יָצַר means 'to form' or 'to fashion,' usually by plan or design (see the related noun יֵצֶר in Gen 6:5). It is the term for an artist's work (the Hebrew term יוֹצֵר refers to a potter; see Jer 18:2–4)." Indeed, as this text suggests, when God "formed" the first human from the ground, he was fashioning a work of art. Cf. Bavinck, *RD*, 2:559: "The body is not a prison, but a marvelous piece of art from the hand of God Almighty, and just as constitutive for the essence of humanity as the soul (Job 10:8–12; Ps 139:13–17; Eccl 12:2–7; Isa 64:8)."

Dei."[94] If this were not the case, then there would be no critical link between the Son incarnate sharing human embodiment with us and his being the image of God in the person of Jesus Christ. Instead, the critical significance of the Son sharing human embodiment with us would be strictly a matter of God's accommodation and condescension to the human physical mode of existence (as wonderfully important as that all is!). As the second or last Adam, however, Christ did not just *accommodate* the divine purpose for humanity in accordance with which the first image-bearer, Adam, was created, he *humanly embodied* it. Irenaeus's engagement with Gnostic heresy, in fact, occasioned him to affirm that redemption in Christ, the only true image of God, encompasses the whole person, including the body.[95] The theological ground, we can say, for why humans are embodied the way they are is because God decided before the foundation of the world to become incarnate as Jesus Christ (cf. Heb 10:5; 1 Pet 1:20).[96]

That the body is included in what comprises humankind's protological image, moreover, is corroborated by its eschatological counterpart, namely, the eschatological image of those redeemed in Christ includes the resurrection and glorification of the body. The underlying hermeneutical principle I accept as valid here is that what gets restored by grace and transformed into the image of Christ all the way to its consummate image-bearing glory has its counterpart or parallel in the protological image in which humanity was created. That principle is an extension of one of the three primary symmetries I presented in

---

94. Clines, "Humanity as the Image of God," 481. Clines, 482, adds, "If God wills his image to be corporeal humanity—union of physical and spiritual (or psychical)—he thereby wills the manner of his presence in the world to be the selfsame uniting of physical and spiritual."

95. E.g., Irenaeus of Lyons, *AH* 5.6.1 (page 567): "Thus also, if any one take away the image and set aside the handiwork, he cannot then understand this as being a man, but as either some part of a man, as I have already said, or as something else than a man. For that flesh which has been molded is not a perfect man itself, but the body of a man, and part of a man. Neither is the soul itself, considered apart by itself, the man; but it is the soul of a man, a part of a man. Neither is the spirit of a man, for it is called the spirit, and not a man; but the commingling and union of all these constitutes the perfect man."

96. So Bavinck, *RD*, 2: 560: "The incarnation of God is proof that human beings and not angels are created in the image of God, and that the human body is an essential component of that image."

Chapter 2 regarding the symmetrical nature of the Son's agency in the work of the divine economy as it relates to the divine image that human beings bear, an image both created and redeemed through Christ.[97] Just as Christ is embodied in glory now, so the day will come when believers likewise will be embodied in consummate glory. Paul describes this in terms of the Lord Jesus Christ transforming "our lowly body to be like his glorious body" (Phil 3:20–21; cf. Rom 8:11; Col 3:4). My argument here thus rests on a theological concept of the *imago Dei* having its fullest and clearest witness in the New Testament, with Christ himself as the incarnate image of God who embodies—as the archetype—the divine purpose for humanity in accordance with which the first Adam was created.

As argued above, the constitutional aspect of the *imago Dei* pertains to its ontological nature, that is, to the human person exhibiting the image-bearing glory of God in all their *being* and *doing*. The ontology on view is the whole person, and as such there is no basis to say that what comprises the human soul is ontologically closer or truer to God than what comprises the human body. An analogy of being from God to the material (bodily) and immaterial (soulish) aspects of the human person applies in its own way to each. In this regard, for example, the words of the psalmist are seen as more than merely figurative: "He who planted the ear, does he not hear? He who formed the eye, does he not see?" (Ps 94:9). Our capacities to see and hear as image-bearers analogously reflect God as the archetype of these.[98] Still, a proper distinction between body and soul is called for as relates to their respective image-bearing glory. With characteristic incisiveness, Bavinck writes,

> Naturally, just as the cosmos is an organism and reveals God's attributes more clearly in some than in other creatures, so also in man as an organism the image of God comes out more clearly in one

---

97. Restating that symmetry here: That the Son is the preexistent image of God through whom humanity is imaged protologically (image of their Creator), so likewise through the Son as the last Adam the redeemed are imaged eschatologically (image of their Redeemer). See subsection, The Theodramatic Fittingness of the Son as Incarnate Redeemer.

98. Certainly, as the case may be, such sensory language is employed at times in a simply figurative anthropomorphic sense (cf. Ps 11:4), but in other instances analogy to the constitutional aspect of the *imago Dei* is valid to recognize.

part than another, more in the soul than in the body, more in the ethical virtues than in the physical powers. None of this, however, detracts in the least from the truth than the whole person is the image of God.[99]

Reminiscent of (or at least analogous to) the Pauline idea expressed in 1 Corinthians 15:39–41, the idea of respective image-bearing glory captures aptly the essence of Bavinck's point. The radical difference between humans and all other creatures "is a difference of creation, not development: it is a *constitutional* difference."[100] That God breathed into the first human the breath of life (Gen 2:7) signals the constituted reality of this difference, which entailed the highest excellencies of the soul.[101] Just as attributes of God's nature are said to be "clearly perceived" in creation, revealing "the glory of the immortal God" to humanity (Rom 1:18–23), so the excellencies of the soul are the clearest marks or characteristics by which the image-bearing glory with which humanity has been constituted may be discerned.[102] "In short," states Calvin,

---

99. Bavinck, *RD*, 2:555.

100. Philip Edgcumbe Hughes, *The True Image: The Origin and Destiny of Man in Christ* (Grand Rapids: Eerdmans, 1989), 51 (emphasis original).

101. The translator's note on Genesis 2:7 in the NET contributes: "The Hebrew word נְשָׁמָה ("breath") is used for God and for the life imparted to humans, not animals. Its usage in the Bible conveys more than a breathing living organism (נֶפֶשׁ חַיָּה). Whatever is given this breath of life becomes animated with the life from God, has spiritual understanding (Job 32:8), and has a functioning conscience (Prov 20:27)." On Genesis 2:7 Kenneth Mathews notes the following: "The man receives his life force from the breath of the Creator himself, hovering over him. *Breathed* is warmly personal, with the face-to-face intimacy of a kiss and the significance that this was giving as well as making; and self-giving at that. Although both animal (7:22) and human life share in this gift of life (2:7), human life enjoys a unique relationship with God. The correspondence between man and his Maker is expressed both by the language of 'image' (1:26–27) and by the metaphor of a shared 'breath.'" Mathews, *Genesis 1–11:26*, 196.

102. In generic terms the characteristics of the soul can be described as all the immaterial endowments that comprise human nature. Self-evidently, much is still left to mystery there and an exhaustive identification of the soul's characteristics would be unrealistic. Certain principal endowments of human nature, however, have been generally recognized as characteristics or faculties of the soul. These include things that fit more or less under such categories as personality, spirituality, rationality, morality, authority, and aesthetics. For a helpful discussion on these, see Hughes, *The True Image*, chapter 5: The Imprint of the Image in Man.

"the many pre-eminent gifts with which the human mind is endowed proclaim that something divine has been engraved upon it."[103]

We would of course be remiss here if we did not duly acknowledge humanity's "aesthetic sense, whereby human beings not only can appreciate the beauty that God has lavished on his creation, but also can create artistic beauty of their own—in painting, sculpture, poetry, and music."[104] As with all aspects of image-bearing, God is the pattern for humanity. Thus, "the primal artistic act was God's creation of the universe out of chaos, shaping the formless into form; and every artist since, on a lesser scale, has sought to imitate him—by selection and arrangement to reduce the chaotic in experience to a meaningful and pleasing order."[105] Indeed, we image not the hidden God, but the revealed God who creates, who recreates, and who delights in the beauty of all his work. It is this revealed God who has acted upon this world through his Son in order to show forth his glory.

THE ETHICAL-RELATIONAL ASPECT OF THE IMAGE OF GOD

The ethical-relational aspect of the *imago Dei* recognizes that bearing God's image is at once intrinsically relational and moral/ethical in nature. I argue that the ethical-relational aspect is grounded on the fact that being an "image-bearer" entails the idea of bearing responsibility to the one whose image is borne, along with responsibility towards other image-bearers and even creation itself. The characteristics of the ethical-relational aspect are an integral part of the form in and through which humans bear the divine image, and it serves as the third principal way that the beauty of human beings is reflected in their image-bearing glory.

The Trinity relating essentially, who as the Father, Son, and Holy Spirit dwell in mutual love and eternal delight with and in one another, is the selfsame Godhead operating economically whose delight in

---

103. Calvin, *Institutes*, 1.15.2, ed. McNeill, trans. Battles.

104. Anthony A. Hoekema, *Created in God's Image* (Grand Rapids: Eerdmans, 1986), 70.

105. Laurence Perrine, ed., *Sound and Sense: An Introduction to Poetry*, 3rd ed. (New York: Harcourt, Brace & World, 1971), chap. 14, quoted in Ryken, "In the Beginning, God Created," 59.

creation was to have direct personal communion with his image-bearers. Having created a diversity of creature kinds, God singled out humankind to bear his image. As God is the pattern of all aspects of image bearing, then for humanity to image God means that it images his relational nature as well. The idea set forth earlier that being made in the divine image identifies one as being a "son" of God points up the first-order nature of this relation (i.e., filial; cf. Acts 17:29). If the *imago Dei* were not intrinsically relational beyond that, the human person as image-bearer would be strictly individualistic by nature and not, as such, relationally cooperative and communal. What this speaks to is the social nature of the human individual. The intersubjective dimension here would seem to imply that our image-bearing is bound in part in relation to another/others. "The human creature," writes Vanhoozer, "is neither an autonomous individual nor an anonymous unity that has been assimilated into some collectivity, but rather a particular person who achieves a concrete identity in relation to others. Human being is inherently *social*."[106] That humans image God's relational nature is evident from a number of angles, not least being "that the only created species with which God entered into conversation was the human."[107] The dialogical relation between God and our primal parents is fundamental to the creation narrative and highlights the human capacity to be addressed by God (Gen 2:16-17; 3:9, 11, 13a) and to respond back (3:10-13). From the creation outset the human-to-human level was meant to operate in this basic dialogical mode as well (2:23; 4:1, 25). Richard Gaffin Jr. sums it up thus: "As God's image-bearers, in our specific and absolute dependence on him as our Creator, we are made to be addressed and, in turn, to address, to see and to respond, to hear and to reply. This is so above all in our relationship to him, who is our pattern and original, and, out of that relationship, in our relationships with others."[108]

---

106. Kevin Vanhoozer, "Human Being, Individual and Social," in *Cambridge Companion to Christian Doctrine*, ed. Colin E. Gunton (Cambridge: Cambridge University Press, 1997), 174–75. The relational focus received significant attention and affirmation in Karl Barth, *CD*, III/1, 176–206 and 288–92.

107. Kevin J. Vanhoozer, *Remythologizing Theology: Divine Action, Passion, and Authorship* (Cambridge: Cambridge University Press, 2010), 319.

108. Richard B. Gaffin Jr., "Speech and the Image of God: Biblical Reflections on

From Genesis 1:27 it is clear that the human individual is created in the image of God, male and female alike. An oft-debated point is whether the third line of this text argues in favor of the relational aspect of the *imago Dei* or merely anticipates the fertility blessing in verse 28a. In my judgment support for the relational aspect makes the most sense.[109] Just as "filling the earth" with image-bearing progeny is an integral part of fulfilling the official aspect of the *imago Dei*, so too, the male/female distinction signals that both genders together—functioning relationally as one—image God in accordance with the divine plan.[110] Implicit in the male/female distinction, moreover, is that the relational nature of humanity is designed by God to operate from a cisgendered perspective. The human person thus relates to God, to other human beings, and to the creation environment from their own self-aware standpoint of being a man or a woman.[111] The *imago Dei* as revealed in Genesis 1:27 is all the more extraordinary in that it finds its full identity equally represented in the individual man and woman as well as in their complementary relations. The significance of the *imago Dei* being identified with both maleness and femaleness is captured wonderfully here by Emil Brunner: "That is the immense double statement, of a lapidary simplicity, so simple indeed that we hardly realize that with it a vast

---

Language and Its Uses," in *The Pattern of Sound Doctrine: Systematic Theology at the Westminster Seminaries: Essays in Honor of Robert B. Strimple*, ed. David VanDrunen (Phillipsburg, NJ: P&R Publishing, 2004), 184. For Barth, these dialogical relations are the hallmark of the *imago Dei*, which he characterizes in terms of an "I-Thou" relationship: "The relationship between the summoning I in God's being and the summoned divine Thou is reflected both in the relationship of God to the man whom He has created, and also in the relationship between the I and the Thou, between male and female, in human existence itself." (*CD*, III/1, 196)

109. For a well represented counter-argument to this view, see Francis Watson, *Text and Truth: Redefining Biblical Theology* (Grand Rapids: Eerdmans, 1997), 298–99.

110. Arguing in favor of the male/female connection to the *imago Dei*, Paul Niskanen, "The Poetics of Adam: The Creation of אדם in the Image of אלהים," *JBL* 128 no. 3 (2009): 431, writes: "What if it is precisely the biological aspect that the writer wishes to emphasize? This seems to be the case, since the phrase is closely connected with the blessing of fertility. But why dissociate it from the idea of the image of God on this count? Is this not also God's image? Has God not been bringing forth life throughout Genesis 1? It would seem that the will and the power to create/procreate are a significant parallel that the author draws between God and humans. In the event that one misses the connection here, it is repeated in Gen 5:1–2."

111. For a relevant discussion as relates to the cisgendered body, see Gregg R. Allison, "Toward a Theology of Human Embodiment," *SBJT* 13 no. 2 (2009): 4–17.

world of myth and Gnostic speculation, of cynicism and asceticism, of the deification of sexuality and fear of sex completely disappears."[112]

The relational nature of humanity not only operates from a cisgendered perspective but it only ever operates from an ethical perspective as well. The ethical aspect of the *imago Dei* means that moral actions and attitudes are a natural and proper part of how humanity relates to God, to other human beings, and to creation. Gerhard von Rad advances this point from an OT perspective in terms of the concept of righteousness:

> There is absolutely no concept in the Old Testament with so central a significance for all the relationships of human life as that of צדקה [righteousness/justice/justness]. It is the standard not only for man's relationship to God, but also for his relationships to his fellows, reaching right down to the most petty wranglings—indeed, it is even the standard for man's relationship to the animals and to his natural environment.[113]

Again, God is the pattern in this respect. The relational and the ethical represent two sides of the same *imago Dei* coin, if you will. For entailed in the concept "image-bearer" is the idea of bearing responsibility to the one whose image is borne, along with responsibility towards other image-bearers and to creation. So while no other creature besides humankind occupies the privileged position of being made in the divine image, only humans are morally held to account before God for imaging him (i.e., "being-like-God") as we have been created to do. It is thus Adam and Eve and no other creature to whom God directed his command in the garden of Eden and who alone were held accountable *as a bearer of his image* (Gen 2:16–17; 3:9–13).

---

112. Emil Brunner, *Man in Revolt: A Christian Anthropology*, trans. Olive Wyon (London: Lutterworth Press, 1939), 346. In reference to Genesis 1:27, Brunner completes his thought, stating, "It seems so incredibly naïve to couple the statement that 'man was made in the image of God' with the statement that God 'created them, one man and one woman.' And yet in the whole history of man's understanding of himself, this statement has only been made *once* and at this point. ... On account of this one statement alone the Bible shines out among all other books in the world as the Word of God."

113. Gerhard von Rad, *Old Testament Theology*, vol. 1: *The Theology of Israel's Historical Traditions*, trans. D. M. G. Stalker (New York: Harper & Row, 1962), 370.

The image in which Adam and Eve were created was not morally neutral or indifferent but "very good" (Gen 1:31); so they both began in right standing before God, their moral character pleasing to him and fully in accord with God's own holy perfection. From the outset of creation the axiom has always been true: "Good fruits presuppose a good tree; one must first *be* before he can *do*."[114] Before the fall, therefore, the actions and attitudes that defined Adam and Eve's relationship to God, to each other, and to creation must have been altogether morally pure (*status integratis*). Their original image-bearing glory as such did not fall short of the glory of God, that is, the way they were to be-like-God. The connatural expression of this "morally pure" condition, as we said earlier, was doxological delight in God. Yet, as Bavinck reminds us, "this is not to be conceived as childlike innocence, but it must not be exaggerated either, as though the original state of integrity were already equal to the state of glory."[115]

The ethical-relational aspect helps us better see what it means for humans to bear God's image in connection with other aspects of the *imago Dei*. Indeed, our constitution as image-bearers is such that no facet of the *imago Dei* is reflected independent of any other facet. Rather, *all facets of the imago Dei operate holistically in an integrity reflecting the glory of the whole image*. The nature of humanity's kingly office, for example, can be seen as a commission to model justice and benevolence, as the ancient pedigree attests: "Ancient oriental kings were expected to be devoted to the welfare of their subjects, especially the poorest and weakest members of society (Ps 72:12–14). By upholding divine principles of law and justice, rulers promoted peace and prosperity for all their subjects."[116] Throughout the Old Testament even the call for God's people to imitate him in sundry ways is effectively a call to live out rightly the ethical-relational aspect of the *imago Dei*. This is exemplified in the following such ways: God's calling his people to treat strangers kindly because that is exactly what they received from him as strangers in Egypt (Exod 23:9); his calling Israel to be holy because he is holy (Lev 11:44); likewise, the good character modeled by a righteous man

---

114. Bavinck, *RD*, 2:558.
115. Bavinck, *RD*, 2:558.
116. Wenham, *Genesis 1–15*, 33.

in Psalm 112 is mimetic of God's own character expressed in Psalm 111 regarding his actions toward the world.[117] Perhaps the most profound example in the Old Testament to throw a spotlight on the ethical-relational aspect of God's image (not excluding any other aspects, of course) is the theophany of God's glory to Moses in Exodus 34:5–7. This is plain by the cardinal qualities wherein God describes himself: compassion, graciousness, slowness to anger, abounding in love and faithfulness, forgiveness and justice (cf. Exod 20:5–6; Num 14:17–23; Pss 86:15; 103:8; 145:8).[118] Narratives such as Abraham's effort to argue for God's own perspective on human affairs (Gen 18:23–33), along with Moses' effort following suit (Num 14:13–19), are reflective of these same attributes of God and show in dramatically vivid ways God's servants imaging them (cf. Rom 9:3).[119]

In the New Testament the ethical dimension of the *imago Dei* is called out in explicit terms. Before the foundation of the world the Father elected sons and daughters into the family of God through Christ that these "should be *holy and blameless* before him" (Eph 1:4; cf. Eph 5:27; Col 1:22; Jude 24). This refers to those who are the members of the body of Christ, the glorified new humanity conformed to his image. The eschatological image, as we discussed earlier, has its protological counterpart; it follows that "holy and blameless" also characterized Adam and Eve's original image-bearing glory. The same hermeneutic applies to Ephesians 4:24 and Colossians 3:10 in which the eschatological image is described in terms of knowledge, righteousness, and holiness. "From this we infer," states Calvin, "that, to begin with, God's image was

---

117. Michael D. Williams, "First Calling: The *Imago Dei* and the Order of Creation—Part II," *Presbyterion* 39 no. 2 (Fall 2013): 84. In n57, Williams adds: "Examples could be multiplied. See, e.g., Deut 10:17ff; 14:1; 16:18ff; 24:17–22; Lev 19:34." Cf. Gentry and Wellum, *Kingdom through Covenant*, 190, n23: "The divine image is particularly revealed in the living out of the Ten Commandments. This is why there could be no image at the centre of Israel's worship—God wanted the commands or instructions in the ark to be imaged in one's actions: this was the divine character embodied in human lives!"

118. R. Ward Wilson and Craig L. Blomberg, "Image of God in Humanity: A Biblical Psychological Perspective," *Themelios* 18 (April 1993): 9.

119. Richard S. Briggs, "Humans in the Image of God and Other Things Genesis Does Not Make Clear," *JTI* 4 no. 1 (Spring 2010): 123.

visible in the light of the mind, in the uprightness of the heart, and in the soundness of all parts."[120]

The unique and inestimable dignity that God has conferred on man and woman alike is of the grandest significance, for what is at stake is a recognition and valuing of the inherent dignity of every human being simply by virtue of their being human and bearers of the divine image. By marking humankind with his own signet (Ezek 28:12), God delighted to value it above all other creature kinds. Human dignity is thus axiologically real, derived from the intrinsic worth and honor with which every human person has by virtue of being created in the divine image.[121] Moreover, this dignity is foundational to the biblical ethic for how humans are to relate to God and each other. As Blocher points out, "Christ joins the first and great commandment with the second which 'is like it'—'You shall love the Lord your God ...you shall love your neighbor ...'; surely the logic behind that is the likeness between God and his image" (cf. Jas 3:9; 1 John 4:20).[122] In the same vein Calvin viewed the *imago Dei* in axiological terms as well as aesthetic. Since both believer and unbeliever alike share the common brand mark of God's image, he rightly exhorts "not to consider men's evil intentions but to look upon the image of God in them, which cancels and effaces their

---

120. Calvin, *Institutes* 1.15.4, ed. McNeill, trans. Battles. Commenting on the Colossians passage, Wilson and Blomberg, "The Image of God in Humanity," 9, offer the following insight: "Then, as we read on from Col 3:10, we see that the renewal of the knowledge of God in the image of our Creator is a moral and interpersonal knowledge, in which we clothe ourselves 'with compassion, kindness, humility, gentleness and patience' (v. 12). We 'bear with each other and forgive whatever grievances' we may have against one another (v. 13). This list of virtues is strikingly similar to Exod 34:6–7."

121. For an insightful treatment exploring the meanings of human dignity, see Gilbert Meilaender, *Neither Beast nor God: The Dignity of the Human Person* (New York: Encounter Books, 2009).

122. Blocher, *In the Beginning*, 86. Along similar lines, Graham Cole notes: "Jesus nowhere describes human beings using image-of-God language, but in regard to Luke 12:24, Matt 10:31 and 12:11–12, Wolterstorff is probably correct when he argues, 'To be a human being is to have worth. Jesus does not indicate what that worth is, other than to say that it is much greater than the worth of birds and sheep and to suggest that it is a worth one has *qua* human being. Presumably, the worth he had in mind was that of bearing the divine image.'" *God the Peacemaker*, 58, n24, quoting Nicholas Wolterstorff, *Justice: Rights and Wrongs* (Princeton: Princeton University Press, 2008), 131.

transgressions, and with its beauty (*pulcritudine*) and dignity (*dignitate*) allures us to love and embrace them."[123]

THE RADICAL FALL FROM ADAM AND EVE'S ORIGINAL IMAGE-BEARING GLORY

Our theological interpretation of the image of God in which Adam and Eve were formed at creation presented the protological starting point in the outworking of the divine plan concerning the fate of human beings. But, the outworking of that plan takes a tragic turn—the fall of Adam and Eve in Genesis 3. Correspondingly, this tragic turn of events radically alters the shape of the christological contours of beauty. The outcome of the moral testing and conflict between good and evil was the fateful fall away from the realization of humanity's identity and destiny as image of God. André LaCocque encapsulates the cosmic ramifications of this: "The coaxing to become like God meant that Adam would pull up or down the whole world with himself into whatever would be the new fate of his choice. The king of the universe pulls everything with him to glory or abjection. His 'dominion' would be actualized in a new and ominous way."[124] God's judgment curse against Adam and Eve, whatever else the ramifications would be, meant from that point forward that humanity would image God in tragic irony. "No category designed for being is adequate to express the perversion of being," writes Henri Blocher. "We must state that after his revolt mankind remains mankind, and also that mankind has radically changed, that he is but a grisly shadow of himself. Mankind remains the image of God, inviolable and responsible, but has become a contradictory image, one might say a caricature, a witness against himself."[125] Although the *imago Dei* proper is retained in humanity, all of what constitutes the image has become radically affected and infected by a condition of depravity. As a consequence, the human condition of fallenness is characterized by

---

123. Calvin, *Institutes* 3.7.6, ed. McNeill, trans. Battles.

124. André LaCocque, *The Trial of Innocence: Adam, Eve, and the Yahwist* (Eugene, OR: Cascade Books, 2006), 160. Encapsulating this holism of creation, Bavinck, *RD*, 2:588, writes, "In Genesis cosmogony immediately passes over into geogony and geogony into anthropogony. The world, the earth, humanity are one organic whole. They stand, they fall, they are raised up together."

125. Blocher, *In the Beginning*, 94.

an image-bearing glory vitiated and compromised in every way relative to Adam and Eve's original image-bearing glory. Evident in the
Genesis 3 narrative is the baleful impact on the image-bearing glory
as comprehended in the three principal aspects of the *imago Dei*—the
official, the constitutional, and the ethical-relational.

Yet for all that the *common curse* brings on humanity, all aspects
of the divine image remain retained in some measure. It would be a
mistake, however, to think of the condition of fallen humanity relative to Adam and Eve's original condition as being just a deprivation of
glory (*privatio gloriae*). It is not mere *deprivation* that now characterizes humanity's image-bearing glory, but rather a *depravation* of glory
(*depravatio gloriae*) relative to Adam and Eve's original condition. And
entailed in that depravation is the inherited guilt of Adam's sin and its
penal corruption, which, again, has radically affected and infected the
entire human race, and continues so. It follows that the image-bearing
beauty reflecting how humans are to be-like-God in the world is correspondingly, and therefore balefully, affected. Since the image-bearing
beauty of human beings is essentially expressed in how they fittingly
reflect being-like-God in the world, it would now be an expressed
beauty that is vitiated and compromised in every way relative to Adam
and Even's original image-bearing beauty.

Of critical importance to recognize in the biblical storyline is that
even though human persons are not explicitly referred to as the "image
of God," the basic concept of it underlies the Bible's narrative development. As James Luther Mays points out, the *imago Dei* "is a structural
theme of the biblical account of God and humankind. [Its] actuality
continues in the calling and destiny of human beings to represent and
resemble God in the world."[126] This is the essence of how Genesis 1:26–28
plays out in salvation history according to the divine plan. Beginning in
Genesis 3:14–15 the incipient idea of the "seed of the woman" becomes
part of the story, which then after Genesis 11 transitions to the Abraham
story—the one through whom God's blessing will be mediated to all
the nations of the earth. That blessing includes the Lord's promise that

---

126. James Luther Mays, "The Self in the Psalms and the Image of God," in *God
and Human Dignity*, ed. R. Kendall Soulen and Linda Woodhead (Grand Rapids:
Eerdmans, 2006), 38–39.

among Abraham's descendants there will be kings (Gen 17:6; cf. 17:16), and yet more critically still, "the scepter shall not depart from Judah" (Gen 49:10)—foreshadowing a king through whom all the nations of the earth will be blessed.[127] In connection with the *imago Dei*, writes Mays, "The story of Israel as told in the OT is broadly a sequel to Genesis 1–11. Israel is a part of the humanity described there and its career concerns all humankind. The Israelites' identity and destiny as the people of the Lord is a movement toward the realization of humanity's identity and destiny as image of God."[128] However, the significance of humanity's creation in the divine image, along with what constitutes this image and its eschatological fulfillment do not come into their fullest and clearest focus until we come to the revelation in the New Testament.[129] There Christ himself is not only identified as the image of God (2 Cor 4:4; Col 1:15), but also as the last or eschatological Adam who embodies the divine purpose for humanity in accordance with which the first Adam was created (cf. Rom 5:14b). In view of how humans were created to fittingly reflect being-like-God in the world, and God's design to see this eschatologically fulfilled through Christ according to his eternal plan, it is fair to say that "the story of the world is the story of God's *anthropos* project."[130]

---

127. For a helpful biblical-theological treatment here, see T. Desmond Alexander, "Royal Expectations in Genesis to Kings: Their Importance for Biblical Theology," *TynBul* 49 no. 2 (1998): 191–212.

128. Mays, "The Self in the Psalms and the Image of God," 39.

129. To this larger point, Briggs, "Humans in the Image of God," 123–24, contributes: "Genesis uses the phrase 'image of God' to set us reading the canonical narrative with certain questions in mind, or, as one might say, 'the image of God' serves as a hermeneutical lens through which to read the OT's subsequent narratives. ... [T]he longer-term project [pertains to] seeing how the canonical narrative will in the end fill out what is left of the anthropological question after it has been transferred into the scripturally primary categories of Israel and the church, and the God behind them who summons us to be readers who are disciples."

130. Mays, "The Self in the Psalms and the Image of God," 43. Colin Gunton is another who accents God's work of creation and his purposes for human beings within creation as being God's project: "Rather like a work of art, Creation is a project, something God wills for its own sake and not because he has need of it. ... [N]o theology of creation is complete without attention being paid to the place of humankind in the project." Colin E. Gunton, "The Doctrine of Creation," in *The Cambridge Companion to Christian Doctrine*, ed. Colin E. Gunton (Cambridge: Cambridge University Press, 1997), 142, 144.

FITTINGNESS OF RETRIBUTIVE JUSTICE

According to the conditions that God had purposed in the garden of Eden, the probationary character of his testing Adam and Eve implied that the Lord would render judgment at the outcome of the time of testing—whether it be the promissory reward of escalated blessings or, conversely, the execution of his judgment curse. The rest is history, as they say, for in our primal parent's fateful fall in Genesis 3, divine judgment was rendered in the form of God's judgment curse.[131] In view of the narrative prominence of the meting out of judgment by God against Adam and Eve, I address the notion of fittingness in reference to retributive justice. I argue that the complementary relation of moral normativity and aesthetic normativity in regard to retributive justice is aptly captured in the notion—*the punishment must fit the crime*. The theological groundwork laid here figures in as part of the aesthetic dimension of redemptive-history, all of which pays forward in Chapter 4 as we address the judgment that God meted out upon Christ in the place of sinners.

Although the meting out of judgment by God is an expression of his holy and righteous character, it expresses at the same time his judicial wrath toward those on the receiving end of such dealings. As Cole reminds us though, "Wrath is not an essential attribute of God. Rather, wrath is how divine holiness justly expresses itself against human sin."[132] The divine administration of this kind of justice, argues Nicholas Wolterstorff, presupposes another form of divine justice—what he calls *primary justice*, which "consists of treating persons with due respect for their worth."[133] Primary justice as such is an aspect of that

---

131. The idea of "meting out justice" is subsumed here in the broader sense of "rendering judgment," as Nicholas Wolterstorff advocates in "Is There Justice in the Trinity?," in *God's Life in Trinity*, ed. Miroslav Volf and Michael Welker (Minneapolis: Fortress Press, 2006), 177: "Rendering judgment comes in three forms: first, rendering a decision in cases of conflict; second, determining whether the accused is guilty of the accusation and declaring the accused guilty if that person is guilty and innocent if not guilty; and third, meting out judgment on one declared guilty."

132. Cole, *God the Peacemaker*, 72. Lister, *God is Impassible and Impassioned*, 179, n21, notes similarly: "God's emotional responsiveness toward his creation is perfectly fitted. Thus, divine wrath is the appropriate, and not excessive, response to creaturely sin and rebellion. Accordingly, God's wrath should not be misinterpreted along the lines of our experience of 'losing it' or 'flying off the handle.'"

133. Wolterstorff, "Is There Justice in the Trinity?," 185. Wolterstorff cites

mutual love and eternal delight within which the Father, Son, and Holy Spirit perichoretically dwell. God's rendering of judgment in human affairs—or *secondary justice*—reflects the primary justice of the Trinity relating essentially in the following way. Just as God's secondary justice involves his rendering what is due a person(s) as something that person(s) deserves, so likewise God's primary justice involves the mutual love and eternal delight between the Father, Son, and Holy Spirit in which also is entailed their infinitely deserving regard for one another. On this latter point, the infinitely deserving regard shared between the persons of the Trinity may be seen as a direct reflection of the infinite dignity intrinsic to each of them.[134] Theologically suggested here is that "when we treat each other justly, we neither merely obey God's injunction to act justly nor merely imitate God's doing of justice within creation. We mirror the inner life of the Trinity."[135] Nothing of God's secondary justice, however, could ever perturb or diminish any his perfections, including his own beatitude. And thus the divine disposition of wrath expressed in the judgment that God renders in human affairs must be seen not as essential to him but as an extrinsic attribute contingent on his decision to create *this* world and—for lack of a better way of putting it—permit the fall. Indeed, both wrath and mercy presuppose a creation that is fallen.

As a critical aspect of secondary justice, the idea of meted-out judgment has to do fundamentally with a retributive theory of punishment, that is, one that views punishment as something that a wrongdoer deserves (their *desert*).[136] The element of desert, then, which involves

---

Deuteronomy 24:19–21 along with Amos 5:24 and Micah 6:8 as examples of precepts in Scripture pertaining to what he calls primary justice.

134. The concept of God's primary justice that I am putting forward is resonant with Barth's characterization of God's glory as well as human glory: "The objective conception of the honor which a man has in himself and which is therefore his due, the dignity which is his and is therefore accepted by others, the magnificence which he displays because he has a right to it, the splendor which emanates from him because he is resplendent. It is in this sense that the New Testament speaks of God's glory or of the glory of Jesus Christ or even of the glory that belongs to us. It refers to the legitimate, effective, and actual self-demonstration, self-expression and self-declaration of a being whose self-revelation in subject to no doubt, criticism or reservation." (CD II/1, 642)

135. Wolterstorff, "Is There Justice in the Trinity?," 187.

136. For a helpful treatment on divine retributive justice, see R. B. Chisholm Jr.,

meted out punishment, is properly included in the domain of secondary justice. The kind of justice that will remain our interest throughout this work is retributive.[137] Because of the inseparable link between desert and justice, the normativity of desert is essentially moral. That is to say, the moral dimension is the normatively robust claim justifying retributive punishment (cf. Rev 20:12-13). Of greater interest for our consideration, however, is the idea philosopher Leo Zaibert advances that the aesthetic normativity of fittingness lends complementary justification to the robust normativity of the moral dimension.[138] In effect it is the aesthetic sense of French *justesse* applied in service of moral *justice* that provides an even more decisive claim in the application of retributive punishment. To claim that a wrongdoer deserves punishment affirms already "a sort of 'fittingness' between certain features and actions of one person on the one hand and another's evaluative attitudes on the other."[139] Reinforcing that point from another angle, Francesco Orsi notes that the fittingness of having a certain attitude toward some person is recognizable as something which is *prior* to whatever particular reasons might be given for having that attitude.[140] The appeal to fittingness among competing courses of action of punishment "is to

---

"Retribution," *Dictionary of the Old Testament Prophets*, ed. Mark J. Boda and J. Gordon McConville (Downers Grove, IL: IVP Academic, 2012), 671-76.

137. We will have to leave aside from our discussions giving consideration to other forms of justice (e.g., reformative justice, restorative justice and distributive justice), as this is simply beyond the scope of this study. As a general point, Cole, *God the Peacemaker*, 77, n38, properly notes "that deterrence, reformative justice, restorative justice and retributive justice are not mutually exclusive."

138. Leo Zaibert, "The Fitting, the Deserving, and the Beautiful," *Journal of Moral Philosophy* 3 no. 3 (November 2006): 348-49.

139. Zaibert, "The Fitting, the Deserving, and the Beautiful," 338.

140. Francesco Orsi, *Value Theory* (New York: Bloomsbury Academic, 2015), 14. Orsi explains, for example, that "a key fits a keyhole, a chord fits a certain melody, a certain trait makes a species fitter for a certain environment, etc. These statements express evaluations of a functional, aesthetical, or biological kind, without directly addressing what anyone should do. [However], there is a similarity between reasons and fittingness that is worth bringing out: certain features of *x* provide reasons for an attitude towards x or an action, just like an attitude towards *x* or an action fits certain features of *x*. In other words, both notions relate objects and their properties with responses. But reasons seem to essentially relate to the agent or the subject of those responses in a way that fittingness need not. Reasons are always reasons for someone to do something, or they are not reasons at all, while a certain attitude might be called fitting prior to being fitting *for someone* to take."

say that [the punishee] ought, other things being equal, to get *that* thing, or that it would be *morally better* that she get it."[141] Applying the "soft" normativity of fittingness with the robust normativity of the moral dimension may thus strongly recommend one scenario of retributive punishment over other equally just options. Moreover, since primary justice consists of treating persons with due respect for their worth, it already involves a sort of fittingness between one person's due respect on the one hand and another's evaluative attitudes and actions on the other. In this way the moral-aesthetic complementary relation is at least suggestive, therefore, that divine secondary justice derives from the primary justice of the immanent Trinity.

Furthermore, in agreement with Oliver Crisp, the nature of divine holiness is such that "God's justice does not permit him to forgive a person their sin without retributive justice being served. So, on this view, the sin of a person must be punished; it cannot remain unpunished."[142] The complementary relation of moral normativity and aesthetic normativity in regard to retributive justice is displayed in the notion — the punishment must fit the crime.[143] The common curse that God's judgment against Adam and Eve brought on humanity exemplifies the aforementioned notion in two basic ways. First, the divine punishment is commensurate with the offense; and secondly, God's judgment curse takes its shape from the nature of the offender. In connection with the former, Crisp advances the idea (rightly so, in my view) that the infinite ontological divide between divine and human corresponds to an infinite divide in dignity. That is to say, since *"the dignity of God is infinite, so the seriousness of an offense committed against God is infinite, or infinitely surpasses that of other [ontological] kinds."*[144] The underlying points of argument are as follows:[145]

1. All sin is against God, who is worthy of infinite regard.

---

141. Zaibert, "The Fitting, the Deserving, and the Beautiful," 338, quoting Serena Olsaretti, ed., *Desert and Justice* (Oxford: Clarendon Press, 2003), 4, emphasis added.

142. Oliver D. Crisp, "Divine Retribution: A Defence," *Sophia* 42 no. 2 (October 2005): 37.

143. Cf. Chisholm, "Retribution," 673-74, for a discussion on the rhetoric of poetic justice.

144. Crisp, "Divine Retribution," 40 (emphasis in the original).

145. The argument here borrows from Crisp, "Divine Retribution," 41.

2. The gravity of an offense against a being is principally determined by that being's worth or dignity.

3. There is an infinite demerit in all sin against God, such that all sin is infinitely heinous.

In order for the judgment God rendered against his offending image-bearers to be commensurate with the offense, therefore, the punishment meted out would issue ultimately in death—judicial, physical, and spiritual death—for the wages of sin, *all* sin in fact, is death. The administration of divine grace in goodness and mercy, which includes the common grace of God preserving humanity in the outworking of his original creational purposes, is not at all precluded in the satisfaction of divine retributive justice.[146] For God not to violate his own holy character, however, such administration of grace requires that the sin of his offending image-bearers cannot remain unpunished. Outside of God's redemptive grace, though, the commensurate punishment issues in death. "God's goodness is much more glorious when it is shown to those who only deserve evil" writes Bavinck. "It then bears the name *grace* (חֵן, תְּחִנָּה, derived from חָנַן, to bow, incline toward; χαρις, from χαρίζομαι)."[147] As we will see later with respect to the person and work of Christ, the redemption issuing for human beings in eschatologically complete, eternal, personal salvation provides the ultimate satisfaction not only of divine retributive justice, but, one could even say, divine restorative and reformative justice through Christ, which itself derives from the primary justice of the immanent Trinity.

The second way that the divine retributive justice against Adam and Eve exemplifies the complementary relation of moral normativity and aesthetic normativity is in how God's judgment curse takes its shape from the nature of the offenders—the offenders here being Adam and Eve as the original creaturely bearers of the divine image. Recall that entailed in the concept "image-bearer" is the idea of bearing

---

146. "The origin of the doctrine of common grace," writes Louis Berkhof, "was occasioned by the fact that there is in the world, alongside of the course of the Christian life with all its blessings, a natural course of life, which is not redemptive and yet exhibits many traces of the true, the good, and the beautiful." *Systematic Theology* (Grand Rapids: Eerdmans, 1996), 432.

147. Bavinck, *RD*, 2:214.

responsibility to the one whose image is borne. The condition of human fallenness in consequence of Adam and Eve's fateful choice can be seen as inversely proportional to the privileged position of image-bearer with which humankind has been dignified. Arguing along the same lines, John Murray states,

> If our analysis is correct that the divine image defines man in his specific character as man, then sin is intensified in its heinousness for the very reason that his identity is to be defined in such digni-fied terms. The higher is our conception of man in his intrinsic essence, the greater must be the gravity of his offense in rebellion and enmity against God. ... Man conceived of as in the image of God, so far from toning down the doctrine of total depravity, points rather to its gravity, intensity, and irreversibility.[148]

The primal drama in Genesis 3 suggests something to the effect that since Adam and Eve failed to image God as they were created to do, God's judgment curse took its shape from the nature of their image-bearing identity. Notably, the *imago Dei* as comprehended in its three principal aspects—the official, constitutional, and ethical-relational—would now reflect a *depravatio gloriae*. Humanity would image God in tragic irony. The fittingness of God's judgment curse is best recognized in how God preserves the dignity of humanity, each and altogether, while having its fallen glory be a witness against itself. On a final note, we need not accept that categories of fittingness are uncorrelated with each other, as in the case here our theological aesthetic sees the fittingness of God's wisdom and righteousness manifest in his judgment curse rendered against his offending image-bearers as being perfectly correlated with the aesthetic fittingness identifiable in its structure and proportion.

Conspectus

In this section I presented the debut of the created order with its inher-ent beautiful order. After God completed his work of day six, the divine appraisal that everything he had made "was very good" (Gen 1:31) sug-gests that the created order was imbued with beauty, about which God

---

148. John Murray, *Collected Writings of John Murray.* vol. 2: *Select Lectures in Systematic Theology* (Edinburgh: Banner of Truth Trust, 1977), 38.

expressed his full delight in the *fait accompli* of his creation. The basic shape of Scripture's overall story pattern, I have argued, corresponds to a theodramatic comedy, or what I call a sublime comedy. The shape of the Bible's overall story is perfectly consonant with our gloss on the creational-re-creational symmetry of the divine plan, except even better, recognizing the literary form of the Bible as a theodramatic comedy points up the surplus of the gloriousness of its consummation ending compared to its creation beginning. Structural elements of the christological contours of beauty stemming out of creation are discerned in the proto-eschaton—that is, pre-redemptive eschatological themes in Genesis 1–2 that clue us in about God's intentions for humanity in accordance with the design and outworking of the divine plan. One primary theme has to do with the notion of sacred time represented by God's Sabbath rest; another has to do with sacred space represented by the garden of Eden, God's garden of Delight. The telos of God's creational intention for humanity in connection with those two themes is the glorification of human beings, who will be confirmed in beatitude, experiencing the pure enjoyment of God's presence.

The central theme of the proto-eschaton is the image of God in which all humans are created, comprehended in three principal aspects—the official, the constitutional, and the ethical-relational. To bear the divine image is to be-like-God in the world according to those principal aspects. The beauty of human beings is expressed by reflecting most fittingly the ways they bear all aspects of the divine image. The principal aspects of the *imago Dei* are summed up as follows: (1) the official aspect means that all humans are created in a filial relationship with God to reflect his glory as his royal priests; (2) the constitutional aspect pertains to its ontological dimension, that is, to the human person (body-soul) exhibiting the image-bearing glory of God in all their being and doing; and (3) the ethical-relational aspect recognizes that bearing God's image is intrinsically relational and ethical in nature, for entailed in the concept "image-bearer" is the idea of bearing responsibility to the one whose image is borne, along with responsibility towards other image-bearers and towards creation. In this light, human dignity is derived from the intrinsic worth and honor with which every human person has by virtue of being created in the divine image.

4

The Incarnation: Beauty Condescending

In set up for this chapter, it will be helpful to restate a key question I posed in the Introduction. In what ways does a theological aesthetic highlight certain aspects of the plan and purposes of God, promised before the ages began, that he has realized in Christ Jesus? In seeking to answer that, the christological contours of beauty developed in this chapter (as well as the next) will show that the Son's fittingness as incarnate Redeemer is the critical lens for seeing God's beauty, serving as well to display the Son's glory in every stage of the theodrama.

In our development of the christological contours of beauty, we are at the pivotal center of the divine plan—the theodrama's midpoint—in the advent of the Son incarnate. In the fullness of time, Christ came as the Redeemer of the world. As Calvin elegantly puts it:

> The Lord held to this orderly plan in administering the covenant of his mercy: as the day of full revelation approached with the passing of time, the more he increased each day the brightness of its manifestation. Accordingly, at the beginning when the first promise of salvation was given to Adam [Gen 3:15] it glowed like a feeble spark. Then, as it was added to, the light grew in fullness, breaking forth increasingly and shedding its radiance more widely. At last—when all the clouds were dispersed—Christ, the Sun of Righteousness, fully illumined the whole earth [cf. Mal., ch. 4].[1]

Our interest here is to develop the christological contours of beauty in regard to four key aspects of the identity of God the Son incarnate,

---

1. Calvin, *Institutes* 2.10.20, ed. McNeill, trans. Battles.

which I summarize below. It will be helpful, however, to reiterate two theological aesthetic points that will be applied in my argumentation below. First, as a basic point, the beauty of redemptive-history can be seen as a function of the fittingness involved in its design and out-working (so Anselm). Second, the beauty of redemptive-history is dramatic, or more preferable, theodramatic. As such, the beauty of redemptive-history pertains to: (a) the person/role of Christ, that is, his being and doing as displayed predominantly in his obedient relation-ship to the Father demonstrated through the experiences of his earthly life; and (b) what happens redemptive-historically, that is, an event's drama in its proximate context seen within the structure and propor-tion of the larger context of salvation history. I refer to the beauty of Christ's identity in terms of theodramatic fittingness and to the beauty of an event in terms of redemptive-historical fittingness. I develop this chapter in four main sections, followed by an excursus:

1. *Christ the Image of God.* I argue that while Christ's identity as the incarnate image of God is the revelation of God's full and unobscured glory in Christ, the perception of it occurred in a dialectic of reveal-ing and concealing. The question this calls up, which we address in the subsequent section, is the following: did the form of Christ's humanity function to hide and/or reveal his glory?

2. *Christ the Form of a Slave.* Here, I offer a theological interpretation of Philippians 2:6–8, addressing Christ's identity as taking the form of a slave. I argue that Christ's humanity in the form of a slave was most befitting for God the Son to take in accordance with his role as the Messiah, being born under the law, to redeem those who were under the law. Thus, God the Son was not operating incognito as Christ in the form of a slave because his true identity was not actually concealed by a "veil of flesh." The beauty of Christ is thus qualified by the theodramatic fittingness that corresponds to the human form his life takes in the economy of salvation.

3. *Christ the Last Adam and the True Israel.* I argue that the theodramatic fittingness of the Son is again demonstrated through his identity as the last Adam and the true Israel. Christ as such recapitulates in his life the history of Adam and God's covenant people Israel,

perfectly fulfilling all that Adam and Israel were called by God to be and do. The Adam-Christ parallel is demonstrated from Romans 5:12–21 and 1 Corinthians 15:44–49, and the Israel-Christ parallel is demonstrated from the events of Jesus' baptism by John and his temptation in the wilderness, all of which highlights the paradigmatic nature of the parallels as basic to the design of the divine plan. Since the parallels between Adam and Christ and between Israel and Christ play a fundamental part in the recapitulative patterning of redemptive-history, they reflect an ingredient aspect of the beauty of redemptive-history, not just by virtue of perceiving the patterning but ultimately in perceiving the "beauty of the Lord" in the person of Christ, whose glory reflects all facets of his messianic identity.

4. *Christ the Transfigured.* Here, I consider Christ's identity as revealed at the event of his transfiguration, offering a theological interpretation involving all three synoptic Gospels (Matt 17:1–9; Mark 9:2–10; Luke 9:28–36). I present a case for the redemptive-historical fittingness of the transfiguration event in terms of its continuity both backward to the OT tradition—keying in on Moses' Sinai experience—and forward to the eschatological hope of God's future triumph in Christ. I further argue that an implicit eschatological anthropology is suggested that serves as a momentous preview of "coming attractions" in the eschatological fulfillment of humanity's identity and destiny as image of God. A critical point of my argumentation is that the theodramatic fittingness of the Son is perfectly conformed to the respective form of his life in the states of his humiliation and exaltation. The radiance of Christ's glory is therefore expressed most fittingly in and through whichever form of his economic identity is in view, his beauty radiating as always from glory to glory.

5. *Excursus: Theological Aesthetic of Isaiah 53:2.* Here, I offer a theological aesthetic of Isaiah 53:2b, addressing Isaiah's (suffering) Servant of the Lord as identified with the person of Christ, described here by the prophet as having "no form or majesty that we should look at him, and no beauty that we should desire him."

The featured theologian whose view on divine beauty is summarized and whose theological perspectives contribute at places throughout this chapter is Hans Urs von Balthasar. Before proceeding to the main sections, I will first describe in brief the essence of Balthasar's theological aesthetic.

HANS URS VON BALTHASAR ON DIVINE BEAUTY

The Swiss Roman Catholic theologian Hans Urs von Balthasar developed his Christian dogmatics under the rubric of the classical triad of transcendental properties of being—"being" as beautiful, good, and true.[2] As Edward Oakes explains, for Balthasar the transcendental relation between the true, the good, and the beautiful informs all of Christian theology—orthodoxy and orthopraxy together: "Balthasar insisted that there can be no reflection on the *truth* of Christian revelation (Part 3) until it is lived out in committed *action* (Part 2), which a Christian will never feel called to do without having first perceived revelation in all its inherent *beauty* (Part 1)."[3] Important here is the idea that there is a certain primacy to "aesthetics" that informs his trilogy's entire theological flow—"Beauty is the word that shall be our first."[4] With this priority Balthasar fixes upon a fundamental ordering principle in the opening set of his trilogy (*The Glory of the Lord*) that comes full circle theologically: "the *pulchrum* appear[s] in its rightful place within the total ordered structure, namely as the manner in which God's goodness (*bonum*) gives itself and is expressed by God and understood by man as the truth (*verum*)."[5] Balthasar's formal innovation thus starts with

---

2. Articulating a coherent treatment of theology in aesthetic, dramatic, and veridical terms, Balthasar's project comprises a fifteen-volume theological trilogy: (1) *The Glory of the Lord: A Theological Aesthetics*, (2) *Theo-Drama: Theological Dramatic Theory*, and (3) *Theo-Logic: Theological Logical Theory*. In his *Epilogue*, trans. Edward T. Oakes (San Francisco: Ignatius Press, 2004), 46, Balthasar explains the rationale behind this enterprise: "Our trilogy, presenting a theological aesthetics, dramatics, and logic, is built from within this mutually illuminating light. What one calls the properties of Being that transcend every individual being (the 'transcendentals') seem to give the most fitting access to the mysteries of Christian theology. From these common properties, three were drawn out for separate emphasis: the beautiful, the good, and the true. We followed this procedure even though the transcendentals are indivisible from, and closely related to, each other. In fact, they were chosen precisely because together they permeate all Being."

3. Edward T. Oakes, "Hans Urs von Balthasar," in *The Oxford Companion to Christian Thought*, ed. Adrian Hastings et al. (Oxford: Oxford University Press, 2000), 744.

4. Hans Urs von Balthasar, *GL*, I, 18.

5. Balthasar, *GL*, I, Foreword.

the perception of beauty, of which he means a kind of theological per-ception—a perceiving of God's revelation that allows the percipient to "apprehend" the object itself. Such apprehension will lead to action (i.e., the good), and only then as one is inside the action can one take up the question of truth properly. "The more obediently [the Christian] thinks," he states, "the more accurately he will see" (cf. John 7:17).[6]

To be clear, because Balthasar holds beauty to be a transcendental property of being he does indeed consider it to be a divine perfection—that is, intrinsic to God's nature.[7] The most basic Balthasarian principle of aesthetics in the divine economy is that "form" (Gestalt)—the form God's revelation takes in the order of creation and redemption—is so constituted as to irradiate from within itself the light or splendor that illuminates its beauty: "The beautiful is above all a *form*, and the light does not fall on this form from above and from outside, rather it breaks forth from the form's interior."[8] The subjective response to the beautiful of God's revelation in the natural realm serves in a sense as "the foun-dation and foreshadowing of what in the realm of [special] revelation and grace will be the attitude of faith."[9] But the content (Gehalt) within the form of God's self-revelation is perceived in a dialectic of revealing and concealing. So "in view of the nature of the reality involved," writes Balthasar, "the human beholder can be brought to such perception only by the grace of God," whereby those made new in Christ are given the "eyes of faith" to perceive what they could not see before.[10]

We arrive appropriately then at the christological basis of Balthasar's theological aesthetic. As he states, "Christian thought has always known that Jesus Christ is the central form of revelation, around which all other elements in the revelation of our salvation crystallize and are grouped."[11] Small wonder why, for the incarnation of the eternal Son is the archetype and the pinnacle of God's self-expression in the works of creation. God thus reveals himself in and through the Son's incarnate

---

6. Balthasar, *GL*, I, 165.
7. Balthasar equates the glory of God with his divinity (see *GL*, VI, 9), as I also have argued.
8. Balthasar, *GL*, I, 151.
9. Balthasar, *GL*, I, 153.
10. Balthasar, *GL*, I, 154.
11. Balthasar, *GL*, I, 154.

form as the superlative means of expression to communicate himself to the world. Indeed, "God's Incarnation perfects the whole ontology and aesthetics of created Being."[12] With regard to humanity, he writes, "What perfection and infinity really are for man, what emanation and encapsulation, self-surrender and being caught up really are, what 'transfiguration', 'deification', 'immortality' really are and what all the great words of aesthetics signify: it is in the Christ-form that all of it has its measure and its true context."[13] And since the whole of creation shares in the revelation of divine glory, through Christ it also will undergo a total transfiguration. Moreover, to perceive with the eyes of faith the divine beauty of the *Christ-form*—to use Balthasar's term—is to perceive the beauty of God's love in and through it and the hidden depths of God's self-revelation to which it points. In regard to Christ being the normative form of God's self-revelation, Balthasar writes,

> Form is a meaningful unity in a multiplicity of organs; in its fundamental articulations—his Incarnation, his preaching of the kingdom and preparing of the Church, his suffering, his solidarity with the dead and reunion with the Father, his return at the end of history—Christ's dramatic form is the simple self-presentation of a single attitude, which is the effective expression of God's love for the world.[14]

Furthermore, the beauty of the Christ-form as the effective expression of God's love for the world, evokes a response of delight from the human beholder made new in Christ.[15] The evocative nature of divine

---

12. Balthasar, *GL*, I, 29. "[T]o be sure," writes Balthasar, "what is fulfilled superabundantly in the Incarnation is what creation had begun: God's expressing and representing himself, the infinite and free Spirit's creating for himself an expressive body in which he can, first of all, manifest himself but, even better, in which he can conceal himself as 'the one who is ineffably exalted above everything which is outside him and which can be conceived.'" Balthasar, *GL*. I, 457.

13. Balthasar, *GL*, I, 477.

14. Hans Urs von Balthasar, *TD*, II, 87.

15. In this regard his theological aesthetics has great affinity with Barth's. A key difference between them, though, is that Balthasar understood divine beauty in ontological terms (i.e., as a divine attribute and thus of the divine essence itself), while Barth did not. See Chapter 2 subsection, Karl Barth on Divine Beauty. Balthasar was an earnest student and admirer of Barth's theology and established a friendship with him over the course of their careers.

beauty, according to Balthasar, stems from the form itself. That is to say, the form of God's revelation as it appears to us is beautiful because the delight that it arouses in us is founded on the fact that, in the form itself, the truth and goodness of its reality are made manifest to us.[16] Balthasar credits the dynamic of this response to the movement that God effects in a person whereby the "divine Spirit en-thuses and in-spires" a Christian *eros* within the person that elicits a delight in or, even more, a being enraptured by the beauty of God's revelation in Christ.[17] By virtue of the condescension of divine love, such a movement effected by God can overcome the human unwillingness and recalcitrance due to sin, embracing even "the most abysmal ugliness of sin and hell."[18] Most importantly, the whole point of being absorbed by the beauty of God's revelation in Christ is that this absorption leads one out of oneself and into the wonder of the form itself.[19] With this, then, we come full circle wherein the beautiful appears in its rightful place within the total ordered structure. Balthasar sums it all up thus: "God does not come primarily as a teacher for us ("true"), as a useful "redeemer" for us ("good"), but to display and to radiate himself, the splendor of his eternal triune love in that 'disinterestedness' that true love has in common with true beauty. For the glory of God the world was created; through it and for its sake the world is also redeemed."[20]

---

16. Balthasar, *GL*, I, 118. Especially evident in this aspect of Balthasar's theological aesthetics is Aquinas' influence.

17. Balthasar, *GL*, I, 121. For a recommended treatment on this area of Balthasar's theological aesthetic, see Stephen M. Garrett, *God's Beauty-in-Act: Participating in God's Suffering Glory* (Eugene, OR: Pickwick Publications, 2013).

18. Balthasar, *GL*, I, 124.

19. As to the subjectively experienced aspect of beauty, Balthasar, *GL*, I, 247, writes: "Before the beautiful—no, not really *before* but *within* the beautiful—the whole person quivers. He not only 'finds' the beautiful moving; rather, he experiences himself as being moved and possessed by it. The more total this experience is, the less does a person seek and enjoy only the delight that comes through the senses or even through any act of his own; the less also does he reflect on his own acts and states. Such a person has been taken up wholesale into the reality of the beautiful and is now fully subordinate to it, determined by it, animated by it."

20. Hans Urs von Balthasar, *My Work: In Retrospect* (San Francisco: Ignatius Press, 1993), 80. The idea of aesthetic disinterestedness, simply put, is that beauty as *beauty* is not desired as a means to another end.

CHRIST THE IMAGE OF GOD

The christological contours of beauty are developed through the lens of Christology and the theme of the image of God in relation to creation, redemption, and consummation. Christology and the image of God theme thus converge here in consideration of Christ's identity revealed as the incarnate image of God. Our interest is simply to point out that while Christ's identity as the incarnate image of God is the revelation of God's full and unobscured glory in Christ, the perception of it occurred in a dialectic of revealing and concealing. The question this calls up is the following: Did the form of Christ's humanity function to hide and/ or reveal his glory? Our theological aesthetic will need to account for the dialectic and the forms of Christ's humanity, which we will do in the next section.

Stepping back for a bit of redemptive-historical perspective, the incarnation of God in the person of Christ was not exactly how the Old Testament saints envisioned God would fulfill their long-awaited messianic expectation. Yet, as J. Andrew Dearman observes, "When interpreters work back to the Old Testament from the claim that 'whoever has seen me as seen the Father' (John 14:9), they find themselves in mysteriously familiar territory."[21] The territory to which Dearman is referring is the fact that God's self-revelation in the Old Testament is represented anthropomorphically in recurring fashion.[22] It is apparent,

---

21. J. Andrew Dearman, "Theophany, Anthropomorphism, and the *Imago Dei*: Some Observations about the Incarnation in the Light of the Old Testament" in *The Incarnation: An Interdisciplinary Symposium on the Incarnation of the Son of God*, ed. Stephen T. Davis et al. (Oxford: Oxford University Press, 2004), 46.

22. The point that God's self-revelation occurs in anthropomorphic terms includes such things as the Angel of the Lord theophanies as well as God being represented in modes of speech which attribute to him human actions, human emotions, and human form. For convenience I am categorizing all forms of human attribution to God in Scripture as anthropomorphisms. However, I take Graham Cole's point that more precise descriptors are in order: "I propose that when Scripture speaks of divine action in a way that is analogous to human action and roles such as 'speaking', 'seeing' and 'walking', the descriptor to employ is 'anthropopraxism'. However, when Scripture uses terms of God that have their analogues in human emotion, then 'anthropopathism' is the more precise descriptor. Lastly, when Scripture ascribes human organs to God or facial features or limbs, then 'anthropomorphism' is the appropriate term. In fact this last category admits of further refinement. When the text speaks of an appearance of God in human form per se, then we are dealing with an anthropomorphic theophany." Cole, *The God*

in other words, that the invisible God had chosen to reveal himself in accommodatingly human form. Indeed, with redemptive historical hindsight, the later revelation that "God was in Christ" (2 Cor 5:19) can be seen to fit within a biblical pattern of his self-disclosure to Israel, while also disclosing a hidden depth of meaning about the *imago Dei*. Dearman puts it this way:

> [T]he incarnation can be seen as the ultimate "fleshing out" of Israel's "portrait" of God and a goal for which anthropomorphism and the *imago Dei* in humankind were preparation. Although naive and limiting in some respects, the anthropomorphism of the Old Testament can be understood as divine preparation, pointing forward to a Christophany/theophany in which the difficulty of "seeing" God has given way to the Lord who appears in the fulness of time.[23]

The "fleshing out" of Israel's "portrait" of God ultimately in the person of Jesus Christ is writ large in John's Gospel—"we have seen his glory, glory as of the only Son from the Father, full of grace and truth" (John 1:14). Alluded to there is the theophany of God's glory to Moses on Mount Sinai, the very same theophany from which the Lord hid Moses in the cleft of the rock (Exod 33–34). Even though Moses is told by the Lord that no one can see God and live (Exod 33:20),[24] the Lord nevertheless assents to his request to show him his glory (albeit in an eclipsed way),[25] answering: "I will make all my goodness (Heb: טוב; LXX:

Who Became Human, 35. Cole's book provides a helpful and much fuller treatment relevant to our present discussion.

23. Dearman, "Theophany, Anthropomorphism, and the *Imago Dei*," 44. For another recommended treatment relevant to this point, see Jacob Neusner, *The Incarnation of God: The Character of Divinity in Formative Judaism* (Philadelphia: Fortress Press, 1988).

24. Other passages that imply this are Genesis 32:30; Deuteronomy 4:33; 5:24, 26; Judges 6:22; 13:22; and Isaiah 6:5.

25. The study note on Exodus 33:18 in the NET states: "Moses now wanted to see the glory of Yahweh, more than what he had already seen and experienced. He wanted to see God in all his majesty. ... God tells him that he cannot see it fully, but in part. It will be enough for Moses to disclose to him the reality of the divine presence as well as God's moral nature. It would be impossible for Moses to comprehend all of the nature of God, for there is a boundary between God and man. But God would let him see his goodness, the sum of his nature, pass by in a flash."

δόξα) pass before you and will proclaim before you my name 'The LORD'" (Exod 33:19). "This is all highly mysterious," writes David VanDrunen,

> Had not Moses been in the cloud, in the intimate presence of God's glory, for many weeks? Wasn't he the man with whom God actually did speak face to face? A precise explanation eludes us. What is clear, however, is that Moses came to realize that as awesome as God's glory in the cloud may have appeared, the full glory of God actually far surpassed it. Moses enjoyed quite a taste of God's glory, but recognized that it was only an appetizer. The 'glory' and 'face' of God that he saw at the top of Sinai was, from another perspective, not even the equivalent of seeing God's 'back.' This 'man of God' (cf. Deut 33:1) rightly desired even greater communion with his Lord. Once again we see that a glory even better—far better—than what the cloud revealed must be in Israel's future.[26]

In response, the Lord self-describes the goodness/glory that he reveals to Moses in terms of cardinal qualities that pertain to God's very nature and character, namely, his compassion, graciousness, slowness to anger, abounding in love and faithfulness, forgiveness, and justice (Exod 34:5–7). The glory that God formerly had to obscure from Moses' gaze would, in the fullness of time, come to its perfect expression in the glory of God in Christ.

Moreover, as "the only one" who has seen God unmediated and intimately and as the embodied Self-expression of God, Christ alone makes known the Father (cf. John 6:46). John drives home this theme in his Gospel with reference to Jesus' repeated statements concerning it: "And whoever sees me sees him who sent me" (John 12:45); "Whoever has seen me has seen the Father" (John 14:9). And as he approached the end of his mission, Jesus says to the Father, "I made known to them your name, and I will continue to make it known" (John 17:26; cf. 8:25–27). And those who come to "see" and "know" the Father through the Son will by virtue of that be the true *worshipers* of the Father through the Son. As Jesus told the Samaritan woman at the well, "But the hour is coming, and is now here, when the true worshipers will worship the Father in

---

26. David VanDrunen, *God's Glory Alone: The Majestic Heart of Christian Faith and Life* (Grand Rapids: Zondervan, 2015), 58.

spirit and truth, for the Father is seeking such people to worship him" (John 4:23). Balthasar captures the overall point in characteristic style:

> As One and Unique, and yet as one who is to be understood only in the context of mankind's entire history and in the context of the whole created cosmos, Jesus is the Word, the Image, the Expression and the Exegesis of God. ... He *is* what he expresses—namely, God—but he is not whom he expresses—namely, the Father. This incomparable paradox stands as the fountainhead of the Christian aesthetic, and therefore of all aesthetics.[27]

John thus portrays Christ as the "revealer" whose glory consists of revealing God the Father (cf. John 12:44–45). The unveiled and unobscured glory of God that Moses yearned to see, and about which he would have to settle for seeing merely its "aftereffects" (Exod 33:23), was fully composed in the person of Christ. Yet the faculties of natural perception were not enabled in themselves for persons to perceive it. "The glory Christ displayed was not perceived by everyone," notes D. A. Carson. "When he performed a miracle, a 'sign,' he 'revealed his glory' ([John] 2:11), but only his disciples put their faith in him. The miraculous sign was not itself unshielded glory; the eyes of faith were necessary to 'see' the glory that was revealed by the sign" (cf. Mark 6:1–6; Luke 10:23–24; John 12:36–41).[28] Unlike Moses' experience, it is not that the glory of God in Christ became self-eclipsed in any way. The dynamic at work was a spiritual one that functioned as a dialectic of revealing

---

27. Balthasar, *GL*, I, 29.

28. D. A. Carson, *The Gospel according to John* (PNTC; Grand Rapids: Eerdmans, 1991), 130. Carson continues, "Then, as the book progresses, the revelation of Jesus' glory is especially tied to Jesus' cross and the exaltation that ensues—and certainly only those who have faith 'see' the glory of God in the Word-made-flesh in events such as these." Beale, *We Become What We Worship*, 270, contributes the related insight: "Directly after the quotation of Isaiah 6:9–10 in Matt 13:14–15, Jesus likewise says, 'but blessed are your eyes, because they see; and your ears, because they hear' (v. 16), which verse 11 has said is the result of a divine gift: 'to you it has been given to know the mysteries of the kingdom of heaven' (so also Luke 8:10). Luke 10:21–24 expands on its earlier reference to Isaiah 6:9–10 in Luke 8:10 and in Matthew 13:16–17, which underscores even more that the reversal of spiritual blindness and deafness into spiritual 'seeing and hearing' is the gift of God and cannot occur by any independent human determination."

and concealing, requiring the eyes of faith to perceive Christ rightly (cf. Luke 24:15–16).

Given that the beauty of Christ is a quality of his glory, it follows that his beauty was also fully unveiled but was only perceivable according to the same dialectic. The beauty of Christ as the God-man, the incarnate image of God, is inherent in and expressed through his human form. Yet it is precisely because he is both fully God and fully man that the form of Christ is sui generis. Christ is as such *Forma formarum*. As we stated earlier, the question the dialectic calls up is the following: Did the form of Christ's humanity function to hide and/or reveal his glory? We will answer that next in the course of considering Christ's taking on the form of a slave, which is to say that he fulfilled his earthly ministry and accomplished his mission, as the traditional terminology puts it, in a state of humiliation.[29]

CHRIST THE FORM OF A SLAVE

From what we have said above, Christ is the image of God made visible in and expressed through the form of his humanity, and thus the beauty of Christ is inherent in and expressed through that same form. I extend that further, here, arguing that the beauty of Christ is qualified by the theodramatic fittingness that corresponds to the human form his life takes in the economy of salvation. That human form during his earthly career was in the form of a slave. My argument entails that God the Son was not operating incognito as Christ in the form of a slave because his true identity was not actually concealed by a "veil of flesh."

It would seem the claim made above—that the unmitigated "beauty of the Lord" is revealed in the beauty of the Christ-form—stands in an uneasy tension with our other claim that the radiance of Christ's glory during his earthly career involves a dialectic of revealing and concealing. Does it make sense to say that the beauty of the Christ-form is unmitigated if the glory of Christ is concealed? And what factor(s)

---

29. Cf. *Westminster Shorter Catechism*: "Q. 27. Wherein did Christ's humiliation consist? A. Christ's humiliation consisted in his being born, and that in a low condition, made under the law, undergoing the miseries of this life, the wrath of God, and the cursed death of the cross; in being buried, and continuing under the power of death for a time."

determined whether Christ revealed his inherent glory or concealed it—did Christ himself suppress or eclipse the radiance of his glory with the veil of his humanity? In answer to these sorts of questions we can begin with recognizing that the "unmitigated" revelation of God in Christ does not mean the "unmediated" revelation of God himself (*Deus nudus*). As the Lord declared to Moses, no one can see God in his immediate glory and live (Exod 33:20). God in this way remains completely hidden to us (*Deus absconditus*). The incarnation of God the Son, however, is the *mediated* revelation of the glory of God in the person of Jesus Christ, the indivisible God-man. And thus the glory that no one can see and live has been made perceivable in and through the mediated form of Christ in whom "the whole fullness of deity dwells bodily" (Col 2:9). Against the unknowable hidden God, then, is the revealed God (*Deus revelatus/Deus manifestus*) who has made himself known in and through the Son incarnate (cf. Matt 11:25–27; Luke 10:21–22). We can therefore qualify the revelation of God's glory in Christ as being unmitigated yet mediated. Bernard Ramm elaborates on this point as follows:

> The communication between this great God and finite, limited man must thus always be a *mediated* communication. This is not a judgment about the "impurity" of the world, which would force God to communicate indirectly lest he contaminate himself with the world. It is based upon the transcendence of Creator over the creature. Therefore, when God comes to humanity in revelation, He comes through *mediators*. The prophetic word is a *mediated* word. The theophany is a *mediated* manifestation of God. The incarnation is the glory of God, *mediated* through the human nature of Christ.[30]

This does not tell us, however, what it means to say that God's glory in Christ operates in a dialectic of revealing and concealing, or clarify the aesthetic dimension pertaining to it. To address these points we will first render a theological interpretation of Philippians 2:6–8, the first half of the Philippians Christ-hymn, from which our constructive argument will be developed.

---

30. Bernard Ramm, "Angels," in *Basic Christian Doctrines*, ed. Carl F. H. Henry (New York: Holt, Rinehart and Winston, 1962), 66–67.

PHILIPPIANS 2:6–8 EXEGETICALLY UNPACKED

What the hymn describes *in nuce* are three different states of God the Son, namely, his preexistence as God, his state of humiliation on earth, and his enthronement/session in heaven.[31] The context that immediately precedes in Philippians 2:1–5 sets up the Christ-hymn to apply as an ethical-relational paradigm. With all of its marvelous Christology compactly presented, Paul not only meant for the hymn to reinforce or inform Christians about the character and grand story of Christ, but especially to inform the believing community on what being like Christ means in their relations with one another—i.e., to "have the same attitude toward one another that Christ Jesus had" (Phil 2:5 NET). On that basic point concerning Paul's purpose of the hymn virtually all biblical scholars agree: Christ is portrayed as the exemplar for the Christian community in their interpersonal relationships, although opinions vary in notable ways on how all this is carried out at both the spiritual and practical levels of the Christian life.[32]

The grammatical and interpretive challenges pertaining to our text are widely acknowledged and debated. "[M]ost of the difficulties with interpretation," states Fee, "lie with the first of the two sentences (Phil 2:6–7), where the ideas are profound and full of theological grist, and the language not at all simple."[33] These ideas are expressed in a sequence of difficult wordings whose meanings we will respectively unpack. The wordings at issue in verse 6 are the following:

---

31. The term "states" refers to "different planes of being" of God the Son's singular history.

32. A noteworthy exception to the "ethical" (or paraenetic) view given here is the "kerygmatic" view, which sees the hymn strictly as portraying the drama of salvation. In her intriguing article on the Christ-hymn, Susan Grove Eastman, "Philippians 2:6–11: Incarnation as Mimetic Participation," *JSPL* 1 no. 1 (Spring 2011): 2, n6, notes the following: "A purely 'kerygmatic' interpretation was argued forcefully by Ernst Käsemann, "A Critical Analysis of Philippians 2:5–11," *JTC* 5 (1968): 45–88; followed by Ralph P. Martin, *Carmen Christi: Philippians 2:5–11 in Recent Interpretation and in the Setting of Early Christian Worship* (Cambridge: Cambridge University Press, 1967), 294–96, 309–11. [Alternatively,] Troels Engberg-Pedersen claims the primary motif of the letter is 'that of *Paul modeling Christ to the Philippians*,' in *Paul and the Stoics* (Louisville: Westminster John Knox, 2000), 91, emphasis original. See pp. 81–130 for a full discussion."

33. Gordon D. Fee, *Pauline Christology: An Exegetical-Theological Study* (Peabody, MA: Hendrickson Publishers, 2007), 375.

v. 6a — ὃς ἐν μορφῇ θεοῦ ὑπάρχων

v. 6b — οὐχ ἁρπαγμὸν ἡγήσατο τὸ εἶναι ἴσα θεῷ

The relationship of the present participle ὑπάρχων ("being") in verse 6a to its verbal connection in verse 6b is debated.[34] Although these translations each nuance the participial phrase differently, the basic meaning with which the hymn starts off remains the same, namely, a confessional statement about Christ's preexistence as God. G. Walter Hansen sets out how the hymn grammatically presents this in its flow of thought through verse 7:

> In this narrative sentence *existing in the form of God* comes before the actions described by the verbs, *he emptied* himself, *taking* the form of a slave and becoming in the likeness of men. This temporal relation of the present participle to the aorist finite verb and the two aorist participles points to the preexistence of *the one existing in the form of God* before he emptied himself, took the form of a slave, and became in the likeness of men.[35]

This understanding represents the consensus view, which affirms that the hymn begins with Christ as preexistent in eternity and then proceeds to describe his incarnation.[36] In this light the phrase μορφή θεοῦ ("the form of God") denotes not merely that which characterizes God's "form" or "shape" in terms of his external appearance or features,

---

34. Most Bibles translate the participial phrase of Philippians 2:6a with either a concessive use or circumstantial use of the participle. The former case is translated along these lines, "Who, though he existed in the form of God," and the latter case along these: "Who, being in the form of God." But then there are some commentators who argue that a causative use of the participle is implied, translating the text in this way: "Who, precisely because he was in the form of God." See Gerald F. Hawthorne, *Philippians*, rev. and exp. by Ralph P. Martin (WBC 43; Waco, TX: Word, 2004), 116.

35. G. Walter Hansen, *The Letter to the Philippians* (PNTC; Grand Rapids: Eerdmans, 2009), 134.

36. In regard to whether Christians would have already had an understanding of Christ's preexistence as God prior to the time of Paul's writing this letter, Larry W. Hurtado, *How on Earth Did Jesus Become a God? Historical Questions about Earliest Devotion to Jesus* (Grand Rapids: Eerdmans, 2005), 101, submits that "in these verses [Phil 2:6–7] the use of compact phrasing without explanation (e.g., 'in the form of God') suggests that readers were expected to recognize what was being referred to, which would mean that well before this epistle the idea of Jesus' 'preexistence' had become a part of Christian belief."

but rather here "form" denotes that which truly characterizes a thing's reality—that reality being Christ's preexistence in the essential nature and character of God.[37] As Peter O'Brien puts it, "On this view the μορφή θεοῦ does not refer to external appearance alone since possession of the form implied participation in its nature or character."[38] From an aesthetic angle this affirms that here form (*Gestalt*) and content (*Gehalt*) are perfectly united (i.e., the nature of God within the form of God is one divine essence that is one life).

From texts like John 17:5 and Hebrews 1:3, a number of commentators make the connection that if "being in the form of God" implies being/participating in the divine nature, then the μορφή θεοῦ is tantamount to the δόξα θεοῦ. In my view this connection is indeed correct. The criticisms brought against this view cite as problematic the following: (1) μορφή and δόξα are not synonymous or equivalent terms, and (2) δόξα does not apply equally to the parallel phrase in verse 7 to render the words by δόξα δούλου.[39] I will address the second point of criticism below when dealing with verse 7, but the first criticism simply "misses the point that verse 6 refers to Christ's eternal δόξα not because μορφή equals δόξα but because the μορφή θεοῦ is δόξα."[40] Hansen derives the same conclusion from the biblical connection between form and the perception of God's manifest glory-presence: "If we conclude that the *form of God* means the glory of God and that the glory of God is intimately related with the being of God, then we will also conclude that the phrase existing in the form of God points to Christ *being in very nature God*."[41] Our work earlier in considering theologically the glory

---

37. L&N 58.2 s.v. μορφή: "the nature or character of something, with emphasis upon both the internal and external form—'nature, character.'"

38. Peter T. O'Brien, *The Epistle to the Philippians: A Commentary on the Greek Text* (NIGTC; Grand Rapids: Eerdmans, 1991), 208. Similarly, Gordon D. Fee, *Paul's Letter to the Philippians* (NICNT; Grand Rapids: Eerdmans, 1995), 207, writes, "This, then, is what it means for Christ to be "in the 'form' of God"; it means "to be equal with God," not in the sense that the two phrases are identical, but that both point to the same reality."

39. O'Brien, *The Epistle to the Philippians*, 208.

40. O'Brien, *The Epistle to the Philippians*, 209, citing Robert B. Strimple, "Philippians 2:5–11 in Recent Studies: Some Exegetical Conclusions," *WTJ* 41 no. 2 (Spring 1979): 261.

41. Hansen, *The Letter to the Philippians*, 138.

of God in the light of the total biblical testimony pays forward here in validating this meaning of "the form of God" in verse 6. To recall, the immanent glory of God comprehends all God's attributes—all that is essential to his nature and character—and is thus identical in meaning to the altogether perfection of God.[42] This coincides well with our claim here that the phrase μορφή θεοῦ refers to Christ's preexistence in the essential nature of God.

Verse 6b essentially expands on what Christ "being in the form of God" means in set up for verse 7. In the syntactical structure of verse 6b, the infinitive phrase εἶναι ἴσα θεῷ ("to be equal with God") at the end of this clause serves as the subject of an implied "to be," with ἁρπαγμὸν at the front operating as the predicate noun. "Put into 'ordinary' English word order," states Fee, "it would thus read, '[He] considered the being equal with God [to be] not *harpagmon*.'"[43] The Greek term ἁρπαγμός is not used anywhere else in the New Testament or the Septuagint (and only rarely in Greek literature), so settling its meaning has posed a challenge for scholars. Notwithstanding, the definition that has become generally accepted now denotes something to be selfishly exploited that is already possessed.[44] Thus, looking at verse 6 altogether, its meaning follows this line of thought: "in the situation of 'being in the form of God,' [Christ] chose not to exploit for his own advantage the equality with God that was involved."[45] The issue pertaining here, then, is not whether Christ gains equality or keeps it. Rather, it pertains to that which characterizes his essential nature, namely, quintessential selflessness. For one so designated as being in the form of God, the meaning of verse 6 stands in diametric contrast to the rapaciousness for prerogative, power, and glory that human rulers (and the deities in the Greco-Roman pantheon), who so often assumed the status of demigod, exploited for their own advantage.[46]

---

42. See Chapter 2 section, Divine Beauty and Divine Glory.

43. Fee, *Pauline Christology*, 380.

44. For a helpful discussion on the possible definitions and alternatives worth noting, see Hansen, *The Letter to the Philippians*, 142–46.

45. Hurtado, *How on Earth Did Jesus Become a God?*, 97.

46. Hansen, *The Letter to the Philippians*, 145–46, aptly summarizes verse 6 as follows: "The first stanza of the hymn lifts the veil between time and eternity to reveal the choice of one existing in the form of God and equal with God. This person

With the preceding in mind, we will segue now to an examination of the sequence of clauses in verse 7, which is given as follows:

v. 7a — ἀλλὰ ἑαυτὸν ἐκένωσεν

v. 7b — μορφὴν δούλου λαβών

v. 7c — ἐν ὁμοιώματι ἀνθρώπων γενόμενος

v. 7d — καὶ σχήματι εὑρεθεὶς ὡς ἄνθροπος[47]

Verse 7a translates simply, "but he emptied himself." This clause begins an extended description that illuminates what is divinely entailed in Christ being in the form of God and choosing not to exploit for his own advantage his equality with God. The obvious question here is—of what exactly did Christ empty himself? Hansen is again instructive in briefly setting out the three main views of Christ's *kenōsis* (as it is referred to) that have sustained attention and adherents: (1) The kenotic theory, (2) The incarnation view, and (3) The servant of the Lord portrait.[48] The kenotic theory, to which the animadversion "incarnation by divine suicide"[49] aptly applies, has little theological merit, in my view, and does not warrant further discussion here.[50] The servant

---

did not view his divine being and rank as something to use for his own selfish advantage. Such a view was inconsistent with his character."

47. The versification of Philippians 2:7 and 8 is according to the versification in the NA28 and UBS4 editions of the Greek text. Some translations, however, break the verses in front of verse 7d, with the only difference being the versification of that material.

48. For his discussion of these views, see Hansen, *The Letter to the Philippians*, 146–50.

49. David J. MacLeod, "Imitating the Incarnation of Christ: An Exposition of Philippians 2:5-8," *BSac* 158 (July-Sept 2001): 317, citing Everard Digges La Touche, *The Person of Christ in Modern Thought* (London: James Clarke, 1912), 355.

50. The post-Hegelian kenotic Christology of the nineteenth/early twentieth centuries, whose leading exponents include Gottfried Thomasius (1802–1875), Wolfgang Friedrich Gess (1819–1891), and Hugh Ross Mackintosh (1870–1936), is not being reckoned with here. Suffice it to say that regarding this school of thought the problematic penchant, as Thomas Thompson so wryly puts it, is to run "the kenosis all the way empty." In this movement the Chalcedonian axioms were plainly compromised in order to introduce the concept of potentiality into the Godhead, and affirm, inter alia, that only some divine attributes pertain to God's relation to the world *ad extra*. The net result was that the orthodox meanings attached to the hypostatic union and the Son's co-divinity were compromised or denied. Regarding this see Thomas R. Thompson, "Nineteenth-Century Kenotic Christology: The Waxing, Waning, and Weighing of a Quest for a Coherent Orthodoxy," in *Exploring*

of the Lord portrait pertains to the debate that persists regarding the hymn's connections to the Servant of the Lord in Isaiah 42–53 and is not critical to our constructive argument.[51] The incarnation view in my judgment offers the soundest interpretation, which I now present.

While the verb κενόω in verse 7a is translated as "emptied" (metaphorically, in context), it can also carry another sense of emptying, "to make void or of no effect; to deprive."[52] In either case what has often been assumed is that κενόω *requires* a genitive qualifier, which would mean for interpreting our present text that Christ "emptied himself" *of something*. According to the incarnation view, this understanding of κενόω is mistaken. It is not that Christ emptied himself *of* something, but that he poured himself out, as it were; perhaps the better picture is that he emptied himself *into* something.[53] And what Christ emptied

---

Kenotic Christology: The Self-Emptying of God, ed. C. Stephen Evans (Oxford: Oxford University Press, 2006), 74–111. For a helpful treatment that addresses contemporary proposals and issues of kenotic theory, see Vanhoozer, *Remythologizing Theology*, chapter 3: The new kenotic-perichoretic relational ontotheology: some "classical" concerns. Another view of Christ's *kenōsis* not included in the three main views that Hansen gives is what Vanhoozer describes as "kenotic panentheism." Kenotic panentheism has gained prominence in recent years among theologians who advocate a distinctly Christian version of panentheism. It can be considered a cousin to the kenotic theory that Hansen discusses. Vanhoozer summarizes it as follows: "Panentheists argue that God, in order to create, voluntarily exercised self-restraint, especially in the realm of power and knowledge, in order to accord creatures the 'room' to be themselves. This involves respecting both the integrity of the process of nature and the free decisions of human beings. Kenosis, in the context of panentheism, refers to God's self-contraction and self-limitation, especially with regard to omnipotence and omniscience, in order to create something other than himself. The argument, briefly, is that God voluntarily empties or limits himself out of love for the world so that the world has the space and freedom to be itself." (130–31).

51. The scholarly consensus widely acknowledges the allusions in Philippians 2:6–11 to the portrait of the Servant of the Lord in Isaiah 42–53. But opinions vary as to the degree of correspondence involved. It is certainly the case that the themes of abasement and exaltation figure prominently in the Servant Song in Isaiah and the Philippians' Christ-hymn. The description of Christ's exaltation in Philippians 2:6–11 clearly alludes as well to Isaiah 45:23. Others argue, however, that the hymn's various linguistic and conceptual links to Isaiah 42–53 should be seen more as general background—echoes not tie lines. For a recommended work of the various views represented, see Ralph P. Martin and Brian J. Dodd, eds., *Where Christology Began: Essays on Philippians 2* (Louisville: Westminster John Knox, 1998).

52. BDAG 539 s.v. κενόω 2. Cf. Romans 4:14; 1 Corinthians 1:17; 9:15; 2 Corinthians 9:3.

53. Cf. Vanhoozer, *Remythologizing Theology*, 430: "The incarnation and cross alike indicate that God is the one who freely pours out his own life for others. Herein

himself into is given in the extended description that follows—his taking the form of a slave, coming in the likeness of human beings, and being found in appearance as a man. We need not be confused terminologically by language of the Son's "emptying himself" and language of his "assuming humanity," which sounds more like the Son's taking humanity up into himself than emptying himself into humanity. While the referent is the same for both, the former is associated with the Son's act of *kenōsis* and the latter is associated better with the Son's hypostatic union as the God-man, Christ Jesus. What the incarnation view of the *kenōsis* means, then, is that "the self-emptying of Christ is the incarnation in the form of a slave of the one existing in the form of God."[54] Or to put it in pithier terms, the Son condescended to descend, and descended by condescending.

By way of contrastive metaphor, verse 7b specifies the form that Christ took in his condescension from "being in the form of God" to his *kenōsis* in becoming incarnate, namely, that of a slave. There is no reason to suppose that μορφή carries any different sense here than it does in verse 6a. Indeed, its parallel use in the hymn is far from incidental. The phrase μορφὴν δούλου thus does not refer to Christ merely having the external appearance of a slave, but implies his participation in the nature or character of a slave. "The combination μορφὴν δούλου here," states Fee, "probably means something close to the corresponding verb in Gal 5:13 (= 'perform the duties of a slave')."[55] Implied in this, then, is the fundamental disposition of Christ's self-emptying wherein he participates in our humanity for the purpose of serving humanity, just as he himself declared—"the Son of Man came not to be served but to serve, and to give his life as a ransom for many" (Mark 10:45). This shows how bound up Christ's taking the form of a slave is with his mission to give his life as a ransom for many. The rest of the Christ-hymn affirms as much. And as Hansen observes, "Whether or

---

is love: that the Son of God actively surrenders his divine status, pouring himself into human form and then pouring himself out to the point of death (Phil 2:6–8)."

54. Hansen, *The Letter to the Philippians*, 147.

55. Fee, *Pauline Christology*, 385. Cf. L&N, 58.2 s.v. μορφή: In view of the lack of a closely corresponding lexical item such as "nature," it may be necessary to restructure the form of Philippians 2:7 as "he became truly a servant."

not this hymn reflects the tradition of the incident in the life of Jesus, where Jesus takes the role of slave and washes his disciples' feet (John 13), that incident illustrates the meaning of this line in the hymn" (cf. Luke 12:37; 22:27).[56]

In condensed strokes, the rest of verse 7 and verse 8 illuminate what Christ taking the form of a slave entailed. As verse 7c spells out, he did so by "coming to be" (γενόμενος) in the "likeness" (ὁμοίωμα) of human beings (or men, ἄνθρωποι). As compared to the present participle ὑπάρχων in verse 6a, which indicates Christ always already having existed as God, the aorist participle γενόμενος indicates an "inception" to his humanity, that is, his "becoming" a human. Expressing the truth of Christ's *always being* and his *historically becoming*, Bavinck puts it simply, "The incarnation is the unity of being (ἐγὼ εἰμί, John 8:58) and becoming (σὰρξ ἐγένετο, John 1:14)."[57] As to the meaning of ὁμοίωμα, the idea carried here is "likeness" in terms of "commonality of experiences" and "similarity of appearance."[58] Although ὁμοίωμα does not contradict or deny that Christ took on the form of a slave *possessing a true human nature*, it still begs the question regarding the degree of similarity between Christ and human beings.[59] Concerning this we need look no further than within the context of the hymn itself. On the one hand, the whole thrust of verses 7–8 depicts Christ's identification with humanity in total self-surrender to accomplish in perfect obedience his mission from the Father. In this essential way of fully identifying with even the least and lowliest, Christ's "likeness" to human beings is the deepest similarity. On the other hand, he remained "in the form of God," fully divine in every respect, and thus he was not just human, he was and is evermore the God-man. Moreover, Christ remained sinless from birth to death, in perfect obedience to the Father who exalted him to the superlative (Phil 2:9–11; cf. Heb 4:15). "The ambiguity of the phrase *in the likeness* [thus] preserves both the similarity of Christ to human beings

---

56. Hansen, *The Letter to the Philippians*, 151.

57. Bavinck, *RD*, 1:380.

58. BDAG 500 s.v. ὁμοίωμα 1, 2.

59. BDAG 500 s.v. ὁμοίωμα 3: In the light of what Paul says about Jesus in general it is probable that he uses our word [in Phil 2:7] to bring out both that Jesus in his earthly career was similar to sinful humans and yet not totally like them.

in his full humanity and the dissimilarity of Christ to fallen humanity in his equality with God and his sinless obedience."[60]

As the last of the clauses in this line of the hymn, verse 7d serves to complement or reinforce by way of repetition the authentic nature of Christ's humanity. The phrase σχήματι ὡς ἄνθρωπος carries a distinct accent on the "externals" or outward appearance of Christ's human form,[61] though no mere simulacrum of a man is in view.[62] The Greek term σχῆμα ("appearance"), in hymnic fashion, links with μορφή (v. 7b) and ὁμοίωμα (v. 7c) "to form a threefold reiteration of the one fundamentally important idea: Christ in the incarnation identified himself with humanity, while he retained his distinctiveness as appearing in a form that could offer obedience to God."[63] The point extended in verse 7d is simply that Christ looked like an ordinary man in every way and to everybody. He was God living out a genuinely human life, albeit appearing so in his state of humiliation while he fulfilled his mission.[64]

The state of humiliation that Christ lived out in fulfillment of his mission is all summed up in verse 8. His condescension from existence in the glory of God to his incarnation in the form of a slave is depicted now as reaching its full depth—a depth out of which radiates his glory. The perfect constancy of Christ's character is reflected over the extended description given in verses 6–8—that is, his not exploiting

---

60. Hansen, *The Letter to the Philippians*, 153.

61. L&N, 58.7 s.v. σχημα: "the form or nature of something, with special reference to its outer form or structure—'form, nature, structure.'"

62. J. Schneider, σχημα, TDNT, 7:956, states, "σχήματι εὑρεθεὶς ὡς ἄντρωπος does not merely express the reality of His humanity. There is special stress on the fact that throughout His life, even to the death on the cross, Jesus was in the humanity demonstrated by His earthly form. The εὑρεθείς expresses the truth that this fact could be seen by anybody, σχημα does not merely indicate the coming of Jesus, or His physical constitution, or the natural determination of His earthly life, or the shape of His moral character. It denotes the 'mode of manifestation.' The reference is to His whole nature and manner as man. In this respect the outward 'bearing' He assumes corresponds to His inner being."

63. Hawthorne, *Philippians*, 120.

64. MacLeod, "Imitating the Incarnation of Christ," 325, quoting idem, *Philippians 2 and Christology* (Leicester, UK: TSF, 1976), 17, puts it like this: "They saw 'the appearance of a man and that was all. They saw ordinariness. They saw nothing to distinguish Him physically. There were no insignia [i.e., no aura, no halo] of His unique divine status. There was only ordinariness, poverty, frailty, unpopularity and human rejection.'"

for his own advantage his equality with God but instead "emptying himself" is reaffirmed in his not exploiting for his own advantage his divinity as the man Jesus Christ "humbling himself." Hansen captures affectively the text and subtext of the hymn's first half:

> The first three stanzas do not lift up our eyes to the heavens to see the wonders of creation; they do not even lift up our hearts by showing us wonderful miracles of healing and deliverance; they take us down, down, down to the deepest, darkest hell-hole in human history to see the horrific torture, unspeakable abuse, and bloody execution of a *slave* on a *cross*. This hymn celebrates the death of a *slave* on *cross* because, although he is forever the one existing in the form of God, he is on that cross by his own deliberate choice to *empty himself* and *humble himself*.[65]

As verse 8 reads, the obedience "to the point of death, even death on a cross" epitomizes Christ's self-humbling, which artfully anticipates in juxtaposition his being "highly exalted" by God in verse 9. That his obedience was rendered to God the Father is implied in the hymn's second half, but not solely to the Father. As we saw above, Christ participated in our humanity in the form of a slave for the purpose of serving humanity. "Christ's acceptance of death, therefore, was ... his ultimate act of obedience to God in his self-giving service to people."[66] Not to be missed here, the narrative of the first half of the hymn is framed for rhetorical effect with the sharpest imaginable contrast between that of the glory of Christ being in the form of God and the ignominy of his death on a cross.

---

65. Hansen, *The Letter to the Philippians*, 158–59. Worth citing here is Martin Hengel's comment, "Jesus did not die a gentle death like Socrates, with his cup of hemlock, much less passing on 'old and full of years' like the patriarchs of the Old Testament. Rather, he died like a slave or a common criminal, in torment, on a tree of shame." Hengel, *Crucifixion* (Philadelphia: Fortress Press, 1977), 90, quoted in MacLeod, "Imitating the Incarnation of Christ," 329.

66. Hawthorne, *Philippians*, 122.

THE UNMITIGATED BEAUTY OF CHRIST
WHILE IN THE FORM OF A SLAVE

Building on the exegetical groundwork of Philippians 2:6–8, I wish to address now the matter mentioned at the beginning of this section that the beauty of Christ while in the form of a slave (i.e., during his earthly career) is an aspect of his glory, which itself involves a dialectic of revealing and concealing. But what does it mean to say that Christ's glory in this form was revealed or, conversely, concealed? And how should we view the aesthetic dimension pertaining to this? That is the focus of our theological interpretation pursued here.

In regard to the incarnation view of Christ's *kenōsis* presented earlier, I argued that the extended description given in Philippians 2:6–8 reflects the perfect constancy of character of the person of Christ who humbled himself in perfect obedience to the Father. O'Brien puts it this way in reference to the Christ-hymn: "Not that he *exchanged* the form of God for the form of a slave, but that he *manifested* the form of God in the form of slave."[67] In Christ God is fully and truly with us as fully and truly one of us. And thus the self-emptying in the incarnation of Christ of the one who was in the form of God is the full embodiment (literally and figuratively) of the heart of God. This means that any ostensible dissonance between the self-revelatory nature of God's actions in Christ during his earthly career and the essential nature of God in himself is not an actual dissonance. Speaking to this same point, Bauckham rightly states, "The identity of God—who God is—is revealed as much in self-abasement and service as it is in exaltation and rule. The God who is high can also be low, because God is God not in seeking his own advantage but in self-giving. His self-giving in abasement and service ensures that his sovereignty over all things is also a form of his self-giving."[68]

With the above discussion in mind, then, I propose that the beauty of Christ is qualified by the fittingness that corresponds to the respective forms of his life in the states of his: (a) pre-incarnate existence,

---

67. O'Brien, *The Epistle to the Philippians*, 216.

68. Richard Bauckham, *Jesus and the God of Israel: God Crucified and Other Studies on the New Testament's Christology of Divine Identity* (Grand Rapids: Eerdmans, 2009), 45.

(b) humiliation, and (c) exaltation. In regard to his economic identity, the respective forms of Christ's life in the states of his humiliation and exaltation each radiate the glory of God with perfect fittingness even though mediated in apparent outward difference.[69] Concerning the state of his humiliation, we must bear in mind that "the incarnation was not the capping or crowning of an incomplete structure; it was a rescue operation. The Son's coming was to save the world (John 3:17; 12:47)."[70] What Christ's state of humiliation involved, writes Balthasar, is "that the God of plenitude ... poured himself out, not only into creation, but emptied himself into the modalities of an existence determined by sin, corrupted by death and alienated from God."[71] Christ's humanity in the form of a slave was no mere guise, though; it was the assumption of form that was most befitting for him to take in accordance with his role as the Messiah, "born under the law, to redeem those who were under the law" (Gal 4:4-5). It would not have been as fitting, in other words, for Christ to have assumed any form in his earthly career other than that which the undertaking of his role as the Messiah called for, namely, the form of a slave. Given how the Messiah was to identify himself with humanity—with even the least and lowliest—while appearing in a form that could offer perfect obedience to God, one discerns the fittingness of the Son rather than the Father or the Spirit undertaking the role of the Messiah in the form of a slave. Yet in that form was nonetheless the radiance of his glory, and expressed naturally by that, the radiating quality of his beauty—a beauty reflective of and dramatized in the self-giving love of God.

The Revealing and Concealing Dialectic of Christ's Glory

We have spoken in this chapter about Christ's glory during his earthly ministry as operating in a dialectic of revealing and concealing, although we have not yet presented if anything else was determinative besides the eyes of faith to "see" his glory. Regarding this, a commonly held view

---

69. Cf. Stephen E. Fowl, *Philippians* (THNTC; Grand Rapids: Eerdmans, 2005), 93: "Indeed, it may be the case that it is precisely Christ's taking on the 'form' of a slave which definitively makes God's glory visible to humans."

70. Hughes, *The True Image*, 14.

71. Balthasar, *GL*, I, 461.

or at any rate a widely purported one is that Christ's actual glory, that is, his divine glory, was hidden or veiled beneath his humanity during his earthly career. In short, Christ's "flesh" acted as a reverse shield to prevent his real glory from being openly seen. Calvin's comments on this are representative:

> [Christ] showed that although he was God and could have set forth his glory directly to the world he gave up his right and voluntarily "emptied himself." He took the image of a servant, and content with such lowness, allowed his divinity to be hidden by a "veil of flesh." ... [So] for a time the divine glory did not shine, but only human likeness was manifest in a lowly and abased condition.[72]

The idea one could naively draw from this, even if not considered implicit here, is that the veil of Christ's flesh could be activated in a kind of "toggle switch" mode whereby his glory could be selectively revealed or concealed as he willed to do depending on the faith of those involved (and in accord with the will of the Father). Even if that idea is patently rejected (rightly so, in my view), the idea that Christ's glory was hidden by the form of his own humanity does not square well with my claim argued earlier that Christ manifested the form of God *in* the form of a slave, and in so doing his life radiated the glory of God's very nature most fittingly. But if Christ's glory was actually concealed by his human form, then God the Son operated totally incognito as Christ in the form of a slave. Indeed, noted theologians *have* advocated just such a view. In his dogmatic study, *The Person of Christ*, G. C. Berkouwer entitles one of his chapters "Christ Incognito?" and cites Emil Brunner as one prominent exponent. He writes that for Brunner "God reveals himself in Jesus Christ but he does it in the total hiddenness of the flesh. ... The main revelational category of Christ's entire life is that of the incognito: revelation in absolute concealment."[73] More recently, Stephen Wellum, following Donald Macleod's lead, states along similar lines that the three movements in Christ's state of humiliation depicted in Philippians 2:7–9

---

72. Calvin, *Institutes* 2.13.2, ed. McNeill, trans. Battles.

73. G. C. Berkouwer, *The Person of Christ*, trans. John Vriend (Grand Rapids: Eerdmans, 1955), 333–34. "Christ Incognito?" is the title to chapter XIII. Berkouwer argues against the incognito view.

altogether amount to *krypsis*, that is, total hiddenness or veiledness of his divine glory. "Taken together," he writes, "these three movements of the divinely exalted Son into the humiliation of Christ become three layers of veiling that temporarily hide his God-equal glory. In this sense, then, we can say that the full *kenōsis* of Christ involved the near-complete *krypsis* ("hiddenness") of his divine glory, but not the loss of his divine nature and attributes."[74]

As Christopher Holmes points out, however, there is good reason to question the assumption that the humanity of Jesus functioned as a veil, for that "suggests a competitive view of the relationship between the divinity of God and the humanity of God which detracts from the truth of God's being as a being which includes humanity."[75] Holmes' point is that God's glory in Christ all during his earthly career is best appreciated not in an apophatic way—that is, as veiled by his humanity—but in a cataphatic way—that is, as revealed in and through his humanity, "which God includes in himself as the very form of his own self-witness."[76] On this view there is no compromise to the Chalcedonian axioms and the orthodox meanings attached to the hypostatic union. The humanity that Christ took on in the form of a slave is simply being affirmed here in the most robustly self-revelatory way. This is in line with our earlier point that Christ's human form was no mere guise; his form was perfectly fitting in accordance with his role as the Messiah. Holmes expands on this:

> God does not include a veil in himself. The humanity of Jesus, his lived life in obedience to his Father's will in fulfillment of Torah, and the existence of all flesh in him, is what the divine Son elects for himself in obedience to his Father. It is not a *veil*; rather, God

---

74. Stephen J. Wellum, *God the Son Incarnate: The Doctrine of Christ* (Wheaton, IL: Crossway, 2016), 171. Wellum cites the following quote from Donald Macleod, *The Person of Christ* (Downers Grove, IL: InterVarsity Press, 1998), 218: "In becoming incarnate God not only accommodates himself to human weakness: he buries his glory under veil after veil so that it is impossible for flesh and blood to recognize him. As he hangs on the cross, bleeding, battered, powerless and forsaken, the last thing he looks like is God. Indeed, he scarcely looks human." (183, n404)

75. Christopher R. J. Holmes, "Disclosure without Reservation: Re-evaluating Divine Hiddenness," *Neue Zeitschrift für systematische Theologie und Religionsphilosophie* 48 no. 3 (2006): 379.

76. Holmes, "Disclosure without Reservation," 376.

reveals himself in the humanity of the Son and accomplishes and fulfills his covenant purposes in him for all flesh.[77]

God the Son, as such, was in no actual way operating incognito as Christ in the form of a slave because his true identity was not actually concealed by a "veil of flesh."[78] The self-revelatory nature of God's actions in Christ during his earthly career means that the essential nature of God—and thus the glory of God—is in fact revealed. To reiterate Bauckham's point earlier, this reveals God not in seeking his own advantage but in self-giving. Holmes is again incisive here:

> If God's glory and majestic splendor is equated with God's propensity for self-giving, then what positive work is left for an account of divine hiddenness? Would it not be better to forsake categories of veiling and unveiling, primary hiddenness and secondary hiddenness, in favor of the *glory* of God which bespeaks God's propensity for self-giving, for giving himself as he is, a self-giving which includes humanity as the place where God presents himself thus.[79]

As counterintuitive as it may at first seem, then, there is good reason to say that God the Son was not incognito as Christ in the form of a slave, nor was the form of his humanity concealing his divine glory. As I have argued the case, the aspect of Christ's fittingness in accordance with his role as the Messiah is an essential element of the reasoning here. A parallel to the counterintuitive sense of God's actions in Christ can be drawn from 1 Corinthians 1:18-25 concerning God's wisdom and power manifest in Christ crucified. To those who are perishing, Paul says, the message of Christ crucified is simply foolishness and weakness to the extreme. Yet believers do well in recognizing that the divine wisdom and power identified there may *seem* counterintuitive to the natural mind, but in no actual way are these attributes incognito. It is the opposite case, for in Christ crucified God's wisdom and power are openly

---

77. Holmes, "Disclosure without Reservation," 378.

78. With regard to the so-called Messianic secret passages in Mark's Gospel, the fact of Christ's being in the form of a slave was not itself his being incognito even if in the course of his mission he conducted himself oftentimes covertly to keep his identity and his mission out of the limelight until the time was right.

79. Holmes, "Disclosure without Reservation," 377.

revealed in theodramatic display at the cross. Our theological aesthetic sees the fittingness of God's *wisdom* and *power* manifest in Christ crucified as being perfectly correlated with the fittingness that characterizes the *beauty* of Christ crucified. For in and through the form of Christ crucified is the radiance of his glory, radiating a beauty reflective of and dramatized in the self-giving love of God.[80] Of course, there is also the matter of the event of Christ's transfiguration, which ostensibly lends support to the idea that Christ's glory indeed *was* hidden by the veil of his own flesh. I address the transfiguration in the last section of this chapter, but suffice it to say for now that the glory of Christ revealed at his transfiguration was likewise most befitting in accordance with the outworking of redemptive-history and the divine purposes at that particular point in Christ's public ministry.

In understanding the respective forms of Christ's life in the economy of salvation as each radiating the glory of God most fittingly, we can affirm without reservation that Christ lived in a real state of humiliation followed by a real change of state in his exaltation. Contra the view put forward by some, I am positing that there was a temporal transition of the forms of Christ's life in the economy of salvation from a real state of humiliation to a real state of exaltation.[81] At the same time, I submit that the revelation of the glory of God in Christ is not at all attenuated or compromised in Christ's former state relative to his latter one, nor is there any aporia here. The temporal distinction between Christ's state of humiliation and his state of exaltation involves

---

80. I address the beauty of Christ crucified in Chapter 5, discussed under Christ's Kingly Glory on the Cross.

81. For example, the proposal by Jeremy R. Treat, "Exaltation in and through Humiliation: Rethinking the States of Christ" in *Christology, Ancient and Modern: Explorations in Constructive Dogmatics*, ed. Oliver D. Crisp and Fred Sanders, (Grand Rapids: Zondervan, 2013), 104, rejects the idea of a clear temporal distinction between Christ's states of humiliation and exaltation. Treat, 104, argues instead the following: "In response to the common understanding of exaltation after humiliation, I propose that the proper view is exaltation *in* humiliation within a broader progression of exaltation *through* humiliation. ... By 'exaltation through humiliation' I am maintaining a general progression from humiliation to exaltation while at the same time showing how they overlap and interrelate." Treat cites Calvin and Barth as key proponents in support of his view. Notwithstanding, in my view there is no need for such redefinition of these states of Christ's life. To do so conflates what ought to be affirmed as temporally separate and distinct.

a redemptive-historical progression that transitions from his culminating work on the cross to his vindication in the resurrection and session
at the right hand of the Father. "The entire state of exaltation from the
resurrection to his coming again for judgment," states Bavinck, "is a
reward for the work that he accomplished as the Servant of the Lord in
the days of his humiliation."[82] Appreciating this through the aesthetic
lens, the forms of Christ's life in the economy of salvation are properly
perceived in terms of the form befitting each state (humiliation or exaltation) with respect to its respective place in redemptive-history. The
"beauty of the Lord" encompasses without dissonance the Christ-form
of both together—Lamb of God and Lion of Judah—as each contributes
most fittingly to the whole. Balthasar puts it like this: "We do not here
have two images alongside each other, as in a diptych consisting of two
complementary halves. Faith (especially Johannine faith) is able to see
both aspects as a unity—God's *kenōsis* in the Synoptics and the Pauline
doxa of the Risen One."[83]

As the glory of God's actions in Christ during his earthly career
was glory revealed not glory concealed, it was the optics given through
faith alone that determined whether or not someone rightly perceived
him (cf. John 9:35–41). The dialectic of revealing and concealing rested
critically on that.[84] The work of the Spirit was required then just as

---

82. Bavinck, *RD*, 3:433. E.g., Luke 24:26; Romans 1:4; Philippians 2:9–11; Hebrews
2:9; 1 Peter 1:11; Revelation 3:21; 5:12–13. For Bavinck's overall discussion relevant to
this, see *RD*, 3:418–36.

83. Balthasar, *GL*, I, 476. In the same vein he writes, *TL*, II, 147: "The exalted
superiority of Jesus Christ, the revelation of the sovereign glory of God, pervades
his entire being. It comprises both his majestic uniqueness ('Which of you can
accuse me of a sin?': John 8:46) and his familiarly 'eating and drinking with sinners
and tax collectors' (Mt 9:11), Tabor, and the Cross. John saw both together in his
concept of glory."

84. This is not at all to undermine, much less contradict, the apostle Paul's
category of "mystery" concerning which he speaks of the advent of Jesus Christ
and his gospel as revelation that is fundamental to and embedded within the Old
Testament scriptures (1 Cor 2:7–8; Rom 16:25–27; et al.; cf. Luke 24: 25–27). D. A.
Carson, "Mystery and Fulfillment: Toward a More Comprehensive Paradigm of
Paul's Understanding of the Old and the New" in *Justification and Variegated Nomism:
The Paradoxes of Paul*, vol. 2, ed. D. A. Carson et al. (Grand Rapids: Baker Academic,
2004), 427, refers to this paradoxical phenomenon as revelation that was "hidden
in plain view." He observes that there are two aspects to this hiddenness. On the
one hand, the mystery "was hidden salvation-historically," and on the other hand,

it has been ever since to impart such optics to those who would "perceive" Christ in the form of his humanity for who he truly is—Lord and Savior over all (cf. Acts 9:1–20).[85] We see Paul explain as much to the Corinthians: "But we impart a secret and hidden wisdom of God, which God decreed before the ages for our glory. None of the rulers of this age understood this, for if they had, they would not have crucified the Lord of glory. … These things God has revealed to us through the Spirit" (1 Cor 2:7–10; cf. Deut 29:4; Luke 23:34; John 16:13–15). Even at the stage of his infancy, the adoration offered by the Magi to the child Jesus presents a striking example of the eyes of faith perceiving him for who he truly is (Matt 2:1–11). Balthasar points likewise to the canticle of an equally notable infancy narrative: "When Jesus is presented in the Temple, there takes place for Luke the eschatological re-entry of the divine glory of Ezekiel's vision into the sanctuary, for Simeon sings: 'My eyes have seen your glory: light for illumination of the Gentiles, and glory of your people Israel' (Luke 2:30–32)."[86] And until he comes again, Christ in his heavenly exaltation will continue to radiate his glory and reveal himself through the work of the Spirit to all those who would rightly perceive him.[87] The key difference between aesthetics and theological aesthetics is identified more plainly now. In the case of the latter, the work of the Spirit enables those with eyes of faith to perceive rightly the objective beauty of the person of Christ, the beauty of the work of Christ (redemption accomplished), and the beauty of Christ's work ongoing through the Holy Spirit (redemption applied).

---

it was (and is) hidden "to the person without the Spirit (1 Cor 2:14)." Explaining the culpability for not perceiving the revelation of Christ, Carson states: "In the wise providence of God the first of these two forms of hiddenness, that which prevailed across history until the coming of Christ, so worked in and through and behind the culpable blindness that the passion and resurrection of the Messiah was brought about simultaneously by human sin and by the wise plan of God (compare Acts 2:27–28 with 1 Cor 2:7–8)." (432)

85. Still, for all believers in this present age, such perceiving of Christ by faith is a weak and partial perception (1 Cor 13:12). In the age to come the redeemed in Christ "shall see him as he is" (1 John 3:2).

86. Balthasar, GL, VII, 319.

87. Along the same lines, Holmes, "Disclosure without Reservation," 379, writes: "God's glory radiates forth—albeit not exhaustively—in such a way that it evokes response to itself by virtue of its disclosure and its continual disclosure to human beings in the risen Jesus who prophetically attests himself in the Spirit."

That very same work of the Spirit, moreover, is also what enables all those faith-filled ones to subjectively experience and grow in delight of the beauty that they have perceived.

CONSPECTUS

We end this section having developed the christological contours of beauty with respect to Christ's identity as taking the form of a slave. A fundamental aspect of the aesthetic dimension pertaining here is the theodramatic fittingness of the Son as incarnate Redeemer revealed in his assumption of that form. Any ostensible dissonance between the self-revelatory nature of God's actions in Christ during his earthly career and the essential nature of God in himself is not a real dissonance. As I have argued the case, the form of a slave was most befitting for God the Son to take in accordance with his role as the Messiah, which itself is all in accordance with the nature of God's self-giving love. An essential element of the reasoning informing our argument is that the glory of God in Christ while he was in the state of his humiliation was actually glory revealed not glory concealed. Figuring importantly in this is the point that the identity of God is revealed as much in his self-abasement and service as it is in his exaltation and rule. God the Son was thus in no actual way operating incognito as Christ in the form of a slave because his true identity was not actually concealed by a "veil of flesh." Accordingly, the glory that no one can see and live has been made perceivable in and through the mediated form of Christ in whom "the whole fullness of deity dwells bodily" (Col 2:9). We concluded that it was the optics given through faith alone by the work of God's Spirit that determined whether or not someone rightly perceived (albeit weakly and incompletely) Christ in the form of his humanity for who he truly is. And in that form the radiance of his glory is expressed most fittingly such that his beauty is always from glory to glory.

CHRIST THE LAST ADAM AND THE TRUE ISRAEL

Our development of the christological contours of beauty continues with respect to Christ's identity revealed as both the last Adam and the true Israel. The aesthetic dimension here again has to do with the theodramatic fittingness of the Son as incarnate Redeemer, although as we will see, in this case the fittingness is revealed in how Christ recapitulates in his life the history of Adam and Israel. The parallels between Adam and Christ and between Israel and Christ play a fundamental part in the recapitulative patterning of redemptive-history, and as such reflect an important aspect of the beauty of redemptive-history. The examples I present below are commonly acknowledged parallels and for our purposes show their paradigmatic nature as basic to the design of the divine plan. In general the recapitulative patterning of redemptive-history reflects in different ways the creational-re-creational symmetry of the plan and is a conspicuous part of the redemptive-eschatological fulfillment of God's original creational purposes.

The idea of recapitulation was mentioned earlier in Chapter 3 concerning the recapitulation of all things in Christ that so defines Irenaeus' theology.[88] While I am not arguing here for a distinctly Irenaean version of recapitulation, the basic idea stemming from it that Christ's life during his earthly career is recapitulative of the Old Testament figures of Adam and Israel is an idea consonant with the witness of the New Testament. As we will see shortly, the event of Jesus' baptism by John highlights the theodramatic fittingness of the Son revealed through his identity as the true Israel. Jesus himself affirms that event as "fitting" in order to fulfill all righteousness. Although *all* righteousness that Jesus was called to fulfill as the Messiah was not fulfilled in the event of his baptism alone, its occurrence just prior to his public ministry serves emblematically for seeing Jesus' whole messianic undertaking as "fitting" in order to fulfill all righteousness.

What recapitulation entails is that represented in the life and ministry of Christ is a correspondence or parallelism to the past history of redemption that is fulfilled or "summed up" in Christ. R. T. France puts it this way: "The patterns discerned in the Old Testament are not only repeated on a higher plane, but they are now finding their final and perfect embodiment."[89] The idea of a representative position (namely,

---

88. See Chapter 2 section, Sublime Comedy: The Theodramatic Form of the Divine Plan, in particular under the discussion, The Irenaean Form of the Theodrama.

89. R. T. France, *Jesus and the Old Testament: His Application of Old Testament Passages to Himself and His Mission* (Downers Grove, IL: InterVarsity Press, 1971), 79.

headship/sonship) with a universal significance applies here as well to the figures of Adam, Israel, and Christ. In recapitulating in his life the history of Adam and Israel, Christ's messianic roles as the last Adam and the true Israel are basic to the consummative fulfillment of all the redemptive covenants (e.g., Abrahamic, Mosaic, Davidic) leading up to the new covenant through which God carries out his original creational purposes. Balthasar frames the point here nicely:

> If Jesus' claim [of equality with God] poses a limit to all questionings, then in him there is not only the fulfillment of all the promises of Yahweh in salvation history, but also, quite naturally, of all the words of promise that the creator had implanted in his Creation—in the cosmos and in man. A "redeemer" who did not make the claim to be the one who fulfilled God's intentions in creation, would be unworthy of belief.[90]

In Chapter 3 we identified God's creational purposes in the concept of the proto-eschaton, which consists of the divine commission to Adam from Genesis 1:28 in conjunction with accompanying themes of the proto-eschaton. In the postlapsarian context the Old Testament reiterates the commission given to Adam (as God's son and head of the human family) and applies it to Israel and her patriarchs, thus giving warrant to understand Israel as a corporate Adam inheriting the position of being God's son. But just as Adam was unfaithful and disobedient, falling short of the glory of God that he was to reflect, so too were God's covenant people Israel throughout their history with the Lord, as the Old Testament amply attests. Christ's life is recapitulative in that he perfectly fulfills all that Adam and Israel were called by God to be and do. Tibor Fabiny captures that idea in describing "Christ [as] the great 'recapitulator' who fulfills both the vocation of Israel and the will of God. However, the vocation of Israel was seen by St. Paul as the vocation of mankind and therefore Christ fulfills not only Israel's history but all human history as well (Eph 1:10)."[91] His recapitulation as such has nothing to do with being simply a prophetic object lesson or

---

90. Balthasar, *GL*, VII, 128–29.
91. Tibor Fabiny, *The Lion and the Lamb: Figuralism and Fulfilment in the Bible, Art, and Literature* (New York: St. Martin's Press, 1992), 58.

mimetic re-dramatization for Israel, but rather is all part of the drama of redemption for humanity. Christ's recapitulation, in other words, serves his redemptive mission, which "involves the substitution of God's righteous history in Christ for our fallen and condemned histories of rebellion." In this way the reality of the Son's incarnation signifies "a message of hope ...which sees both the end to the history of fallenness and the new beginning of a history that merges with eternity."[92]

CHRIST THE LAST ADAM

The symmetrical design of the divine plan according to the redemptive-eschatological fulfillment of God's original creational purposes is perhaps nowhere more evident than in the correspondence to which the New Testament attests between the first Adam and Christ as the last (or second) Adam. The theodramatic fittingness of the Son revealed through his identity as the last Adam is integral to the orchestrated correspondence between Adam and Christ in the outworking of redemptive-history. Christ's mission from the Father involved doing the work set before him as the second Adam. In this regard Christ did what the first Adam was supposed to do, namely, remain unswervingly obedient in loving fealty to the Father in the face of all temptation to do otherwise, for he never acquiesced to Satan any lordship.[93] Christ's own justification as our Adamic representative plays a crucial role in the theodrama of triumph and redemption. For Christ's justification involves the Father's pleased acceptance of his meritorious life and death that he earned for the salvation of many (cf. Isa 53:10–12; Heb 5:8–9), and entails "the death he died he died to sin, once for all, but the life he lives he lives to God" (Rom 6:10). The parallel between Adam and Christ plays an elemental part in the recapitulative patterning of redemptive-history and as such reflects an ingredient aspect of its aesthetic dimension. The Adam-Christ parallel is brought out explicitly in three instances of Paul's letters—Romans 5:12–21 and 1 Corinthians 15:21–22, 44–49. I will

---

92. Graeme Goldsworthy, *Gospel-Centered Hermeneutics: Foundations and Principles of Evangelical Biblical Interpretation* (Downers Grove, IL: IVP Academic, 2006), 223, 228.

93. For a thorough treatment on the correspondence between the first Adam and Christ as the last Adam, see Brandon D. Crowe, *The Last Adam: A Theology of the Obedient Life of Jesus in the Gospels* (Grand Rapids: Baker Academic, 2017).

set out a brief treatment of Christ as the last Adam from Romans 5:12-21 and 1 Corinthians 15:44-49, highlighting key theological elements that demonstrate its recapitulative character.[94]

Christ the Last Adam in Romans 5:12-21

In Romans 5:12-21, Paul expresses in rather straightforward terms that Adam and Christ, respectively, are decisive for humanity—Adam for the old humanity and Christ for the new humanity. Paul's concern has to do with the universal impact of Adam's act of sin compared to Christ's act of righteousness—the former brings condemnation and death to all humanity while the latter brings justification and life eternal to all those who are "in Christ." As Douglas Moo writes, "The parallel, as Paul stresses throughout this paragraph, is that, in each case, a critical spiritual condition has been introduced into human history 'through' the act of 'one man.'"[95] It is by virtue of its analogous universal impact that Christ's obedience is recapitulative of Adam's disobedience (Rom 5:19). The idea of recapitulation is implicit in Christ's headship role as the last Adam, which is why Paul calls the first Adam a "type" (τύπος) of Christ (Rom 5:14).[96]

In verse 12 Paul begins by attributing to "one man" (Adam) the universal sin that has invaded the world. It becomes more discernible later in the passage, but implicit to his argument is the theological understanding that Adam's disobedience against God in Genesis 3,

---

94. Biblical scholars have long acknowledged that this Adam-Christ parallel is likewise recognizable—to cite one prominent example—in the account of Jesus' temptation in the wilderness. Noteworthy in the case of Luke's Gospel, the temptation account follows the genealogy of Jesus Christ that ends with "Adam, the son of God" (3:38). Meredith Kline's remarks in *Kingdom Prologue* are representative: "Scripture's identification of Jesus as a second Adam is therefore another facet of its identification of him as the representative seed of the woman of Genesis 3:15. Particular mention may be made of the relevant data in the Gospel accounts of Jesus' temptation-encounter with Satan, where the parallelism of our Lord's experience to that of the first Adam is most pronounced." (144) I agree that the correspondence is valid and more could be said about it here, but I defer to take up the account of Jesus' temptation in the wilderness in my treatment of Christ as the true Israel in the subsection following.

95. Moo, *The Epistle to the Romans*, 339.

96. BDAG 1020 s.v. τύπος 6: an archetype serving as a model (*type, pattern, model*); 6c: of the *types* given by God as an indication of the future, in the form of Adam: τύπος του μέλλοντος ('Αδάμ) *a type of the Adam to come* (i.e., of Christ) Rom 5:14.

which resulted in the divine judgment of his death, is at the causal root of why sin and death "reign"—that is, that sin and death inflict and afflict all humanity. Although the consequence of Adam's trespass is death's universal reign (Rom 5:17), it is conjunctively true that all human beings merit or deserve that divine judgment (Rom 5:12, "because all sinned"). Notwithstanding the theological complexities here, it is clear enough that Paul regards Adam and Christ as representative-corporate figures. In Moo's words, "For Paul, Adam, like Christ, was a corporate figure, whose sin could be regarded at the same time as the sin of all his descendants."[97] Christ's obedience, however, results in the reign of life for "those who receive the abundance of grace and the free gift of righteousness" (Rom 5:17)—except in this case, for such who receive this "free gift," it is wholly unmerited and ill-deserved.[98] It is with this extravagant gratuitousness of God's grace in view that Paul asserts a fortiori "how much more" believers will "reign in life" through Christ. In sum, Adam is the representative of humanity under whose headship is the reign of sin and death, whereas Christ is the representative of a new humanity under whose headship is received the free gift of righteousness by the grace of God and the reign in life eternal through him.

Christ the Last Adam in 1 Corinthians 15:44–49

Unlike Paul's concern in the Adam-Christ parallel in Romans 5, which has to do with the universal impact of Adam's act of sin compared to Christ's act of righteousness, in 1 Corinthians 15:44–49 the matter Paul wishes to address concerns the nature of the resurrection body. Leading up to our passage, Paul uses a series of analogies from everyday life to underscore the essential contrast between the human body belonging to our earthly life in this present age, and the human body of those who are redeemed "in Christ" belonging to the future heavenly life in the age to come. The nature of the earthly human body versus the heavenly one is contrasted in the following terms: perishable/imperishable (1 Cor 15:42), dishonor/glory, weakness/power (1 Cor 15:43), and of particular significance in verse 44 a "natural body" ($\sigma\tilde{\omega}\mu\alpha$ $\psi\upsilon\chi\iota\kappa\acuteo\nu$) versus a

---

97. Moo, *The Epistle to the Romans*, 328.

98. On this, Moo, *The Epistle to the Romans*, 339, notes, "This gift is specified to be 'righteousness,' here clearly the status of a new relationship with God."

"spiritual body" (σῶμα πνευματικόν). With respect to this latter contrast, Gordon Fee writes, "Most likely ...[Paul] here intends to describe a 'body adapted to the final life of the Spirit,' whereas the first 'body' is that which is adapted to the present earthly life, characterized by ψυχή."[99] The vital difference here in regard to the human body is a transformational one, but it is nevertheless still a human body in both cases. For this reason, Paul "is intent on emphasizing the fact that the risen Christ *continues to have a body that is related to his life as a human being*."[100] Recalling Paul's earlier analogy of Christ as the firstfruits (1 Cor 15:23), it follows that in the resurrection those who belong to Christ will continue also to have a body that is related to their life as a human being, albeit one that is ontologically characterized not by ψυχή but by πνεῦμα. Thus, for the new humanity redeemed in Christ, which is brought to its eschatological realization in the world to come, essential continuity as embodied human persons is maintained.[101]

The Adam-Christ parallel is made explicit in verse 45: "'The first man, Adam, became a living person (ψυχὴν ζῶσαν)'; the last Adam became a life-giving spirit (πνεῦμα ζῶσαν)" (NET). Here Paul applies Genesis 2:7 (LXX) to underscore the difference in his preceding claim between the "natural body" of those "in Adam" and the "spiritual body" of those "made alive in Christ" (1 Cor 15:22). The tenor of Paul's argument here, involving certain comparisons between Adam and Christ, takes the form *a minore ad maius*, but this is not simply from a lesser to a greater *in degree*. For Christ's messianic identity as the last Adam goes beyond his being just a supreme version of the first Adam. He is, we might say, the Adam nonpareil in which the fullness of deity dwells bodily while still being altogether genuinely human.

Concerning verse 45 the following points are recognized.[102] First, in Paul describing Christ as the last (ἔσχατος) Adam, Christ is depicted as representing humanity's ultimate status. In other words, he is an

---

99. Fee, *Pauline Christology*, 116.

100. Fee, *Pauline Christology*, 516. Italics original.

101. On arguments for bodily continuity in the Pauline account of resurrection, see N. T. Wright, *The Resurrection of the Son of God* (Minneapolis: Fortress Press, 2003), 209–398.

102. With debts here to Hans Burger, *Being in Christ: A Biblical and Systematic Investigation in a Reformed Perspective* (Eugene, OR: Wipf & Stock, 2009), 172.

eschatological figure to the first Adam's *creational* status. Second, the Adamic moniker applied to Christ is meant to imply his representative role for humanity, and the nature of this role, Paul teaches, involves his being "a life-giving spirit"—that is, the source of eternal spiritual life. It is worth noting that the text offers little support for the idea that Christ becomes the last Adam *in his resurrection*. What the text does support is that in his resurrection Christ became a life-giving spirit/ Spirit over against Adam who was only ever a life-receiving human being. "In referring to Christ as a 'life-giving πνευμα,'" observes Fee, "Paul envisions the risen Christ as assuming the *eschatological* role that God played at the beginning."[103]

The thrust of verses 46–49 is that there is an eschatological order and a respective ontological fittingness that pertains, on the one hand, to the nature of the human body identified with our earthly life in this present age and, on the other hand, to the body that believers will have in the age to come. In verses 47 and 48, Paul again alludes to Genesis 2:7 and now characterizes "the first man" (Adam) as "the man of dust" and "the second man" (Christ) as "the man of heaven," which respectively denotes that Adam and Christ are representative heads of different orders of existence for humanity. Since "the Lord God formed the man of dust from the ground" (Gen 2:7), the kind of bodily existence Adam represents is strictly an earthly one belonging to this present age. Christ's human body—that is, his *ante-mortem* human body—was also of that same kind during his earthly career (Rom 8:3); but the kind of embodied existence he represents in his resurrection is now "of heaven," that is, of an empyreal kind belonging to the age to come for those who are redeemed "in Christ."

Yet it is clear that this means more than our present bodies merely being uninfected and unaffected by sin. Fee puts it this way:

> Christ in his humanity, through death and resurrection, has not simply identified with us as human beings but has set a future resurrection in motion—as the new creation with its eventual realization of a new body, fully adapted to the life of the future. And all

---

103. Fee, *Pauline Christology*, 118.

of this because in his incarnation he bore a body that was truly in keeping with that of Adam.[104]

We could therefore say that the nature of the "natural body" versus the "spiritual body" is effectively one of fittingness corresponding to which age is in view—the present earthly one or the future eternal one. In relation to this temporal earthly life the bodily fittingness corresponds to "the one made of dust," but in relation to eternal life the bodily fittingness corresponds to "the one from heaven" (1 Cor 15:48 NET). In verse 49, Paul concludes, "Just as we have borne the image of the man of dust, we shall also bear the image of the man of heaven." As Fee notes, "The eschatological goal of [Christ's] redemptive work lies with our being transformed into that same image, so that the goal of the first creation will be finally realized in the second."[105] Two connections here to our theological aesthetic are worth pointing out. First, the "spiritual body" to which Paul refers affirms the eschatological realization of the constitutional aspect of the *imago Dei*. And second, evident in this Adam-Christ parallel is the nature of the Bible's story pattern as a theodramatic comedy, which points up the surplus of the gloriousness of its consummation ending compared to its creation beginning.

Christ the True Israel

Just as we saw above with respect to the Adam-Christ parallel, the parallel between God's covenant people Israel and Christ is basic to the recapitulative patterning of redemptive-history and reflects an aspect of its aesthetic dimension. For Christ likewise recapitulates in his life the history of Israel, representatively fulfilling all that God's covenant people Israel were called to be and do. Moreover, given that Israel's sonship is recognized as a positional status she inherited from God in connection with the commission Adam was given as God's son, it is fair

---

104. Fee, *Pauline Christology*, 517.

105. Fee, *Pauline Christology*, 119. This coheres nicely with the concept of the proto-eschaton that we presented in Chapter 3 in which the theme of the *imago Dei* has a central role in the eschatological latency that would be actualized according to the divine plan. See in particular the subsection, The Glory of the Image of God in Humans. Our treatment here of this particular area is intentionally brief, as we will address it in more detail in the Chapter 6 section, Humans Immortal in Final Fittingness: Redeemed as Glorious.

to say that implicit in the idea of recapitulation here is Christ's sonship as the embodiment of Israel whose identity and destiny he fulfills. Thus, just as the New Testament attests to a correspondence between the first Adam and Christ as the second Adam that is recapitulative in nature, so likewise we can say—though Scripture does not put it in these terms—that the New Testament attests to a similar correspondence between Israel as a corporate Adam inheriting the position of being God's son and Christ as the "second Israel." A further way the redemptive-eschatological fulfillment of God's original creational purposes can be justifiably understood, therefore, is as Christ's mission from the Father in doing the work set before him as the second Israel.

To the question, "Who did Jesus think he was?," N. T. Wright responds, "The first answer must be: Israel-in-person, Israel's representative, the one in whom Israel's destiny was reaching its climax. He thought he was the Messiah. Jesus' actions, his message, his warning, and his welcome, make sense only within this framework."[106] Indeed, the patterns of God's working in the history of Israel are featured throughout the Gospel narratives. R. T. France observes,

> Jesus saw his mission as the fulfillment of the Old Testament scriptures; not just of those which predicted a coming redeemer, but of the whole sweep of Old Testament ideas. The patterns of God's working which the discerning eye could trace in the history and institutions of Israel were all preparing for the great climax when all would be taken up into the final and perfect act of God which the prophets foretold. And in the coming of Jesus all this was fulfilled. That was why he could find "in *all* the scriptures the things concerning himself".[107]

---

106. N. T. Wright, *Jesus and the Victory of God* (Minneapolis: Fortress Press, 1996), 538. Wright expands on this idea elsewhere, stating: "Jesus of Nazareth was conscious of a vocation: a vocation, given him by the one he knew as 'father,' to reenact in himself, what, in Israel's scriptures, God had promised to accomplish all by himself. He would be the pillar of cloud and fire for the people of the new exodus. He would embody in himself the returning and redeeming action of the covenant God." *The Challenge of Jesus: Rediscovering Who Jesus Was and Is* (Downers Grove, IL: InterVarsity Press, 1999), 123.

107. France, *Jesus and the Old Testament*, 79–80. Affirming the same point, Balthasar, *GL*, VII, 55, writes, "Had Jesus not borne the whole history of Israel with

Scholars and Gospel commentators have rightly given much attention to the various patterns and motifs in which the Gospels feature
Jesus as recapitulating Israel. For our purposes it will be sufficient to
demonstrate this from two prominent accounts, both of which are
included in all three synoptic Gospels—Jesus' baptism and his temptation in the wilderness.[108] Viewed together as narratively interde-
pendent, these accounts of Jesus' life representatively mirror (i.e.,
recapitulate) Israel's exodus through the waters of the Red Sea and
her testing in the wilderness.

CHRIST THE TRUE ISRAEL RECAPITULATED IN THE BAPTISM OF JESUS

Our interest here is to lay out the key aspects in the event of Jesus'
baptism that recapitulate Israel's passage through the Red Sea during
their prototypal first exodus history. For this, I draw primarily from
the account given in Matthew's Gospel. Joel Kennedy encapsulates this
correspondence as follows: "In Israel's exodus, God leads his people out
of Egypt through water and into the wilderness for testing (Deut 8:2–5),
which is also the pattern recapitulated by Jesus in Matthew 3:13–4:11."[109]
That sequence of events for Israel comes prior to their task of taking
the land of promise; for Jesus they come just prior to the public ministry
he is to undertake.

There are several clues within the baptism narrative (Matt 3:1–17)
suggestive of Jesus recapitulating Israel's exodus experience. John's
baptizing people from Jerusalem and all Judea and all the region about
the Jordan is set in the wilderness (Matt 3:1) just as Israel's experience
of passing through the waters of the Red Sea takes place in the wilderness (Exod 13:18). The quotation of Isaiah 40:3 by the Baptist (Matt 3:3)

God in himself, then he could not have been the final word of the history of God
with Israel (and therein the world)."

108. This is not at all to suggest that John's Gospel lacks a vibrant testimony
of Jesus' recapitulation of Israel. See, e.g., D. A. Carson, "John and the Johannine
Epistles" in *It Is Written: Scripture Citing Scripture: Essays in Honour of Barnabas
Lindars, SSF*, ed. D. A. Carson and H. G. M. Williamson (Cambridge: Cambridge
University Press, 1988), 245–64.

109. Joel Kennedy, *The Recapitulation of Israel* (Tübingen: Mohr Siebeck,
2008), 177.

lends support to the idea that the exodus motif is in view.[110] Of course, the element of water being centrally involved and the action of Jesus coming up out of the water in his baptism (Matt 3:16) evoke the rending of the waters for Israel (Exod 14:21–22). Moreover, by the narrative slowly narrowing in focus until it is exclusively upon Jesus, "Matthew signals Jesus' unique role, and it is fundamentally a representational role, embodying Israel in his recapitulation of her history."[111] Also telling is that Jesus came to the Jordan for the express purpose of being baptized by John (Matt 3:13), especially so since John's was a baptism of *repentance*. In so doing, Jesus shows himself to be obedient to the call to *Israel* for repentance in full compliance with God's righteous requirements. And thus by submitting to John's baptism, Jesus is identifying representatively with his people Israel, and fulfilling all righteousness (3:15; cf. 5:17–18). As Murray Rae puts it, Jesus came to be baptized "not in confession of his own sin, but shouldering the corporate guilt of his people and offering a true repentance on their behalf, though not, as it turns out, on behalf of Israel alone, but on behalf of the whole of humanity."[112]

Integral to Jesus' baptism being recapitulative of Israel's exodus through the Red Sea is that it signifies him as the inaugurator of the

---

110. For recommended works on the new exodus theme, see the Markan account given by Rikki E. Watts, *Isaiah's New Exodus in Mark* (Grand Rapids: Baker Academic, 2000); the Johannine account given by Paul S. Coxon, *Exploring the New Exodus in John: A Biblical Theological Investigation of John Chapters 5–10* (Eugene, OR: Resource Publication, 2015); the Lukan account given by David W. Pao, *Acts and the Isaianic New Exodus* (Eugene, OR: Wipf & Stock, 2016); and the exodus paradigm within the wider biblical-theological landscape given by Bryan D. Estelle, *Echoes of Exodus: Tracing a Biblical Motif* (Downers Grove, IL: IVP Academic, 2018).

111. Kennedy, *The Recapitulation of Israel*, 171.

112. Murray A. Rae, "The Baptism of Christ" in *The Person of Christ*, ed. Stephen R. Holmes and Murray A. Rae (London: T&T Clark, 2005), 132. Illuminating the point here further is the extended quote Rae cites by G. B. Caird, *The Gospel of Saint Luke* (Harmondsworth: Penguin Books, 1963), 77: "Jesus went to be baptized … not for private reasons but as a man with a public calling. John had summoned all Israel to repentance and with Israel Jesus too must go. He dwelt in the midst of a people with unclean lips and could not separate himself from them. Rather he must be fully identified with them in their movement towards God. If he was to lead them into God's kingdom, he himself must enter it by the only door open to them. He must be their representative before he could be their king. He must be *numbered with the transgressors* before he could see the fruit of the travail of his soul (Isa 53:11–12)." (original italics)

new exodus with the dawning of the messianic age. Whatever else may be said of it, that Jesus employs the notion of "fittingness" in response to the resistance John has to baptizing him—"Let it be so now, for thus it is *fitting* (πρέπω)[113] for us to fulfill all righteousness" (3:15)—comports with seeing this orchestrated correspondence as an ingredient part of the theological aesthetic of redemptive-history. In the case here, then, our theological aesthetic sees the fittingness of God's wisdom and righteousness manifest in Christ's role as Israel-in-person in full compliance with God's righteous requirements as being perfectly correlated with the beauty of Christ's theodramatic fittingness in the event of his baptism as part of the recapitulative patterning of redemptive-history.

Jesus' baptism by John is met with a dramatic combination of two revelatory events—the descent of the Spirit upon Jesus (Matt 3:16), and the voice of God the Father from heaven declaring, "This is my one dear Son; in him I take great delight" (Matt 3:17 NET).[114] That seal of the Father's good pleasure affirms in a clarion way the purposive obedience of Jesus to fulfill all righteousness. Commenting on the baptism narrative, Balthasar writes:

> Jesus' initiative attains immediately to its fulfillment, for he "rises up" out of the waters, and his act of "coming up from beneath" is answered by the "coming down from above" of the "Spirit (of God)": here we see that incarnation is the encounter, to the point of identification, of the Israel who has been made ready and the God of the covenant who descends to Israel.[115]

Highlighted here as well is the identity of Jesus as God's *Son*, which coincides with his representative role as Israel-in-person (cf. Matt 2:15; Hos 11:1). Already in the opening line of his Gospel, Matthew identifies Jesus as the messianic son of David, reinforcing further the idea of Jesus

---

113. L&N 66.1 s.v. πρέπω: to be fitting or right, with the implication of possible moral judgment involved.

114. Commentators have widely noted that the Father's words likely involve allusions to Psalm 2:7, Isaiah 42:1, and maybe Isaiah 41:8; others suggest Genesis 22:2, 12, or Jeremiah 38:20 LXX. The study note on Matthew 3:17 in the NET adds: "God is marking out Jesus as his chosen one (the meaning of '[in him I take] great delight'), but it may well be that this was a private experience that only Jesus and John saw and heard (cf. John 1:32–33)."

115. Balthasar, *GL*, VII, 56.

being the embodiment of Israel whose destiny he will fulfill. It is in this thick sense of Israel's sonship that Christ's messianic identity entails him being "the true Israel."

Jesus' obedience is defining of his whole mission, of course, and therefore his fulfilling all righteousness is not brought to its completion simply by this act alone of submitting to John's baptism. Within the larger scope of his mission, Jesus submits to John's baptism "as the one who will redeem his people, already programmatically expressed at Matthew 1:21 (cf. Matt 20:28)."[116] Christ's messianic identity as the true Israel is thus divinely orchestrated for salvific purpose in connection with Christ's role as Savior of Israel and, indeed, of the whole world. The baptism of repentance to which John called Israel, and to which Jesus submitted as Israel's representative, is fitting with the suffering that comes to increasingly define Jesus' path of obedience. The likely allusion to Isaiah 42:1 in Matthew 3:17 already suggestively identifies Jesus with Isaiah's (suffering) Servant of the Lord. Still, Matthew 16:21 marks a key turning point wherein we learn more explicitly that Jesus' call to obedience will "take on a new shape, the shape of suffering."[117] It is not surprising, then, that in Luke's Gospel, for example, Jesus speaks to his disciples of his impending passion and crucifixion using baptism imagery: "I have a baptism to be baptized with, and how great is my distress until it is accomplished!" (Luke 12:50). Mark in his Gospel records a similar statement by Jesus (Mark 10:38). Considering things from a wide angle perspective, one commentator put it this way: "The Baptism is ... the first step in the redeeming work of Christ. It is not only the beginning of the ministry, it is also the beginning of the passion."[118] Indeed, it is only through the path of suffering and death that Jesus' unswerving obedience fulfills all righteousness to perfection.

---

116. Kennedy, *The Recapitulation of Israel*, 161.

117. Brandon D. Crowe, *The Obedient Son: Deuteronomy and Christology in the Gospel of Matthew* (Berlin: De Gruyter, 2012), 202. Crowe also notes that just before this Peter confesses Jesus to be "the Christ, the Son of the living God" (Matt 6:16). The first half of the Gospel thus climaxes in a confession that combines the concepts of the Davidic Messiah and divine sonship. (203)

118. Rae, "The Baptism of Christ," 134, quoting John R. H. Moorman, *The Path to Glory: Studies in the Gospel according to Luke* (London: SPCK, 1963), 39.

CHRIST THE TRUE ISRAEL RECAPITULATED
IN THE TEMPTATION OF JESUS

Our consideration of Christ's identity as the true Israel continues in
the temptation narrative recounted in Matthew 4:1–11. In the wake of
Jesus' baptism, he is then "led up by the Spirit into the wilderness to be
tempted by the devil" (4:1). Reminiscent here is how the Lord led Israel
by the Spirit out of Egypt and into the wilderness (cf. Isa 63:14). But
before considering further the correspondence between Jesus' situation and Israel's, a more primeval connection in play here is also worth
pointing out. On the battleground of the wilderness, Satan is shown
for the first time confronting Jesus outright—not the seed of the serpent but the serpent itself engages here in deadly business against the
promised seed of the woman (Gen 3:15). The temptation circumstances
and event were hardly adventitious. We are reminded here again how
the sovereign purposes of God are masterfully orchestrated in all these
things defining of Jesus' life. While the three major temptations come
at the end of Jesus' fast of forty days, Luke's account notes that Jesus
had been tempted by the devil throughout that time (Luke 4:2).[119]

Basic to the recapitulative character of Jesus' experience to that of
Israel's are the following parallels: "Both are times of hardship and
testing, preparatory to the undertaking of a special task (the conquest
of the promised land, and the ministry of Jesus). Both suffer hunger, a
hunger deliberately inflicted by God to teach a lesson. The forty days
of Jesus' fast reflects the forty years of Israel's wandering."[120] The narrowing in exclusively upon Jesus that we saw in the baptism narrative
continues on in the temptation narrative. As Kennedy notes, "Jesus

---

119. In addition, the brief account of Jesus' temptation in Mark's Gospel
includes the detail that he was with "the wild animals" (θηρίον, 1:13). In light of
our earlier point that Jesus' baptism is fitting with the suffering that increasingly
will define his path of obedience, it is possible that Mark's reference to the wild
animals involves an allusion to Leviticus 26:22 LXX, which speaks of "the wild
beasts" (θηρίον) in the context of enumerated covenant curses that the Lord would
send as a sign of judgment against Israel should they walk in disobedience. If this
reading of Mark's Gospel is correct, it suggests that in Jesus' temptation experience
he is representatively identifying with his people Israel who have long been under
the covenant sanctions of the Lord's judgment. On this view the idea of suffering
that would characterize Jesus' path of obedience is here again being anticipated.

120. France, *Jesus and the Old Testament*, 51.

alone received the divine approval as the Son and now he is led into the wilderness to be tested alone as the Son."[121] In this testing/temptation experience, Jesus recapitulates in his life three testing events that occurred during a critical period in Israel's early history.[122] All three of these events for Israel occurred during the forty years of their wandering in the wilderness, which was the Lord's punishment for their faithlessness to follow the plan of conquering Canaan (Num 14:33–34; Josh 5:6). We are also told that the Lord wanted to test Israel to reveal whether they would keep his commandments or not, and thus reveal what was in their heart (Deut 8:2).

As narrated in Matthew's Gospel, Jesus' temptation experience corresponds in the same chronology to three tests that Israel experienced, recounted in Exodus 16, 17, and 32. To each of his three temptations by the devil, Jesus responds by quoting a text of scripture from Deuteronomy 6–8 that in each case is linked to a failure by Israel as recounted in Exodus. Moreover, the section of Deuteronomy from which Jesus quotes depicts God speaking through Moses to his son Israel as they are poised to enter the land that had been promised to them, and warning Israel not to follow the failures of their past. Jesus' use of these scriptural quotations is a key aspect of the temptation narrative that portrays him as hearing and obeying God's voice in Deuteronomy, and thus as recapitulating in his own life that part of Israel's history faithfully at every point where Israel had failed.

In the first test as presented in Matthew, the devil's stratagem ostensibly is to call into question the divine Sonship of Jesus and challenge him to prove it by performing the miraculous: "If you are the Son of God, command these stones to become loaves of bread" (Matt 4:3). "This focus on Jesus as Son relates back to the divine voice in 3:17," explains Kennedy, but the authentication of his Sonship by doing the called-for miracle is not the real test here. The critical issue at stake in the devil's challenge concerns "whether [Jesus] will obey God's will, fulfilling the righteousness he had just announced to John in 3:14, as well as a temptation for Jesus to abandon his mission as servant."[123] To the challenge issued by

---

121. Kennedy, *The Recapitulation of Israel*, 185.

122. With debts here to Kennedy, *The Recapitulation of Israel*, 186–89.

123. Kennedy, *The Recapitulation of Israel*, 193.

the devil in this first test, Jesus responds in Matthew 4:4 by quoting Deuteronomy 8:3b (LXX), a scripture that had been addressed to Israel in reference to their experience recounted in Exodus 16.[124] Depicted there in Exodus is Israel's rebellion, which was likewise related to food. When the people are tested by hunger along the course of their journey in the wilderness, they complain against Moses and Aaron because they see no prospect for food, and grumble that at least in Egypt they always had ample food to enjoy (16:3). The Lord in turn responds to Moses that he will rain bread from heaven for them, which serves as a test as to whether they will follow his law or not (16:4). This is all background relevant to Deuteronomy 8:1–6, and verses 2–3 particularly so, which point up the Lord's provision of manna in connection with Exodus 16:4.

Evident here is how Jesus' testing is recapitulative of Israel's: both Israel and Jesus are put in a situation of hunger and the test is whether they will remain faithful and obedient in their privation or in disobedience betray a self-centered and disloyal heart. The devil directed his device, of course, for Jesus to repeat the disloyalty and rebellion of Israel. More to the point, "The devil is tempting Jesus to misuse, not his divine *powers*, but his *relationship* with his Father by failing to respond to his Father's love with trust."[125] In response, Jesus quotes the command of Deuteronomy 8:3b, prefacing it with "It is written" (γέγραπται), and thus signaling the binding character of God's word upon his own life as "a man" (ὁ ἄνθρωπος). The first test thus recapitulates the lesson that whole-hearted trust in, and obedience to, God's word is paramount.[126]

In the first test, Jesus responded to the devil with a quotation from Scripture that rebutted with learned precision the temptation challenge issued at him. Now, in the second test, the devil tries to turn the tables on Jesus by quoting Psalm 91:11–12 to entice Jesus, since he is the Son of God, to test God to see whether he will prove true to the word of his promise. The bait is set with the question implied here—do not the words of Deuteronomy 8:3b hold true here too? As the devil presents it,

---

124. With debts to Kennedy, *The Recapitulation of Israel*, 196–200.

125. William L. Kynes, *A Christology of Solidarity: Jesus as the Representative of His People in Matthew* (Lanham, MD: University Press of America, 1991), 33.

126. Along the same lines, France, *Jesus and the Old Testament*, 52, states, "This, then, is for [Jesus] the essence of the temptation, and this lesson he, like Old Testament Israel, must learn if he is to be worthy of the title 'Son of God'."

if Jesus would cast himself down from the pinnacle of the temple (the setting appears to be a visionary one), he could count on the angels to come to his aid and miraculously rescue him from harm. It is not insignificant that the devil prefaces his quotation of Scripture by using the same "it is written" that Jesus used earlier in Matthew 4:4. The devil's stratagem appears to be along these lines: "If you truly live by every word that proceeds from God's mouth then you will heed his promise in Psalm 91."[127] On closer examination of Psalm 91, however, nothing in the text suggests the appropriateness of taking any such risky action or putting oneself presumptuously in the way of a life-threatening danger. The thrust of the psalm's broader context has to do with the security of the person who trusts in the Lord throughout the circumstances of life, promising protection from outward dangers (Ps 91:3, 5–8, 10, 12–13) as well as security in the endeavors of that person (Ps 91:11–12).

The devil for his part abstracts the verses from their context and distorts their meaning as if one may presume to "dare" God to keep the word of his promises. But Jesus sees right through the presumptuousness in the challenge issued by the devil. He will not presume upon God by daring his protection, for to do so would be again to misuse his relationship with his Father. In response, Jesus quotes the command of Deuteronomy 6:16: "Again it is written, 'You shall not put the Lord your God to the test.'" In this portion of Deuteronomy, God is impressing upon Israel through his servant Moses that they take utter care to worship and serve him alone. In context Deuteronomy 6:16 is not just a general command to not put God to the test, but is a command for Israel to not test God *as they had tested him at Massah*, reflecting there on the experience of Israel recounted in Exodus 17:2–7. Recapitulating Israel's history in regard to the test they had faced in Exodus 17, "Jesus likewise is tempted to force God's hand to see whether he really is with his Son, and will meet his need as he has promised."[128] But Jesus remains faithful where Israel had failed (cf. Ps 95:7b–11); his refusal to test God reveals he had heeded the warning of Deuteronomy 6:16 as well as having discriminated rightly the intent of Psalm 91 that God protects the faithful.

---

127. Kennedy, *The Recapitulation of Israel*, 201. With debts to Kennedy, *The Recapitulation of Israel*, 202–6.

128. France, *Jesus and the Old Testament*, 52.

Like the second test, the devil's third temptation involves another visionary setting, this time to an unspecified mountain on which he shows Jesus "all the kingdoms of the world and their glory," and then proffers, "All these I will give you, if you will fall down and worship me" (Matt 4:8b–9). Quite plainly, the devil challenges Jesus far more brazenly than in the two previous temptations. A progression in the nature of the temptations is discernible. Satan's first two salvos call into question the Father's commitment to Jesus. Would Jesus *turn to* the Father in obedient trust to sustain as well as protect him? The subversive nature of the devil's third salvo, however, is laced with full blown idolatry. Would Jesus *turn from* the Father in a betrayal of the highest treason? It is hardly fanciful to surmise that the force of this temptation upon Jesus was *not* the lure of receiving immediate rule over the kingdoms of this world by an instant *quid pro quo* of submission to Satan. More plausible, I submit, is that the force of this temptation is related to the growing sense Jesus had of the cup that the Father would be giving him to drink (Matt 26:39), a cup that was full of suffering and death. Here, the devil offered him an easy bypass.

For the first time in response to the devil's temptations, Jesus rebukes him with the command, "Be gone, Satan!," and then quotes Deuteronomy 6:13,[129] "For it is written, 'You shall worship the Lord your God and him only shall you serve'" (Matt 4:10). In this section of Deuteronomy, Moses is admonishing the people that once they arrive in the land God promised, they must not forget the Lord who redeemed them from Egypt (6:10–12), and "not go after other gods" (6:14).[130] Later in Deuteronomy, the rank idolatry of the golden calf incident recounted in Exodus 32 is explicitly referenced in 9:7–21, 25–10:5. Deuteronomy 10:12–22 then rounds things out with a call for Israel to fear and serve only the Lord, repeating the command of 6:13 in 10:20. The recapitulative character of Jesus' experience to that of Israel's can be seen through the quotation of Deuteronomy 6:13 in connection with the golden calf incident of Exodus 32. In this third test, Jesus recapitulates

---

129. The wording of the quotation from Deuteronomy 6:13 differs from the LXX in substituting "worship" for "fear" in the first line; in the second line the word "only" is an interpretive expansion.

130. With debts here to Kennedy, *The Recapitulation of Israel*, 210–12.

Israel's history at the mountain, namely, their being tempted to surrender themselves to undisguised idolatry to fast-track what God had promised. Israel failed the test most egregiously, whereas Jesus' use of Deuteronomy evidences his obedient hearing of that text, staying true to God alone. The irony is rich: Jesus' refusal of Satan's kingdoms means he will now inaugurate his own (Matt 4:17). William Kynes ties it up nicely: "This forms a fitting climax to the narrative not only because idolatry was thought to be Israel's most grievous sin, but also because it alludes to the ending of the gospel in which the triumphant Son of God through his obedience and faithfulness to his Father receives far more than that which Satan had offered (28:18)."[131] Just as in the episode of Jesus' baptism, our theological aesthetic sees the fittingness of God's wisdom and righteousness manifest in Christ's role as Israel-in-person in full compliance with God's righteous requirements as being perfectly correlated with the beauty of Christ's theodramatic fittingness in the event of his temptation experience as part of the recapitulative patterning of redemptive-history.

Conspectus

We end this section having contributed to the christological contours of beauty with respect to Christ's identity as the last Adam and the true Israel. The operative concept I applied here is "recapitulation," which is to say that Christ recapitulates in his life the history of Adam and Israel. Thus, represented in the life and ministry of Christ is a correspondence or parallelism to past history of redemption that is fulfilled or "summed up" in Christ. The Adam-Christ parallel was demonstrated from Romans 5:12–21 and 1 Corinthians 15:44–49, and the Israel-Christ parallel from the events of Jesus' baptism by John and his temptation in the wilderness, all of which highlights the paradigmatic nature of the parallels as basic to the design of the divine plan. The theodramatic fittingness of the Son revealed through his identity as the true Israel is especially highlighted in the event of Jesus' baptism, with Jesus himself affirming that event as "fitting" in order to fulfill all righteousness. Although *all* righteousness that Jesus was called to fulfill as the Messiah was not

---

131. Kynes, *A Christology of Solidarity*, 34.

fulfilled in the event of his baptism alone, its occurrence just prior to his public ministry serves emblematically for seeing Jesus' whole messianic undertaking as "fitting" in order to fulfill all righteousness. Christ's recapitulation as such serves his redemptive mission wherein the righteousness that Christ altogether fulfills as the Messiah becomes the free gift of righteousness by the grace of God to all those whose salvation hope is found in Christ. The parallels between Adam and Christ and between Israel and Christ reflect an important aspect of the beauty of redemptive-history, not just by virtue of perceiving the recapitulative patterning but ultimately in perceiving the "beauty of the Lord" in the person of Christ, whose glory reflects all facets of his messianic identity.

CHRIST THE TRANSFIGURED

In this final section we develop the christological contours of beauty in regard to Christ's identity as revealed at the event of his transfiguration. Recorded in all three synoptic Gospels (Matt 17:1–9; Mark 9:2–10; Luke 9:28–36), it is fair to say that no other event in the Gospel narratives outside of Jesus' death on the cross is more pregnant with signification and mystique.[132] The event of Christ's transfiguration stands out in its own arresting way as an example of how God orchestrated the episodes defining of Jesus' life. The theological aesthetic principle we have employed earlier likewise will be employed in argument here, namely, that the theodramatic fittingness of the Son is perfectly conformed to the respective form of his life in the states of his humiliation and exaltation. The significance of the transfiguration event is presented in terms of three main parts: (1) the redemptive-historical fittingness of the transfiguration; (2) the epiphanic significance of Jesus' Sonship; and (3) the implicit eschatological anthropology. What all of this conveys is a theologically thicker sense of the identity of Christ and the purpose of his mission.

Before proceeding in our theological interpretation of the transfiguration event, it will be helpful first to summarize it from the common elements and narrative thread found in all three versions of

---

132. A corroborating testimony of the transfiguration story is given in 2 Peter 1:16–18.

the synoptic accounts. The narrative common to all the Synoptics preceding the transfiguration event unfolds in the following sequence:[133] (1) Peter's confession that Jesus is the Messiah; (2) Jesus' charge not to divulge this to others; (3) Jesus' prediction of his coming suffering, death and resurrection; and (4) his call to those who want to be his disciples to follow him in self-sacrifice. Soon after these things take place, Jesus takes Peter, James, and John up to a mountain site and he becomes "transfigured before them" (Mark 9:2), that is, his bodily appearance, garments and all, become magnificently luminous.[134] Right then, Moses and Elijah appear in the scene in conversation with Jesus. In a somewhat bemused response to Jesus, Peter suggests that three tents (shelters) be built, one each for Jesus, Moses, and Elijah. A cloud manifesting the veiled presence of God then overshadows Jesus and the disciples, and a voice out of the cloud announces that this is my beloved/chosen Son and commands the disciples, "Listen to him!" In the next instant the disciples see no one with them except Jesus. On the descent down the mountain, Jesus charges them to tell no one about what they had seen until after his resurrection, and a discussion follows (except in Luke) concerning the coming of Elijah. The inexorable direction for Jesus from this point on is to Jerusalem, his city of destiny, and the events of his passion that await him there. To accomplish his redemptive mission, the path forward must be realized first by way of suffering and death, and only then to realize his entrance into glory (Luke 24:26).

THE REDEMPTIVE-HISTORICAL FITTINGNESS OF THE TRANSFIGURATION

The public ministry of Jesus that was inaugurated at his baptism comes to a crescendo in theodramatic fashion at his transfiguration. As Arthur Ramsey puts it, "The Transfiguration seems to stand at a watershed in the ministry of Jesus, and to be a height from which the reader looks down on one side upon the Galilean ministry and on the other side upon the *Via Crucis*."[135] The transfiguration thus marks a crucial transition

---

133. W. L. Liefeld, "Transfiguration" in *Dictionary of Jesus and the Gospels*, ed. Joel B. Green and Scot McKnight (Downers Grove, IL: InterVarsity Press, 1992), 834.

134. The term "transfiguration" goes back to the Vulgate's *transfiguratus est*.

135. Ramsey, *The Glory of God and the Transfiguration of Christ*, 101.

in Jesus' ministry. The issue of his identity and the purpose of his mission converge there in revelation unlike anytime up to that point. An appreciation of the redemptive-historical fittingness of the transfiguration event involves discerning its redemptive-historical signification, which has to do with its continuity both backward to the Old Testament tradition and forward to the eschatological hope of God's future triumph in Christ. Thus, in the literary sense, the transfiguration has the characteristics of, and functions in the wider Gospel narrative as, a Janus-type episode whose associated imagery and motifs look backward and forward in redemptive-history. These motifs and imagery, involving a constellation of allusions and intertextual connections, are intertwined in significance, simultaneously pointing back to the Old Testament tradition and pointing ahead to the dawning of the messianic age. As I will unpack in my theological interpretation, the transfiguration entails Mosaic, eschatological (apocalyptic), and enthronement connotations. Along with this, each of the synoptic accounts accent different aspects of the event. All of this plays together in comprising its fullness of meaning, a fullness that, to be sure, makes it slippery to theologically interpret. As such, our theological interpretation will draw from the more salient motifs and imagery that, generally speaking, scholars have recognized.

Continuity Backward to Moses-Mount Sinai

The interpretation of the transfiguration in the light of Moses' Sinai experience has a long history in Christian exegesis.[136] Our immediate focus here will be limited to this aspect of continuity to the Old Testament tradition. "Allusions to the exodus context have been noted by many," write David Pao and Eckhard Schnabel. "Two texts are particularly relevant for this account: Exod 24:9–18; 34:29–45."[137] Although certain elements of difference exist between the synoptic accounts, the aforementioned point holds true for all of them. In the example

---

136. See, e.g., Dale C. Allison, *The New Moses. A Matthean Typology* (Minneapolis: Fortress Press, 1993), 243–48.

137. David W. Pao and Eckhard J. Schnabel, "Luke" in *Commentary on the New Testament Use of the Old Testament*, ed. G. K. Beale and D. A. Carson (Grand Rapids: Baker Academic, 2007), 311.

given here in regard to Mark's Gospel, the following parallels between the transfiguration event and Moses' Sinai experience are typical of those cited:[138]

Mark	Event	Exodus	Event
9:2a	six days	24:16	six days
9:2a	three disciples	24:1, 9	Aaron, Nadab, and Abihu
9:2b	ascent of mountain	24:9, 12–13	ascent of Sinai
9:2b-3	Jesus' transfiguration	34:29	Moses' glory on the face
9:7b	God's presence in the clouds	24:15–16, 18	God's presence in the clouds
9:7b	God's voice from the clouds	24:16	God's voice from the clouds

The aspects of the transfiguration alluding to these elements of Moses' Sinai experience need not be taken in any strict correspondence, and certain points may be arguable. "Of course, the parallels are not exact," writes Rikki Watts. "These are paradigmatic moments, not precisely constructed replicas."[139] But when considered with all the Old Testament intertextuality with which Mark frames his narrative, the imagery and allusions to Moses' Sinai experience were unmistakably recognized by all three synoptists.

Expanding a bit more on the parallels between the transfiguration and Sinai events. Mark and Matthew both begin their transfiguration story with the same time reference indicating that the transfiguration occurs "six days" after the conversation at Caesarea-Philippi; Luke says it was "after eight days." This differential makes the allusion to Exodus 24:16 more tenuous in the view of some commentators, but as a rule not at the expense of discounting the overall symbolism to

---

138. The parallels listed here borrow from Simon S. Lee, *Jesus' Transfiguration and the Believers' Transformation: A Study of the Transfiguration and Its Development in Early Christian Writings* (Tübingen: Mohr Siebeck, 2009), 23.

139. Rikki E. Watts, "Mark" in *Commentary on the New Testament Use of the Old Testament*, ed. G. K. Beale and D. A. Carson (Grand Rapids: Baker Academic, 2007), 186.

the Moses-Mount Sinai motif.[140] The three disciples, Peter, James, and John, who accompany Jesus up the mountain as he enters God's manifest glory-presence have their Sinai parallel in the three named men, Aaron, Nadab, and Abihu (along with seventy unnamed elders), who accompany Moses on his ascent to do the same. Indeed, Elijah is the only other Old Testament figure to go up on Mount Sinai (Horeb) and experience meeting with God and seeing his glory (1 Kgs 19:8–13). While the description of Jesus' transfigured appearance in terms of its dazzling radiance carries clear eschatological connotations (more on this below), it also recalls how Moses' face shined with a reflection of the divine glory he had seen. The presence of the cloud at the site of the transfiguration, its overshadowing of Jesus and his disciples, and God's voice that projects from it, together exhibit the same pattern as at Mount Sinai with Moses (and Joshua, his assistant). Moreover, Matthew mentions the cloud's brightness (17:5), which is reminiscent of God's shekinah glory (Exod 40:35; 1 Kgs 8:10–11).

Continuity Forward to Eschatological Hope

That the redemptive-historical orientation of the transfiguration is fundamentally to the future seems perhaps self-evident. From this perspective the episode serves as a momentous preview of "coming attractions" that are integral to the eschatological design of the divine plan. When Jesus' appearance transfigured before the disciples, all three synoptists describe his clothing comparably to being "white as light" (Matt 17:2). Far from being incidental, this detail contributes to the apocalyptic tenor of the whole scene, for during that moment the disciples saw Jesus transform "from an earthly form into a supraterrestrial, which is denoted by the radiance of the garments, [and] suggests the context of apocalyptic ideas."[141] Matthew's highlighting that Jesus' face "shone

---

140. As one example, Dorothy Lee, *Transfiguration* (London: Continuum, 2004), 69, goes with this explanation in regard to Luke's version: "Luke disregards Mark's calculation of six days, with its overtones of Moses on Mount Sinai, and rounds the number to a week, making it smoother and less abrupt than Mark's reckoning." Another possibility is that Luke is drawing a connection to the eighth day assembly of the annual Feast of Tabernacles (Lev 23:36).

141. Behm, μεταμορφόω, *TDNT*, 4:758. Clothing of such a dazzling nature is characteristic of how heavenly beings are described in Jewish apocalyptic writings. As

like the sun" (17:2; cf. Rev 1:16) only enhances this tenor, and along with this, his choice of the term "vision" (ὅραμα) in reference to the event (17:9) brings out connections to the theme of the Danielic Son of Man. In Daniel's vision, the "Ancient of Days" [God] is garbed in clothing as "white as snow, and the hair of his head like pure wool" (Dan 7:9), with a fiery radiance surrounding his presence. And the "one like a son of man" approaches the Ancient of Days and receives authority and kingdom (Dan 7:13-14).[142] "If this is correct," states Craig Evans, "then the transfiguration should be understood as a visual verification of Jesus' claim to be the 'son of man' who will come in the glory of his Father with the holy angels (Mark 8:38; Dan 7:10)."[143]

The brilliant light, the luminescent face, the dazzling white clothes—in short, the whole optical phenomenon of Jesus' irradiant appearance—projects patent apocalyptic overtones. Although the same sense is implicit in Matthew and Mark, Luke alone captures the image of Jesus' full irradiance with the term "glory" (δόξα, 9:32). "The glory," writes Lee, "which will be fully manifest in God's future—in the banquet at the end time and the establishing of peace and harmony on the earth (Isa 11:6-9; 25:6-10a)—is anticipated in the face and raiment of Christ on the mount of transfiguration."[144] Adding to the uniqueness, even mystique, of the event comes the appearance of Moses and Elijah in the scene. Noticeable in Mark's account is the reversed chronological placement

---

Lee, *Transfiguration*, 16, points out, "The angelic beings who stand in the presence of God are clothed in radiant white garments (Mark 16:5; 2 Macc 11:8). By extension, the righteous in heaven will also be clothed in white, wearing celestial garb as befits their status and abode (e.g. 1 Enoch 62:15; 2 Enoch 22:8-10; 4 Ezra 2:39; Rev 3:5; 6:11; 7:9, 13-14; 19:14)."

142. Relevant to this, A. D. A. Moses, *Matthew's Transfiguration Story and Jewish-Christian Controversy* (JSNTSup 122; Sheffield, England: Sheffield Academic Press, 1996), 91-92, writes: "It is notable that Matthew's transfiguration pericope (17:1-8) is preceded and followed by two Son of Man sayings (16:27; 16:28 and 17:9; 17:12). ... [T]hese Son of Man sayings when taken together form a Danielic Son of Man *inclusio*, which has direct bearing on Matthew's theology of the transfiguration. ... Matthew's use of the term ["Son of Man" found in Dan 7:13-14] reflects the conviction that those verses provided a pattern which it was Jesus' mission to fulfill. For the *majority* of Matthew's distinctive uses are set in the context of the future vindication and glory of the Son of Man and many of the relevant passages echo Daniel 7 themes: clouds, heaven, coming, glory, kingdom, judgment and the like."

143. Craig A. Evans, *Mark 8:27–16:20* (WBC 34B; Waco, TX: Word, 2001), 36.

144. Lee, *Transfiguration*, 73.

of introducing Elijah before Moses (9:4). The most likely reason for this priority in the name order is the eschatological orientation with which Mark wants to stamp his narrative. Expectations in Judaism recognized Elijah's apocalyptic role in particular as the harbinger of the Lord—the eschatological prophet of whom it was written: "Remember the law of my servant Moses, the statutes and rules that I commanded him at Horeb for all Israel. Behold, I will send you Elijah the prophet before the great and awesome day of the LORD comes" (Mal 4:4-5; cf. John 1:21, 45). That Moses and Elijah together may be seen to summarize the Law and the Prophets is fair to say, but not simply by virtue of presuming their respective representation of these categories. As Rikki Watts explains, the Malachi connection here is elucidative: "The traditional view that Moses represents the law and Elijah the prophets is essentially correct because in Malachi, Elijah the representative prophet will call the people back to the law of Moses."[145] In regard to their signification at the mount of transfiguration, then, "[t]he presence of Moses and Elijah testify to the inbreaking of the great and terrible day of the Lord, and that Jesus, who alone of the three is clothed in glory and whose word is identified with God's, is mysteriously the Lord whom Israel seeks and who will indeed come suddenly to his temple (Mal 3:1)."[146]

Epiphanic Significance of Jesus' Sonship

A noteworthy, if subtle, aspect of the transfiguration that the Lukan version suggests is its role in strengthening Jesus, serving "as a fortifying for the cross, so that the will to the cross might be free and complete."[147] Following just days after having told his disciples of his imminent suffering and death (9:22), Jesus "went up on the mountain to pray" (9:28). Given the subject of exchange between Jesus, Moses, and Elijah (9:30-31),

---

145. Watts, "Mark," 187. Regarding the next verse (4:6), Watts writes, "Elijah's task—"to turn the hearts of the parents to their children" and vice versa—though sometimes taken to mean righting the family dislocations of 2:10-16, seems best understood in the light of the immediately preceding reference to Moses as the restoration of the postexilic faithless generation to the covenant loyalty of the ancient forefathers." (189)

146. Watts, "Mark," 187.

147. Adolf Schlatter, *The History of the Christ: The Foundation for New Testament Theology*, trans. Andreas J. Köstenberger (Grand Rapids: Baker Books, 1997), 298.

it is quite plausible such fortification occurred. "The transfiguration ... appears to be the answer of the Father to the prayer of the Son," writes S. Lewis Johnson. That answer "is not the removal of the cross; that cannot be prevented. It is rather a revelation of the glory of the kingdom to come, designed to encourage the Son as he moves toward his atoning sufferings."[148] In Matthew, at the climax of the transfiguration the voice of the Father declares his paternal delight in his Son just as he had done at Jesus' baptism. In Mark and Luke the wording of the heavenly testimony paralleling the baptism and transfiguration accounts is more approximate. All the same, the echoes of Psalm 2:7 and Isaiah 42:1 reverberate in the Father's pronouncement to the disciples that this is my beloved/chosen Son. In the substance of these allusions the aspects of Christ's identity as messianic king and (suffering) Servant of the Lord are respectively brought out even as they are brought together into one historical figure, Jesus. The things concerning "the traditional hopes that had attached to Psalm 2 of a victorious king-messiah," writes Watts, "Jesus will do, ... but his wielding a rod of iron and shattering the nations like pots (Ps 2:9) will come through the power of redeeming death and resurrection."[149] The eschatological majesty thus glimpsed at the transfiguration is that to which Christ is destined as chosen Son, but what can only be fulfilled by way of the cross.

It might appear at first glance that the self-humbling epitomized in the Son's *kenōsis* (described in Phil 2:6-8), and which so defines his messianic servanthood, is allowed a momentary exception in the case of his transfiguration as he proleptically manifests his glory to come. The question here is simply whether the grandiose display of Christ's eschatological majesty momentarily belies his disposition in condescension. I submit it does not, for the constancy of character that Christ reflects is evident even in, or better, especially in, his moment of transfiguration. As Adolf Schlatter relates, "The event revealed the greatness of renunciation Jesus took upon himself through the way to the cross. By

---

148. S. Lewis Johnson, "The Transfiguration of Christ," *BSac* 124 (April-June 1967), 135-36. Although the transfiguration account is not included in John's Gospel, our present discussion is evocative of John 12:27-28 in which the Son's inner turmoil, God's glorification, and the Father's voice are all involved.

149. Watts, "Mark," 186.

stepping from so intimate a communion with God that he was capable of transfiguration into the pain and struggle of the cross, the liberty and greatness of the will to the cross became apparent."[150] Thus, in that extraordinary moment, Christ dramatizes-in-epiphany the same self-humbling condescension that characterizes his *kenōsis* proper (Phil 2:7). One could even say a *kenōsis* of an analogous, if indeed lesser, sort was dramatized, namely, Christ emptied himself from the form of his proleptic glory back to the form of a slave. In this way the transfiguration serves to magnify Christ's constancy of character even as his passion draws near. All of this is consistent with our affirmation that the glory of the Son incarnate is revealed as much in his self-abasement and service as it is in his exaltation and rule. On this note, Lee remarks, "the beloved Son, revealed in heavenly glory and beauty on the mountain as the harbinger of God's future, and the suffering of the Son of Man, dying in desolation on the cross, are one and the same person."[151] What the community of the faithful of all the ages will someday come to fully perceive and delight in is that the beauty of the Lord encompasses both without dissonance.

IMPLICIT ESCHATOLOGICAL ANTHROPOLOGY

Although the transfiguration was an extraordinary revelatory event in Christ's earthly career, it is important to keep in mind that the incarnation of God the Son is itself already the mediated revelation of the glory of God in the person of Jesus Christ, the indivisible God-man. Accordingly, it was not just the human part of Christ that became transfigured, nor just the divine part, but rather the whole person of Christ

---

150. Schlatter, *The History of the Christ*, 296. Schlatter continues, "It was therefore not natural necessity that forced him to die; even less did death face him because the Father forsook him. He was so close to him that he already saw his own glory, and yet he humbled himself to the cross, precisely because God was present to him in a way made visible at the transfiguration."

151. Lee, *Transfiguration*, 32. Similarly, W. D. Davies and Dale C. Allison Jr., *Commentary on Matthew VIII–XVIII: A Critical and Exegetical Commentary on the Gospel According to Saint Matthew*, vol. II (ICC; Edinburgh: T&T Clark, 1991), 706, write: "As God's Son it is Jesus' lot to participate in the polarities … of human experience. This is because the Son of God is the Messiah (16:16), and that means the eschatological man, in whom the eschatological pattern of suffering-vindication, tribulation-salvation must play itself out."

became transfigured. Thus, "the transformation touched the inner man, the form, the nature—a kind of foregleam of the resurrection body perhaps."[152] At the same time, a theologically thicker understanding of the transfiguration can be gained in light of canonical texts that help put in sharp relief the divinity of Christ, or conversely, his humanity. As a model example with respect to the former, Kevin Vanhoozer calls attention to the ending remark in Matthew's account—"And when they lifted up their eyes, they saw no one but Jesus only" (17:8)—in connection with Moses' speaking with God on Mount Sinai. As he explains,

> We are meant to see the contrast between Matt 17:6–8 and what Deut 4:11–16 says happened when God spoke on Sinai. ... The people heard God's voice, were afraid, but "saw no form; there was only a voice" (Deut 4:12). By contrast, in Matthew the disciples were afraid, and saw only Jesus. Matthew's account identifies Jesus by putting him in the spot hitherto reserved for God only. Who is Jesus? Not merely a greater than Moses but YHWH in the flesh.[153]

In this case, then, the transfiguration story enhances our view of Christ's true divinity. But this applies not just in regard to his divinity, the transfiguration story can enhance our view of Christ's true humanity as well. "It is not, therefore, only the eternal reality of God's glory that is made evident," writes Matthew Steenberg, "but the unending reality too of his humanity."[154] For the radiance of Christ's incarnate form showed forth the glory of God in humanity as it will be brought to eschatological completion by God for the redeemed in Christ (cf. Col 3:4).

Relevant to the present discussion is our treatment earlier of Christ as the last (ἔσχατος) Adam.[155] Paul's depiction of Christ as "the man of heaven" in 1 Corinthians 15:45–49 resonates theologically with the synoptic depiction of Christ transfigured. The latter image provides

---

152. Johnson, "The Transfiguration of Christ," 136.

153. Kevin J. Vanhoozer, "Theological Commentary and 'The Voice from Heaven': Exegesis, Ontology, and the Travail of Biblical Interpretation" in *On the Writing of New Testament Commentaries: Festschrift for Grant R. Osborne on the Occasion of his 70th Birthday*, ed. Stanley E. Porter and Eckhard J. Schnabel (Boston: Brill, 2013), 294.

154. M. C. Steenberg, "Two-Natured Man: An Anthropology of Transfiguration," *Pro Ecclesia* 14 no. 4 (Fall 2005): 418.

155. See above subsection, Christ the Last Adam, in particular under the discussion, Christ the Last Adam in 1 Corinthians 15:44–49.

a striking indication of the heavenly form that became Christ's when he ascended into heaven and entered the state of his exaltation, seated at the right hand of God. As we also pointed out in that discussion, the nature of his resurrection body is something empyreal—what Paul calls a spiritual body ($\sigma\tilde{\omega}\mu\alpha$ $\pi\nu\epsilon\upsilon\mu\alpha\tau\iota\kappa\acute{o}\nu$) in contradistinction to a natural one ($\sigma\tilde{\omega}\mu\alpha$ $\psi\upsilon\chi\iota\kappa\acute{o}\nu$)—and as such it corresponds most fittingly not to the present earthly age but to the eschaton, the age to come. As relates here to the transfiguration, I argue the following: even though Christ's incarnate form was eschatologically transformed in the brief time of his transfiguration (being a kind of prolepsis of his resurrection body), his manifest glory on that mountain site was *not* a more true, more real, or even more unveiled glory than his glory revealed in the form of a slave all during his earthly career. Given that Christ's glory was not hidden or veiled beneath his humanity, the glory that Christ manifested in both conditions—in the form of a slave and in his transfigured form—was equally the true, real, and unveiled glory of God in Christ. Accordingly, we can posit the following: in the event of the transfiguration, the form of glory that belonged to Christ while in the state of his humiliation (i.e., all during his earthly career) changed momentarily to reveal prolepti-cally that form of glory he would soon come to possess in the state of his exaltation, and as he will so appear at his parousia.[156] To encapsulate a critical point of our argumentation, then, the theodramatic fittingness of the Son is perfectly conformed to the respective form of his life in the states of his humiliation and exaltation.

In understanding the nature of Christ's transfiguration as being in part an anthropological revelation, it intimates "what we will be," for "when [Christ] appears we shall be like him, because we shall see him as he is" (1 John 3:2). Of consequence here is the correlation specific to Matthew's Gospel between the eschatological anthropology implicit in the transfiguration and the eschatological interpretation given by Christ of the parable of the weeds of the field (Matt 13:36–43).[157] Just as

---

156. Cf. William L. Lane, *The Gospel according to Mark: The English Text with Introduction, Exposition, and Notes* (NICNT; Grand Rapids: Eerdmans, 1974), 314, writes, "The transfiguration was a momentary, but real (and witnessed) manifes-tation of Jesus' sovereign power which pointed beyond itself to the parousia, when he will come 'with power and glory' (Mark 13:26)."

157. Including the context preceding the transfiguration account, both

Jesus' face "shone like the sun" (Matt 17:2), so likewise after the final judgment "the righteous will shine like the sun in the kingdom of their Father" (Matt 13:43; cf. Dan 12:3). Relevant to our argument here and previously, Stephen Barton ties in nicely several themes, stating:

> Just as Jesus obediently "fulfills all righteousness" at his baptism and subsequently shines like the sun at the transfiguration, so too, disciples of Jesus who obey his commands will shine like the sun with God as their Father. So a close corollary is established between Jesus the eschatological Son of God and followers of Jesus as "sons" of God (cf. [Matt] 5:9, 16). Thus, Matthew's transfiguration has an implicit theological anthropology at its heart, following on from its strong sonship christology and related to the key theme of "righteousness."[158]

Conspectus

We conclude this section and this chapter having elucidated the christological contours of beauty in regard to Christ's identity as revealed at the event of his transfiguration. As I have presented the case, the glory of Christ revealed at his transfiguration was a real episode during his earthly career that was most befitting in accordance with the divine purposes at that particular point in Christ's public ministry. As evident by its constellation of allusions and imagery, the scene of Christ's transfiguration was divinely orchestrated so as to highlight its continuity backward to the Old Testament tradition in connection with the exodus context and forward to the eschatological hope of God's future triumph in Christ. The epiphanic significance of Jesus' Sonship is revealed at the climax of the transfiguration when the Father declares his paternal delight in his Son just as he had done at Jesus' baptism. At that point especially, I have argued, the transfiguration serves to magnify the constancy of Christ's character in the self-humbling that was dramatized when he returned from his proleptic glory in intimate

---

narratives make mention of the coming of the Son of Man as the eschatological judge, the involvement of his angels as agents of judgment, and his kingdom.

158. Stephen C. Barton, "The Transfiguration of Christ according to Mark and Matthew: Christology and Anthropology" in *Resurrection*, ed. Friedrich Avemarie and Hermann Lichtenberger (WUNT 135; Tübingen: Mohr Siebeck, 2001), 244.

communion with the Father back to the form of a slave to embrace his destiny of death on the cross. Furthermore, in understanding the nature of Christ's transfiguration as being in part an anthropological revelation, the radiance of Christ's incarnate form showed forth the glory of God in humanity as it will be brought to eschatological completion by God for the redeemed in Christ. Given that Christ's glory was not hidden or veiled beneath his humanity, the glory that Christ manifested in both conditions—in the form of a slave and in his transfigured form—was equally the true, real, and unveiled glory of God in Christ. The radiance of Christ's glory is thus expressed most fittingly in and through whichever form of his economic identity is in view, his beauty radiating as always from glory to glory. The perspective this chapter offers of the christological contours of beauty corroborates our thesis, namely, that the Son's fittingness as incarnate Redeemer is the critical lens for seeing God's beauty, serving as well to display the Son's glory in every stage of the theodrama.

EXCURSUS: THEOLOGICAL AESTHETIC OF ISAIAH 53:2

> For he grew up before him like a young plant,
>> and like a root out of dry ground;
>> he had no form or majesty that we should look at him,
>> and no beauty that we should desire him.

In the midst of the portrait of the Servant of the Lord in Isaiah 42–53, the fourth "Servant Song" of Isaiah (52:13–53:12) reverberates with the themes of abasement and exaltation. The Servant's exaltation forms the poem's bookends within which we find a highly disturbing image of the Servant, a solitary figure described in visually shocking and ignominious terms. As to the note of triumph that frames the Servant's work, "[t]here is a reason why that point is made at the beginning and at the end of the poem. It is because nothing in between looks in the least like victory, certainly not any victory that proud, dominating humans can conceive of."[159] Writ large in this Servant Song are themes of sin and righteousness, grace and judgment, suffering and subsequent glory. Our interest is to offer a theological aesthetic of Isaiah 53:2b, addressing

---

159. John N. Oswalt, *Isaiah* (NIVAC; Grand Rapids: Zondervan, 2003), 570.

Isaiah's (suffering) Servant of the Lord as identified with the person of Christ, described here by the prophet as having "no form or majesty (Heb: הָדָר; LXX: δόξα) that we should look at him, and no beauty (Heb: מַרְאֶה; LXX: κάλλος) that we should desire him."

In the theological interpretation of Philippians 2:6–8 put forward earlier in the chapter, I noted the Christ-hymn's various linguistic and conceptual links to Isaiah 42–53, and how the prominent themes of abasement and exaltation figure commonly. The whole thrust of our earlier argument regarding Christ's identity as taking the form of a slave is all of a piece with the Isaianic description in 53:2b of the Servant of the Lord being bereft of any majesty or beauty to the commonplace perception of him. As we see this Servant figure even more shockingly described just before in Isaiah 52:14 and just after in 53:3, there is nothing regal nor notably attractive about him as far as the eyes could tell, nothing about his external appearance or position that anyone would be drawn or allured to. In other words, apparent ignobility and unprepossessing appearance is how the fourth Servant Song prophetically characterizes the messianic Servant of the Lord.

The correspondence between Christ's identity as taking the form of a slave is one with his messianic identity as taking the form of the Isaianic Servant of the Lord. The theological aesthetics according to the train of our argument is that Christ's humanity in the form of a slave—transposed in context here as the Isaianic Servant of the Lord—was most befitting for God the Son to take in accordance with his role as the Messiah, which itself is all in accordance with the nature of God's self-giving love. A fundamental aspect of the aesthetic dimension pertaining here is the theodramatic fittingness of the Son as incarnate Redeemer revealed in his assumption of the form of the Isaianic Servant of the Lord. Any ostensible dissonance between the self-revelatory nature of God's actions in Christ in his assumption of that form and the essential nature of God in himself is not a real dissonance. The beauty of Christ is thus qualified by the theodramatic fittingness that corresponds to the human form his life takes as incarnate Redeemer in the economy of salvation.

The parallel we can draw to the Christ-hymn is that the Son's *kenōsis* in becoming incarnate in the form of a slave is in effect depicted by

Isaiah in terms of the Servant of the Lord's apparent ingloriousness and off-putting appearance. Regarding the Servant figure in Isaiah 53:2b, John Oswalt comments:

> The Christian thinks inevitably of Jesus Christ: a baby born in the back-stable of a village inn. This would shake the Roman Empire? A man quietly coming to the great preacher of the day and asking to be baptized. This is the advent of the man who would be heralded as the Savior of the world? No, this is not what we think the arm of the Lord should look like. We were expecting a costumed drum major to lead our triumphal parade. Our eyes are caught and satisfied by superficial splendor. This man, says Isaiah, will have none of that. As a result, our eyes flicker across him in a crowd and we do not even see him. His splendor is not on the surface, and those who have no inclination to look beyond the surface will never even see him, much less pay him any attention.[160]

It is this depiction of Christ which, for Balthasar, encapsulates the revelation of the heart of God. "No truth of revelation," he writes, "from the Trinity to the Cross and Judgment, can speak of anything else than of the glory of God's poor love—which of course is something much different than what we here below imagine by the name love. No, it is Spirit and Fire."[161] In his humiliating death on the cross, the glory of God's actions in Christ reveals in the most theodramatic way the divine love that expresses itself in unreserved self-giving for the sake of others. Such a "poverty-stricken" obedience is only understandable, explains Balthasar, as "an obedience that lies beyond the limits of what is possible to man upon earth, as the most absolute proclamation to the world of God's disposition of love."[162] Yet in that self-giving obedience

---

160. John N. Oswalt, *The Book of Isaiah, Chapters 1–39* (NICOT; Grand Rapids: Eerdmans, 1986), 382–83.

161. Hans Urs von Balthasar, "Geist und Feuer," *Herder Korrespondenz* 30 (1976): 72–82, here 82, quoted in Edward T. Oakes, *Pattern of Redemption: The Theology of Hans Urs von Balthasar* (New York: Continuum, 1994), 298.

162. Balthasar, *GL*, VII, 232. Relevant as well here, Balthasar *TL* II, 141, writes: "God's love is almighty because it can do anything that lies within the imaginable compass of infinite love. This omnipotence is neither limited nor disturbed by the worldly antithesis of wealth and poverty. ... We can demonstrate this in terms of the economy of salvation. Once again, could anyone be poorer than God the Father,

is demonstrated the supreme "human realization of the divine dispo-sition of Jesus Christ."[163] Thus, in the same way that Christ's humanity in the form of the Isaianic Servant of the Lord is counterintuitive to the natural mind, so too is the divine nature of which Balthasar speaks. In the sense that we are talking about here, the essential nature of God in himself does not consist of power *without* weakness but power *in* weakness—*seeming* weakness, that is. "His apparent weakness is actu-ally the effect of his almighty power, for everything is his doing," writes Philip Hughes. "The amazing truth is that in Christ, our seemingly weak, poor, despised, fellow, God was reconciling the world to himself (2 Cor 5:19)."[164] The glory of God in Christ while he was in the state of his humiliation presents to mere ocular perception an image of his person that is altogether dissident to the perception of the unveiled glory of the Son in the form of his humanity to those with eyes of faith. On this view, Isaiah 53:2b "implies that his true intrinsic beauty is hidden from people because they look at him entirely from a human standpoint," unlike those who are given the eyes of faith to perceive what they could not see before.[165]

Belonging to the state of Christ's humiliation from the time and circumstances of his birth and up through his death, his voluntary poverty identifies in an essential way his solidarity with all human beings, even the least and lowliest. The remarkable ease with which Jesus connected to folk of all rank and station, especially common folk

---

who cannot spare his Son because he loves the world so much; could anyone be poorer than the Son, who for our sake 'empties himself of his divine form and takes the form of a slave' (Phil 2:6-7), who, 'though he was rich, made himself poor out of generosity in order to enrich you by his poverty' (2 Cor 8:9), so that, following Christ, the Apostle is 'familiar with satiety and hunger, superfluity and depriva-tion', 'because I can do all things in the one who strengthens me' (Phil 4:12f)? The power of love therefore transcends the antithesis between poverty and wealth (it is both at once)."

163. Balthasar, *GL*, I, 670. Balthasar continues on, "We ought not here, more-over, to speak of an opaque christological dialect that destroys all form; rather, its structure is truly visible to faith, so overpowering is it for man's spirit and senti-ment to realize that the most glorious aspect of God's glory is precisely this divine disposition that becomes manifest in Christ's condescension."

164. Hughes, *The True Image*, 233.

165. Geoffrey W. Grogan, *Isaiah*, vol. 6, ed. Tremper Longman III and David E. Garland (EBC; Grand Rapids: Zondervan, 2008), 800.

and social outcasts, reflects this solidarity. In God reconciling the world to himself through Christ, the poverty of Christ embraces our own spiritual bankruptcy. As subsequent verse of this Servant Song puts it (Isa 53:4–6 NET):

> But he lifted up our illnesses, he carried our pain;[166]
>> even though we thought he was being punished,
>> attacked by God, and afflicted for something he had done.
>
> He was wounded because of our rebellious deeds,
>> crushed because of our sins;
>> he endured punishment that made us well;
>> because of his wounds we have been healed.[167]
>
> All of us had wandered off like sheep;
>> each of us had strayed off on his own path,
>> but the LORD caused the sin of all of us to attack him.[168]

And out of Christ's self-forfeiture of life ("because he willingly submitted to death," 53:12b) came his resurrection triumph ("he will divide the spoils of victory with the powerful," 53:12a),[169] and no sinner need be left in their own poverty of sin and misery. In Balthasar's words, "the righteous bring their righteousness, the scribes the weight of their

---

166. The study note on Isaiah 53:4 in the NET clarifies: "Illness and pain stand by metonymy (or perhaps as metaphors) for sin and its effects, as vv. 11–12 make clear."

167. The study note on Isaiah 53:5 in the NET further adds: "Continuing to utilize the imagery of physical illness, the group acknowledges that the servant's willingness to carry their illnesses (v. 4) resulted in their being healed. Healing is a metaphor for forgiveness here."

168. The translator's note on Isaiah 53:6 in the NET explains that "elsewhere the Hiphil of פָּגַע (paga`) means 'to intercede verbally' (Jer 15:11; 36:25) or 'to intervene militarily' (Isa 59:16), but neither nuance fits here. Apparently here the Hiphil is the causative of the normal Qal meaning, 'encounter, meet, touch.' The Qal sometimes refers to a hostile encounter or attack; when used in this way the object is normally introduced by the preposition -בְּ (bet, see Josh 2:16; Judg 8:21; 15:12, etc.). Here the causative Hiphil has a double object—the Lord makes 'sin' attack 'him' (note that the object attacked is introduced by the preposition -בְּ). In their sin the group was like sheep who had wandered from God's path. They were vulnerable to attack; the guilt of their sin was ready to attack and destroy them. But then the servant stepped in and took the full force of the attack."

169. The study note on Isaiah 53:12a in the NET points out that "the servant is compared here to a warrior who will be richly rewarded for his effort and success in battle."

learning and arguments, the tax-collectors and sinners their guilt, those who seek help their sickness, the demoniacs the fetters of their possession, and the poor the burden of their poverty. ...For in this encounter, each one is required to leave what he was before"—and namely so, at the cross.[170]

Manifested economically, all reflections of the beautiful expressed in God's outward works (*pulchritudo Dei ad extra*) are perceivable as an aesthetic quality of God's extrinsic glory. Given that beauty is integral to God's essential nature, moreover, that reality in and of itself does not require that God conform his self-revelation to our this-worldly norms and notions of the beautiful. Keeping that in mind, fundamental to our theological aesthetic is the premise that everything God does is perfectly fitting—and hence beautiful in its God-glorifying nature. To put it another way, theological aesthetics situates the beautiful as an entailment of whatever ways God displays his glory, that is, whatever is God-glorifying, most especially through the person and work of Christ. How theological aesthetics may or may not conform to our norms and notions of the beautiful or to our conceptualization of fittingness does not drive how we must understand and appreciate it. The plan of God as revealed in the economies of revelation and redemption in which all things are summed up in Christ Jesus drives the form and content of its theological aesthetics. With respect to Isaiah 53:2b, then, the gulf between the aesthetics versus theological aesthetics as it pertains to the Isaianic Servant of the Lord is quite patent, in the polarity between what to mere natural perception is attractive or impressive and what is revealed (cf. 53:1 with Rom 10:16–17, 21). A theological aesthetic apprehension involves the work of the Spirit enabling those with eyes of faith to perceive rightly the objective beauty of Christ in his assumption of that form, and that very same work of the Spirit is also what enables all those faith-filled ones to subjectively experience and grow in delight of the beauty that they have perceived. An essential element of the reason informing our argument is that the identity of God is revealed as much in his self-abasement and service as it is in his exaltation and rule. Again, in the way Balthasar is wont to express it, "God is not, in

---

170. Balthasar, *GL*, VII, 120.

the first place, 'absolute power', but 'absolute love', and his sovereignty manifests itself not in holding on to what is its own but in its abandonment."[171] And thus, the glory of God in Christ while he was in the state of his humiliation was actually glory revealed not glory concealed.

Our basic conclusion as it pertains to a theological aesthetic of Isaiah 53:2b remains unaltered from that which I have already argued for in this work—it is the optics given through faith alone by the work of God's Spirit that determines whether or not someone rightly perceives (albeit weakly and incompletely) Christ in the form of this humanity for who he truly is. And in that form the radiance of his glory is expressed most fittingly such that his beauty is always from glory to glory. With that whole picture in mind, we will round off our excursus with a befitting excerpt from Augustine's marvelous exposition of Psalm 44 (*Enarrationes in Psalmos 44*):

> Let the Bridegroom come forth and show himself to us, and let us love him. But if we find any trace of ugliness in him, let us love him not. What a strange thing! He found plenty of ugly features in us, yet he loved us; but if we find anything ugly in him, we must not love him. It is true that he put on our flesh in such a way that it could be said of him, *We saw him, and there was no fair form or comeliness in him* (Isa 53:2), but if you take account of the mercy that caused him to be reduced to such a state, he is beautiful even in his deformity. The prophet was speaking from the standpoint of the Jews when he said, *We saw him, and there was no fair form or comeliness in him.* Why is that so? Because his lowly state was no use to them *for understanding.* For all who do understand, the truth that *the Word was made flesh* (John 1:14) is supremely beautiful. A friend of the Bridegroom prayed, *Far be it from me to boast, save in the cross of our Lord Jesus Christ* (Gal 6:14). It would be a mean-spirited thing merely not to be ashamed of it; you must boast of it. Why did Christ have neither fair form nor comeliness? Because Christ crucified was a scandal to the Jews, and foolishness to Gentiles. But in what sense was he fair of form on the cross? Because God's foolishness is wiser than human wisdom, and God's weakness more powerful than human strength.

---

171. Hans Urs von Balthasar, *Mysterium Paschale: The Mystery of Easter*, trans. Aidan Nichols (San Francisco: Ignatius Press, 2005), 28.

Let us therefore, who believe, run to meet a Bridegroom who is beautiful wherever he is. Beautiful as God, as the Word who is with God, he is beautiful in the Virgin's womb, where he did not lose his godhead but assumed our humanity. Beautiful he is as a baby, as the Word unable to speak, because while he was still without speech, still a baby in arms and nourished at his mother's breast, the heavens spoke for him, a star guided the magi, and he was adored in the manger as food for the humble. He was beautiful in heaven, then, and beautiful on earth: beautiful in the womb, and beautiful in his parents' arms. He was beautiful in his miracles but just as beautiful under the scourges, beautiful as he invited us to life, but beautiful too in not shrinking from death, beautiful in laying down his life and beautiful in taking it up again, beautiful on the cross, beautiful in the tomb, and beautiful in heaven. Listen to this song to further your understanding, and do not allow the weakness of his flesh to blind you to the splendor of his beauty. The supreme and most real beauty is justice: if you can catch him out in any injustice, you will not find him beautiful in that regard; but if he is found to be just at every point, then he is lovely in all respects. Let him come to us, so that we may gaze on him with the eyes of our spirit, as he has been delineated for us by the prophet who sang his praises, and began, *My heart overflows with a good word* [Ps 45:1].[172]

---

172. Augustine, *Exposition of Psalm 44*, in *Expositions of the Psalms, 33–50*, ed. John E. Rotelle, trans. Maria Boulding (Hyde Park, NY: New City Press, 2000), 283. Leading in to this portion of his exposition of Psalm 44, the Gospel of John was an evident source of Augustine's inspiration in writing this.

5

The Cross: Beauty Redeeming

In this part of the theodrama—the midpoint of the biblical meta-story whose theodramatic form we characterized in Chapter 3 as a sublime comedy—the reversal out of tragedy into triumph that God had promised in the protevangelium plays out climactically as he reconciles the world to himself through Christ's atoning sacrifice and subsequent heavenly rule. Our interest in the last chapter concerned four key aspects of Christ's identity during his earthly career. In this chapter the christological contours of beauty will be developed in reference to Christ's work on the cross and God's work through Christ in the state of his heavenly exaltation. These efforts will demonstrate: (a) the Son's fittingness in the states of his humiliation and exaltation serves to display his glory appropriately; (b) the fittingness of God's retributive judgment meted out upon Christ; and (c) God's reconciling operations through the reign of Christ evince the beautiful nature of his work. I develop this chapter in three main sections as follows:

1. *The Depth of Beauty in the Form of the Cross.* I address two aspects in reference to Christ's work on the cross: (1) The Fittingness of Christ's High Priestly Mediatorship. Here, I offer a theological interpretation of Hebrews 2:10 and 7:26. I argue that because Jesus had to be made perfect through his sufferings in the state of his humiliation so that consequently he could enter the state of his exaltation to accomplish his high priestly intercession, the Son's fittingness in the form of his humanity corresponds perfectly to the respective form of his life in the states of his humiliation and exaltation. (2) Christ's Kingly Glory on the Cross. I argue that Christ's identity as revealed on the

cross magnifies the majesty of the unveiled glory of God in Christ for those with eyes to see it. The account of the penitent criminal who perceives Jesus' true identity on the cross offers a strong witness to this point.

2. *The Fittingness of God's Retributive Justice at the Cross.* I argue that the judgment God meted out upon Christ in the place of sinners was fitting—and hence beautiful (i.e., God-glorifying)—as that which the Son justly deserved as the one who for our sake God made to be sin, though he himself knew no sin. As such, due proportionality between punishment and "crime" was properly transacted in Christ's penal substitutionary death. The perfect equipoise of God's righteous holy love exemplifies the beauty of his glory in everything he does.

3. *The Already but Not-Yet Beauty of God's Reconciling Work through Christ the Exalted King.* I argue that, as represented in the body of Paul's letter to the Ephesians, God's reconciling operations through the reign of Christ display his beauty fundamentally in the form of an already but not-yet unity and harmony operating in the spheres of human-divine relations and human-human relations in the perfecting of his church.

THE DEPTH OF BEAUTY
IN THE FORM OF THE CROSS

The argument of our theological aesthetic entails that the Son's glory is displayed appropriately in each stage of the theodrama, and is qualified by the fittingness that corresponds to the form of his humanity. I consider that point here with respect to Christ's role as our high priestly mediator in light of how the author of Hebrews describes Christ's being qualified to become our high priestly mediator as a function of his respective fittingness in the states of his humiliation and exaltation. For his high priestly role, Christ's work on the cross is the necessary fulfillment of being qualified in the state of his humiliation and the prerequisite of being qualified in the state of his exaltation. The second case I consider in this section concerns the display of the Son's glory on the cross in reference to the account of the penitent criminal next to Jesus who perceives his true identity. Calvin's insights in particular are pressed into service here.

The Fittingness of Christ's High Priestly Mediatorship

In two verses that concern Christ's role as our high priestly media-tor—Hebrews 2:10 and 7:26—the author of Hebrews describes God's redemptive work through Christ in terms of its fittingness. I argue that in being made perfect through his sufferings to become our high priestly mediator before the Father, the Son's fittingness in the form of his humanity corresponds perfectly to the respective form of his life in the states of his humiliation and exaltation. The Son's glory is thus displayed appropriately in each stage of the theodrama.

The author of Hebrews takes up the notion of fittingness in direct reference to God's creational and redemptive work through Christ: "For it was fitting (πρέπω) that he [God], for whom and by whom all things exist, in bringing many sons to glory, should make the founder of their salvation perfect through suffering" (2:10). With regard to Hebrews 2:10, since all things are not only *by* God but also *for* him, "the goal of his redemptive work is thoroughly in line with his creative work. And 'since he created people for glory, it is *fitting* that he should provide a way for them to reach this end.'"[1] Earlier in Hebrews the Son is described as the agent "through whom also he [God] created the world" (Heb 1:2). Evident here is the symmetrical role of the Son's agency in the divine economy, as the work of creation is through the Son and the work of redemption also is accomplished through the Son. God's "bringing many sons to glory" through the work of Christ is fundamental to the redemptive-eschatological fulfillment of his original creational pur-poses. It was entirely fitting, writes William Lane, "with the primal intention celebrated in Psalm 8 that God should graciously decree that his Son identify himself with the human condition and rescue

---

1. Regarding the sonship of believers in Hebrews 2:10, William Lane, *Hebrews 1–8* (WBC 47A; Waco, TX: Word, 1991), 56, writes: "The motif of God's leading of many sons is familiar from the OT, particularly in connection with the Exodus from Egypt, where the divine initiative is frequently stressed (e.g., Exod 3:8, 17; 6:6–7; 7:4–5). The writer understands the goal of God's leadership to be entrance into the glory (δόξαν) envisioned in the statement from Ps 8:6b (LXX), which he has cited in v. 7, 'crowned with glory [δόξῃ] and splendor.' The redemptive associations of the term *glory* are apparent in the subsequent phrase "their salvation" (τῆς σωτηρίας αὐτῶν). The reference is to the heritage reserved for the redeemed in the world to come (cf. v. 5)."

humanity through his own humiliation and death. The sufferings of Jesus were appropriate (ἔπρεπεν) to the goal to be attained and were experienced in accordance with God's fixed purpose."[2] In this way the tragic incongruence between Psalm 8's depiction of human beings and the depravation of glory (*depravatio gloriae*) that characterizes all of humanity's image-bearing glory becomes fully rectified in Christ.

The passage from Hebrews 2:10-18 develops in train of thought from the Son's solidarity with God's people ("the offspring of Abraham," verse 16) in his *humanity* to his solidarity as their *high priest* (verses 17-18). That train of thought connects the term *it is fitting* (verse 10) with the terms *had to be* (verse 17).[3] The focus concerns the Son's preparation to be made "perfect" (verse 10) in order "to be made like his brothers in every respect," and thereby become "a merciful and faithful high priest" (verse 17). The common element singled out as befitting for Christ to be made perfect as the "founder" (ἀρχηγός;[4] cf. Heb 12:2) of salvation and to become a high priest," is the sufferings through which he had to pass (Heb 2:10, 18). Christ's being made perfect through sufferings as our Adamic representative is thus all of a piece with his becoming our high priestly mediator. As we saw earlier, the baptism of repentance to which John called Israel, and to which Jesus submitted as Israel's representative, was fitting with the suffering that comes to increasingly define Jesus' path of obedience. A further aspect of the theodramatic fittingness of God's purposes in Jesus' sufferings can be seen in how Jesus recapitulates in his life the history of Israel by representationally embodying the "psalms of lament."[5] James Mays puts it well:

---

2. Lane, *Hebrews 1-8*, 55.

3. While the first part of verse 17—"[Jesus] *had to be* (ὀφείλω) made like his brothers in every respect"—carries an obligatory sense, the train of thought develops in coordination with verse 10's "it is fitting." It makes the most sense to understand the sense of necessity in verse 17 not as being an absolute necessity of the case but as being a conditional necessity of the case, i.e., given (conditional on) God's purposes that lay behind the meaning of verse 10.

4. L&N 36.6 s.v. ἀρχηγός: "a person who as originator or founder of a movement continues as the leader—'pioneer leader, founding leader.' In order to indicate clearly the significance of ἀρχηγός in Heb 2:10, it may be important to employ a translation such as 'who established a way of salvation and leads people to it.' But it is also possible to understand ἀρχηγός in Heb 2:10 as meaning only the 'initiator' or 'founder.'"

5. For a recommended essay relevant to this point, see Bruce N. Fisk, "See My

The identification of Jesus with the self who speaks in the psalms is the sign of the representative and corporate reality of his passion. He suffers and prays with all those whose suffering and praying is represented by such prayers. He enters into their predicament. The hurt and cry of that great choir of pain is gathered into his life and voice. Henceforth the voice of affliction in these psalms is inseparable from the voice of Jesus. They are the liturgy of his incarnation, the language of his assumption of our predicament.[6]

It is fitting according to God's purposes, therefore, that in being made perfect (τελειόω) through the sufferings he endured, Jesus is able to identify perfectly with his brothers and sisters. In this context "Christ's being perfected is a vocational process by which he is made complete or fully equipped for his office" (cf. Heb 5:8-10; 7:28).[7] It is thus also fitting that Jesus is made perfect as high priest of his people through his sufferings so that he would be perfectly qualified to come before the Father in priestly service. "Even though he was Son, intimately linked with God," notes Alan Mitchell, "he was made to endure that suffering, which was not merely incidental to his priesthood but was constitutive of it."[8]

The language of "fittingness" is again employed in Hebrews 7:26 in reference to Christ as our high priest: "For it was indeed fitting (πρέπω) that we should have such a high priest, holy, innocent, unstained, separated from sinners, and exalted above the heavens." Leading up to this

---

Tears: A Lament for Jerusalem (Luke 13:31-35; 19:41-44)" in *The Word Leaps the Gap: Essays on Scripture and Theology in Honor of Richard B. Hays*, ed. J. Ross Wagner et al. (Grand Rapids: Eerdmans, 2008), 147-78. Although everything written about Jesus in the Law and the Prophets also must be fulfilled (Luke 24:44), here I am only emphasizing how Jesus embodies the psalms of lament in his life and death.

6. James L. Mays, *The Lord Reigns: A Theological Handbook to the Psalms* (Louisville: Westminster John Knox Press, 1994), 51.

7. O'Brien, *The Letter to the Hebrews*, 107. Cf. Lane, *Hebrews 1-8*, 57: "The statement that Jesus was 'perfected through suffering' draws upon a special nuance of the verb τελειουν in the LXX. In ceremonial texts of the Pentateuch the verb is used to signify the act of consecrating a priest to his office (Exod 29:9, 29, 33, 35; Lev 4:5; 8:33; 16:32; 21:10; Num 3:3). ... This cultic sense of the verb clarifies the meaning of τελειωσαι in v. 10 and explains the close association of the ideas of perfection and consecration in vv. 10-11."

8. Alan C. Mitchell, "The Use of πρέπειν and Rhetorical Propriety in Hebrews 2:10," *CBQ* 54 no. 4 (October 1992): 698.

point in Hebrews 7:11–25, the author has been arguing on the basis of Psalm 110:4 that Jesus is the priest to arise after the order of Melchizedek whose exalted status supersedes the Levitical priesthood, and whose priestly mediation is incomparably more effective where the Levitical priests' was not. With respect to his atoning work, the theme of Christ's kingship does not advance the author's message as does the priesthood of Christ. Although Christ's regality cannot be separated from his priestly ministry, in the presentation of Hebrews the victory by which Christ (our Adamic representative) wins back humanity's regal station is accomplished through Christ's priestly office (our Adamic mediator). Gerald Wilson observes that the kingly context that begins Psalm 110, recalling the throne promised to David and his descendants (2 Sam 7:11–16; Ps 89:34–37), takes a decided twist in verse 4:

> The claim in 110:4a that "Yahweh has sworn and will not change his mind" ... makes the unexpected completion of God's proclamation—"You are a priest forever, according to the order of Melchizedek" (110:4b)—even more startling. Contrary to all expectation, the one who is commissioned here is *priest* and not *king*! Thus the ambiguity [in 110:2b] permitted by the choice of the term רדה ("exercise authority") becomes an essential preparation for the sudden reversal accomplished in 110:4b as an enduring priesthood replaces an eternal (human) kingship![9]

What becomes evident, then, is a transformation of the Davidic kingship to a Davidic priest-king. As both a priest after the order of Melchizedek and the greater Davidic Scion, the paradigm of Christ's atonement combines both the role of king with its leading association of the *Christus Victor* motif, and the role of priest with its leading association of mediating penal substitutionary sacrifice. "Like the mysterious king of Salem in days of yore," writes Douglas Farrow, "he would unite the functions of the two historic institutions by which the divine blessings were mediated to Israelite society" (cf. Zech 6:12–13).[10] As we would

---

9. Gerald H. Wilson, "King, Messiah, and the Reign of God: Revisiting the Royal Psalms and the Shape of the Psalter" in *The Book of Psalms: Composition and Reception*, ed. Peter W. Flint and Patrick D. Miller Jr. (Boston: Brill Academic, 2005), 399.

10. Douglas Farrow, *Ascension Theology* (London: T&T Clark, 2011), 6.

expect, Christ's identity united as priest-king coincides with the basic description of the official aspect of the *imago Dei* that we presented in Chapter 2—that is, humans are created in a filial relationship with God to reflect his glory as his royal priests.[11]

Furthermore, according to Hebrews 7:26, what makes it most fitting for Jesus to be our high priest can be seen as a compound function of his character, achievement, and status. With regard to Jesus' character, it is summed up as being "holy, innocent, and unstained." Although the three terms overlap in meaning, Lane helpfully delineates each of them as follows:[12]

1. "holy" (ὅσιος) appears in Hebrews only here. In the LXX it describes those whose relationship to God and to others reflects fidelity to the covenant (Pss 12:1; 18:26; 32:6; 79:1-2; 132:9, 16; 149:1-2). The term resumes the motif of Jesus' obedient relationship to the Father demonstrated through the experiences of his earthly life (5:7-8).

2. "innocent" (ἄκακος) is used in the LXX predominantly with a passive and moral significance. It was an appropriate term for denoting the moral qualification of Jesus to be high priest. It signifies not only that Jesus was guileless in his relationship with other people, but that he was not touched by evil.

3. "unstained" (ἀμίαντος) denotes cultic purity. The cultic imagery is used figuratively to express the qualification of this high priest to enter the presence of God.

Taken in tandem, what all the terms describe is the sinlessness that befits Jesus as our high priest. There is a direct correlation between Jesus' sinlessness and the sufferings through which he had to pass to be perfectly qualified to come before the Father as our high priestly mediator. In the suffering that came to increasingly define Jesus' path of obedience, and climactically so in his passion, he "experienced the full force of temptation without once yielding to it. There is no question of his fitness to appear in the presence of God; he is the Holy One of

---

11. The idea of Christ's identity united as priest-king is borne out also in the book of Revelation with the depictions of Christ as the King of kings and Lord of lords and as the Lamb who was slain (Rev 5:6, 12; 17:14; 22:3).

12. With debts here to Lane, *Hebrews 1–8*, 191–92.

God, free from all guile and defilement."[13] And as such Jesus had proved for all time in his obedient relationship to the Father demonstrated through the experiences of his earthly life his fittingness to serve as our high priest.

The two other marks that Hebrews 7:26 points up to show the fittingness of Jesus to be our high priestly mediator follow on naturally from the first. That Jesus is described next as being "separated from sinners" assumes the moral perfection of his character just stated. It is true that during his earthly career Jesus' sinlessness already set him apart from sinful humanity. But here "the emphasis falls upon his actual entrance before the divine presence, where he accomplishes the ministry of intercession."[14] And so the third mark of fittingness is simply a corollary of the ones preceding, namely, Jesus' status—he is now "exalted above the heavens." Indeed, with the background of Psalm 110 in mind, what the event of Christ's transfiguration revealed proleptically concerning his majestic enthronement in heaven is indirectly affirmed here as having become actualized in his exaltation. But more to the point, Christ's exalted status as a high priest after the order of Melchizedek is a consequence of his having offered himself once for all as a single sacrifice for sins (Heb 7:27). Only such a high priest as this—"who has been made perfect forever" (Heb 7:28)—is fittingly qualified to fulfill his priestly office and secure eternally acceptance with God on behalf of his people. As the author of Hebrews later declares, "For by a single offering he has perfected for all time those who are being sanctified" (Heb 10:14).

Thus the plan of redemption required Jesus to be fittingly qualified to become our high priestly mediator. Considering Hebrews 2:10 and 7:26 in tandem, this means that in the state of his humiliation Jesus had to be made perfect through his sufferings so that consequently he could

---

13. F. F. Bruce, *The Epistle to the Hebrews* (NICNT; Grand Rapids: Eerdmans, 1990), 176.

14. Lane, *Hebrews 1–8*, 192. Cf. Bruce, *The Epistle to the Hebrews*, 179, n88: "The high priest of Israel, while not personally free from sin, was ceremonially set apart from his fellows for the proper discharge of his sacred functions. But Jesus has no need to be set apart in any such ceremonial manner; his separation is, on the one hand, inward and moral, and, on the other hand, the consequence of his being now exalted to the right hand of God, withdrawn from the midst of a sinful world."

enter the state of his exaltation to accomplish his high priestly intercession. In that way the Son's theodramatic fittingness corresponds perfectly to the respective form of his life in the states of his humiliation and exaltation, and thus in every stage of the theodrama the Son's glory is always fittingly manifest. Our theological aesthetic thus sees the fittingness of God's masterful wisdom in Christ's being made perfect through his sufferings to become our high priestly mediator before the Father as being perfectly correlated with the beauty of Christ's theodramatic fittingness in the states of his humiliation and exaltation.

Christ's Kingly Glory on the Cross

The central element of our thesis is that the Son's fittingness as incarnate Redeemer is the critical lens for seeing God's beauty, serving as well to display the Son's glory in every stage of the theodrama. The unveiled glory he displayed during his earthly career, I have argued, was in the form of a slave because this was the form that was most fitting for him to assume as the Messiah in the state of his humiliation. Christ crucified takes the display/revelation of his glory to a whole other level because in this event of the theodrama the form of his humanity on the cross was literally cruciform—the form that was most fitting as Sin-bearer. I argue that Christ's identity as revealed on the cross magnifies the majesty of the unveiled glory of God in Christ for those with eyes to see it. The account of the penitent criminal who perceives Jesus' true identity on the cross offers a strong witness to this point. Calvin's insights in particular are pressed into service here.

Although Calvin had contended that during Christ's earthly career, "the divine glory did not shine, but only human likeness was manifest in a lowly and debased condition,"[15] it seems elsewhere he was drawn to modify such language as he contemplated the illimitable divine love dramatized on the cross. For example, just as the glory of the Lord that was revealed to Moses on Mount Sinai highlighted God's merciful goodness, his faithful love, and his justice (Exod 34:5-7), Calvin likewise is struck by the nonpareil grace and goodness manifest in the glory

---

15. Calvin, *Institutes* 2.13.2, ed. McNeill, trans. Battles.

of Christ's work on the cross, which he accomplished for humanity—indeed for all creation:

> For in the cross of Christ, as in a magnificent theatre, the inestimable goodness of God is displayed before the whole world. In all the creatures, indeed, both high and low, the glory of God shines, but nowhere has it shone more brightly than in the cross, in which there has been an astonishing change of things, the condemnation of all men has been manifested, sin has been blotted out, salvation has been restored to men; and, in short, the whole world has been renewed, and every thing restored to good order.[16]

The theater imagery Calvin uses highlights the dramatic tenor that necessarily characterizes the event of Christ crucified. The display of the Son's glory in every stage of the theodrama, while qualified by the fittingness that corresponds to the form of his humanity, is a dramatic display represented in his person and work, and never more so than on the cross. Moreover, the perspective here accords with what we have emphasized along the way, namely, that the goal of God's redemptive work is thoroughly in line with his creative work. Perceptively, Calvin sees that by Christ bearing our sin, death, and curse (and thereby freeing us from them), the depth of love he discloses on the cross points up his glory and majesty more so than it would even beholding his session at the right hand of the Father:

> And this fruit [of the atonement made for us] swallows up all the ignominy of the death of Christ, that his majesty and glory may be more clearly seen than if we only beheld him sitting in heaven; for we have in him a striking and memorable proof of the love of God, when he is so insulted, degraded, and loaded with the utmost disgrace, in order that we, on whom had been pronounced a sentence of everlasting destruction, may enjoy along with him immortal glory.[17]

---

16. John Calvin, *Commentary on the Gospel according to John*, trans. William Pringle (Grand Rapids: Baker Book House, 1979), 73 (commenting on John 13:31); see also Randall C. Zachman, *Image and Word in the Theology of John Calvin* (Notre Dame, IN: University of Notre Dame Press, 2007), 276–79.

17. John Calvin, *Commentary on the Book of the Prophet Isaiah*, trans. William Pringle (Grand Rapids: Baker Book House, 1979), 131 (commenting on Isa 53:12).

The essence of Calvin's point is consonant with a critical line of our argument, namely, that the glory of God in Christ is revealed as much in his self-abasement and service as it is in his exaltation and rule. And in the event of Christ's atoning work on the cross, God's sovereign purposes are manifest as the foreordained means by which he dramatizes the fullness of his self-giving love—and thus magnifies the fullness of his majestic glory.[18]

In his commentary on Matthew 27:35, Calvin writes, "[Christ] suffered nothing which the Holy Spirit does not declare to belong truly and properly to the person of the Redeemer."[19] And nowhere is the paradoxical juxtaposition between Christ's incarnate state of poverty and his kingship more acute than in his crucifixion. In his crucifixion as a convicted criminal, and his placement in the prominent center between two other convicted criminals, Christ's ignominy becomes both an iconic and ironic dramatization of his majesty. It is because the form (*Gestalt*) and content (*Gehalt*) of God's self-revelation in Christ—that is, the character of the Son within the form of Christ—are perfectly united, that the essential nature of God—and thus the glory of God—is truly and properly revealed. As I have argued, though, that glory is perceived in a dialectic of revealing and concealing. "If one fails to see the form of Jesus it is not because the objective evidence is insufficient," explains Balthasar, "but because of the guilt of a 'darkness' which does not see, recognize, or receive the Light. ... Thus, the guilt is not excused by the hiddenness; rather, the latter becomes the judgment of guilt. The hiddenness is the objective proof that the guilty have not wanted to see" (cf. John 9:39).[20] In a true sense, Jesus Christ as the crucified God-man (cf. 1 Cor 1:23; 2:2) holds up a mirror that evinces and exposes the depravation of glory that characterizes every human being *qua* sinner.[21]

---

18. Commenting on John 13:32, Calvin, *Commentary on the Gospel according to John*, 74, concludes: "For the death of the cross, which Christ suffered, is so far from obscuring his high rank, that in that death his high rank is chiefly displayed, since there his amazing love to mankind, his infinite righteousness in atoning for sin and appeasing the wrath of God, his wonderful power in conquering death, subduing Satan, and, at length, opening heaven, blazed with full brightness."

19. John Calvin, *Commentary on a Harmony of the Evangelists, Mark, Mark, and Luke*, trans. William Pringle (Grand Rapids: Baker Book House, 1979), 299.

20. Balthasar, *GL*, I, 522.

21. To illustrate the point, we might appropriate a concept from the field of

Calvin likewise states, "If it be objected, that never was there any thing less glorious than the death of Christ, which was then at hand, I reply, that in that death we behold a magnificent triumph which is concealed from wicked men."[22] For this reason the regal nature of Christ, and the glory of God's love and goodness that reflected as the brightest mirror in his death, can only be perceived over Christ's visible abasement by those with eyes of faith.[23] Such eyes perceive Christ in the humility of faith and are not offended at his outward state, but are instead drawn to him.

In reference to the scene of Jesus standing before Pilate, Calvin writes:

> The supreme and sole Judge of the world is placed at the bar of an earthly judge, is condemned to crucifixion as a malefactor, and— what is more—is placed between two robbers, as if he had been the prince of robbers. A spectacle so revolting might, at first sight, greatly disturb the senses of men, were it not met by this argument, that the punishment which had been due to us was laid on Christ, so that, our guilt having now been removed, we do not hesitate to come into the presence of the Heavenly Judge.[24]

---

ecosystem biology to say that Christ himself is the "indicator species" for the whole world. In the field of ecosystem biology, an indicator species is an organism whose presence serves as a measure of the health of its ecosystem as a whole. Indicator species can signal a change in the biological condition of a particular ecosystem, and thus may be used as a proxy to diagnose the health of an ecosystem (e.g., a species may indicate an environmental condition such as a disease outbreak, pollution, species competition, or climate change). Using this idea as a rough analogy, then, Christ himself is the indicator species for the "ecosystem" that is the whole world, serving as the measure of humanity's identity and destiny as God created it to be, and providing the true diagnosis of (and remedy for) its spiritual condition.

22. Calvin, *Commentary on the Gospel according to John*, 164 (commenting on John 17:1). Cf. Balthasar, *TD*, II, 63–64: "It is true that the phenomenon of Jesus— the mortal man who died and rose again—floods individual existence and world history with radiant light, but this fullness of light is unbearable to our 'moth eyes' (as Aquinas says following Aristotle). Thus for Paul, God's wisdom as manifested in the Cross of Jesus seems like 'folly.' The Cross emits what Dionysius calls the 'bright darkness of God.'"

23. Calvin, *Institutes* 2.16.13, ed. McNeill, trans. Battles, comments, "For since only weakness appears in the cross, death, and burial of Christ, faith must leap over all these things to attain its full strength."

24. Calvin, *Commentary on a Harmony of the Evangelists, Mark, Mark, and Luke*, 288. (commenting on Matt 27:24)

The irony is extreme indeed. The seeming poverty of this self-forfei-ture of life, however, serves to disclose to those with eyes of faith Jesus' messianic identity as the Redeemer-King. For Calvin, this beggars belief. Commenting on Luke 23:42 with regard to the penitent criminal who perceives Jesus' true identity, he declares, "I know not that, since the creation of the world, there ever was a more remarkable and striking example of faith."[25] Given Jesus' state of mutual abjection, all natural reasoning conspires against making any sense as to why *this* robber at *this* time would perceive Christ's true majesty. Even so, those with eyes of faith *are* able to see Christ crucified in the majesty of his kingly glory, and thus *are* able to glorify him rightly. For the penitent criminal crucified next to Jesus it was the optics given through faith alone by the work of God's Spirit that enabled his perceiving Jesus' unveiled glory. Calvin continues his train of thought on this remarkable and striking example of faith:

> A *robber*, who not only had not been educated in the school of Christ, but, by giving himself up to execrable murders, had endeavored to extinguish all sense of what was right, suddenly rises higher than all the apostles and the other disciples whom the Lord himself had taken so much pains to instruct; and not only so, but he adores Christ as a *King* while on the gallows, celebrates his *kingdom* in the midst of shocking and worse than revolting abasement, and declares him, when dying, to be the Author of life.[26]

In addition to receiving Christ as his Redeemer-King, the robber also perceived, with faith-filled eyes, that Christ's kingdom was not from this world (cf. John 18:36). It is evident how powerful its impact was on Calvin, for he is amazed at how this robber looked towards Christ with eyes of faith—given the apparent fate of their lives—in absolute trust and assurance: "Hence we infer how acute must have been the eyes of his mind, by which he beheld life in death, exaltation in ruin, glory in shame, victory in destruction, a *kingdom* in bondage."[27] From a

---

25. Calvin, *Commentary on a Harmony of the Evangelists, Mark, Mark, and Luke*, 311.
26. Calvin, *Commentary on a Harmony of the Evangelists, Mark, Mark, and Luke*, 311.
27. Calvin, *Commentary on a Harmony of the Evangelists, Mark, Mark, and Luke*, 311 (commenting on Matt 27:35).

natural perspective, if ever there was a point in Jesus' public life when we might want to insist that his glory was hidden by his humanity, it would be his crucifixion. Calvin's reflections on this scene support a key claim of our argument that the self-revelatory nature of God's actions in Christ during his earthly career means that his essential nature, his glory, is revealed—in this case even and most majestically in the depth of love he discloses on the cross. The perception of the penitent criminal suggests that the glory was always displayed, just not always perceived by everyone.

In the state of his total ignominy, Christ's kingly glory is thus epitomized in his death on the cross.[28] Of consequence here, Bernard Ramm suggests that the royal motif aptly captures the displayed character of God's glory: "If there is a bridge which connects the visible glory of the Lord with his essential being, it is that of the kingship. ... The royal kingship becomes one of the richest sources of analogies in the OT for the doctrine of God. The *kābôd* of the earthly king becomes the analogue for the *kābôd* of the Lord" (cf. Pss 22:28; 24:7–10).[29] For the visible glory of the Lord in the Old Testament to which Ramm refers has come in the fullness of time in the person of Jesus Christ, in whom the fullness and majesty of deity dwells bodily (Col 2:9). The account of the penitent criminal is a strong witness that Christ's identity as revealed on the cross magnifies the majesty of his unveiled glory for those with eyes to see it. Apropos here is the strong connection Scripture indicates between the beauty of God and his manifest glory, namely, his majesty, kingship, and splendor.[30] The cruciform of Christ on the cross, perhaps better said, magnifies the beauty of the glory of God's self-giving love.

---

28. Donald Macleod, *Christ Crucified: Understanding the Atonement* (Downers Grove, IL: IVP Academic, 2014), 37: "The underlying theological fact is that the dying of Christ is a kingly act, not merely in the sense that he dies royally and with dignity, but in the sense that his dying is his supreme achievement for his people: the act by which he conquers their foes, secures their liberty and establishes his kingdom."

29. Bernard Ramm, *Them He Glorified: A Systematic Study of the Doctrine of Glorification* (Grand Rapids: Eerdmans, 1963), 19.

30. See the Chapter 2 section, Beauty—A Divine Attribute?

THE FITTINGNESS OF GOD'S
RETRIBUTIVE JUSTICE AT THE CROSS

The experience of Jesus being made perfect through his sufferings was undergone in its most concentrated and horrific form in the execution of God's judicial wrath poured out upon him on the cross in the place of sinners. To accomplish his mission for which the Father had sent him meant he had to drink to the full the cup that the Father had given him (John 18:11). Our interest here considers the fittingness of that cup in terms of the judicial wrath meted out upon Christ. In this case we are asking, if everything God does is beautiful in how he glorifies himself, on what basis can we say that the judgment God meted out upon Christ in the place of sinners is fitting in terms of being duly proportional to the collective "crime" committed against him? Of relevance here is our discussion in Chapter 3 on the fittingness of retributive justice.[31] But before developing that point as it relates to the punishment that Christ bore on the cross, it will be helpful first to briefly lay out what we are saying is at the vital center—the essence—of the penal substitution theory of Christ's atonement as informed by the Old Testament background of atonement in Israel's ritual worship legislation. Following that I will address the dimension of fittingness in reference to divine retributive justice being satisfied in the work of God's wrath poured out on Christ.

THE CONCEPT OF ATONEMENT IN THE OLD TESTAMENT

The concept of atonement is central to the reconciling act of God in Christ. Its theological importance in the Old Testament is evident from the general role atonement played in Israel's sacrificial system, notably in Leviticus on the Day of Atonement provisions, as well as its prominence in the Passover narrative in Exodus. The underlying concern of the Old Testament's whole ritual worship legislation centered around the presence of God in the midst of Israel.[32] Fundamental to this was the focus on community holiness and purity oriented toward faithful worship of the Lord. The dwelling of God in the tabernacle, and later

---

31. See Chapter 3 subsection, Fittingness of Retributive Justice.

32. For the discussion in hand, I was helped by Richard E. Averbeck, "כָּפַר," *NIDOTTE*, 2:681–701; and Averbeck, "Leviticus," *NIDOTTE*, 4:906–22.

in the temple, in the form of the glory cloud gave a visible sign of the Lord's presence and made the entire structure holy. "Within the nation as a place of God's presence there was a graduated spectrum of holiness," explains Richard Averbeck,

> that extended from the Most Holy Place in the tabernacle to the community outside the tabernacle complex. It included not only the spatial dimension but also the personal dimension (from the priests to the Levites to the people), the sacrificial dimension (from holy to most holy offerings), and the temporal dimension (from the weekly Sabbath to the annual festival holy days).[33]

Thus, the basic concern of Leviticus' so-called Holiness Code (notably Lev 17-27) begins with the sanctification of the tabernacle and priests, but it extended to the whole national life of all the people. Similarly, the Day of Atonement regulations in Leviticus 16 show that thorough atonement had to be made for both the tabernacle and the people, that is, to cleanse the tabernacle on behalf of the priests/people, and to cleanse the people from all their sins.[34]

Although the idea of "cleansing" corresponds to "atonement" in connection with the base meaning of כָּפַר ("to wipe away/wipe clean/ purge"), to make atonement for human life in Deuteronomic history sometimes carries the sense of "to ransom" in regard to the overall effect of the action (e.g., Exod 30:11-16).[35] But with respect to Leviticus 17:11—"For the life of the flesh is in the blood, and I have given it for you on the altar *to make atonement* (לְכַפֵּר) for your souls, for it is the blood that makes atonement by the life"—the blood or "life" of a slaughtered animal is instrumental in the act of atoning. Whether in this case the

---

33. Averbeck, "Leviticus," *NIDOTTE*, 4:911-12. For a recommended treatment on this topic, see Philip Peter Jenson, *Graded Holiness: A Key to the Priestly Conception of the World* (JSOTSup 106; Sheffield, England: JSOT Press, 1992).

34. Averbeck, "כָּפַר," *NIDOTTE*, 2:696-697, proposes that the results or benefits of making atonement fall into three main categories: *consecration* (changes the status of someone/something by shifting them from the realm of the common to the realm of the holy); *purification* (changes their condition from unclean to clean); or *forgiveness* (the people will be forgiven for violating any of the Lord's commands, cf. Lev 4-5).

35. Averbeck, "כָּפַר," *NIDOTTE*, 2:690. See Jay Sklar, *Sin, Impurity, Sacrifice, Atonement: The Priestly Conceptions* (Sheffield: Sheffield Phoenix Press, 2005), 160ff. Sklar argues that כָּפַר means primarily "to make a ransom."

expiatory work of atonement is best understood as a "wiping away" of human sin (i.e., "to wipe clean with" blood, the blood serving metaphorically as a detergent-like cleanser) or as an "effective ransom" for the sins of the people, either way the purpose is a propitiatory one, namely, that of averting the wrath of God by offering the life of a substitute.[36]

The New Testament depicts how Christ's death atoned for the sin of the world (cf. John 1:29) on the same fundamental basis given above for the same fundamental purpose—averting the wrath of God by offering the life of a substitute.[37] Hebrews 2:17, for example, describes Jesus as having become "a merciful and faithful high priest in things relating to God, to make atonement (ἱλάσκομαι) for the sins of the people" (NET). The corresponding Old Testament background connected to Jesus' role as high priest is the Day of Atonement rituals. The apostle John, on the other hand, identifies Jesus not as the high priest but as the sacrificial victim: "he himself is the atoning sacrifice (ἱλασμός) for our sins, and not only for our sins but also for the whole world"; further on he states, "[God] loved us and sent his Son to be the atoning sacrifice (ἱλασμός) for our sins" (1 John 2:2 and 4:10 NET, respectively). Henri Blocher is instructive here regarding Jesus' role as both high priest and sacrificial victim in his making atonement for the sins of the people:

> [S]ince sin-bearing for atonement is ascribed both to the animal
> victim *and to the priest* (Exod 28:38; Lev 10:17), we should think of the
> two of them together substituting for sinners before God. Drawing

---

36. Reminiscent of such signification involving God's wrath being averted is the account of the Lord's Passover in Exodus 12:12-23: "For I [the Lord] will pass through the land of Egypt that night, and I will strike all the firstborn in the land of Egypt, both man and beast; and on all the gods of Egypt I will execute judgments: I am the LORD (v.12). ... For the LORD will pass through to strike the Egyptians, and when he sees the blood on the lintel and on the two doorposts, the LORD will pass over the door and will not allow the destroyer to enter your houses to strike you (v. 23)." For a recommended treatment on this topic, see Emile Nicole, "Atonement in the Pentateuch," in *The Glory of the Atonement: Biblical, Historical and Practical Perspectives: Essays in Honor of Roger Nicole*, ed. Charles E. Hill and Frank A. James III (Downers Grove, IL: InterVarsity Press, 2004), 35-50.

37. H.-G. Link, "ἱλάσκομαι," *NIDNTT*, 3:148: The three Greek words used in the New Testament that correspond in meaning to forms of כפר are ἱλάσκομαι (propitiate, expiate, conciliate, make gracious, be gracious); ἱλασμός (propitiation, propitiatory sacrifice); and ἱλαστήριον (that which expiates or propitiates, means of propitiation, mercy-seat).

into the presence of God was a matter of life and death—no human being could see his face and live, for his holiness does not tolerate the tiniest trace of evil and his wrath is a devouring flame—and the priest, especially the high priest when he entered the Most Holy Place, risked his life on behalf of the people; Exodus 28:35 expresses the consciousness of that danger. His safe return could be called a resurrection *en parabolē* like that of Isaac (Heb 11:19). If we consider therefore the pair of victim and priest—and Jesus was the antitype of both—the sacrificial type is remarkably complete, and the "metaphor" highly adequate.[38]

In one other *locus classicus*, the apostle Paul writes, "God publicly displayed him [Jesus] at his death as the mercy seat (ἱλαστήριον) accessible through faith. This was to demonstrate his righteousness, because God in his forbearance had passed over the sins previously committed" (Rom 3:25 NET).[39] Here, Jesus is identified either as a place of atonement or a sacrifice of atonement.[40] The significant point in Paul's use of the concept ἱλαστήριον is that the ἱλαστήριον is an atonement for human sin. Considering these things altogether, then, Jesus is "represented and explained ... as a vicarious sacrificer, a vicarious sacrifice, and [plausibly] a vicarious place of sacrifice."[41] Christ's atoning sacrifice thus combines all the elements of being substitutionary, expiatory, and propitiatory.[42] And fundamentally on that basis, "the issues that

---

38. Henri Blocher, "Biblical Metaphors and the Doctrine of the Atonement," *JETS* 47 no. 4 (December 2004): 642.

39. The translator's note on Romans 3:25 offers the following: "The word ἱλαστήριον may carry the general sense 'place of satisfaction,' referring to the place where God's wrath toward sin is satisfied. More likely, though, ... Paul is saying that God displayed Jesus as the 'mercy seat,' the place where propitiation was accomplished." In the LXX, ἱλαστήριον is used consistently to translate כַּפֹּרֶת (mercy seat/atonement seat).

40. Both readings are defensible; although the LXX background favors the former reading, the connection to God's forbearance shown in not punishing sins previously committed favors the latter reading.

41. Averbeck, "כָּפַר," *NIDOTTE*, 2:701.

42. Not to be overlooked here, the Day of Atonement rituals involved the high priest taking two goats and casting lots to determine one to be the sacrificial sin offering and the other to be sent away into the wilderness. The former was killed and its blood sprinkled on the mercy seat of the ark of the covenant; the other became the "scapegoat" on which the high priest laid his hands and confessed the sins of the people of Israel, transferring them in effect to the goat. The scapegoat

would cause God's wrath to be turned against us are wiped away, expiation," and thus "there is no reason for God to be angry anymore—he is 'propitiated.'"[43]

The Fittingness of God's Meted Out Judgment upon Christ

With the above background in mind, recall from Chapter 3 that retributive justice involves meted out punishment that a wrongdoer deserves (their *desert*). Concerning the meting out of judgment by God, it is an expression of the altogether perfection of his holy character, which takes prominent form in the execution of his judicial wrath. According to the traditional evangelical view (more or less) of the penal substitution theory, God's judicial wrath is poured out upon Christ in the place of sinners in the perfect vindication of his justice. God's justice is wholly upheld in meting out the judgment that Christ bore, while the issues that would cause God's wrath to be turned against evildoers who justly deserved to die are wiped away—God is "propitiated." Insofar as this representation (albeit only partial) is valid, then, what is evident here is that the *penal* dimension of Christ's substitutionary atonement pertains to (at least in a basic way) divine retributive justice being satisfied. We should note here as well that while the background relevant to speaking of Christ's punishment in terms of the satisfaction of divine justice relates analogously to that of a judicial court, the broader redemptive-historical background informing this relates to God's covenant lawsuit against Israel for her tragic record of covenant-breaking ("vengeance for the covenant," Lev 26:25). And thus in his messianic identity as the true Israel, Christ bore on the cross the divine punishment on behalf of Israel for her repeated failure of covenant faithfulness, though not on Israel's behalf only. As Vanhoozer puts it, "Jesus is ... the one who, unlike Adam and Israel, successfully passes the test of covenant faithfulness, even though it cost him his life"[44]

---

was then released into the remote wilderness. In his work of redemption as the long-awaited Messiah, Jesus embodied and fulfilled once for all time the role of both the goat of the sin offering and the living goat that bore the iniquities of the people into oblivion.

43. Averbeck, "כָּפַר," *NIDOTTE*, 2:700.

44. Kevin J. Vanhoozer, *Faith Speaking Understanding: Performing the Drama*

The moral-aesthetic normativity of fittingness as it relates to the punishment that Christ bore on the cross has critically to do with the notion of due proportionality between punishment and crime (i.e., sin), in short, "the punishment must fit the crime."[45] In terms of the theological aesthetics broadly considered, we have sound reason to affirm that the judgment rendered by the Father was perfectly fitting—and hence beautiful in its God-glorifying nature—as that which the Son justly deserved as the one who for our sake God made to be sin, though he himself knew no sin (more on this below). In Chapter 3 I argued for the fittingness of retributive justice, except there it was in relation to God's judgment curse against Adam and Eve. As one might expect, the underlying points of argument I set forth in that discussion apply likewise to our present one. Tagging once more off of Oliver Crisp's work, our basic claim here is that in the penal substitution of Christ, the divine retributive punishment fits the crime.[46] That is to say, the judgment that God meted out upon Christ in the place of sinners is justly commensurate to the collective "crime" committed against him. The premise assumed here is "that in the case of divine-human relationships, the status of the person offended (God) is of crucial importance in determining the severity of the punishment to be meted out. Sin against a being of infinite honor and worth has consequences for the sinner that are themselves infinite."[47] With respect to the claim that in

---

of Doctrine (Louisville: Westminster John Knox Press, 2014), 109. In his messianic role as the last Adam and the true Israel, then, Christ's penal substitution extends retroactively all the way back to the outset of creation, encompassing descendants of the first Adam, the head of the human family.

45. Cf. Anselm in Cur Deus Homo 1.20 (Basic Writings, ed. and trans. Williams, 281) directs his discussion on the point that recompense ought to be proportionate to sin, and that human beings cannot make recompense on their own.

46. As it turns out, Crisp, who provided grist for our argumentation in Chapter 2, applies in a later essay the same points of his argument to the topic of Christ's penal substitution. See Oliver D. Crisp, "The Logic of Penal Substitution Revisited," in The Atonement Debate: Papers from the London Symposium on the Theology of Atonement, ed. Derek Tidball et al. (Grand Rapids: Zondervan, 2008), 208-27.

47. Crisp, "The Logic of Penal Substitution Revisited," 213. This idea seems to be behind Anselm's reply to his conversation partner, the monk Boso, in Cur Deus Homo 1.21 (Basic Writings, ed. and trans. Williams, 281): "You have not yet come to grips with how serious sin is." Likewise, to the question, "Whether Sin Incurs a Debt of Punishment Infinite in Quantity?, Aquinas, ST Ia IIae, q. 87, a. 4, writes: "Further, quantity of punishment corresponds to quantity of fault, according to Deut 25:2.

Christ's penal substitution the divine retributive punishment fits the crime, the line of argument runs something like this:[48]

1. God is worthy of infinite regard.

2. The gravity of an offense against a being is principally determined by that being's worth or dignity.

3. There is an infinite demerit in all sin against God, such that all sin is infinitely heinous (cf. Jas 2:10).

4. Divine justice is retributive and inexorable, that is, it is in the nature of God to punish sin inexorably because it is heinous to him and divine justice must be perfectly satisfied.

5. Sin requires an infinite punishment.

6. Satisfaction for sin must be made either in the punishment of the sinner or in the person of a vicar.

Crisp himself seems to find this view of the penal substitution theory wanting on account of it violating the bounds of what constitutes proper justice.[49] In his view it is not a morally coherent position to claim that God metes out the infinite punishment due sinners upon Christ as their innocent vicar. Admittedly, one can certainly sympathize (intuitively or in more explicable terms, however so) with Crisp's basic

---

Now a sin which is committed against God, is infinite: because the gravity of a sin increases according to the greatness of the person sinned against (thus it is a more grievous sin to strike a sovereign than a private individual), and God's greatness is infinite. Therefore an infinite punishment is due for a sin committed against God."

48. Applied in my own argumentation here are points Crisp sets out in Crisp, "The Logic of Penal Substitution Revisited," 209 and 213, the first three of which we previously employed in the Chapter 3 subsection, Fittingness of Retributive Justice.

49. Notably, in Crisp, "The Logic of Penal Substitution Revisited," 223, he states that the central problem with penal substitution is that "it is not possible for the sin and guilt of one individual to be transferred to another individual. Even if penal substitution means only that the penal consequences of sin are transferred from the sinner to Christ, there is still the transference of the penal consequences of sin to contend with, and it seems monumentally unjust to punish an innocent party in the place of a guilty one for a penal debt. Perhaps God can relax his justice to the extent that he can accept a vicarious satisfaction of the infinite debt owed by human beings instead of punishing them. If God can do this, it is a legal arrangement that has no obvious parallel in human penal transactions and still appears to be unjust, even if it is not arbitrary. And this problem alone poses serious difficulties for the traditional arguments for penal substitution."

criticism here, namely, the seeming moral impropriety of judicially transferring the guilt and retributive punishment that belongs to one party over to another party (an innocent other party at that). To my mind, though, the critical question is whether any purely human penal transactions can serve as a legitimate parallel by which the penal substitution theory in question here can be adjudicated. If, as Crisp surmises, it is a legal arrangement that has no obvious parallel in human penal transactions, then may not this suggest rather that it is a sui generis arrangement that in fact does allow for, indeed is designed for, perfect justice to be upheld in Christ's atoning work? An affirmative answer in my judgment seems a perfectly reasonable and recommendable way to go. The human administration of justice is, in a real sense, incomparable to that of God's.[50] The moral coherency of penal substitution, moreover, becomes arguably much more robust if one other critical point of argument is admitted: once for all divine satisfaction for sin requires that the status of the vicar (Jesus) be equal to the status of the person offended (God).

Granting this additional point of argument would seem to adequately address the criticism of penal substitution's so-called moral incoherency. Not least it comports well with the biblical witness, for to Christ as vicar belongs at once the infinite dignity native to his divine Sonship and the merited glory and honor to which the Father has highly exalted him in connection with his Adamic Sonship. "An attempt to grasp the righteousness of Christ's substitution does not fittingly begin from the notion of Jesus Christ as one individual among many," writes Jeremy Wynne. "The argument proceeds rather from the premise that only as the Incarnate Son and second Adam is he eminently able and worthy to undergo the punishment of our sin, to represent us before the judgment seat of God, and so to impart to us his own righteousness as a free gift (cf. Rom 5:15–17)."[51] Thus, our claim that the judicial propriety of

---

50. For a recommended treatment relevant to this point, see by John W. Wenham, *The Enigma of Evil: Can We Believe in the Goodness of God?* (Grand Rapids: Zondervan, 1985), 44–50.

51. Jeremy J. Wynne, *Wrath among the Perfections of God's Life* (London: T&T Clark, 2010), 170. Wynne continues, "It is on the basis of Jesus Christ's person as the God-man that he is uniquely able to bear the severity and to endure the efficacy of wrath's exercise. A robust doctrine of the incarnation is likewise the basis for

Christ's penal substitutionary sacrifice has no direct parallel in human penal transactions coincides with the fact that Christ's hypostatic union is itself sui generis, having no human parallel.

The notion of Christ's infinite dignity in particular has been traditionally put forward as a basis to appreciate better how his suffering on the cross for a temporally finite duration could commensurately satisfy the divine justice of infinite punishment due sinners. In the words of Dutch theologian Herman Witsius (1636–1708), the concept of infinite dignity suggests how "the sufferings of Christ, though of short duration, were equivalent to the eternal sufferings of the damned; and the sufferings of a single person sufficed for the redemption of the many myriads of the elect."[52] The nineteenth-century American Reformed theologian R. L. Dabney (1820–1898) illustrates this point to good effect:

> A stick of wood, and an ingot of gold are subjected to the same fire. The wood is permanently consumed: the gold is only melted, because it is a precious metal, incapable of natural oxidation, and it is gathered, undiminished, from the ashes of the furnace. But the fire was the same! And then, the infinite dignity of Christ's person gives to His temporal sufferings a moral value equal to the weight of all the guilt of the world.[53]

---

asserting that no other human, not even humanity in its entirety, could undergo the judgment and destruction of God's wrath both justly and without being lost to death." Cf. Calvin, *Institutes* 2.12.2, ed. McNeill, trans. Battles: "Finally, since as God only he could not suffer, and as man only he could not overcome death, he united the human nature with the divine, that he might subject the weakness of the one to death as an expiation of sin, and by the power of the other, maintaining a struggle with death, might gain us the victory." Germane to the discussion here as well is Anselm's dialogue in *Cur Deus Homo* 2.6–11 (*Basic Writings*, ed. and trans. Williams, 293–304).

52. Herman Witsius, *Sacred Dissertations on What Is Commonly Called the Apostles' Creed*, vol. 2, trans. Donald Fraser (Escondido, CA: The den Dulk Christian Foundation, 1993), 40. Along the same lines, Francis Turretin, *IET*, vol. 2, Topic XIV, Quest. XI, Sec. XXX, states: "Although money has no higher value in the hand of a king than in that of a captive, still the head and life of a king are of more value than the life of a vile slave (as the life of David was reckoned of more worth than that of half the Israelite army, 2 Sam 18:3). In this way, Christ alone ought to be estimated at a higher value than all men together. The dignity of an infinite person swallows up and absorbs all the infinities of punishment due to us." (437)

53. R. L. Dabney, *Lectures in Systematic Theology* (Grand Rapids: Zondervan, 1972), 505.

It is in this overall light, therefore, that the judicial wrath of God poured out on Christ is seen to satisfy the demands of divine retributive justice and propitiate God's wrath against evildoers who had deserved to die.[54] As such, due proportionality between punishment and crime would appear to be properly transacted in Christ's substitutionary death. In accord with the biblical witness, we have sound reason to believe that the judgment God meted out upon Christ in the place of sinners is justly commensurate to the collective "crime" committed against him (cf. Rom 3:26; Col 2:13–14; Rev 5:9).[55] On the basis of the argument put forward, the divine retributive punishment was designed perfectly to fit the crime.[56] This schema of divine retributive punishment, in other words, is not merely *plausibly just* but truly *beautifully just*. How so? Because everything God does is beautiful in whatever ways he displays his glory. And what God does theodramatically here

---

54. In arresting terms, Calvin, *Institutes* 2.16.5, ed. McNeill, trans. Battles, writes of the satisfaction of divine justice involved: "To take away our condemnation, it was not enough for [Christ] to suffer any kind of death: to make satisfaction for our redemption a form of death had to be chosen in which he might free us both by transferring our condemnation to himself and by taking our guilt upon himself. ... But when he was arraigned before the judgment seat as a criminal, accused and pressed by testimony, and condemned by the mouth of the judge to die—we know by these proofs that he took the role of a guilty man and evildoer. ... Thus we shall behold the person of a sinner and evildoer represented in Christ, yet from his shining innocence it will at the same time be obvious that he was burdened with another's sin rather than his own. ... This is our acquittal: the guilt that held us liable for punishment has been transferred to the head of the Son of God [Isa 53:12]. We must, above all, remember this substitution, lest we tremble and remain anxious throughout life—as if God's righteous vengeance, which the Son of God has taken upon himself, still hung over us."

55. Worth noting is that Jesus' final dying utterance, τετέλεσται (John 19:30), generally rendered as "it is finished," may also mean "paid in full" (BDAG 997 s.v. τελέω 3: to pay what is due).

56. Cf. Bavinck, *RD*, 3:402: "For though the sin that entered the world through Adam manifests itself in an incalculable series of sinful thoughts, words, and deeds, and though the wrath of God is felt individually by every guilty member of the human race, it is and remains the one indivisible law that has been violated, the one indivisible wrath of God that has been ignited against the sin of the whole human race, the one indivisible righteousness of God that has been offended by sin, the one unchangeable eternal God who has been affronted by sin. The punishment of Christ, therefore, is also one: one that balances in intensity and quality the sin and guilt of the whole human race. ... That punishment, after all, was laid on him who was not an individual on a level with other individuals but the second Adam head of the human race, both Son of Man and Son of God."

in displaying his glory is pour out his judicial wrath upon Christ in the place of sinners in the perfect, commensurate vindication of his justice. What is truly beyond our ken is that within the life of God in himself, God enacted this display of his absolute perfection according to his perfect knowledge, will, and beatitude. On display here is the True, the Good, and the Beautiful in perfect correlation and unity.

In no way, furthermore, does the penal dimension of Christ's substitutionary death take away from or take precedence over the motivation and operation of divine love involved. The remedy that God in his wisdom and power procured in Christ is bound up with his illimitable love demonstrated on the cross. The apostle Paul puts it like this: "in Christ God was reconciling the world to himself, not counting their trespasses against them" (2 Cor 5:19). The new covenant in Christ's blood whereby divine justice is satisfied and judicial wrath is averted involves equally and together God the Father so loving the world that he gave his only Son (John 3:16) to be the atoning sacrifice for our sins (1 John 4:10; Rom 5:6-9) and God the Son laying down his life for us (Eph 5:2; 1 John 3:16), demonstrating his love for us in so doing (Gal 2:20; Rom 5:8; Rev 1:5).[57] George Hunsinger rightly characterizes the atonement schema accordingly: "The wrath of God is removed (propitiation) when the sin that provokes it is abolished (expiation). Moreover, the love of God that takes the form of wrath when provoked by sin is the very same love that provides the efficacious means of expiation (vicarious sacrifice) and therefore of propitiation."[58] The outworking of God's plan of redemption comes to its masterful climax wherein the anger that must condemn the sinner unites in perfect expression with the mercy that would pardon him.[59] In this way Christ's forensic work on the cross is identifiable as part of the wonder of the perfect equipoise of God's

---

57. Cf. John Murray, *Redemption Accomplished and Applied* (Grand Rapids: Eerdmans, 1955), 78: "Of Calvary the spirit is eternal love and the basis eternal justice. It is the same love manifested in the mystery of Gethsemane's agony and of Calvary's accursed tree that wraps eternal security around the people of God. ... That is the security which a perfect atonement secures and it is the perfection of the atonement that secures it."

58. George Hunsinger, *The Eucharist and Ecumenism: Let Us Keep the Feast* (Cambridge: Cambridge University Press, 2008), 173-74.

59. Balthasar, *TD*, III, 119, sees this idea as indicative of a drama in the very heart of God, which also informs to a large degree his understanding of the Trinity relating

righteous holy love, where this perfect expression of the strictest vindicative justice is reconciled with the most condescending mercy.[60] In this way as well, it is fair to say, that perfect equipoise of God's righteous holy love exemplifies the beauty of his glory in everything he does. Our theological aesthetic thus sees the fittingness of God's wisdom and righteous holy love manifest in the execution of God's judicial wrath poured out on Christ in the place of sinners as being perfectly correlated with the beauty of Christ's theodramatic fittingness in the event of his penal substitutionary atonement.

THE ALREADY BUT NOT-YET BEAUTY OF GOD'S RECONCILING WORK THROUGH CHRIST THE EXALTED KING

According to our argument the respective forms of Christ's life in the states of his humiliation and exaltation each radiate the glory of God in Christ most fittingly. The glory of the Son in the state of his humiliation is epitomized in its most majestic display in his death on the cross. And having fully accomplished his mission from the Father, "God has highly exalted him and bestowed on him the name that is above every name" (Phil 2:9). What the event of Christ's transfiguration revealed proleptically concerning his majestic enthronement in heaven has become actualized in his exaltation. Now the majesty of the Son's glory is perfectly conformed to the form of his life in the state of his heavenly exaltation/session at the right hand of the throne of God. At the heart of our thesis is the idea that everything God does is beautifully God-glorifying. Here, I am giving treatment to that idea in reference to God's reconciling operations through the reign of Christ. The stage

---

essentially, that is, the life of the immanent Trinity. This aspect of Balthasar's theology requires much more attention than we can give in this study, though.

60. Herman Witsius, *The Economy of the Covenants between God and Man: Comprehending a Complete Body of Divinity*, vol. 1, trans. William Crookshank (Escondido, CA: The den Dulk Christian Foundation, 1990), Book II, Chap. I, Sec. III (164). Relevant to this point, Cole, *God the Peacemaker*, 51, properly reminds us that "holiness is an essential attribute of God. Wrath is not. Wrath is an expression of holiness in certain contexts. Likewise, love is an essential attribute of God, but mercy is not. Mercy is how love acts in certain contexts. Some theologians make the category mistake of treating holiness, love and wrath as though all three were essential divine attributes."

of the theodrama I am assuming is that the new order of creation has been inaugurated in an already but not-yet order of reality governed under the preeminence of Christ's heavenly rule.

I argue that, as represented in Paul's letter to the Ephesians, God's reconciling operations through the reign of Christ display his beauty fundamentally in the form of an already but not-yet unity and harmony operating in the spheres of human-divine relations and human-human relations in the perfecting of his church.[61] To be clear, I am not contending that the aesthetic dimension is in any sense the preeminent dimension of God's work through Christ. My argument here is only that the forms of God's reconciling operations through Christ clearly evince the beautiful nature of his work, reflected centrally in and for his church. I will characterize in brief compass the nature of God's reconciling work through Christ as evidenced in the main body of Ephesians and then draw together concluding comments regarding the theological aesthetics as relates to my argument.

Our consideration in Ephesians of God's reconciling operations through the reign of Christ is bound up with the idea that God's reconciling all things to himself involves their being in some sense "summed up" (ἀνακεφαλαιόω)[62] in Christ (Eph 1:10). The basic idea Paul describes here commentators widely agree on, namely, that the mystery of God's plan of salvation involves uniting the entirety of the cosmos in

---

61. With debts to Julien Smith's work in *Christ the Ideal King*, whose schematic of Ephesians I follow in my own development. Julien Smith, *Christ the Ideal King: Cultural Context, Rhetorical Strategy, and the Power of Divine Monarchy in Ephesians* (WUNT 2/313; Tübingen: Mohr Siebeck, 2011), specifically, chap. 4: "Ephesians: Is There a King in This Text?" Smith does not include the final section of Ephesians 6:10-20 in his formal breakdown of God's reconciling operations through Christ's rule primarily because the recurrent emphasis of the letter is on the peace, unity, and harmony of the church, which she already shares with Christ eschatologically. Paul then shifts the emphasis in the last section of the letter on exhorting the church to put on the full armor of God and stand firm against the hostile spiritual powers that Christ has already and altogether triumphed over. See Smith, *Christ the Ideal King*, 238. My treatment here will follow in the same course as Smith and not include Ephesians 6:10-20.

62. L&N 63.8 s.v. ἀνακεφαλαιόω: "to bring everything together in terms of some unifying principle or person—'to bring together.' ἀνακεφαλαιώσασθαι τὰ πάντα ἐν τῷ Χριστῷ 'to bring everything together in Christ' Eph 1:10." The only other use of this verb in the New Testament is in Romans 13:9, where the whole law is said to be "summed up" in the command to love one's neighbor.

Christ; this reaches its fullness in the consummation of all things when through Christ history itself is summed up.[63] Peter O'Brien puts it this way: "Christ is the one *in whom* God chooses to sum up the cosmos, the one in whom he restores harmony to the universe."[64] In Ephesians the sense of restoration does indeed pertain to the "summing up" idea, but the overall substance of the letter suggests much more than the idea of *mere* restoration. The reconciliation of the fractured cosmos that God has accomplished in an "already but not-yet consummate" way through the reign of Christ—*this* seems to be the outworking of that key metaphor, the summing up of all things in and through Christ (cf. Col 1:18-20).

In Ephesians 2:1-10, the fundamental "fracture" Paul is addressing concerns the reality that, apart from Christ, all humans are alienated from God, following the course of this world as those who are dead in their trespasses and sins (Eph 2:1-3). Smith summarizes the passage thus: "Formerly, the gentile audience was spiritually dead, held in thrall by malevolent powers, as were formerly the author and his fellow Christians. Now, as a result of God's mercy and love, author and audience alike have been made alive with Christ and enthroned with him in the heavenlies, as an enduring demonstration of God's favor."[65] Here the reconciling work of God through Christ does specifically concern restoration, the restoration of the broken relationship between humans and God. Indeed, absent this reconciled relationship to God, the apostle says elsewhere we are God's *enemies*: "For if while we were enemies we were reconciled to God by the death of his Son, much more, now that we are reconciled, shall we be saved by his life" (Rom 5:10).[66]

---

63. Smith, *Christ the Ideal King*, 197, argues that "this plan to sum up (ἀνακεφαλαιώσασται) all things through Christ is the quintessential metaphor for God's redeeming activity in Ephesians."

64. Peter T. O'Brien, *The Letter to the Ephesians* (PNTC; Grand Rapids: Eerdmans, 1999), 111–12.

65. Smith, *Christ the Ideal King*, 208.

66. Worth pointing out here, Paul is not saying that in the first instance *we* are the ones who consider God as *our* enemy but rather *God* is the one who considers us as *his* enemies (cf. Rom 1:18). That is the context in which we become reconciled to God. It points to the fact that reconciliation is God's initiative, procured by an objective something outside of ourselves, namely, the death of his Son in realized history (cf. 2 Cor 5:18; Col 1:21-22).

According to our Ephesians passage, in addition to Christ's reconciling work removing our alienation before God, it also means the change from being held in thrall by malevolent powers to being enthroned with Christ in the heavenlies (cf. Acts 26:18; Col 1:13). The lives of all those who are in Christ's fellowship are therefore "no longer characterized by domination by the powers, but rather by the good works for which God created them" (Titus 2:14).[67] The first consequential aspect is identified in negative terms in which the redeemed are liberated *from* something; the second in positive terms in which the redeemed are liberated *for* something. The liberation *from*—what Balthasar calls the fruit of the reconciliation event—covers the gamut of liberation "from slavery to sin (Rom 7; John 8:34), from the devil (John 8:44; 1 John 3:8), from the 'world powers' (Gal 4:3; Col 2:20), from the power of darkness (Col 1:13), from the law (Rom 7:1) and from the 'law of sin and death' (Rom 8:2) and ...from the 'wrath to come'(1 Thess 1:10)."[68] To be sure, the telos of what humans are liberated "from" is at the same time realized in what they are liberated "for"—not only to be delivered from God's curse and the thrall of malevolent powers, but to be brought through Christ by the Spirit into loving union and communion with God as partakers in the *ad intra* life that is itself the Trinity (cf. John 17:20–26).[69] P. T. Forsyth captures the overall idea here nicely:

> To deliver us from evil is not simply to take us out of hell, it is to take us into heaven. Christ does not simply pluck us out of the hands of Satan, He does so by giving us to God. He does not simply release us from slavery, He commits us in the act to a positive liberty. He does not simply cancel the charge against us in court and bid us walk out of jail, He meets us at the prison-door and puts us in a new way of life. His forgiveness is not simply retrospective, it is, in the same act, the gift of eternal life.[70]

---

67. Smith, *Christ the Ideal King*, 208.

68. Balthasar, *TD*, IV, 242.

69. "Union with Christ" is the underlying theological idea of being brought through Christ by the Spirit into loving union and communion with God as partakers in the *ad intra* life that is itself the Trinity. To be clear, then, the kind of phrasing I am using of being "brought through Christ by the Spirit into communion with God" is equivalent to the Pauline concept of being in union with Christ by the Spirit, or simply the theological expression Paul frequently uses, namely, to be "in Christ."

70. P. T. Forsyth, *The Work of Christ* (Eugene, OR: Wipf & Stock, 1996), 202.

Of course, all of this will not be fully realized until the eschaton (cf. Eph 1:21; 2:7); nevertheless, by virtue of Christ's rectifying the problem of human sin and removing our alienation before God, the harmony of that broken relationship is restored, and the prerequisite is settled for the unity and harmony that will characterize further aspects of Christ's reconciling work.

If Christ's reconciling work of removing the alienation between human beings and God is operating in the sphere of human-divine relations, the next "fracture" Paul addresses in Ephesians 2:11–22 describes Christ's reconciling work as operating notably in the sphere of human-to-human relations. Here, God's reconciling operations through the reign of Christ are being realized between formerly hostile ethnic groups, notably the reconciliation of Gentile to Jew within the church. What Paul has in view is that in both groups together being reconciled to God through the death of Christ (Eph 2:16), a new corporate entity united to Christ is formed—"that he might create in himself one new man in place of the two" (Eph 2:15)—or what Paul simply distinguishes elsewhere as "the church of God" (1 Cor 10:32; cf. John 10:16; 11:52).[71]

Correspondingly, the ethnic catholicity of the gospel summed up in the Great Commission (Matt 28:18-20) gives visible form to, and serves as an expression of, the reconciling work of Christ before the entire world. As Vanhoozer expresses,

"This koinōnia is indeed the very being of the Church as a sign, instrument, and foretaste of what God purposes for the whole human family." The church, as public spire, is the vanguard of the realization of this plan. As such, the church is the public truth of Jesus Christ, and not only truth, but also the public goodness and public beauty of God's plan of redemption.[72]

---

71. Paul likewise brings out the corporate unity of both old and new covenant saints in Christ in Galatians 3:16-29 in which the seeds (verse 16, heirs of the Abrahamic promise) are recognized now as the seed (verse 29, referring to these same heirs), being unified in the promised seed of Abraham, which is Christ (verses 16, 19).

72. Kevin J. Vanhoozer and Owen Strachan, The Pastor as Public Theologian: Reclaiming a Lost Vision (Grand Rapids: Baker Academic, 2015), 21, citing Lesslie Newbigin, "Trinity as Public Truth" in The Trinity in a Pluralistic Age: Theological Essays on Culture and Religion, ed. Kevin J. Vanhoozer (Grand Rapids: Eerdmans, 1997), 8.

Concerning those who are in Christ's fellowship (or put otherwise, those who are in union with Christ) Paul makes this especially clear in Colossians 3:11: "Here there is not Greek and Jew, circumcised and uncircumcised, barbarian, Scythian, slave, free; but Christ is all, and in all"—what Scot McKnight calls "a fellowship of differents."[73] The import of this is that "in the new order, already set in motion through Christ's death and resurrection, the value-based distinctions between people— ethnicity, status, gender—no longer maintain."[74] The ethnic harmony constituted on earth through Christ's reconciling work reflects a vital facet of God's will being done on earth as it is in heaven, and centrally so within Christ's church (cf. Rom 15:5–7).

Following Smith's schematic of God's reconciling work through Christ, the accent in Ephesians 4:1–16 is on Christ as the benefactor supreme of his body, the church. Already in the letter's opening *berakah*, in fact, God's blessings for the church mediated through Christ are proclaimed: "Blessed be the God and Father of our Lord Jesus Christ, who has blessed us in Christ with every spiritual blessing in the heavenly places" (Eph 1:3). The prayer culminates in grand fashion, expressing that Christ fills the universe as its exalted king (Eph 1:20–21), and the church is the special realm of his munificent rule—"the fullness of him who fills all in all" (Eph 1:22–23; cf. Acts 20:28).[75] Thus, as a thematic thread within the letter, Christ is properly understood as "God's vicegerent, the cosmically enthroned king through whom God blesses his people."[76] The notion of Christ as the supreme benefactor of the church

---

73. See Scot McKnight, *A Fellowship of Differents: Showing the World God's Design for Life Together* (Grand Rapids: Zondervan, 2014).

74. Gordon D. Fee, *Pauline Christology: An Exegetical-Theological Study* (Peabody, MA: Hendrickson Publishers, 2007), 486.

75. Smith, *Christ the Ideal King*, 217–18. The study note on Ephesians 1:23 in the NET adds: "The idea of *all in all* is either related to the universe (hence, he fills the whole universe entirely) or the church universal (hence, Christ fills the church entirely with his presence and power)."

76. Smith, *Christ the Ideal King*, 187. Smith summarizes the great extent of these blessings as the *berakah* unfolds: "God is blessed for having blessed the audience with every spiritual blessing in the heavenly places through Christ (1:3). God moreover chose them through him (Christ) (1:4). God preordained them for adoption through Jesus Christ unto himself (1:5). God graciously bestowed his grace upon them through the beloved (1:6). Through him (the beloved), they have redemption through his blood (1:7). God set forth his good pleasure (planned to effect his

in Ephesians 4:1–16 is seen notably in his giving gifts to her for the building up of the unity of the body of Christ. Indeed, the church into which people from every tribe and language and nation have been/are being called is itself emblematic of this unity; just as the apostle says, "There is one body and one Spirit … one hope … one Lord, one faith, one baptism, one God and Father of all" (Eph 4:4–6; cf. Rom 12:4–5).

The apostle's christologically refocused quotation of Psalm 68:18 [68:19 MT; 67:19 LXX] in Ephesians 4:8 highlights in vivid imagery God's blessings for the church mediated through Christ;[77] this in turn is expanded on in Ephesians 4:7–16. In 4:8, Paul makes use of the divine warrior theme in citing Psalm 68, which celebrates Yahweh as the Warrior-God who subverts the forces of evil for the salvation of his people. A prominent element in the psalm is blessing after victory and enthronement, but unlike the psalm, Christ as the divine warrior is portrayed not as the *receiver* of tribute but rather as the *giver* of gifts. In Ephesians 4:9, the apostle continues his christological perspective of Psalm 68:18, posing this question with respect to Christ: "Now what is the meaning of 'he ascended,' except that he also descended to the lower regions, namely, the earth?" (NET). Exactly what Paul meant here in juxtaposing Christ's ascent with his descent is not altogether clear, but a plausible reading is that Christ's triumph over the powers and authorities is in view. "The descent of Christ in verse 9," writes Timothy Gombis, "is

---

purpose) through him (1:9). God's plan for the fullness of time is to sum up all things through the Christ (1:10)." (186)

77. The study note on Ephesians 4:8 in the NET comments: "It has sometimes been suggested that the author of Ephesians modified the text he was citing in order to better support what he wanted to say here. Such modifications are sometimes found in rabbinic exegesis from this and later periods, but it is also possible that the author was simply citing a variant of Ps 68 known to him but which has not survived outside its quotation here. Another possibility is that the words here, which strongly resemble Ps 68:19 MT and LXX (68:18 ET), are actually part of an early Christian hymn quoted by the author." However, the view taken here is that Psalm 68:18 is christologically refocused by Paul, as Timothy G. Gombis explains: "The author [of Ephesians] has no intention of quoting Ps 68:19 MT verbatim, but rather has in mind the full narrative movement of the entire psalm. He thereby appropriates the imagery of Yahweh ascending his throne after victory and refocuses it christologically. Consequently Christ is depicted as the triumphant divine warrior who defeats his enemies in his death, ascends his throne as the exalted and victorious Lord, and blesses his people with gifts." Gombis, "Cosmic Lordship and Divine Gift-Giving: Psalm 68 in Ephesians 4:8," *NovT* 47 no. 4 (2005): 379–80.

a reference to his descent to the grave—the abode of the dead—and has in view his death by which he triumphed over his enemies."[78] On this view, the ascent of Christ is taken to be an ascent of victory. More specifically, it is a victorious ascent because he had already disarmed and triumphed over these enemies by his atoning death on the cross (Col 2:15).

As Paul continues his train of thought to his own question—"What is the meaning of 'he ascended'?"—he adds in Ephesians 4:10: "He, the very one who descended, is also the one who ascended above all the heavens, in order to fill all things" (NET). Having vanquished his enemies, in other words, Christ rightfully ascended to his heavenly enthronement as the exalted king of the universe. Insofar as this is a fair reading of the text, "the ascent of Christ is the triumphant procession of the conquering Warrior to his throne, from which he will bless his people with gifts."[79] Paul expands on Christ's munificence toward his church, shown in apportioning the gift of grace to each member of the body of Christ (Eph 4:7), and endowing the church in the form of leadership gifts with some as apostles, some as prophets, some as evangelists, and some as pastors and teachers (Eph 4:11). The body of Christ will in this way be brought "to the unity of the faith and of the knowledge of the Son of God—a mature person, attaining to the measure of Christ's full stature" (Eph 4:13 NET). Thus God's blessings for the church mediated through Christ by the Spirit to those "in Christ" are a constitutive part of the unity of the church. From Paul's perspective, it is fair to say, the church is the evident centerpiece of God's work of summing up all things in Christ. All of this, remarks Smith, "should be understood in the context of the overall vision of God reconciling the cosmos through Christ."[80]

---

78. Gombis, "Cosmic Lordship and Divine Gift-Giving," 378. To note, scholarly opinion varies on what the descent of Christ means here. In my judgment the reading selected is preferable (cf. Rom 10:6–7), but alternative readings include taking it as a reference to the incarnation itself; or the underworld (hell), where Jesus is thought to have descended during the three days between his death and resurrection; or happening *after* the ascent and thus referring to the descent of the Spirit at Pentecost.

79. Gombis, "Cosmic Lordship and Divine Gift-Giving," 379.

80. Smith, *Christ the Ideal King*, 219.

Having just emphasized that Christ's gifts to his church are meant largely to build up her members in the unity of the faith and to the full measure of maturity in Christ, the apostle focuses in Ephesians 4:17–5:21 on summoning them to a distinctive *kind* of life. Here he develops further his earlier exhortation that those who have been called by Christ must live lives worthy—that is, befittingly (ἀξίως)—of the calling to which they have been called (Eph 4:1; cf. Phil 1:27; Col 1:10).[81] Further on, Paul is just as keen to proscribe any lifestyle or habits that are unbefitting the lives of members of Christ's church (e.g., Eph 5:3–4). As we will address in Chapter 6, an important element of our theological aesthetic is the idea that living a life worthy of one's calling involves living out fittingly one's identity in Christ.[82] The thrust of Paul's message here is clear enough: understanding what one's identity in Christ is about carries with it the mandate of discipleship to live in full accordance with that identity (cf. Col 2:6–7).[83] After pointing up the contrast of those who are "alienated from the life of God because of the ignorance that is in them, due to their hardness of heart" (4:18; cf. Col 3:5–7), Paul quickly follows it with pronouncing, "But that is not the way you learned Christ!" (4:20; cf. John 17:3; Gal 4:9; 2 Cor 5:16; Phil 3:10). In Ephesians 4:22–24, Paul addresses in three overlapping injunctions what "learning Christ" means for living out fittingly one's identity in Christ. Christians are to "put off your old self, which belongs to your former manner of life and is corrupt through deceitful desires" (Eph 4:22); "be renewed in the spirit of your minds" (Eph 4:23); and "put on the new self, created after the likeness of God in true righteousness and holiness" (Eph 4:24). How this all is to take form and expression in the lives of believers is set forth in the verses following. Furthermore, just as the call throughout the Old Testament for God's people to imitate him in various ways amounted to a call to live out rightly the ethical-relational aspect of the

---

81. BDAG 94 s.v. ἀξίως: worthily, in a manner worthy of, suitably.

82. The matter of living out fittingly one's identity in Christ will be taken up in Chapter 6 in the section, Being Conformed to the Image of Christ: God's Work of Forming and Making Beautiful His Children.

83. Employing Passover imagery, Paul admonishes the Corinthian believers likewise to conform their lives to who they *now* are in Christ: "Cleanse out the old leaven that you may be a new lump, *as you really are unleavened*. For Christ, our Passover lamb, has been sacrificed" (1 Cor 5:7).

imago Dei, in like respect does Paul enjoin his audience, "Therefore be imitators of God, as beloved children" (Eph 5:1). This is all of a piece with the charge Paul then gives to walk in love in accord with Christ's example of love for us (Eph 5:2; cf. 4:32), because for those who are in Christ's fellowship, the *imitatio Dei* and *imitatio Christi* are one and the very same thing. Jesus himself characterizes how all those who are in his fellowship are to imitate him as a testimony to all people in terms of the *agapē* they have for one another: "A new commandment I give to you, that you love one another: just as I have loved you, you also are to love one another. By this all people will know that you are my disciples, if you have love for one another" (John 13:34–35). In so doing followers of Christ demonstrate in the purest way what it means to have truly "learned Christ."

Smith suggests the audience may have understood the idea of *learning Christ* "as shorthand for leading virtuous lives enabled by the presence of their king, the risen and exalted Christ in the church."[84] In any case, the enablement to fittingly live out one's identity in Christ had been adumbrated earlier in the letter (e.g., Eph 1:13; 2:10; 3:16–17, 19–20). The bottom line is that "because ethical behavior is dependent upon God, who now dwells in them through Christ, the possibility for such behavior may now be actualized."[85] Thus the enablement through union with Christ to live distinctively Christ-like lives is essential for the Christian community to fittingly live out her identity in Christ, both individually and corporately, and to be imitators of Christ in their relations with one another.

Lastly, consistent with the redeeming activity Paul sets out in Ephesians, the issues he addresses in 5:22–6:9 are to be fully appreciated as yet another facet of Christ's reconciling work, which here entails effecting the harmonious functioning of relations within the family household. The context of this passage has to do with the so-called *Haustafel* or "household code," whose basic form back then prescribed rules within the context of the family estate regarding the proper relations between husbands and wives, fathers and children, and masters

---

84. Smith, *Christ the Ideal King*, 230–31.
85. Smith, *Christ the Ideal King*, 230–31.

and slaves.[86] As was the case in the ancient Roman world, one's status in society was effectively determined as a function of these sets of oppositions. Paul's point is that as members of God's family, our status is no longer correlated to whether or not one is a Jew, slave, or female. Paul thus adapts this basic form and applies it to exhort the body of Christ in two clear ways:[87]

1. Submission and obedience on the part of the subordinate parties (wives, children, slaves) is to be carried out "as to the Lord," "in the Lord," "as to Christ," or "as slaves of Christ."

2. The behavior of the superordinate parties (husbands, fathers, masters) toward those subordinate to them is likewise to be modeled upon Christ's relationship to the church. Husbands are to love their wives as Christ loved the church (Eph 5:25); fathers are to bring up their children in the instruction and admonishment of the Lord (Eph 6:4), and masters are to treat their slaves in a way that reflects the impartiality of their master in heaven (Eph 6:9).

Christ is once again given as the exemplar for the Christian community to model in their relations with one another. Yet the same spiritual basis we have seen all along must apply: the Christ-like harmony that households are called to reflect has its source solely in and through Christ, who himself nourishes and cherishes the members of his own body (Eph 5:29–30; cf. John 15:5; Col 2:19). And precisely because Christ is the one who effects this by his Spirit, harmony in accord with this Pauline *Haustafel* can be/is being realized in the functioning of relations within the family household in demonstration of Christ's reconciling rule. According to Smith, "the household is viewed primarily as a microcosm of the church rather than the state. As in the household, so in the church and so in the cosmos."[88] In this light the Pauline *Haustafel* is not

---

86. Other examples of *Haustafel* that occur in the New Testament include Colossians 3:18—4:1; Titus 2:1–10; and 1 Peter 2:18–3:7.

87. See Smith, *Christ the Ideal King*, 236–37.

88. Smith, *Christ the Ideal King*, 238. The idea implicit in Paul's theological worldview that God establishes through the reign of Christ a certain eschatological harmony between himself and the cosmos, church, and household is not altogether unique, however. The Hellenistic thought-form still present in Paul's day affirmed similar patterns of cosmological correspondence existing between God, ruler, and

directed to instruct believers first and foremost in how to fittingly live out their identity in Christ as members of society, but rather in how to do so within the church, his body and the special realm of his munificent rule.[89] Any and all rectification of this disharmony through Christ by his Spirit represents another facet of God's will being done on earth as it is in heaven. Bound up with all this is Christ's love for the church and the summing up of his purposes to "present the church to himself as glorious—not having a stain or wrinkle, or any such blemish, but holy and blameless" (Eph 5:27 NET).

Conspectus

The christological contours of beauty are extended here to the already but not-yet order of reality governed under the preeminence of Christ's heavenly rule. That order of reality involves the reconciliation of the fractured cosmos that God has accomplished in an "already but not-yet consummate" way through the reign of Christ. I have argued that, as represented in the body of Paul's letter to the Ephesians, God's reconciling operations through the reign of Christ display his beauty fundamentally in the form of an already but not-yet unity and harmony operating in the spheres of human-divine relations and human-human relations in the perfecting of his church. It may be worth reiterating here that according to our theological aesthetic whatever work God does through Christ by his Spirit in the economy of salvation is a work that, by definition, manifests his glory—his essential nature. Thus, my argument does not restrict or denote unity and harmony as signifying qualities that pertain strictly to God's beauty. God's nature cannot be parsed in such terms. However, I am arguing that it is proper to recognize unity and harmony in the divine work of making whole what has

---

state, and this framework of thought may have resonated with his Ephesian audience. A helpful overview regarding such Hellenistic influence is found in Willis Peter De Boer, *The Imitation of Paul: An Exegetical Study* (Kampen, Netherlands: J. H. Kok, 1962). See specifically 1–13, and 24–28.

89. Smith, *Christ the Ideal King*, 237, writes: "Within the letter's argument, there seems to be little concern that Christian households function harmoniously so that the social order of the state may be preserved. Rather, the letter is anxious to preserve unity in the church, and sees the household as an integral element within that."

been fractured as being marks that accord with and evince God's beautiful nature. In my characterization of Paul's theological perspective in Ephesians, I have shown that God's reconciling operations through the reign of Christ are exemplified in the following ways:

- *Ephesians 2:1–10:* By virtue of Christ's rectifying the problem of human sin and removing our alienation before God, the harmony of that broken relationship is restored, and the prerequisite is settled for the unity and harmony that will characterize further aspects of Christ's reconciling work.

- *Ephesians 2:11–22:* The realizing of unity and harmony between formerly hostile ethnic groups, beginning with the reconciliation of Gentile to Jew within the church. In both groups together being reconciled to God through the death of Christ, a new corporate entity united to Christ is formed—the church of God.

- *Ephesians 4:1–16:* The notion of Christ as the supreme benefactor of the church is seen notably in the building up of the body of Christ in the unity of the faith and to the full measure of maturity in Christ through the blessings/gifts she receives through him.

- *Ephesians 4:17–5:21:* The enablement through union with Christ to live distinctively Christ-like lives is essential for the Christian community to fittingly live out her identity in Christ, both individually and corporately, and to be imitators of Christ in their relations with one another.

- *Ephesians 5:22–6:9:* As members of God's family, our status is no longer correlated to one's status in society. The Christ-like harmony that family households are called to reflect has its source solely in and through Christ, who himself nourishes and cherishes the members of his own body. The idea implicit in Paul's theological worldview is that God establishes through the reign of Christ a certain eschatological harmony between himself and the cosmos, church, and household. Bound up with all this is Christ's love for the church and the summing up of his purposes to "present the church to himself as glorious—not having a stain or wrinkle, or any such blemish, but holy and blameless" (Eph 5:27).

In all these ways a divine work of making whole what has been fractured is directed in the perfecting of Christ's church, which evinces

God's beautiful nature. And in a myriad other ways God's reconciling operations through the reign of Christ advances toward the redemptive-eschatological fulfillment of his will being done on earth as it is in heaven, which will be summed up consummately in Christ. In the age to come, a fractured cosmos will be ultimately transformed into a consummative kingdom characterized, among other things scarcely imaginable, by its unity and harmony—that is, its perfect *shalom*.

6

Re-creation: Beauty's Denouement

The Son's fittingness as incarnate Redeemer, as I have argued it, is the critical lens for seeing God's beauty, serving as well to display the Son's glory in every stage of the theodrama. The theodrama comes at last to its denouement in the consummation of all things through the Son—the Alpha and the Omega (Rev 1:8; 21:6; 22:13)—the one through whom all things were made and the one in whom all things will eventually be summed up (Eph 1:10). The working of the Trinity in the economy of consummation is the same, mutatis mutandis, as I described previously with respect to the economies of creation and redemption: the Father consummates, but always through the Son in the Spirit; the Son consummates, but always from the Father in the Spirit; the Spirit consummates, but always from the Father through the Son, so that the Father together with the Son and the Spirit pursue and accomplish the consummation that belongs to God alone. In this stage is the eschatological realization of all things being reconciled to God through Christ in the Spirit, and God's original creational purposes manifest in their consummative fulfillment, all worked out according to the design of the divine plan. In his sermon, "Approaching the End of God's Grand Design," Jonathan Edwards celebrates the masterfully directed working and intimacy of "this great design" in eloquent fashion: worth quoting at length.

> There is a time coming wherein this great design will be completed: the scheme finished and work done, and it will be proclaimed, as in the text, "It is done." Notwithstanding the greatness of the work, the mighty opposition, so long a-doing and so long waited for: things

seem to go backwards and not forwards; yet the time is coming—
and certainly will come—when it will be seen, actually finished.
Angels shall see it. The church of God shall see it despite wicked men,
persecutors, opposers, and devils. Nothing shall hinder it. God's
great ends will be obtained: all his ends will be obtained, and by his
own means. After all this seeming confusion and vast succession
of strange and wonderful revolutions, everything shall come out
right at last. There is no confusion in God's scheme; he understands
his own works and every wheel moves right in its place. Not one
mote of dust errs from the path that God has appointed it; he will
bring order at last out of confusion. God don't [sic] lose himself in
the intricate endless moves of events that come to pass. Though
men can't see the whole scheme, God sees. The course and series
of events in divine providence is like the course of a great and long
river with many branches and innumerable windings and turnings
which often seems to go backwards. Like the motion of a chariot,
the revolutions of divine providence are like the manifold turnings
of the wheels of a chariot.[1]

We also are approaching the end of God's grand design and will
finish at the end of the Bible's story, the happy-ever-after ending of the
sublime comedy for the redeemed in Christ.

Our theological aesthetic in this chapter concerns God's work of
forming and making beautiful his children in reference to both this
present age and its consummative fulfillment in the age to come. That
work has in view how humans were created to reflect being-like-God
in the world, and God's redemptive-eschatological design to see that
purpose fulfilled through Christ. This will be developed in relation to
the themes of sonship, image bearing, and the church. In relation to our
theological aesthetic, the subject of the damned in hell is considered,
followed by the relation between creation and new creation, and lastly,
the theodrama's ending as a sublime comedy. Our featured theologian
to conclude with is Jonathan Edwards. I develop this chapter in four
main sections as follows:

---

1. Jonathan Edwards, "Approaching the End of God's Grand Design," *WJE* 25:121.

1. *Being Conformed to the Image of Christ: God's Work of Forming and Making Beautiful His Children.* I argue that Christian fittingness, understood as God's people living in conformity to their identity in Christ, is both modeled after Christ's theodramatic fittingness during his earthly career as represented in the Scriptures, and based on Christ, as the incarnate image of God, being the full measure of the image in which humans were created and thus the full measure of the image-bearing glory inherent in and expressed through his human form. Christian fittingness as such is based on Christ being the archetype of humanity and for humanity. I address this at the level of Christian individuals and at the level of the church. (1) God's Work of Forming and Making Beautiful Each of His Children. I break this aspect down in two parts: (a) Living Out the Truth of Our Adoptive Sonship; and (b) Bearing the Image of Christ Theodramatically. (2) God's Work of Forming and Making Beautiful His Church.

2. *Humans Immortal in Final Fittingness: Redeemed as Glorious.* In the coming age is the eschatological realization of humanity's identity and destiny as image of God. These will be the sons and daughters of God who will, at that time, reflect their consummative transformation into the image of Christ. At that time the identity and destiny of the church will be represented in her form as the glorified Bride of Christ. In all respects the fittingness of God's people will be complete for sharing eternal life with God and in God because in all respects Christ is the archetype of humanity and for humanity through whom the redeemed are imaged eschatologically. I unpack this in three parts: (1) Beloved Sons and Daughters with Whom the Father Is Well Pleased; (2) Image-Bearers Glorified; and (3) The Church without Spot or Wrinkle: The Bride of Christ Made Beautiful and Glorified.

3. *Humans Immortal in Final Fittingness: Damned as Glory-less.* Assumed here is the traditional view of hell, understood as a realm of eternal, conscious torment of all those who, under the final sentence of divine judgment, are thus damned and consigned there. Our interest concerns how this area of doctrine fits within the application of our theological aesthetic, whose fundamental premise is that everything God does is beautiful (i.e., God-glorifying). The argumentation I propose considers the aspect of fittingness and the motif of glory in regard to the divine judgment of damnation rendered against the

creature made in God's image. The section is divided into two parts:
(1) Damnation: The Miserific Death; and (2) The Damned: Loss of
Sonship, Loss of Image, Loss of Glory.

4. *The Eschaton: The Beginning of the Eternity of All Things.* In the age to
come, the reconciliation of the fractured cosmos that God has accomplished through Christ will reflect the beauty of God in a glorified
new creation when God proclaims at last, "Behold, I am making all
things new" (Rev 21:5). The relation between the original creation
(*creation originalis*) and the new creation (*creation nova*) seen in the
broad outworking of God's plan points up the integral nature of the
glorification of the creation with the glorification of the new humanity in Christ. I present a theological interpretation in evidence of
that point. Lastly, the sublime comedy ending of the theodrama is
presented as the beautiful beginning of the eternity of all things for
the people of God. Uniquely characterizing the sublime comedy, the
eschatological fulfillment of God's master plan thus brings something
incomparably and everlastingly more glorious than its protological
beginning. The section is divided into two parts: (1) New Creation:
Creatio Originalis Becomes *Creatio Nova*; and (2) The Sublime Comedy:
The Happy-Ever-After Ending Begins.

JONATHAN EDWARDS ON DIVINE BEAUTY

Widely recognized as one of the premier philosopher-theologians of
America, and perhaps her most famous colonial era pastor, Jonathan
Edwards preached and promoted an essentially orthodox Calvinist
theology, which was informed by his exceptionally robust theological aesthetic vision of reality. In his dissertation *On the Nature of True
Virtue*—part of Edwards' most mature work—he encapsulates this
vision as a reality that all derives from God, redounds back to God, and
encompasses all of creation:

> God is not only infinitely greater and more excellent than all other
> being; but he is the head of the universal system of existence; the
> foundation and fountain of all being and all beauty; from whom
> all is perfectly derived, and on whom all is most absolutely and
> perfectly dependent; *of whom*, and *through whom*, and *to whom* is all
> being and all perfection; and whose being and beauty is as it were

the sum and comprehension of all existence and excellence: much
more than the sun is the foundation and summary comprehension
of all the light and brightness of the day.[2]

Indeed, for Edwards, the altogether perfection of God in himself
(*in se*) is identified preeminently in terms of his divine beauty: "God
is God, and distinguished from all other beings, and exalted above 'em,
chiefly by his divine beauty."[3] In characterizing the nature of beauty,
Edwards adopts the basic view that beauty—whether divine or created— involves a particular relational quality or dynamic that exists
between things. "All beauty," Edwards states in his early writing in
"The Mind," "consists in similarity or identity of relations."[4] As Louis
Mitchell points out, the ambit of terms Edwards uses in connection with
or synonymously for beauty include symmetry, proportion, harmony,
agreement, consent, union, and love.[5]

Moreover, emphasized in Edwards' theory of aesthetics is that the
quality of beauty expressed between beings involves a kind of agreement with or consent to each other. Such consent operates as a kind
of conformity to Being in general (or God). We should note here as
well that Edwards subsumes beauty in all its facets under the more
comprehensive term—excellency. Linking excellency with beauty in
terms of the notion of consent, he remarks in "The Mind," "Excellency
may be distributed into greatness and beauty. The former is the degree
of being, the latter is being's consent to being."[6] In his mature work

---

2. Jonathan Edwards, "On the Nature of True Virtue," *WJE* 8:551. "On the Nature
of True Virtue" is the second of a dissertation pair that Edwards intended to be
published together; "Concerning the End for Which God Created the World" is the
first. Paul Ramsey writes in the "Editor's Introduction": "The one is the mirror image
of the other; the 'end' for which God created the world must be the 'end' of a truly
virtuous and holy life. The present volume reproduces the unity and the sequence
of the component parts of the original edition of *Two Dissertations*" (*WJE* 8:5).

3. Jonathan Edwards, *Religious Affections*, *WJE* 2:298. In distinguishing God from
all other beings, Edwards at times applies the more metaphysical appellation to
God as the "Being of beings," or as he also puts it, "Being in general."

4. Jonathan Edwards, "The Mind no. 1," *WJE* 6:334.

5. Louis J. Mitchell, "The Theological Aesthetics of Jonathan Edwards," *Theology
Today* 64 (2007): 37.

6. Edwards, "The Mind no. 62," *WJE* 6:381–82. Along related lines in "The Mind
no. 1" he writes: "This is a universal definition of excellency: the consent of being to
being; or being's consent to entity. The more the consent is, and the more extensive,

this same idea is again used synonymously for beauty—for example, "Beauty does not consist in discord and dissent, but in consent and agreement."[7] Beauty exists between beings, therefore, in a relational dynamic involving the consent of being to being, such that the capacity to consent itself presupposes beings capable of volition and love. In Edwards' theological aesthetic, the notion of the consent to being has as its basis the social ontology of God's Being. His conception of beauty as involving "consent" and "agreement" thus provides the key philosophical link for identifying God's divine beauty with God's *Trinitarian* beauty. A kernel of this thought can be seen in one of his miscellanies: "One alone cannot be excellent, inasmuch as, in such a case, there can be no consent. Therefore, if God is excellent, there must be a plurality in God; otherwise there can be no consent in him."[8] Thus a "unity" can be excellent, but not a "singularity," that is, unity in a monadic sense.

However, in "The Mind," Edwards expresses the excellence of God's beauty in explicitly Trinitarian terms: "God's excellence consists in the love of himself. ... But he exerts himself towards himself no other way than in infinitely loving and delighting in himself, in the mutual love of the Father and the Son. This makes the third, the personal Holy Spirit or the holiness of God, which is his infinite beauty, and this is God's infinite consent to being in general"—that is, God's consent within himself or intra-Trinitarian consent.[9] And so the consent of being to being in God is the infinite consent between the Father and the Son,

the greater is the excellency" (*WJE* 6:336). According to Wallace E. Anderson, the editor of this *WJE* volume, the notions of consent and agreement that Edwards uses in his conception of excellency are associated with his early training in the Ramist system of logic and Locke's definition of truth. In the "Editor's Introduction," *WJE* 6:90-91, he writes: "The notions of agreement and disagreement that Edwards introduces in ['The Mind'] probably take their rise from the formal disciplines, especially logic, to which he was devoted as a student. In the Ramist system of logic, in particular, these terms had an established use in the classification of 'arguments' or reasons that should be searched out and applied to a subject matter in explaining or proving something about it. ... John Locke's definition of truth as 'the joining or separating of signs, as the things signified by them do agree or disagree with one another,' and of knowledge as 'the perception of the connection or agreement, or disagreement and repugnancy, of any of our ideas,' seem to have an even more direct bearing upon Edwards' explanation of excellency."

7. Edwards, "On the Nature of True Virtue," *WJE* 8:541.
8. Jonathan Edwards, "Misc. no. 117," *WJE* 13:285.
9. Edwards, "The Mind no. 45," *WJE* 6:364.

a consent that consists of the infinite love each has *for* the other, and the eternal delight each has *in* the other. This, writes Edwards, "is the harmony and excellency and beauty of the Deity"—a beauty that is itself the personal distinction of the Holy Spirit, the third person of the Trinity.[10] And this immeasurable fullness of love and delight within the Godhead—the very expression of his beauty *ad intra*—is what, for Edwards, explains God's natural and essential disposition to create, to emanate *ad extra* the fullness of his beauty, which he does out of his own infinite regard for himself. Thus, in his dissertation "Concerning the End for Which God Created the World," Edwards writes:

> As there is an infinite fullness of all possible good in God, a fullness of every perfection, of all excellency and beauty, and of infinite happiness. And as this fullness is capable of communication or emanation *ad extra*; so it seems a thing amiable and valuable in itself that it should be communicated or flow forth, that this infinite fountain of good should send forth abundant streams, that this infinite fountain of light should, diffusing its excellent fullness, pour forth light all around. And as this is in itself excellent, so a disposition to this in the Divine Being must be looked upon as a perfection or an excellent disposition.[11]

Bound up with God's fullness of Being, moreover—again, "a fullness of every perfection, of all excellency and beauty, and of infinite happiness"—is the glory of God *ad intra*. The glory is distinguished from the fullness of God, however, in that God's internal glory involves intra-Trinitarian relations of glory. That is to say, although none of the Persons of the Trinity has "a distinct essence" of all their own, each does have "a distinct glory," "a relative glory, or glory of relation."[12] In Edwards' schema, the relational dynamic of God's Triune glory operates

10. Edwards, "Misc. no. 293," *WJE* 13:384. As Edwards states in another of his miscellanies, "The Holy Spirit is the act of God between the Father and the Son infinitely loving and delighting in each other. Sure I am, that if the Father and the Son do infinitely delight in each other, there must be an infinitely pure and perfect act between them, an infinitely sweet energy we call delight" ("Misc. no. 94," *WJE* 13:260).

11. Jonathan Edwards, "Concerning the End for Which God Created the World," *WJE* 8:432–33.

12. Jonathan Edwards, "On the Equality of the Persons of the Trinity," *WJE* 21:146.

as a communicative outflow, or perhaps better, overflow in that his "external glory is only the emanation of his internal glory."[13]

But whether internal or external, God's glory is inseparable from all his fullness of perfection and beauty, whose glorious emanation *ad extra* is the enactment and expressed work of creation itself.[14] And because the Holy Spirit is the harmony and excellency and beauty of the Deity, it is his role to bring beauty to the world: "It was more especially the Holy Spirit's work to bring the world to its beauty and perfection out of the chaos, for the beauty of the world is a communication of God's beauty."[15] We need only add here that, for Edwards, the communication of God's beauty in creation must be understood in Trinitarian terms. Mitchell offers the following reframing of Edwards' Triune aesthetic: "In Edwards' doctrine of the Trinity, the Father is the 'Lover,' the source of love; the Son is the "Beloved," the object of the Father's love; and the Holy Spirit is 'Love,' the relatedness within the Godhead. In aesthetic categories one could say that the Father is the 'Beautifier;' the Son is the 'Beautiful;' and the Holy Spirit is 'Primary Beauty.'"[16]

Furthermore, the beauty of the world communicated by the Person of the Holy Spirit is perceivable and experienceable by spiritual and moral beings "who see the beauty there is in true virtue ... by the frame of their own minds, or a certain spiritual sense given them of God."[17] In Edwards' theological aesthetic, all true virtue is intrinsically beautiful, though not all beauty is intrinsically virtuous. The nature of true virtue is that "which renders any habit, disposition, or exercise of the heart truly beautiful."[18] The "truly beautiful" referred to here is what Edwards calls primary beauty; in his parlance this consists in consent

---

13. Edwards, "Concerning the End for Which God Created the World," *WJE* 8:529.

14. Cf., Edwards, "On the Nature of True Virtue," *WJE* 8:550: "For as God is infinitely the greatest being, so he is allowed to be infinitely the most beautiful and excellent: and all the beauty to be found throughout the whole creation, is but the reflection of the diffused beams of that Being who hath an infinite fullness of brightness and glory."

15. Edwards, "Misc. no. 293," *WJE* 13:384.

16. Louis J. Mitchell, "Jonathan Edwards on the Experience of Beauty," *Theology Matters* 9 no. 6 (November/December 2003): 7.

17. Edwards, "On the Nature of True Virtue," *WJE* 8:620.

18. Edwards, "On the Nature of True Virtue," *WJE* 8: 539.

and union of heart to Being in general (i.e., God), and subsidiarily to spiritual/moral beings in particular. The kind of concord and consent that characterizes primary beauty manifests itself in true harmony of relationships between people; such harmony may be evident in social community and, by the same token, in the church. The highest expression of true virtue, of course, is love, which Mitchell sums up here in aesthetic terms: "Thus to experience love is to experience beauty; to be loving is to beautify; to be filled with love is to be beautiful."[19]

To experience primary beauty, however, is not to privilege a subjectivist view of beauty over an objectivist one. For Edwards, the objective nature of primary beauty is founded on the objective relations of consent/conformity to Being in general. At the same time, Edwards affirms the subjective dimension of primary beauty in terms of the delight or aesthetic pleasure it elicits in the dynamic of its presence or perception. Regarding the beauty of true virtue he states, "They immediately perceive pleasure in the presence of the idea of true virtue in their minds, or are directly gratified in the view or contemplation of this object."[20] But it is especially as human beings experience God's saving grace that they are infused by the Holy Spirit with religious/spiritual affections that accord with the beauty and delight of God's nature. As he expresses in his "Treatise on Grace," this occurs through what Edwards calls a "sense of the heart": "The first effect of the power of God in the heart in regeneration, is to give the heart a divine taste or sense, to cause it to have a relish of the loveliness and sweetness of the supreme excellency of the divine nature."[21] Moreover, it is through perceiving the objective beauty of Christ by the saving grace of God's Spirit that "this sight of the divine beauty of Christ … bows the will and draws the hearts of men."[22]

---

19. Mitchell, "Jonathan Edwards on the Experience of Beauty," 7.

20. Edwards, "On the Nature of True Virtue," *WJE* 8:620.

21. Jonathan Edwards, "Treatise on Grace," *WJE* 21:174. In his sermon "True Grace, Distinguished from the Experience of Devils," *WJE* 25:636, Edwards likewise states, "This sense of divine beauty is the first thing in the actual change made in the soul in true conversion, and is the foundation of every thing else belonging to that change."

22. Edwards, "True Grace, Distinguished from the Experience of Devils," *WJE* 25:635.

Lastly, for Edwards there is a kind of beauty that, in contrast to primary beauty, is not intrinsically virtuous, at least not in a true virtue sense. He calls this secondary beauty. Unlike primary beauty, which we already know as the proper and peculiar beauty of spiritual and moral beings, secondary beauty "is not peculiar to spiritual beings, but is found even in inanimate things: which consists in a mutual consent and agreement of different things in form, manner, quantity, and visible end or design; called by the various names of regularity, order, uniformity, symmetry, proportion, harmony, etc."[23] But while secondary beauty does not directly reflect true virtue, it nevertheless functions in countless ways as an analogical reflection of the true, spiritual original beauty—that is, primary beauty. As Edwards puts it, it simply "pleases God to observe analogy in his works," such that secondary beauty appears beautiful to human beings by virtue of a divinely given instinct or by design of a law of nature. In this way God makes "an agreement or consent of different things, in their form, manner, measure, etc. to appear beautiful, because here is some image of a higher kind of agreement and consent of spiritual beings."[24] On Edwards' view, one could therefore say, there is a "consent" between primary and secondary beauty.

BEING CONFORMED
TO THE IMAGE OF CHRIST

"In 1904, less than six years before his death, William James made a revealing statement in response to a questionnaire circulated by his former student James Pratt. To the question, 'Do you believe in personal immortality?' James answered, 'Never keenly, but more strongly as I grow older.' 'If so, why?' 'Because I am just getting fit to live.'"[25] James'

---

23. Edwards, "On the Nature of True Virtue," *WJE* 8:561.

24. Edwards, "On the Nature of True Virtue," *WJE* 8:564, 566. For Edwards, secondary beauty applies just as much to things immaterial as it does to material. For his take on various examples and expressions of secondary beauty, see Edwards, "On the Nature of True Virtue," *WJE* 8:562–74.

25. This quote borrows from Carol Zaleski, "In Defense of Immortality," read at the Ingersoll Lecture given at Harvard Divinity School on March 16, 2000. Known as an American philosopher, psychologist, and physician, William James was one of the leading thinkers of the late nineteenth century.

response resonates nicely with the concept of Christian fittingness inasmuch as disciples of Christ, as they mature in having "learned Christ," come to increasingly realize and experience in the freedom of the Spirit that they likewise are "just getting fit to live." A core point of the christological contours of beauty has to do with our formation as Christian disciples. The beauty of that formation is that vital part of God's work in this present age of forming and making beautiful his children, which is all about their being conformed to the image of his Son. The work of spiritual formation involves Christians living out fittingly their identity in Christ, which is part and parcel of the progressive work of spiritual transformation that God through Christ by the Spirit does in us. That central purpose of spiritual transformation in the plan of salvation is integral to the church of God—the Bride of Christ—being formed and "adorned" in preparation for her nuptial union with Christ.

Two christological premises that recognize Christ as the archetype of and for humanity lay behind this idea. First, the Son's theodramatic fittingness in the form of his humanity is the critical lens for seeing God's beauty, and served to display his glory appropriately during his earthly career. Second, as the incarnate image of God, Christ is the full measure of the image in which humans are created, and thus the full measure of the image-bearing glory inherent in and expressed through his human form. Based on the theodramatic fittingness of Christ, I argue that the concept of Christian fittingness is God's people living in conformity to their identity in Christ, and serves as a fundamental aspect of their spiritual formation. Christian fittingness as such operates at the level of Christian individuals as well as at the level of the church worldwide. Michael Horton expands on the overall idea here in properly pneumatological terms:

> Through the Spirit, all that is done by Christ for us, outside of us and in the past, is received and made fruitful within us in the present. In this way, the power that is constitutive of the consummation (the age to come) is already at work now in the world. Through the Spirit's agency, not only is Christ's past work applied to us but his present status in glory penetrates our own existence in a semirealized manner. The Spirit's work is what connects us here and now

to Christ's past, present, and future. ... The Spirit shapes creaturely reality according to the archetypal image of the Son.[26]

Our growing in conformity toward the full measure of Christ's image involves in this present age a divine work in which we are enabled to grow spiritually in image-bearing glory in and through our human form as we live out fittingly our identity in Christ (cf. Luke 6:40).[27] In this dynamic God's work of forming and making beautiful each person in Christ translates to a progressive work of spiritual transformation that corresponds to their image-bearing glory being transformed from glory to glory. "Observe, that *the design of the gospel* is this," writes Calvin, "that the image of God, which had been effaced by sin, may be stamped anew upon us, and that the advancement of this restoration may be continually going forward in us during our whole life, because God makes his glory shine forth in us by little and little."[28] At the level of the church worldwide, the church's conformity to the pattern of Christ's life in this present age, I propose, corresponds to the state of his humiliation and translates in the broadest sense to a participation in his sufferings according to the working of the Spirit of Christ risen and exalted.

To some extent the work of God as it relates to believers being conformed to the image of Christ was presented already in different terms. Notably, Paul's exhortation in Philippians 2:5 to "have the same attitude toward one another that Christ Jesus had;" and his summons to the Ephesian Christian community to live according to how they have "learned Christ," which effectively carries a mandate of discipleship whose aim is for Christians to live in full accordance with their identity in Christ. The more generalized notion applying here is our growth in maturing to the measure of Christ, both individually and corporately. Admittedly, all aspects of God's work that bear upon the individual

---

26. Michael S. Horton, *People and Place: A Covenant Ecclesiology* (Louisville: Westminster John Knox Press, 2008), 21.

27. In the words of Irenaeus, "Now God shall be glorified in His handiwork, fitting it so as to be conformable to, and modeled after, His own Son. For by the hands of the Father, that is, by the Son and the Holy Spirit, man, and not [merely] a part of man, was made in the likeness of God." Irenaeus of Lyons, *AH* 5.6.1 (page 566).

28. John Calvin, *Commentary on the Epistles of Paul the Apostle to the Corinthians*, trans. John Pringle (Grand Rapids: Baker Book House, 1979), 187 (commenting on 2 Cor 3:18, italics mine).

Christian's conformity to the image of Christ and those that bear upon the worldwide church's are all of a piece of the same unitive work. As Gordon Fee states:

> Christ's saving work is not only (re-)creating a people for God's name, but also, at the same time, this people is to be part of the new creation, who in their own lives and in their life *together* are God's image-bearers on this planet. And this is why Paul's energies are given almost totally to exhorting and encouraging his congregations to live out this calling as God's people wherever they are.[29]

What we can also say here is that for God's people to live in accordance with their identity in Christ is for them to improvisationally live out the Father's will on earth in accord with his will in heaven (cf. Matt 6:10). The section is divided into two basic parts: (1) God's Work of Forming and Making Beautiful Each of His Children; and (2) God's Work of Forming and Making Beautiful His Church.

GOD'S WORK OF FORMING AND MAKING BEAUTIFUL EACH OF HIS CHILDREN

The work of God's forming in beauty his people, beginning in this present age, is integral to the master design of what James Mays refers to as "the story of God's *anthropos* project."[30] God's forming his people Israel in the Sinai narratives is a vivid Old Testament example of that project (cf. Deut 8:2-6). We understand in natural terms that at the most basic level any creative work involves bringing something from an unformed condition to one of particular form with its given aesthetic characteristics in mind. For the person who is recreated in the image of Christ, that idea applies in spiritual terms too, except the person re-created in Christ is described more properly as having been brought

---

29. Gordon D. Fee, *Pauline Christology: An Exegetical-Theological Study* (Peabody, MA: Hendrickson Publishers, 2007), 487-88. Consonant with this basic point is how Paul applies the imagery of the temple in 1 Corinthians 3:16 in reference to the church, and then applies the same imagery in 6:19 in reference to the individual believer.

30. James Luther Mays, "The Self in the Psalms and the Image of God" in *God and Human Dignity*, ed. R. Kendall Soulen and Linda Woodhead (Grand Rapids: Eerdmans, 2006), 43.

out of a condition of spiritual *malformity* into an already but not-yet condition of spiritual *conformity*. Seen in connection with one's spiritual maturation, the believer's conformity to the image of Christ is a function of what I refer to as Christian fittingness. Put more formally, Christian fittingness pertains to the "dynamic" of growing in Christ-like character as one whose identity is already "stative" in Christ.[31] Out of this dynamic issues the outward expressions of one's life in ways befitting that identity, all of which are part of the progressive transformation of one's "not-yet perfected" conformity to the image of Christ. Arthur Ramsey encapsulates the telos in view: "Man when he is raised up with Christ in glory, will be man as God created him to become, ... like unto Christ's perfect manhood."[32] The idea of fittingness is not denoted simply by the display of conduct befitting a disciple of Christ, although that is most certainly entailed. But "conduct befitting" might only speak to the outward form (*Gestalt*) of one's life (i.e., one's outward expression) and not necessarily to the inner content (*Gehalt*) of it (i.e., one's inner character). The essence of this point we see reflected in Jesus' words to the Pharisees in Luke 11:39–41: "But the Lord said to him, 'Now you Pharisees clean the outside of the cup and the plate, but inside you are full of greed and wickedness. You fools! Didn't the one who made the outside make the inside as well? But give from your heart to those in need, and then everything will be clean for you" (cf. Luke 16:15).[33]

---

31. The following description by George W. Peters, *A Biblical Theology of Missions* (Chicago: Moody Press, 1972), 63, is representative of what I mean by the Christian's identity being already "stative" in Christ: "It is a divine reality entering the human being to transform his fundamental disposition, cleanse him from sin and unrighteousness, redeem him from bondage and corruption, impart to him the nature of God, recreate in him the image of Christ, make him a child of God, a member of the household of God, and qualify him through the gift of the Holy Spirit to live a life of true discipleship in the midst of a world almost destitute of the consciousness of God and eternity." In this holistic description of the present-age work of God in which he marks and seals those who are his own (2 Tim 2:19), God calls his children to embrace by faith their recreated identity in Christ and empowers them by his Spirit to pursue a life of true discipleship.

32. Ramsey, *The Glory of God and the Transfiguration of Christ*, 151.

33. The study note on Luke 11:41 in the NET expands of this, stating: "The expression everything will be clean for you refers to the agreement that should exist between the overt practice of one's religious duties, such as almsgiving, and the inner condition of one's heart, including true love for God and the poor; one is not only to wash the outside of the cup and plate, but the inside as well, since

The deeper notion of fittingness with which we are concerned has everything to do with the degree of conformity between the outward expression of one's life and one's "not-yet perfected" character—all of which, admittedly, is known perfectly only to God.[34]

It is not difficult to see how fittingness understood this way has significant resemblances to Jonathan Edwards' view of the aesthetic complexion of true virtue (see on Edwards above). The standard for us as always is Christ, for in him there is perfect conformity between the outward expression of his life and the glory of his character. As Vanhoozer puts it, "A disciple is one who seeks to speak, act, and live in ways that *bear witness to the truth, goodness, and beauty of Jesus Christ*."[35] To apply an aesthetic concept I introduced at the outset of this project, the idea of "fittingness-intensity" advanced by Nicholas Wolterstorff may be helpfully adopted here.[36] Fittingness-intensity functions as an evaluative measure of the aesthetic merit of some work or thing. Adapting this to our current discussion, fittingness-intensity refers from a theological aesthetic angle to the degree of conformity between the believer whose identity as a new creation (2 Cor 5:17) is "already" in the image of Christ and the qualitative measure of his or her "being conformed in the present" to that image. The dynamic of growing in Christ-like character means believers participate theodramatically— that is, in their being and doing as displayed in their obedient relationship to the Father through the Son by the Spirit, demonstrated through the experiences of their lives. It is thus an active participation. "Call it eschatological participation, a this-age taking part in the reality of the age to come."[37]

---

as Jesus said, God created the inside too. Religious duties are not to be performed hypocritically, i.e., for the applause and esteem of people, but rather they are to be done out of a deep love for God and a sensitivity to and concern for the needs of others. Then, everything will be clean, both hearts and lives."

34. Thus, my notion of Christian fittingness is much more than the outward sense. It carries, rather, the full-orbed sense that Vanhoozer articulates as "right thinking, desiring, and doing alike, involving all the disciple's faculties: cognitive, affective, and dispositional." Kevin J. Vanhoozer, *Faith Speaking Understanding: Performing the Drama of Doctrine* (Louisville: Westminster John Knox Press, 2014), 147.

35. Vanhoozer, *Faith Speaking Understanding*, 20 (italics original).

36. See the associated discussion in the Introduction.

37. Vanhoozer, *Faith Speaking Understanding*, 126.

LIVING OUT THE TRUTH OF OUR ADOPTIVE SONSHIP

Since God's forming and making beautiful his children at its most basic relational level is a matter of the "sons" of God being conformed to the image of his Son, we will address the aspect of our sonship first. A point essential to the theological aesthetics being set forth here is that Christ is *Forma formarum* to which those who are re-created in him are conformed: "For those whom [God] foreknew he also predestined to be conformed to the image of his Son, in order that [his Son] might be the firstborn among many brothers" (Rom 8:29). The tight connection we have noted before between "sonship" and "image of God"—indicative of how sonship is bound up with image-bearing—is corroborated here, though now, of course, our identity as a new creation in Christ relocates our image-bearing in the messianic Son of God, the Son incarnate. As Adolf Schlatter also points out, our conformity to the image of the Son is at once an identification of brotherhood with him: "Now it is God's purpose to make those he calls to be like the form of his Son, because the Son is to obtain many brothers. As the firstborn he is to be placed above many brothers. Their induction into sonship is at the same time the induction into brotherhood with the Son of God."[38] In this way Paul reinforces the idea of our adoptive sonship and fellow heirship with Christ he had just set out, beginning in Romans 8:14. God's creational intention was always for humans to be and to bear his image in *filial* relationship with him.

In this present age God's work of forming and making beautiful each person in Christ is properly considered a work of spiritual formation, albeit radical in its effect on our inner character belonging to our new self identity in Christ (Eph 4:24; Col 3:10). To this same point, Julie Canlis writes, "Spiritual formation is all about entering this Father-Son relationship, about living out the truth of our adoption. It is *formation as relation*."[39] Our adoptive status as a son or daughter of God is not a fictive designation but one whose basis is constituted judicially and

---

38. Adolf Schlatter, *Romans: The Righteousness of God*, trans. Siegfried S. Schatzmann (Peabody, MA: Hendrickson Publishers, 1995), 193.

39. Julie Canlis, "Living as God's Children" in *Evangelical Calvinism: Essays Resourcing the Continuing Reformation of the Church*, ed. Myk Habets and Bobby Grow (Eugene, OR: Pickwick, 2012), 346.

relationally through Christ by the Spirit to those in union with Christ.[40] In Johannine terms this correlates to God's conferral on disciples of Christ the status of being his beloved children: "But to all who have received him [i.e., Jesus]—those who believe in his name—he has given the right to become God's children (τέχνα θεοῦ)" (John 1:12 NET; cf. John 11:51–52; 1 John 3:1).

In his exposition of "The Lord's Prayer," Calvin understood that the designation "children of God" counted as the highest term of endearment:

> Therefore God both calls himself our Father and would have us so address him. By the great sweetness of this name he frees us from all distrust, since no greater feeling of love can be found elsewhere than in the Father. Therefore he could not attest his own boundless love toward us with any surer proof than the fact that we are called "children of God."[41]

Such freedom from all distrust concerning God as our Father is the blessed consequence of an adoptive sonship characterized by freedom from bondage and filial intimacy with the Father. Thus in Galatians 4 Paul depicts how we were no better off than a slave both to the world and to the curse of the law (Gal 4:3, 5; Gal 3:13), but now our sonship through Christ means the Father has brought us to know him by the Spirit in the deepest filial relation as "Abba! Father!" (Gal 4:6; cf. Rom 8:15). Our spiritual formation is lived out of the dynamic of this filial relationship in virtue of no longer being in spiritual thralldom of any kind (cf. John 8:34–36; Rom 8:1–4; Gal 5:13), but rather having received— to put it in Trinitarian terms—an adoptive sonship from the Father through the Son in the Spirit.[42] Thus by the Spirit's *confirming* work, believers are given both the access and ability to take up the *ipsissima*

---

40. With respect to believers' adoptive status that Paul highlights in Romans 8:15, the Greek term υἱοθεσία was originally a legal technical term for adoption as a son with full rights of inheritance. BDAG 1024 s.v. notes, "a legal t.t. of 'adoption' of children, in our lit., i.e. in Paul, only in a transferred sense of a transcendent filial relationship between God and humans (with the legal aspect, not gender specificity, as major semantic component)."

41. Calvin, *Institutes* 3.20.6, ed. McNeill, trans. Battles.

42. Garner, "Adoption," 104, sums it up this way: "Thus, by the work of the messianic Son, those once under the curse of the law (Gal 4:5) now live as transformed

verba of the Son—Jesus' Abba-cry to the Father (Mark 14:36). And by the Spirit's *transforming* work, many sons are brought to their fully realized eschatological glory (Rom 8:23; cf. Heb 2:10). To be given such access and ability to take up Jesus' Abba-cry to the Father is indicative of the already but not-yet living reality of being brought through Christ by the Spirit into loving union and communion with God as a partaker in the *ad intra* life that is itself the Trinity (cf. John 17:20–26). Complementing all this is an earlier inference we made from Ephesians 1:3–6, that although God delights perfectly in all of the divine plan, our adoption as sons through Christ seems to be at the heart of it.

What is brought out here in sharp relief theologically is the third primary witness of the symmetrical nature of the Son's agency in the work of the divine economy: That as an analogue of the only-begotten Son's relationship to the Father, the Son of God as incarnate Redeemer procures adoptive sonship for all those he redeems, so that these may become beloved sons of God the Father.[43] The key premise underlying this claim is that the Father's expressed love for the Son, identified in dramatic terms at points during the Son's earthly career, is the same paternal love he extends in covenantal union with his adopted sons and daughters redeemed through the Son (cf. John 17:23, 26). Jesus' baptism by John as well as the climax of his transfiguration are two supreme episodes in which the Father's voice from heaven declares, "This is my beloved Son, with whom I am well pleased." What the aforementioned premise entails—and what I am suggesting—is that these dramatic declarations of the Father's love for his Son and his delight in him are freighted with theological import *that points beyond* the Father's relationship with his only-begotten Son (while never of course superseding it). That is to say, a theologically thicker meaning is indicated beyond the commentary generally found regarding the Father's declaration of belovedness for his Son. Here, I am extending Calvin's theological interpretation on John 15:9—"As the Father has loved me, so have I loved you. Abide in my love." Quoting Calvin:

---

sons in the freedom of the life-giving Spirit (cf. 1 Cor 15:45), a freedom in and for obedience."

43. See Chapter 2 subsection, The Economic Fittingness of the Son as Incarnate Redeemer.

[Jesus] intended to express something far greater than is commonly supposed; ... for it was rather the design of Christ to lay, as it were, in our bosom a sure pledge of God's *love* towards us. ... [Jesus] is distinguished by this title, that he is *the beloved Son*, in whom the will of the Father is satisfied (Matt 3:17). But we ought to observe the end, which is, that God may accept us in him. So, then, we may contemplate in him, as in a mirror, God's paternal love towards us all; because he is not *loved* apart, or for his own private advantage, but that he may unite us with him to the Father.[44]

More specifically, then, what I am suggesting is that the Father's declaration, given twice over in the scheme of Jesus' public ministry, can be appreciated as a divine speech act whose illocutionary force communicates the same sense of belovedness to adoptive sons and daughters redeemed through the Son.[45] The perlocutionary force of this speech act thus ultimately obtains in the conferral of the right to be counted among God's children. Perceiving the Father's declaration as speech act in this way is not exactly equivalent to positing the distinction between redemption accomplished and redemption applied, but a loose kind of resemblance can be accepted here.

---

44. Calvin, *Commentary on the Gospel according to John*, 112. Echoing Calvin on this point, Julie Canlis states, "The declaration of belovedness at the baptism was a declaration *for us*, who are in Christ. It is the 'pledge of our adoption,' whereby we may 'boldly call God himself our Father.'" Canlis, "Living as God's Children," 341, citing Calvin, *Commentary on a Harmony of the Evangelists, Mark, Mark, and Luke*, 206, on Matthew 3:17.

45. In his excellent pastoral commentary on the parable of the prodigal son, Henri J. M. Nouwen, *The Return of the Prodigal Son: A Story of Homecoming* (New York: Doubleday, 1994), 39, captures this idea wonderfully: "As the Beloved of my heavenly Father, 'I can walk in the valley of darkness: no evil would I fear.' As the Beloved, I can 'cure the sick, raise the dead, cleanse the lepers, cast out devils.' Having 'received without charge,' I can 'give without charge.' As the Beloved, I can confront, console, admonish, and encourage without fear of rejection or need for affirmation. As the Beloved, I can suffer persecution without desire for revenge and receive praise without using it as a proof of my goodness. As the Beloved, I can be tortured and killed without ever having to doubt that the love that is given to me is stronger than death. As the Beloved, I am free to live and give life, free also to die while giving life. Jesus has made it clear to me that the same voice that he heard at the River Jordan and on Mount Tabor can also be heard by me. ...The somewhat stiff hands of the father rest on the prodigal's shoulders with the everlasting divine blessing: 'You are my Beloved, on you my favor rests.'"

We will round things off in drawing together how our filial relationship with the Father and our fraternal relationship with the Son relates to our spiritual formation. Because our adoptive sonship by the Father is at the same time our brotherhood with the Son, our spiritual formation as God's children means being formed in character to become like our "elder brother" (cf. Gal 4:19; Heb 2:11), who in character is perfectly like his Father. For the outward expression of the messianic Son of God always was and is in perfect conformity to the glory of his character, a glory described as "the radiance of the glory of God and the exact imprint of his nature" (Heb 1:3a). Of consequence here is the account in John 8 of Jesus' exchange with the Jews as he taught in the temple courts, especially verses 38–44. Two spiritual truths emerge from Jesus' trenchant criticism of his interlocutors. The first is premised on the point that, to put it bluntly, a person is either a child of God the Father or a child of the devil.[46] Not exactly mincing any words to the Jews he is addressing, Jesus tells them that they are children of the devil (John 8:38, 41, 44), while testifying of himself that he always does those things that please the Father (John 8:29). Spiritually speaking, "Like father, like son" in character and conduct is the implicit attestation here. Bradley Green puts it aptly: "As Jesus sees it, *persons do the works of their Father*, whoever that Father is."[47] The other spiritual truth here—this time more explicitly stated, and which I am broadly applying—is that all those who truly have God as their Father will also truly love Jesus, for he came from the Father and was sent by him (John 8:42). Or as Jesus conversely put it, "Whoever hates me hates my Father also" (John 15:23; cf. 5:23). Together, both these spiritual truths drawn from the narrative of John's Gospel accord with and reinforce how our spiritual formation as God's children means being formed in character to become like Jesus, who in character is perfectly like his Father. In succinct terms, Dutch pastor and theologian Hendrikus

---

46. Consistent with this, John describes those who are spiritually unregenerate as being "of the devil" (1 John 3:8), while "God's seed abides" in those who are spiritually regenerate (3:9). The former are "the children of the devil" but the latter are "the children of God" (3:10; cf. Matt 13:36–43).

47. Bradley G. Green, *Covenant and Commandment: Works, Obedience and Faithfulness in the Christian Life* (Downers Grove, IL: InterVarsity Press, 2014), 37.

Berkhof put it this way, "We are adopted as sons in order that we may behave as sons."[48]

In consequence of having become sons of God the Father through the Son in the Spirit, believers become heirs of the kingdom of God. As Paul puts it, "So you are no longer a slave, but a son, and if a son, then an heir through God" (Gal 4:7). Sonship through Christ thus implies heirship through God—indeed, heirs of God and also fellow heirs with Christ—as "partakers of the promise in Christ Jesus through the gospel" (Eph 3:6; Rom 8:16–17). "A son does not inherit the title 'son,'" notes Richard Bauckham. "Rather his being a son is the basis for his inheriting other things from his father."[49] One could hardly overestimate how this heirship through God opens up for the saints in Christ an untold wealth of spiritual capacity to be-like-Christ through the work of the Spirit.

Bearing the Image of Christ Theodramatically

As I stated earlier, our growing in conformity toward the full measure of Christ's image involves in this present age a divine work in which we are enabled to grow spiritually in image-bearing glory in and through our human form as we live out fittingly our identity in Christ. The dynamic of growing in Christ-like character means believers participate in their being and doing. It is thus an active participation in which all those recreated in Christ bear his image theodramatically. The underlying hermeneutical principle I accept as valid is that the protological image in which humanity is created has its counterpart or parallel in what gets restored by grace and transformed into the image of Christ all the way to its consummative image-bearing glory. To recall from Chapter 3, the attributes that properly characterize our image bearing are identifiable in terms of three principal aspects: (1) official (royal priest), (2) constitutional (whole person, i.e., body-soul), and (3) ethical-relational. As with bearing the protological image, no facet of imaging Christ is reflected independent of any other facet. For although our transformation into Christ's image is yet "in-progress," it still is a reflection in-progress of the glory of Christ's whole image.

---

48. Hendrikus Berkhof, *The Doctrine of the Holy Spirit* (Richmond, VA: John Knox Press, 1964), 74.

49. Bauckham, *Jesus and the God of Israel*, 200.

The dynamic of being transformed into Christ's image implicates the complete interdependence of the official, constitutional, and ethical-relational aspects of image-bearing. Inasmuch as this interdependence operates holistically in an integrity reflecting the glory of Christ's whole image, it resists any effort to being formally schematized.[50] For our royal identity and destiny is bound up altogether with our priestly, which is altogether bound up with the ethical-relational dimension as expressed by the whole human person, body and soul. Nevertheless, in all the various ways the New Testament either explicitly or implicitly calls for believers to reflect the image of Christ in their lives, a certain dimension of image bearing is at times represented in a more pronounced or apparent way than others; in other instances the interdependence of all three principal aspects of image bearing is equally apparent. Our approach here is to consider several Pauline imperatives, which highlight particular ways believers are called to conform their lives to their identity in Christ, and in so doing reflect the image of Christ in their being and doing.

Colossians 3 summons believers to live out fittingly their identity in Christ as those who have died with Christ and have been raised with him (Col 3:1-4). The fact that believers "have been raised with Christ ... where Christ is, seated at the right hand of God" (Col 3:1) affirms their new self identity in Christ in its royal hue. "This idea fits quite well with believers' identification with Christ's resurrection and sovereign kingship," states G. K. Beale.[51] Based on one's new self identity in Christ, therefore, practices and expressions of the old self are to be "put to death" or "put off" (Col 3:5-9) in virtue of having "put on the new self, which is being renewed in knowledge after the image of its creator" (Col

---

50. Cf. James G. Samra, *Being Conformed to Christ in Community* (London: T&T Clark, 2006), 107: "Paul does not define 'being conformed to Christ,' but his use of the concept in connection with 'righteousness' (Rom 8:29-30), 'glory' (2 Cor 3:18-4:6; Phil 3:21), 'mind' (Rom 12:2), 'body' (1 Cor 15:42-55; Phil 3:21), 'inner man' (2 Cor 4:15), 'Spirit/spiritual' (Rom 8; 1 Cor 15:44-49; 2 Cor 3:17-18), 'resurrection' (1 Cor 15:44-55; Phil 3:8-11), 'salvation' (Phil 3:20-21) and 'Adam' (1 Cor 15:44-49) suggests a holistic idea including both the material and non-material aspects of man. ... To be conformed to the image of Christ is to become like Christ so that the character of Christ is manifested in the life of the believer."

51. G. K. Beale, *A New Testament Biblical Theology: The Unfolding of the Old Testament in the New* (Grand Rapids: Baker Academic, 2011), 451.

3:10). Relevant to the latter verse, Paul had earlier enjoined his audience "to walk in a manner worthy—that is, befittingly (ἀξίως)—of the Lord, fully pleasing to him, bearing fruit in every good work and increasing in the knowledge of God" (Col 1:10). The thrust of the whole passage in Colossians 3 clearly emphasizes the ethical-relational dimension of our image-bearing, but implicit here as well is the official aspect in connection with the divine commission of Genesis 1:28. For the allusion in Colossians 3:10 to Genesis 1:26–27 relates back to the same allusion in Colossians 1:15 speaking of Christ as "the image of the invisible God," which also ties back to the allusion in Colossians 1:6 and 10 to Genesis 1:28. Specifically, the command in Genesis 1:28 to "subdue, rule, and fill the earth" reflects in a creaturely way God's own kingship and his creative work through filling the earth with other image-bearing sons and daughters of God. While the creational sense of Genesis 1:28 has to do with physical progeny, its allusion in Colossians takes on a redemptive-eschatological sense in fulfilling this commission by way of the gospel "bearing fruit" in the whole world and the lives of God's children "bearing fruit" likewise. "It may be important to recall," explains Beale, "that part of 'ruling and subduing' in Genesis 1:26–28 was to 'be fruitful and multiply and fill' the earth not only with literal but also, after the fall, spiritual children who would join Adam in reflecting God's image and in his kingly dominion over the earth."[52] Discerned in all this is how God's creational intention for humanity is carried through in his plan of salvation through the gospel promise that becomes fulfilled in Christ.

Important to note here is that while the dynamic of God's work of forming each person in Christ translates to a progressive work of *spiritual* transformation, the constitutional aspect—specifically here the *body* aspect—of our image bearing is nonetheless an essential aspect in and through which God works spiritually to form each person in Christ. For our growing in conformity toward the full measure of Christ's image involves a divine work in which we are enabled to grow in image-bearing glory in and through our human form as we live out fittingly our identity in Christ. For example, the constitutional aspect of image bearing is implicit in the call both to "present your bodies as

---

52. Beale, *A New Testament Biblical Theology*, 451.

a living sacrifice" and "be transformed by the renewal of your mind" (Rom 12:1–2; cf. Col 3:10), the latter of which concerns the domain of noetic activity being conformed to the truth and understanding as it is found in Christ. And although "our physical body is wearing away" (2 Cor 4:16 NET), our body is nonetheless, as John Barclay puts it, "the necessary expressive medium of the Christ-sourced life." While it may seem paradoxical to affirm, even our presently-wearing-away body is not extraneous, let alone antithetical, to God's interim work of transforming us into the image of Christ. The fact that the spiritual transformation God works in his children only ever is the case in the whole human person implicates the human body in this dynamic in its unity with the soul. As Barclay explains,

> Once appropriated by sin, the body is reappropriated by Christ. The very location where sin once held most visible sway, and where its former grip still draws our bodily selves towards death, is now the location where the "newness of life" breaks through into action, displaying in counterintuitive patterns of behavior the miraculous Christ-life which draws our embodied selves towards the "vivification" (Rom 8:11) or "redemption" (Rom 8:23) of the body.[53]

Thus, since any and all progress of being conformed to the image of Christ entails by God's design the whole person, it attests implicitly, and undergirds our gospel hope, that the image of those redeemed in Christ includes the resurrection and glorification of their body (cf. Phil 3:21). But on this side of eschatological glory—the penultimate side—God calls his children to live in the freedom of the Spirit in all ways befitting to their new self identity in Christ.[54]

---

53. John M. G. Barclay, "Under Grace: The Christ-Gift and the Construction of a Christian Habitus," in *Apocalyptic Paul: Cosmos and Anthropos in Romans 5–8*, ed. Beverly Roberts Gaventa (Waco, TX: Baylor University Press, 2013), 69. Barclay continues: "Even when speaking of the body, Paul is talking about a system of loyalties and alignments which appears to go 'deeper' than this or that particular practice: at issue is what he calls τὸ φρόνημα—either of the Flesh or of the Spirit (Rom 8:6–8)—which governs the body while being expressed not outside or behind it, but precisely in the physical deployment of its 'limbs.'"

54. Developing the larger point here under the idea of "Improvisatory Discipleship," Vanhoozer, *Faith Speaking Understanding*, 191, writes, "Disciples improvise each time they exercise Christian freedom fittingly, in obedient response

Paul's discussions in 1 Corinthians 6:13-20 and 2 Corinthians 6:14-7:1 serve as an exemplary pair of texts highlighting the interdependence of the believer's priestly identity in Christ with the ethical-relational and constitutional aspects of imaging Christ through the expressive medium of his or her body. This interdependence is evident in 1 Corinthians 6 where Paul is addressing the issue of sexual immorality engaged in by believers: "The body is not meant for sexual immorality, but for the Lord, and the Lord for the body" (1 Cor 6:13). The case in point Paul calls out concerns being "joined to a prostitute" (1 Cor 6:16). Paul condemns any such activity on three grounds. In the first place, the whole person—one's body included—is joined to Christ as a member of his body (1 Cor 6:15-17). The gist of Paul's argument here is that "being a 'member of Christ' in 'one spirit' precludes being 'one flesh' with the prostitute. The two are incompatible bodily relationships."[55] Secondly, Paul points out that such sexual immorality qualifies ignobly and uniquely as itself a reflexive sin, that is, a sin against one's own body (1 Cor 6:18). Lastly, Paul invokes the cultic imagery of the temple that he used earlier (1 Cor 3:16-17) to impress upon the saints that as members joined to Christ, each person's own "body is a temple of the Holy Spirit" who indwells them (1 Cor 6:19). Because Christ procured in redemption the whole person, all those redeemed in him are thus called to glorify God in and with their body (1 Cor 6:20). The priestly aspect of image-bearing draws naturally from the context of the community of God's people each and altogether being identified as the temple of the Holy Spirit. For just as the Lord's presence made holy the entire structure of the temple in Jerusalem, so likewise does the presence of God through his Spirit consecrate each believer as holy.[56] In this way the believer's priestly identity in Christ is accented along with

---

to the gracious word of God that set it in motion. Improvising to the glory of God is ultimately a matter simply of being who one has been created to be in Christ, so that one responds freely and fittingly as if by reflex or second nature: 'Where the Spirit of the Lord is, there is freedom' (2 Cor. 3:17)."

55. James W. Thompson, *Moral Formation according to Paul: The Context and Coherence of Pauline Ethics* (Grand Rapids: Eerdmans, 2011), 50-51.

56. The believer's priestly identity in Christ is brought out vividly with temple imagery as well in 1 Peter 2:4-6, with all believers likened to "living stones ... being built up as a spiritual house, to be a holy priesthood, to offer spiritual sacrifices acceptable to God through Jesus Christ." Christ is the foundation "stone" of this

the ethical-relational and constitutional aspects in a call to live out the implications of that identity by keeping oneself/one's body holy and pure.

In 2 Corinthians 6:14–7:1, Paul applies the same theo-logic as above except here he calls believers to remain consecrated to the Lord: "Do not be unequally yoked with unbelievers" (2 Cor 6:14). In the rhetorical questions and imperatives that follow it is clear that Paul's basic concern is for believers to separate themselves from unholy/impure associations or personal entanglements because *they are consecrated to the Lord*. Paul argues this by once again identifying believers as the temple of God's indwelling presence: "What agreement has the temple of God with idols? For we are the temple of the living God" (2 Cor 6:16). The imperatives in verse 17 drawn from the OT stress God's will for believers to live out the implications of that identity. As James Thompson observes, "The imperatives 'Come out from among them and be separate, says the Lord' and 'Do not touch anything unclean,' drawn from the exilic prophets (Isa 52:11; Ezek 20:34, 41), are fundamental to Israel's identity as the elect and holy people."[57] Here again the believer's priestly identity in Christ is accented along with the ethical-relational and constitutional aspects. The priestly garments that Aaron and his sons wore "for glory and for beauty" (Exod 28:40) apply now spiritually to the children of God through Christ so that these, being enabled in the Spirit, may worship the Lord truly in the "splendor of holiness" (1 Chr 16:29). Paul's concluding summons bespeaks of how our transformation into Christ's image is yet in-progress, being also a dynamic in which we are called to actively play our part. Thompson sums it up accordingly: "[Paul's] final challenge in this section, 'Let us cleanse ourselves from every impurity of the flesh and of the Spirit, completing holiness in the Lord' (7:1), indicates the expectation that, although God has called the people to holiness, they must implement this call in their own lives" (cf. 1 Thess 4:1–8).[58]

---

new temple that continues to be built up by living stones until its completion at the end of the age.

57. Thompson, *Moral Formation according to Paul*, 52.
58. Thompson, *Moral Formation according to Paul*, 53.

God's Work of Forming and Making
Beautiful His Church

Zooming out from the work of God that bears upon the individual Christian's conformity to the image of Christ, God's wider plan of spiritual transformation in the plan of salvation involves the church of God—the Bride of Christ—being formed and adorned in preparation for her nuptial union with Christ. As Thompson rightly states, "Spiritual formation is corporate formation. The church is not a collection of individuals who devote themselves to spiritual formation but a community that shares the destiny of Christ together. ... Those who are being conformed no longer live for themselves (Rom 14:7; 2 Cor 5:15) but share the destiny of the crucified Lord."[59] That destiny ultimately is a glorious destiny, one in which Christ "present[s] the church to himself as glorious—not having a stain or wrinkle, or any such blemish, but holy and blameless" (Eph 5:27 NET). In the advance toward all things being summed up in Christ, this is consistent with how God's reconciling operations through the reign of Christ involve the building up of the body of Christ in the unity of the faith and in Christ-like harmony toward the full measure of maturity in Christ. Yet in the extended outworking of God's redemptive-historical purposes, the mode of glory the church of God reflects in this time between the times is in fitting with the mode of glory Christ reflected in the state of his humiliation. Following a line of argument Calvin takes, the glory of the church in this present age is not manifested in earthly terms of visible splendor and majesty, but such glory is eschewed for the adornment of a humbled position that attests to the glory of God's power perfecting his work in weakness (cf. 2 Cor 12:9–10).[60] For Calvin, the prophetic statement identified with Christ in Isa 53:2—"he had no form or majesty that we should look at him, and no beauty that we should desire him"—is derivatively emblematic of the church as well.[61] As Bonnie Pattison relates, Calvin considered that

---

59. James W. Thompson, *The Church according to Paul: Rediscovering the Community Conformed to Christ* (Grand Rapids: Baker Academic, 2014), 125.

60. The immediate discussion draws from Bonnie Pattison, "Splendor and Beauty in Calvin's Ecclesiology: The Aesthetic and Ethical Implications of Calvin's Christology for the Spiritual Worship of the Church" (paper presented at the Sixteenth Century Society Conference, New Orleans, LA, October 16, 2014).

61. Pattison, "Splendor and Beauty in Calvin's Ecclesiology." Pattison quotes

Christ's kingdom as manifested in and through the church bears witness most faithfully in "an aesthetic of simplicity and its corresponding ethic of moderation."[62] His commentary on Isaiah 49:18 is reflective of this:

> The true ornament of the Church ... [is] a great number of children, who are brought to her by faith and guided by the Spirit of God. This is the true splendor; this is the glory of the Church, which must be filthy and ugly, ragged, and mangled, if she have not these ornaments. ... But the true dignity of the Church is internal, so far as it consists of the gifts of the Holy Spirit, and of progressive faith and piety. Hence it follows, that she is richly provided with her ornaments, when the people, joined together by faith, are gathered into her bosom, to worship God in a proper manner.[63]

Despite what may appear to the world as unremarkable—perhaps common, lowly, and unrefined, if not seemingly ridiculous and despised by the world (1 Cor 1:26-29)—the church advances adorned in true, albeit presently unperfected and blemished, spiritual beauty. Following the same pattern of life as her Bridegroom, the Bride of Christ is being formed and made beautiful in this present age through her advance as it were in the state of humiliation.

In this time between the times the church is thus being conformed to the pattern of Christ's earthly career, corresponding to the state of his humiliation, as the requisite pathway to "the glory that is to be revealed to us" (Rom 8:18), corresponding to the state of his exaltation. In this way the life God's people share in union with Christ through the Spirit is a real participation in his personal history—a sharing in the same pattern of life through death (cf. John 12:23-26). It is because we "already" participate in life-sourcing union with Christ that we presently experience the power of his resurrection (even if subjectively it

---

Calvin, *Commentary on Isaiah* 53:2: "This must be understood [that these words] relate not merely to the person of Christ, who was despised by the world, and was at length condemned to a disgraceful death; but to his whole kingdom, which in the eyes of men had no beauty, no comeliness, no splendor, which, in short, had nothing that could direct or captivate the hearts of men to it by its outward show."

62. Pattison, "Splendor and Beauty in Calvin's Ecclesiology."

63. Pattison, "Splendor and Beauty in Calvin's Ecclesiology," quoting Calvin, *Commentary on Isaiah* 49:18.

feels so partial). In the apostle Paul's words, "But we have this treasure in jars of clay, to show that the surpassing power belongs to God and not to us" (2 Cor 4:7). By the same token, because the community of the faithful at large is "not yet" fully glorified in union with Christ, she also participates presently in his sufferings. From this perspective a strong correlation exists between the church's participation in Christ's sufferings in the broadest sense and her being conformed to the image of Christ according to the working of the Spirit of Christ risen and exalted.[64] Between Christ's first coming and his return in glory, then, the church as such is called to advance not as the *church militant* but as, if you will, the *church humilitant*.

In accordance with the church's conformity to the pattern of Christ's life, a notable if also subtle point of theological import stands in connection with the descent of the Spirit upon Jesus at his Jordan-baptism and "the same Holy Spirit, with which the church was baptized at Pentecost." As we saw in Chapter 4, Jesus' baptism by John was anticipatory of the suffering and death that came to increasingly define Jesus' path of obedience. The parallel import here, as Richard Gaffin Jr. observes, is that "the Pentecostal Spirit is as well the Spirit of suffering, although this tends to be 'the spiritual gift no one is talking about.'"[65] Indeed, it is the very givenness of Christian suffering the apostle Paul is keen to stress: "For it has been granted to you that for the sake of Christ you should not only believe in him but also suffer for his sake" (Phil 1:29)—that is, whatever sufferings that come in connection with being a Christian and living so, not merely such suffering as is common to human experience (cf. Matt 5:11–12; 10:16–18, 22; John 15:18–25). Importantly, Paul says nothing indicating that faith in Christ is essentially ingredient to all believers while suffering for his sake applies only to some. Rather, believing in Christ and suffering for the sake of Christ are divinely

---

64. Cf. David Peterson, *Possessed by God: A New Testament Theology of Sanctification and Holiness* (Grand Rapids: Eerdmans, 1995), 118: "Suffering can be a means of confirming faith, producing endurance, proving character, and strengthening hope (Rom 5:3–4). But it can only be so for those who are convinced of God's promises and have that hope of sharing his glory in the first place (Rom 5:2)."

65. Richard B. Gaffin Jr., "The Usefulness of the Cross," *WTJ* 41 no. 2 (Spring 1979): 239, adapting the title of an article on suffering by L. Samuel, "The Spiritual Gift No One Is Talking About," *Christianity Today* 21 (Jan 21, 1977): 10–12.

designed correlates for the church's conformity to Christ. The apostle Peter posits the same point as integral to being a disciple of Christ: "If when you do good and suffer for it you endure, this is a gracious thing in the sight of God. For to this you have been called, because Christ also suffered for you, leaving you an example, so that you might follow in his steps" (1 Pet 2:20–21; cf. 1 Pet 4:1–2, 12–19; 5:8–9).[66] God's power is thus directed at making beautiful the Bride of Christ even in and through her participation in her Bridegroom's sufferings. Jonathan Edwards expresses along similar lines:

> True virtue never appears so lovely, as when it is most oppressed: and the divine excellency of real Christianity, is never exhibited with such advantage, as when under the greatest trials: then it is that true faith appears much more precious than gold; and upon this account, is found to praise, and honor, and glory. ... [Such trials] tend to cause the amiableness of true religion to appear to the best advantage; ... they tend to increase its beauty, by establishing and confirming it, and making it more lively and vigorous, and purifying it from those things that obscured its luster and glory.[67]

Moreover, what Paul says of his own aim—"that I may know [Christ] and the power of his resurrection, and may share his sufferings, becoming like him in his death" (Phil 3:10)—implies by extension that sharing in Christ's sufferings is itself an essential form that his resurrection power takes in the life of his church. Paul's theo-logic here is worth noting. The resurrection power that undergirds all believers in Christ is not a spiritual dynamic separate from that which produces conformity to Christ's death (cf. 2 Cor 4:7–11). As Gaffin puts it, "Resurrection-eschatology is eschatology of the cross, and the theology of the cross is the key signature of all theology that would be truly 'practical' theology."[68]

Drawn together in Romans 8 are several of the themes we have developed that are integral to the master design of God's *anthropos*

---

66. Cf. G. K. Beale and Mitchell Kim, *God Dwells among Us: Expanding Eden to the Ends of the Earth* (Downers Grove, IL: InterVarsity Press, 2014), 109: "Suffering is not an automatic lever to release the life of Christ in us, but suffering is the occasion that we look for Christ's life to flow in us (2 Cor 4:10–11)."

67. Edwards, *Religious Affections*, WJE 2:93–94.

68. Gaffin Jr., "The Usefulness of the Cross," 236.

project—that is, that work of God's forming and making beautiful his children through their being conformed to the image of Christ. The sense of Paul's statement in verse 17 is not that our participation in Christ's sufferings is a precondition or prerequisite to the right to be counted among God's children (cf. Rom 8:9), but rather that it is *concomitant* with our adoptive sonship. The church's sharing in Christ's sufferings, we may better say, is a form of her glory until Christ returns—just not her consummative glory. For God brings to vital spiritual effect in and for his church any and all suffering for the sake of Christ. It all serves his purposes in the design of the divine plan as a fitting means in his work of preparing the Bride for her glorification with Christ in the age to come. For this reason Paul proclaims, "The sufferings of this present time are not worth comparing with the glory that is to be revealed to us" (Rom 8:18). In and through all such providence, God works his good purposes (Rom 8:28) for his adoptive sons to be conformed to the image of his Son according to an already but not-yet eschatological participation (Rom 8:29-30). In the age to come, even our adoption as sons of God will undergo an eschatological transformation that becomes fully revealed (Rom 8:19) with the redemption of our bodies (Rom 8:23).

Conspectus

Having completed his mission from the Father, Christ is in his heavenly exaltation seated at the right hand of the throne of God. Working all things now through Christ's heavenly rule, God calls his children to live in the freedom of the Spirit in all ways befitting to their identity in Christ—that is, to walk in a manner befittingly of the Lord. That has been the focus of the christological contours of beauty here, namely, our formation as God's people in Christ. The beauty of that formation is that vital part of God's work in this present age of forming and making beautiful his children, which is all about their being conformed to the image of his Son. I have argued that, based on the theodramatic fittingness of Christ, the concept of Christian fittingness is God's people living in conformity to their identity in Christ, and serves as a fundamental aspect of their spiritual formation. Christian fittingness as such is based on Christ being the archetype of humanity and for humanity, which consists of two basic premises. First, the Son's theodramatic fittingness in the form of his humanity served to display his glory appropriately during his earthly career. And second, as the incarnate image of God, Christ is the full measure of the image in which humans are created, and thus the full measure of the image-bearing glory inherent in and expressed through his human form. The dynamic of Christian fitting-ness, moreover, operates at the level of Christian individuals as well as the level of the church worldwide. My argumentation looked at each level separately but acknowledges that all aspects of God's work that bear upon the individual Christian's conformity to the image of Christ and those that bear upon the worldwide church's are all of a piece of the same unitive work.

In reference to spiritual formation at the level of Christian individuals, I argued that at its most basic relational level it pertains to our adoptive status as a son or daughter of God. Our spiritual formation is lived out of the dynamic of this filial relationship, which we have from the Father through the Son in the Spirit, and means being formed in character to become like our "elder brother," who in character is perfectly like his Father. I proposed a theological interpretation, the gist of which is that the belovedness the Father expressed for the Son during Jesus' public ministry (his baptism and transfiguration) can be appreciated as a divine speech act whose illocutionary force communicates the same sense of belovedness to adoptive sons and daughters redeemed through the Son. The perlocutionary force of this speech act ultimately obtains in the conferral of the right to be counted among God's children. I further argued that the dynamic of growing in conformity to the image of Christ involves the restoration by grace of the *imago Dei* as comprehended in its three principal aspects—the official, constitutional, and ethical-relational. That dynamic implicates the complete interdependence of these aspects. In bearing Christ's image, believers participate theodramatically. I demonstrated this through examining several Pauline imperatives that highlight particular ways believers are called to conform their lives to Christ.

In reference to spiritual formation at the level of the church world-wide, I argued the mode of glory the church of God reflects in this time between the times is in fitting with the mode of glory Christ reflected in the state of his humiliation. God's work of spiritual formation is seen in how the church is conformed to the pattern of Christ's earthly career, corresponding to the state of his humiliation, as the requisite pathway to "the glory that is to be revealed to us" (Rom 8:18), corresponding to the state of his exaltation. God's power is thus directed at making beautiful the Bride of Christ even in and through her participation in her Bridegroom's sufferings.

HUMANS IMMORTAL IN FINAL FITTINGNESS: REDEEMED AS GLORIOUS

As I have presented it, God's work in this present age of forming and making beautiful his children and altogether his church involves his people growing in conformity toward the full measure of Christ's image as they live out fittingly their identity in Christ. That is a vital part of God's *anthropos* project in the already but not-yet order of reality governed under the preeminence of Christ's heavenly rule. In the denouement of eschatological events, the "not-yet" of promised reality is come. In that coming age is the eschatological realization of humanity's identity and destiny as image of God. These will be the sons and daughters of God who will, at that time, reflect their consummative transformation into the image of Christ. At that time the identity and destiny of the church will be represented in her form as the glorified Bride of Christ. In all respects the fittingness of God's people will be complete for sharing eternal life with God and in God because in all respects Christ is the archetype of humanity and for humanity through whom the redeemed are imaged eschatologically. "The Word of God who dwelt in man, and became the Son of man," wrote Irenaeus, did so "that He might accustom man to receive God, and God to dwell in man, according to the good pleasure of the Father."[69] Here, once again, we see the principle of *connaturality* in effect (only like can know like) — God's people will fully appreciate the glory of God when they themselves are fully glorified in him (cf. 1 Cor 2:11–12; 13:12; 15:48–49).

The stage of the theodrama in view here, then, assumes the bodily return of Christ, which ushers in the age to come and the consummation of all things. Mindful of the magnitude of theological complexities

---

69. Irenaeus of Lyons, *AH* 3.30.2 (page 367).

involved here, and bracketing out any discussion of the nature of the millennium, our theological aesthetic in this section pertains only to the new humanity redeemed in Christ. The section is divided into three parts: (1) Beloved Sons and Daughters with Whom the Father Is Well Pleased; (2) Image-Bearers Glorified; and (3) The Church without Spot or Wrinkle: The Bride of Christ Made Beautiful and Glorified.

Beloved Sons and Daughters with Whom the Father Is Well Pleased

Just as Israel's adoptive sonship heads Paul's list in Romans 9:4 of her elect privileges, we likewise begin with adoptive sonship as that dearest and most precious privilege believers come to know in a consummative way in virtue of their filial relationship with the Father through the Son in the Spirit. As I have argued the matter, this is the highest end in which God's creational intention for humanity—that is, to be and to bear God's image in filial relationship with him—is carried through in his plan of salvation through the gospel promise that becomes fulfilled in Christ. The earlier inference we made from Ephesians 1:3–6 bears repeating, that although God delights perfectly in all of the divine plan, our adoption as sons and daughters through Christ seems to be at the heart of it. The apostle John's words anticipate its unsurpassable intimacy and fullness: "See what kind of love the Father has given to us, that we should be called children of God; and so we are. ... Beloved, we are God's children now, and what we will be has not yet appeared; but we know that when he appears we shall be like him, because we shall see him as he is" (1 John 3:1–2). Even already in this present age, as we have discussed, God begins that re-creational work of bringing each child of his to be more like Christ, that is, so forming in spiritual beauty each person in Christ by their becoming more and more like him. In the age to come the glory of each believer's spiritual formation, which was always a function of their filial relationship with the Father through Christ by the Spirit, means that their conformity to the image of Christ, who in character perfectly images his Father, will be fully realized at his parousia when "we shall see him as he is."

Implicit here, and perhaps even taken for granted, is that, whatever else may be said of it, the most fundamental way saints "shall be like him" corresponds to the same relation the messianic Son of God has with the Father, namely, as his Father-God. Pertinent to this are Jesus' post-resurrection words to Mary Magdalene: "Go to my brothers and say to them, 'I am ascending to my Father and your Father, to my God and your God'" (John 20:17).[70] In line with our earlier treatment, this pertains to understanding the Father's expressed love for the Son as being the same paternal love he extends in covenantal union with his adoptive sons and daughters redeemed through the Son. In this way, too, Jesus' prayer to the Father in John 17, offered for the sake of all those whom the Father has given him—"that the love with which you have loved me may be in them, and I in them" (verse 26)—becomes fully realized in glorified sons and daughters of the living God who will, at that time, reflect their consummative transformation into the image of Christ.

While Christ's life and atoning death are the fitting means of redemption to bring "many sons to glory," it is only when Christ returns in his exalted glory that these sons come to fully partake in the "glory and honor" with which they have been crowned. Only then will they fully partake in the glory and honor with which Jesus himself has been crowned on their behalf (Heb 2:9–10; cf. Ps 8:4–6). Fast-forwarding to John's closing vision in the Apocalypse, the recipients of that glory and honor are even described in the first person pronominal form in terms of their filiation with the Father: "The one who conquers will have this heritage, and I will be his God and he will be *my* son" (21:7). This represents the consummative fulfillment of that same sense of belovedness the Father expressed for the Son during his earthly career, here extended in covenantal union with his adopted sons and daughters redeemed through the Son.[71] Ultimately, all those who enter the

---

70. Jonathan Edwards, "True Saints, When Absent from the Body, Are Present with the Lord," *WJE* 25:234, posits along the same lines, "The saints by virtue of their union with Christ, and being his members, do in some sort, partake of his child-like relation to the Father; and so are heirs with him of his happiness in the enjoyment of his Father. The spouse of Christ, by virtue of her espousals to that only begotten son of God, is as it were, a partaker of his filial relation to God, and becomes the 'King's daughter' (Ps 45:13), and so partakes with her divine husband in his enjoyment of his Father and her Father, his God and her God."

71. See above subsection, God's Work of Forming and Making Beautiful Each

kingdom of heaven are those who do the will of their heavenly Father (Matt 7:21). These are children of God, conquerors through their persevering fealty to him and holding fast to their faith in him (cf. 2 Tim 2:12). More could be said on this, of course, but let it suffice here to consider the description Douglas Farrow offers, comparing the estate of our sonship to that of the holy angels with God dwelling in our midst through the person of Jesus Christ glorified by the power of the Spirit: "We will not live and move, as they do, *coram Deo*; we will live and move with Christ *in Deo*. We will be deified by the Spirit, knowing God by way of God."[72] This will be, truly, the beatific life. In the balance of this chapter are offered various considerations or conceptions as to what such "deification by the Spirit" may entail or be like in the eschaton (either suggestive from Scripture or at times theologically speculative).

IMAGE-BEARERS GLORIFIED

For every believer, the progressive work through the Spirit of being transformed into the image of Christ from one degree of glory to another will be perfected at last in glorification upon Christ's return. Therein is fulfilled God's creational intention for humanity in its identity and destiny as image of God, an image restored by grace and transformed into the image of Christ all the way to its consummative image-bearing glory. Thus, in the eschatological fulfillment of God's *anthropos* project, the radiance of our image-bearing beauty—in whatever are its many-splendored dimensions—will be reflected from glory to glory. Our interest here is simply to offer a brief treatment on the eschatological fulfillment of the three principal aspects of image bearing for the new humanity redeemed in Christ.

As the constitutional aspect of image bearing concerns the whole person, body and soul, it pertains most directly to that "living hope through the resurrection of Jesus Christ from the dead" (1 Pet 1:3),

---

of His Children, in particular under the discussion, Living Out the Truth of Our Adoptive Sonship.

72. Douglas Farrow, *Ascension Theology* (London: T&T Clark, 2011), 150. Farrow later adds, "Has anything like this ever been said in treating of the destiny of man? Yet it is no violation of the canons of caution to speak of having an end that is higher, not merely in degree but in kind, than that of the angels, not if the *homoousian* is true" (152).

realized in *our* bodily resurrection from the dead (cf. Acts 24:15). *The Westminster Confession of Faith* sums up that hope thus: "All the dead shall be raised up, with the selfsame bodies, and none other (although with different qualities), which shall be united again to their souls forever. The bodies of the unjust shall, by the power of Christ, be raised to dishonor: the bodies of the just, by his Spirit, unto honor; and be made conformable to his own glorious body."[73] To this latter point, the redeemed will have a body that is as it were biologized pneumatically with the life-giving Spirit of Christ. This bodily re-creation by the Spirit corresponds to the postmortem body in which Christ was raised as the firstfruits from the dead—what the apostle Paul in 1 Corinthians 15:44 calls a spiritual body (σῶμα πνευματικόν) in contradistinction to a natural one (σῶμα ψυχικόν). For each human being it is still nevertheless a human body and thus an essential continuity is maintained.[74] Although what we will be has not yet appeared, the prolepsis of Christ's transfiguration is the only materially realized intimation in Scripture of how "those who belong to Christ" will be like him as relates to his glorified human form, that is, when at his coming these "shall also bear the image of the man of heaven" (1 Cor 15:23, 49; cf. Matt 13:43).[75] As Jonathan Edwards conceives it, in our bodily glorification we are endowed with the excellence and enjoyment of every exercise of body or mind in its harmonious operation with the soul. "This harmony will be in its perfection in the bodies of the saints after the resurrection," writes Edwards. "Every part of the saints' refined bodies shall be as full of pleasure as they can hold; and that this will not take the mind off from, but prompt and help it in spiritual delights, to which even the delight of their spiritual bodies shall be but a shadow."[76] Elsewhere, in regard to the faculties of the soul (whatever those may fully entail), Edwards

---

73. *Westminster Confession of Faith* 32.2–3.

74. This continuity is seen in the above-mentioned confessional statement in which the term "selfsame bodies" underscores the continuity between our bodies adapted to the present earthly life, characterized by ψυχή, and bodies adapted to the final life of the Spirit, characterized by πνευμα. In my judgment this coheres with understanding the human body as the divinely ordained expressive medium purposed for the telic fulfilling of each person's identity in being and bearing the divine image, specifically as conformed to the image of God in Christ.

75. Arguable here as well is the account of Jesus' appearance to Saul in Acts 9.

76. Jonathan Edwards, "Misc. no. 95," *WJE* 13:263.

likewise proclaims, "Every faculty of the soul will be employed and exercised, and will be employed in vastly more lively, more exalted exercises than they are now, though without any labor or weariness."[77]

The eschatological fulfillment of the ethical-relational aspect of image-bearing means that in a fully realized way we become in pure and holy character who we already are in Christ. Our bodily redemption is at the same time our completed spiritual redemption from sin in which our recreated and glorified selves live everlastingly in the freedom of the *non posse peccare* and of the *non posse mori* (cf. John 11:25; Heb 9:27–28). The relations of human society in the new heavens and earth—however these consist—will operate at the interpersonal level in perfect conformity to Christ's character. Since there will be no need to administer among the saints any sort of retributive justice, nor for that matter justice (as we know it) of the reformative or restorative kind, what will ultimately characterize the ethical-relational dimension of all interpersonal relationship is best regarded as a reflection of the primary justice that characterizes the mutuality within the Godhead. In this respect our image-bearing glory will be reflective of that mutual love and eternal delight between the Father, Son, and Holy Spirit in which also is entailed their infinitely deserving regard for one another.[78] The intersubjective dimension of our image bearing implies that it is bound in part in relation to others. As such, we should expect the ethical-relational aspect to reflect the glory of its full relational nature being expressed in its cooperative and communal character. Edwards offers an apposite picture of such society:

> [The saints] are employed so as in some way to be subservient to each other's happiness under God; because they are represented in Scripture as united together as one society, which can be for no other purpose but mutual subserviency. And they are thus mutually subservient by a most excellent and perfectly amiable behavior, one towards another, as a fruit of their perfect love one to another.[79]

---

77. Jonathan Edwards, "Serving God in Heaven," *WJE* 17:259.
78. See Chapter 3 subsection, Fittingness of Retributive Justice.
79. Jonathan Edwards, *Charity and Its Fruits*, Sermon 15, *WJE* 8:384.

The capstone of all this is that the profound dignity conferred by God on man and woman alike by virtue of being created in his image is eschatologically fulfilled through Christ, thereby escalating that dignity to such a degree as one can only receive by way of union with Christ.

And finally, the official aspect of image-bearing will be eschatologically fulfilled through how the redeemed of all the ages come to share in the glory and honor of Christ's High Kingship and High Priesthood. Indeed, the exaltation conferred on them is "by a sort of reflected dignity, the exaltation of their elder brother."[80] It is thus through the dual offices of Christ's kingship and priesthood that the elect calling and office of the saints as "a chosen race, a royal priesthood, a holy nation, a people for [God's] own possession" (1 Pet 2:9) attain their purposed end.[81] In John's eschatological vision the redeemed are described likewise "as a kingdom and priests to serve our God, and they will reign on the earth" (Rev 5:10 NET).[82] The vocation to which the children of Israel were called of serving as a "kingdom of priests" among the nations (Exod 19:5-6), then, has been fulfilled in Christ as the true Israel, and through him becomes fully realized by those who are the spiritual children of Abraham.

The community of the saints as royal priests of God is, again, how John portrays them in the final chapter of his vision. In Revelation 22:3, worship of the Lamb of God is shown as a priestly doxological action by those identified as his servants. That the priestly dimension is in view here is implied by the unmediated access granted all who worship the Lamb to "see his face," for "his name will be on their foreheads" (Rev 22:4). It is notably this latter clause, observes William Dumbrell, that evokes "reference to Israel's origins and to the tabernacle account of Exodus 25-31, since we are immediately reminded of the inscription

---

80. Dabney, *Lectures in Systematic Theology*, 847.

81. Here Peter has strung together allusions and quotations from Exodus 19:5-6; 23:22 (LXX); Isaiah 43:20-21; and Malachi 3:17.

82. The translator's note on Revelation 5:10 in the NET offers the following: "The reference to 'kingdom and priests' may be a hendiadys: 'priestly kingdom.'" In the only two other times in Revelation that the apostle refers to believers explicitly as "priests," he portrays them either as a priestly "kingdom" (βασιλεία) or as priests who forevermore will "reign" (βασιλεύω) with Christ (Rev 1:6; 20:6).

'Holy to the Lord' engraved on the forefront of Aaron's mitre (28:38)."[83] Integral to the official aspect of image bearing we see represented here, the royal dimension is underscored in how all such servants redeemed by the Lamb "will reign forever and ever" with the Lamb (Rev 22:5). The accent on the royal dimension, moreover, is depicted throughout Revelation in terms of the vicegerency of the saints in their glory as victors/conquerors.[84] To those with an ear to hear what the Spirit says to the churches, our exalted Lord says: "Behold, I stand at the door and knock. If anyone hears my voice and opens the door, I will come in to him and eat with him, and he with me. The one who conquers, I will grant him to sit with me on my throne, as I also conquered and sat down with my Father on his throne" (Rev 3:20-21; cf. Rev 2:25-28).

The above biblical imagery depicting the official aspect of image bearing certainly *does not* suggest its eschatological realization as being associated with a life for the saints of blessed *stasis*. Still, an open question remains: what will it look like in real terms for the communion of saints as a kingdom of priests to have dominion and authority, to rule and to reign under Christ, to worship and serve our Father-God in the new heavens and earth? Scripture does not spell out such things. To put it in more Johannine terms—what we will be doing and how we will be doing it has not yet appeared. Worth considering here, even if speculatively, is the idea that in the age to come God will reward each of his children gratuitously, that is, in such a way that takes nothing away from his work of sheer grace, according to the measure of faithful service each one had performed in regard to the responsibilities and gifts God had entrusted them with in this present age. Leaving aside the larger question of the validity and nature of heavenly rewards, the parable of the talents (Matt 25:14-30), along with the parable of the

---

83. William J. Dumbrell, *The End of the Beginning: Revelation 21-22 and the Old Testament* (Eugene, OR: Wipf & Stock, 2001), 160.

84. In this regard, Christopher A. Beetham, "From Creation to New Creation: The Biblical Epic of King, Human Vicegerency, and Kingdom," in *From Creation to New Creation: Biblical Theology and Exegesis*, ed. Daniel M. Gurtner and Benjamin L. Gladd (Peabody, MA: Hendrickson Publishers, 2013), 253, writes: "Disciples who overcome will share in Christ's rule over the nations in fulfillment of Psalm 2 (Rev 2:26-27; cf. 3:21). They are exhorted to 'hold fast' so that no one may 'seize your crown,' that is, the right to rule in the new creation-kingdom of God (Rev 3:11-12)."

ten minas (Luke 19:11–27), suggest potentially that saints are rewarded with apportioned ruling authority and responsibilities in the coming age. Presuming this to be the case (*ex hypothesi*), then, suggests that under our greatest reward (enjoying God himself), saints will take sheer pleasure in whatever "office" responsibilities God apportions. Jesus' declaration, "My Father is working until now, and I am working" (John 5:17), said in reference to the work of healing Jesus did on the Sabbath during his days of public ministry, may be instructive here. For whatever office responsibilities the saints are apportioned in the age to come can be seen perhaps as the Sabbath-rest version of the ongoing work of the Father's will being carried out by the saints in the economy of consummation. Bavinck rounds this out nicely:

> The service of God, mutual communion, and inhabiting the new heaven and the new earth undoubtedly offer abundant opportunity for the exercise of these offices, even though the form and manner of this exercise are unknown to us. That activity, however, coincides with resting and enjoying. The difference between day and night, between the Sabbath and the workdays, has been suspended. Time is charged with the eternity of God. Space is full of his presence.[85]

THE CHURCH WITHOUT SPOT OR WRINKLE: THE BRIDE OF CHRIST MADE BEAUTIFUL AND GLORIFIED

The picture that Scripture paints of God's people in the coming age coincides nicely with the answer to the first question of the *Westminster Larger Catechism*: "Q. 1. What is the chief and highest end of man? A. Man's chief and highest end is to glorify God, and fully to enjoy him forever." This is only true, however, if the corporate-ecclesiological dimension is seen as vitally constitutive of this. Lesslie Newbigin offers the underlying theo-logic:

> In the final consummation of God's loving purposes we and all creation will be caught up into the perfect rapture of that mutual love which is the life of God himself. What is given to us now can only be a foretaste, for none of us can be made whole till we are made whole together. The very meaning of the word salvation is that it is

---

85. Bavinck, *RD*, 4:729.

a making whole, a healing of that which sunders us from God, from one another, and from the created world. The idea of a salvation that is a completed experience for each of us privately, apart from the consummation of all things, is a monstrous contradiction in terms.[86]

Eschatologically, the identity and destiny of the church is represented in her form as the glorified Bride of Christ—God's *anthropos* project on a corporate scale. This is, as such, the form of the church consummate described in terms of her holy splendor "as glorious—not having a stain or wrinkle, or any such blemish, but holy and blameless" (Eph 5:27 NET). For Edwards, as well, this all accords with the telos of God's grand design:

> The creation of the world seems to have been especially for this end, that the eternal Son of God might obtain a spouse, toward whom he might fully exercise the infinite benevolence of his nature, and to whom he might, as it were, open and pour forth all that immense fountain of condescension, love, and grace that was in his heart, and that in this way God might be glorified.[87]

Bridal or spousal language in reference to the church in her form as the glorified Bride of Christ does not show up in John's Apocalypse until the closing vision of a new heaven and a new earth in Revelation 21. As I will argue, there are good grounds for understanding the identity of the holy city—the new Jerusalem—which descends from God out of heaven and is prepared as a bride "adorned or made beautiful" (κεκοσμημένην)[88] for her husband (Rev 21:2), as being the church glorified. With the new order of creation having been inaugurated, this present age is the already but not-yet order of reality in which God is doing that preparation of making his church beautiful for her end-time glorification as the wife of the Lamb (Rev 19:7–8). In a sense, then, the revelation of Jesus Christ (Rev 1:1) is not made complete until there is

---

86. Lesslie Newbigin, *The Household of God: Lectures on the Nature of the Church* (New York: Friendship Press, 1954), 147.

87. Jonathan Edwards, "The Church's Marriage to Her Sons, and to Her God," *WJE* 25:187.

88. L&N 79.12 s.v. κοσμέω "to cause something to be beautiful by decorating—'to beautify, to adorn, to decorate, adornment, adorning.'"

the revelation at last of his Bride. In Edwards' words, "Thus the church of Christ (toward whom and in whom are the emanations of his glory and communications of his fullness) is called the fullness of Christ: as though he were not in his complete state without her; as Adam was in a defective state without Eve."[89]

In line with the interpretation argued by Robert Gundry, the vision John is describing here is not of the new heavens and earth per se, but of the new *city*—the new Jerusalem.[90] And while it is true typically that reference to a polis means both the inhabitants of that city as well as the actual place of dwelling itself, it appears that the new earth in its entire scope is what serves as the saints' dwelling place. "The new Jerusalem is a dwelling place, to be sure," explains Gundry. "But it is God's dwelling place in the saints rather than their dwelling place on earth."[91] We see a similar conceptual link between the heavenly polis and the assembly of the saints in Hebrews 12:22-23: "But you have come to Mount Zion, the city (πόλις)[92] of the living God, the heavenly Jerusalem, and to myriads of angels, to the assembly and congregation (ἐκκλησία) of the firstborn" (NET). In this light the signification of the new Jerusalem is not essentially *habitative* in nature but *ecclesiological*, depicting in nuptial imagery the covenantal union of Bridegroom and Bride, that is, Christ and his church. I am agreeing, therefore, with the position of those who would make a categorial distinction between the new earth as essentially a habitative domain of sacred spacetime and the new Jerusalem as essentially the ecclesiological communion of all the saints.[93]

---

89. Edwards, "Concerning the End for Which God Created the World," *WJE* 8:439.

90. With debts here to Robert H. Gundry, "The New Jerusalem: People as Place, Not Place for People" in *The Old Is Better: New Testament Essays in Support of Traditional Interpretations* (Tübingen: Mohr Siebeck, 2005), 400-406.

91. Gundry, "The New Jerusalem," 401.

92. The translator's note in the NET states: "*Grk* 'and the city'; the conjunction is omitted in translation since it seems to be functioning epexegetically—that is, explaining further what is meant by 'Mount Zion.'"

93. Other commentators interpret the new Jerusalem to be synonymous with the new earth ("habitative") along with all the saints ("the Bride") who dwell in it. See, for example, Mark B. Stephens, *Annihilation or Renewal? The Meaning and Function of New Creation in the Book of Revelation* (Tübingen: Mohr Siebeck, 2011), 232-34. I will seek to substantiate the "ecclesiological" interpretation.

John had already signaled in Revelation 19:7–8 that the time has come for the marriage of the Lamb to his Bride, who are the saints clothed and ready in the pure fine linen of their righteous deeds. And it is this "adornment" of the Bride of Christ for her husband that John likens in 21:2 to the new Jerusalem having been "made ready" for her bridal debut at the debut of the new creation. It is not until 21:9–11, however, that "the Bride, the wife of the Lamb" is identified in explicit terms with "the holy city Jerusalem coming down out of heaven from God, having the glory of God."[94] The glory of God, indeed, is signified in the bridal adornment of purity, the holiness of the glorified saints. This adornment of holiness reflects the promised blessings of the prophets, notably Isaiah, concerning the future restoration of Israel as a "bride/wife" and God as the "bridegroom/husband" (cf. Isa 52:1; 54:5–8; 61:10; 62:1–5; Hos 2:19–20).[95] All of this becomes ultimately fulfilled by the church, Jew and Gentile alike as heirs of the Abrahamic promise—true Israel as the new corporate entity united to Christ—in her end-time glorification as the wife of the Lamb. It is worth noting how the marriage imagery itself, with its timbre of joy and intimacy, is reflective too of the beatific life of the saints with God.

The intimate communion implicit between God and those whom he redeems had been intimated already in John's vision of the saints as those clothed in robes made white in the blood of the Lamb whom he will shelter with his presence (Rev 7:13, 15; cf. Ezek 16:8–10). The bridal union of Christ and his church essentially reflects the eschatological fulfillment of God's overarching covenantal purposes, which can be

---

94. Cf. Jonathan Edwards, "Nothing upon Earth Can Represent the Glories of Heaven," *WJE* 14:137–38: "It is called 'new Jerusalem' in contradistinction to that which was so glorious in Solomon's time, which was a type, and is to be taken as including both the glorified church of God, the triumphing assembly of the saints, and their reward, or the glories of heaven, the place of their abode. It appears to be the former, that is, the congregation of the persons of the saints, by the latter end of the second verse, where this new Jerusalem is said to be 'prepared as a bride adorned for her husband,' and by the ninth verse, where it is called 'the Lamb's wife.'"

95. The translator's note on Hosea 2:19 in the NET offers the following: "The text contains an allusion to the payment of bridal gifts. The Lord will impute the moral character to Israel that will be necessary for a successful covenant relationship (*contra* 4:1)."

taken to underlie the proclamation in Revelation 21:3: "And I heard a loud voice from the throne saying, 'Behold, the dwelling place of God is with man. He will dwell with them, and they will be his people, and God himself will be with them as their God.'" Reminiscent here, again, are the promised blessings of the prophets concerning the future restoration of Israel in terms of God's dwelling with his people in a new covenantal way (cf. Jer 31:31–33; Ezek 36:24–28; 37:26–28; 43:7). The eschatological trajectory of God's dwelling in the midst of his people thus becomes perfectly realized in the consummative fulfillment of our union with God through Christ, domiciling in the fellowship of God's presence in glorious Spirit-filled communion (cf. John 14:23). It is likely from the testimony of Jesus' words to the Philadelphians in Revelation 3:12 that the triple name he promises to write on all those who conquer (cf. 21:7)—"the name of my God, and the name of the city of my God, the new Jerusalem, which comes down from my God out of heaven, and my own new name"—suggests a Trinitarian formulation in which "new Jerusalem" is a way of speaking about the presence of God's Spirit with the community of the faithful, whom the Lord calls pillars in his temple. In reference to this Spirit-filled communion, writes Edwards, the heavenly state is "a state in which this shall be, as it were, the only gift or fruit of the Spirit, as being the most perfect and glorious, and which being brought to perfection renders others, which God was wont to communicate to his church on earth, needless."[96]

That the dimensions of the new Jerusalem described in Revelation 21:15–17 are cubical in shape recalls the same shape of the Most Holy Place in Israel's tabernacle and temple, the Holy of Holies (1 Kgs 6:20). The fullness of God's dwelling presence with his people made explicit in Revelation 21:3 is heightened further as the Most Holy Place of the new creation. As Geerhardus Vos notes, "The peculiarity of the representation here is that, in dependence on Isaiah 4:5, 6, the area of the tabernacle and temple are widened so as to become equally co-extensive with the entire New Jerusalem."[97] The fellowship of God's presence in glorious Spirit-filled communion is now recognized to mean "that the perfected saints [themselves] will be God's most sacred dwelling place. ...

96. Edwards, *Charity and Its Fruits*, Sermon 15, *WJE* 8:368.
97. Vos, *Biblical Theology: Old and New Testaments*, 155.

Thus the whole of the city has the glory of God because the whole of the city is the holy of holies, filled with the glory of his presence" (cf. Ezek 48:35).[98] Given this limning of things, it comes as no surprise that John then begins Revelation 21:22—"Now I saw no temple in the city"— because ostensibly it would seem that the new Holy of Holies shining with the glory of God is an entire city-temple. But John then immediately adds, "because the Lord God—the All-powerful—and the Lamb are its temple" (NET). With this it becomes apparent that the new creation is new as well in this respect: "while the church is the temple where God dwells, God is the Spirit-Temple where the church dwells."[99] To put it another way, the consummation is realized in God dwelling with his people so intimately, it is appropriate to describe the communion of the saints as the church deified by the Spirit, living and moving with Christ *in Deo* like a Bride made beautiful in her glory, living and moving in covenantal union with her Lord in his glory.

The corporate-ecclesiological dimension of beauty in all this may perhaps be considered the *summum bonum* of all creaturely *summum bonums*, surpassing however it may, even the glory magnified in and experienced by each son and daughter of God. The phenomenon involved here, I am suggesting, is an aesthetic entailment that relates to the perceivable and experienceable effect achieved when the whole of something can be said to be greater than the sum of its parts. That is to say, the glorification of the ecclesiological body of Christ, whose glory is experienced in relationship with each other and altogether as one family with God through Christ in the Spirit, surpasses in some magnified or intensified way the individual glory of each son and daughter of God in their unique glorified self. It is beyond us now to envision such a perfected reality and rhythm of life with God. But we can at least stoke our imagination with illustrative similes or conceptualizations evocative of such beatific unity in diversity.[100] Aesthetic examples

---

98. Gundry, "The New Jerusalem: People as Place, Not Place for People," 405.

99. Kline, *Images of the Spirit*, 26.

100. Cf. Stephen H. Webb, *The Divine Voice: Christian Proclamation and the Theology of Sound* (Grand Rapids: Brazos Press, 2004), 239: "When we imagine heaven, we must rely on descriptions that we know will fall short of their object, yet when we enter heaven, we will realize that those descriptions were feeble but appropriate ways of stimulating our delight."

lend themselves especially to such illustration. Peter Leithart cites the following one from Roger Scruton's observation on music: "In music, all distance between movements is abolished, as we confront a single process in which multiplicity is simultaneously preserved and overridden. No musical event excludes any other, but all coexist in a placeless self-presentation. ... It is as though these many currents flowed together in a single life, at one with itself."[101] In some such living dynamic as may be likened to this illustration, the spousal meaning of Christ and his church is fulfilled. As Edwards states, though, until that day arrives of the church in her form as the glorified Bride of Christ, "there further remains the need of every member to be brought into being: all brought home to Christ, their souls perfectly sanctified, bodies glorified. Both body and soul then realize complete glory, consisting in perfect purity, perfect union, and perfect blessedness—not merely that happiness that is enjoyed by separate spirits, but the love that unites them all."[102]

HUMANS IMMORTAL IN FINAL FITTINGNESS: DAMNED AS GLORY-LESS

The stage of the theodrama we have had in view assumes the bodily return of Christ, which ushers in the age to come and the consummation of all things. In accord with the sequence of events in the apocalyptic storyline it also assumes that consequent upon Christ's return is the bodily resurrection of the dead of all the ages (along with the rapture of all who are still alive), involving as part of this the final judgment. It is, at the same time, understood as the great and terrible Day of the Lord, notably for those who are God's enemies. With applied concision, Christopher Beetham captures its terrifying eventfulness:

> The story of the Creator-King climaxes with the final battle, defeat, and destruction of the satanic usurper of Adam's throne (Rev 20:7–10). The dead are raised and judged. The image-bearers who refused to repent and cease from their rebellion, as evidenced by their deeds,

---

101. Peter J. Leithart, *Traces of the Trinity: Signs of God in Creation and Human Experience* (Grand Rapids: Brazos Press, 2015), 95, citing Roger Scruton, *The Aesthetics of Music* (Oxford: Clarendon Press, 1997), 338–39.

102. Jonathan Edwards, "Approaching the End of God's Grand Design," *WJE* 25:120.

are thrown into the lake of fire (20:11–15). Judgment accomplished, God consummates his new creation.[103]

The extension of our theological aesthetic in this section assumes the traditional view of hell—that is, I am assuming and upholding with church tradition the doctrine of hell, understood as a realm of eternal, conscious torment of all those who, under final sentence of divine judgment, are thus damned and consigned there.[104] We might otherwise characterize hell as a spacetime realm entailing everlasting exile or excommunication from God's spacetime realm of life. Our interest here concerns how this area of doctrine fits within the application of our theological aesthetic, whose fundamental premise is that everything God does is beautiful in its God-glorifying nature. Thus, as regards the outworking of the divine plan centrally in the fate of the creature made in God's image, our theological aesthetic here pertains to the judgment of damnation upon unredeemed sinners. The argumentation I propose, admittedly speculative at points, considers the aspect of fittingness and the motif of glory in regard to the divine judgment of damnation rendered against the creature made in God's image. The section is divided into two parts: (1) Damnation: The Miserific Death; and (2) The Damned: Loss of Sonship, Loss of Image, Loss of Glory.

Damnation: The Miserific Death

"When the Son of Man comes in his glory, and all the angels with him, then he will sit on his glorious throne. ... Then he will say to those on

---

103. Beetham, "From Creation to New Creation: The Biblical Epic of King, Human Vicegerency, and Kingdom," 253.

104. Typologically foreshadowing this final judgment are three examples the apostle Peter gives, showing how God has judged in times former and will judge again at the end of the age: the apostate angels, the flood of Noah's time, and Sodom and Gomorrah (2 Pet 2:4–9). Glimpsed in these examples are both the final redemption and the final judgment to come. In the domain of systematic theology across the evangelical spectrum, the traditional doctrine of hell has retained general, albeit tenuous, support, and indeed in recent times it has become noticeably more controverted in both systematic and philosophical theology. See, for example, the recent multi-view work by Preston Sprinkle, ed., *Four Views on Hell*, 2nd ed. (Grand Rapids: Zondervan, 2016), which presents the traditional view of hell (eternal conscious torment) alongside three prominent alternative positions: Annihilationism (conditional immortality); Universalism (ultimate reconciliation); and Purgatory (a Protestant proposal).

his left, 'Depart from me, you cursed, into the eternal fire prepared for the devil and his angels.' ... And these will go away into eternal punishment, but the righteous into eternal life" (Matt 25:31, 41, 46). The scene Jesus is describing is part of a powerful discourse on the final judgment that relates to each person's ultimate and eternal destiny, whether unto eternal life or unto eternal death. But this eternal fire is not the fire of a refiner. For just as the Adamic fall in Genesis 3—in a penultimate sense—casts in sharp relief how humanity is morally held to account before God for imaging him as she has been created to do, so now we see how in an ultimate sense the judgment of damnation casts in the sharpest relief for eternity this same moral accountability. Interestingly, according to Hebrews 6:1-2 eternal judgment is an elementary doctrine of the Christian faith. Yet on this side of the eschaton a certain shroud of mystery and mysteriousness surround the revelation concerning eternal damnation. In mightily understated terms, Francis Turretin writes, "But what [eternal death] is or in what infernal punishments consist, it is not easy to define."[105] I will not presume to offer an easy definition either. It is fair to say, however, that the damned in hell are nonetheless within the compass of the outworking of the divine economy. But it is an aporia of the highest magnitude to reconcile that aspect of the outworking of the divine economy as being part of God's original creational purposes—what I had represented in the basic themes of the proto-eschaton in Chapter 3. I propose simply that the damned in hell do not in any way participate in God's original creational purposes, which are revealed in their eternal fullness in the consummation when all things become summed up in Christ. The idea of the damned in hell not being part of God's original creational purposes would seem to be a fair inference (or at least a suggestive point) drawn from Matthew 25:41 where Jesus describes the ultimate fate of the damned as being banished "into the eternal fire prepared for the devil and his angels." On this view the future realization of eternal damnation is considered in some way as

---

105. Francis Turretin, *IET*, vol. 3, Topic XII, Quest. VII, Sec. IV (605). Notwithstanding Turretin's comment, he goes on to affirm infernal punishments "of all kinds in the soul as well as in the body." Note, unless otherwise stated, all references to "the damned" refer to humans who are judged as such at the final judgment.

being an obverse reality from that of God's fully realized creational intention. Exactly how such an obverse reality is explained as being within the compass of the outworking of the divine economy but not as part of God's original creational purposes I will just leave at this—to reissue the words of Turretin—it is not easy to define.

"With flaming fire [Christ] will mete out punishment on those who do not know God and do not obey the gospel of our Lord Jesus. They will undergo the penalty of eternal destruction, away from (ἀπό) the presence of the Lord and from the glory of his strength" (2 Thess 1:8–9 NET). The eternal destruction identified here is itself defined by that which characterizes this penal judgment, namely, the exiling "presence of the Lord," taken as synonymously parallel to the "glory of his strength" (cf. Jude 24).[106] It is fair to say, moreover, that the retributive punishment, destruction, and exclusion comprehended in Paul's description is bound up with the banishment Jesus will pronounce against all those whose claim to be among his followers is fraudulent. In that final day of reckoning he will "declare to them, 'I never knew you; depart from me, you workers of lawlessness'" (Matt 7:23; cf. Matt 25:1–12; Luke 13:23–30). Even more expressly, I suggest, is that Jesus' own cry of dereliction from the cross in some real sense touches on the meaning of eternal destruction (more on this below). Taken together, passages such as 1 Corinthians 15:28, Colossians 1:20, and Philippians 2:9–11 are seen to support the idea of God's unchallengeable rule in the reconciliation of all things through Christ's kingly reign. Preeminently this affirms that when all evil is ultimately destroyed, all sinning ceases. In agreement with Shawn Bawulski, this means even the damned will bow the knee to Jesus and confess him as Lord, albeit "in subjection, shame, and defeat—not with contrived and insincere external lip service but as

---

106. See Douglas F. Moo, "Paul on Hell" in *Hell Under Fire*, ed. Christopher W. Morgan and Robert A. Peterson (Grand Rapids: Zondervan, 2004), 106–8; and BDAG 106 s.v. ἀπό 5: to indicate cause, means, or outcome. Cf. also Isaiah 2:10, 19, 21. Moo notes additionally that "the various word groups that Paul uses to depict the fate of unbelievers are interrelated. In the same context, for instance, Paul can shift from 'perish' to 'condemn' (2 Thess 2:9–12); from 'condemnation' to 'death' (Rom 5:12, 18; 2 Cor 3:6, 7, 9); from 'condemnation' to 'wrath' (Rom 2:1–5); from 'punish' to 'wrath' to 'destroy' (2 Thess 1:8–10); and from 'perish' to 'judge' (Rom 2:12). Clearly Paul uses these different word groups to describe the same reality" (94).

an expression of their internal recognition of [his] undeniable worth, goodness, and righteousness."[107]

Those who are ultimately damned will come to possess no beatific life. Rather, they will experience the presence of the Lord in an unimaginably opposite way—one I am hazarding to call the *miserific death*.[108] All the descriptions mentioned above in connection with the future reality of eternal destruction/punishment are meant to convey in the most visceral and extreme terms the infernal nature of the miserific death. It is not unduly extreme to see the second death for the damned (Rev 21:8) as their being consigned as it were to eternal horror participation. That is to say, the eternal punishment experienced by the damned will be in some real sense a horror of God-forsakenness. As Henri Blocher suggests, the reconciliation of all things through Christ subsumes this in some such way as this:

> If sinners ultimately glorify God, they do reach in a paradoxical way the telos of all creatures as such. And they know it, since they now see the truth of their lives; they see their evil works—which they now abhor—as included in God's plan, by his permissive will, and used for his purposes. ... They are excluded from the fellowship of God; they cannot "enjoy him for ever." ... [T]heir thought is fixed in the knowledge that, through their very deprivation, they glorify God and agree with him.[109]

---

107. Shawn Bawulski, "Reconciliationism, A Better View of Hell: Reconciliationism and Eternal Punishment," *JETS* 56 no.1 (March 2013): 133. Bawulski, citing O'Brien, *The Epistle to the Philippians*, 243, then adds, "As O'Brien points out, this is in significant accord with Isa 45:20ff. (which is drawn from in Phil 2:9-11), where the future reality of universal worship is an irrevocable truth (v. 23) and at the same time 'all who have raged against him will come to him and be put to shame' (v. 24)."

108. I adapted the term "miserific death" from the affecting phrase C. S. Lewis uses—"Miserific Vision"—in the second book in his Space Trilogy, *Perelandra: A Novel* (New York: Scribner, 2003), 96: "As there is one Face above all worlds which merely to see is irrevocable joy, so at the bottom of all worlds that face is waiting whose sight alone is the misery from which none who beholds it can recover. And though there seemed to be, and indeed were, a thousand roads by which a man could walk through the world, there was not a single one which did not lead sooner or later either to the Beatific or the Miserific Vision."

109. Henri Blocher, "Everlasting Punishment and the Problem of Evil," in *Universalism and the Doctrine of Hell*, ed. Nigel M. de S. Cameron (Grand Rapids: Baker, 1992), 310.

The eternal fixed remorse Blocher proposes is the absolute obverse of the doxological delight that characterizes the beatific life. Certainly on this point, Jonathan Edwards concurs: "The wicked, at the day of judgment, will see everything else in Christ, but his beauty and amiableness."[110] It follows in Edwards' theological aesthetic, though, that since what he calls primary beauty consists in consent and union of heart to Being in general (i.e., God), and presupposes such consent and union of heart by beings capable of volition and love, Edwards does not agree that for the damned all sinning ceases, even though evil itself will be ultimately destroyed.[111]

Contrariwise, in my judgment the damned will not have the capacity to operate in the power of their freedom to persevere in hatred against God. So, for example, the imagery in Mark 9:43-48 of undying devouring worm and unquenchable consuming fire—recalling the final word of the prophecy of Isaiah (66:24)—is taken up by Jesus as a powerful warning of the eternal consequences of rebellion against God. While accepting the point earlier that the reconciliation of all things through Christ subsumes the fallout of all such consequences for the damned, Blocher proposes that the metaphorical language of the fire and the worm is regarded best as something like a "self-condemning conscience" that issues in "burning" or "gnawing" remorse. Such remorse would be reflective of "a right attitude, attuned to God's own judgment, towards the past sinful lives," that is, a kind of eternal "remorse-in-agreement with God."[112] Such consequence is the obverse destiny of how the *Westminster Larger Catechism* answers its first question—the damned will indeed glorify God, but are never to enjoy him forever. Thus in

---

110. Edwards, "True Grace, Distinguished from the Experience of Devils," *WJE* 25:634.

111. E.g., in reference to the damned, Jonathan Edwards, "Misc. no. 282," *WJE* 13:380, writes, "Although the strength of their pain is very great ... yet the strength of their malice is proportionably great; which puts them forward industriously to pursue their works of malice, even in the midst of pain."

112. Blocher, "Everlasting Punishment and the Problem of Evil," 306-7. Cf. Edwards, "True Grace Distinguished from the Experience of Devils," *WJE* 25:634: "They will have a sense of [Christ's] great majesty, that will be, as it were, infinitely affecting to them. They shall be made to know effectually, *that he is the Lord*. They shall see what he is, and what he does: his nature and works, shall appear in the strongest view."

Edwardsian terms we could say that such remorse is a kind of consent, but one that is absolutely devoid of any joy and delight.[113] Presumably, the body of those who are damned befits the infernal nature of the miserific death. On this view the aesthetic notion of fittingness applies to those who are ultimately damned in how the outward form (*Gestalt*) of their miserific death is perfectly befitting the inner content (*Gehalt*) of their horror of God-forsakenness. For just as "the eyes of [Adam and Eve] were opened, and they knew that they were naked" (Gen 3:7) after eating of the fruit of the tree of the knowledge of good and evil, so also, I submit, will the eyes of the damned be opened in apprehending their eternal judgment, acutely aware of just how naked and ashamed before the Lord they are. But in this final condition of remorse, repentance will not be an option. As Blocher explains, "Repentance has a future, it enters the open future; remorse relates only the past. The remorse of the gnashed teeth and gnawing worm relates only to the past."[114] In speaking of the dual destiny of those who "sleep" in death, the prophet Daniel gives one of the closest descriptions we have in the Old Testament to this very idea: "And many of those who sleep in the dust of the earth shall awake, some to everlasting life, and some to shame and everlasting contempt" (Dan 12:2).[115]

This conception, moreover, is consistent with the idea I put forward in Chapter 3 that the execution of God's secondary justice—applying here with respect to eternal damnation—involves a fittingness between the retributive punishment a person deserves on the one hand (i.e., a person under final sentence of divine judgment) and another's evaluative attitudes and actions on the other (i.e., as God has and does with

---

113. Cf. Consonant with this view is the theological aesthetic of Anselm. As Frank Burch Brown notes, "Anselm says only that any ugliness in the order of things would ultimately be intolerable to God; and because hell is designed to remedy [i.e., rectify] the ugliness of sin, he implies—without stating it outright—that hell should be seen as in some way beautiful." Brown, "The Beauty of Hell: Anselm on God's Eternal Design," 340.

114. Blocher, "Everlasting Punishment and the Problem of Evil," 307.

115. Tremper Longman III, *Daniel*, NIVAC (Grand Rapids: Zondervan, 1999), 304, comments, "The problem of retribution is a huge one in the Bible, particularly in the Old Testament. ... Daniel 12, however, makes it clear that the wicked will ultimately get what they deserve—destruction and shame."

respect to that person).[116] In this case God's evaluative attitude toward unredeemed sinners reflects the fact that all sin is heinous to him, and since divine justice must be perfectly satisfied, there is perfect fittingness with eternal punishment "away from the presence of the Lord" (cf. Ps 5:4). This extension of our theological aesthetic thus sees the fittingness of God's holiness and righteousness manifest in his final judgment of eternal damnation rendered against unredeemed sinners as being perfectly correlated with the fittingness that characterizes the beauty of God's unchallengeable rule in the reconciliation of all things through Christ's kingly reign.[117] A theological point worth noting here is that the disposition God reveals in the economies of revelation and redemption is that he takes no pleasure in the death of the wicked (Ezek 18:23; 33:11). In the economy of consummation, however, God is revealed as righting for all time all that is wrong as it pertains both to those who are redeemed in Christ and those who are not. God's disposition as will be revealed in the economy of consummation is better considered, I would suggest, not in terms of how he takes no pleasure in the death of the wicked, but rather how he delights in summing up all things in Christ, which includes his judgment of damnation upon unredeemed sinners in the final judgment.

THE DAMNED: LOSS OF SONSHIP, LOSS OF IMAGE, LOSS OF GLORY

"And this is eternal life, that they know you the only true God, and Jesus Christ whom you have sent" (John 17:3; cf. Ps 36:9; John 1:4; 12:46–50). As is implicit here in Jesus' high priestly prayer to the Father, eternal life does not merely equate to a state of immortal existence any more than eternal death (i.e., damnation) equates to a state of annihilated existence. Rather, what ultimately is defining of eternal life is being restored in right relationship to God the Father through his Son Jesus Christ in glorious Spirit-filled communion. The event of the eschatological resurrection is when that becomes fully realized for the redeemed

---

116. See Chapter 3 subsection, Fittingness of Retributive Justice.

117. Recall from Chapter 2 that Scripture indicates a strong connection between the beauty of God and his manifest glory, namely, his majesty, kingship, and splendor; see the section, Beauty—A Divine Attribute?

in Christ (cf. John 6:40, 54; 11:25–26). I have referred to this as the beatific life, whose obverse reality is the miserific death. The latter we will now consider in relational terms: What does it mean relationally to be under final sentence of divine judgment, never to be restored in right relationship to God the Father through his Son Jesus Christ? Our discussion earlier on 1 John 3:1–2 regarding believers' filial relationship with the Father through Christ would seem to imply the negating of that relation with those who are ultimately damned. Considered from that perspective, I offer the following *theologoumenon.*

If the most fundamental way saints "shall be like Christ" corresponds to the same relation he has with the Father, namely, as his Father-God, then those who are ultimately damned are eternally severed from that relation. Their relation to the Son will not be in any sense fraternal, and they will not know God in any sense as *Father.* Like the apostate angels, the damned will indeed know the only true God, and Jesus Christ whom he has sent (cf. Matt 8:29; Jas 2:19), but they will have no filial relationship with the Father. They will know the only true God and Jesus his Son in the worst light possible for them—as the only true Judge of the universe. To recall the dire warning of Jesus, "But I will warn you whom to fear: fear him who, after he has killed, has authority to cast into hell. Yes, I tell you, fear him!" (Luke 12:5; cf. John 3:36; 17:2). For the damned will be judged by Christ (Acts 17:31; Rev 20:11–15) and the judgment rendered is a judicial act that will render void any right to be counted a child of God. The judgment of damnation thus implies the judicial stripping of any status of sonship. The damned as such will be disqualified from being considered even offspring of God (Acts 17:29). Even that final separation pronounced by Jesus of the sheep from the goats, picturing the final judgment of all humanity, lends support to the idea of a termination of filial relationship with the Father for those who are damned. Christ himself will say to the sheep on his right, "Come, you who are blessed by my Father, inherit the kingdom prepared for you from the foundation of the world." But to the goats on his left, Christ will say, "Depart from me, you cursed, into the eternal fire prepared for the devil and his angels" (Matt 25:34, 41).

As I alluded to earlier, the horror of the miserific death is captured in some real sense as a horror of God-forsakenness. Albeit theologically speculative, the horror of God-forsakenness experienced by Christ in those unfathomable moments on the cross surrounding his cry of dereliction, while sui generis and incomparable in its own right, is perhaps suggestive of some form of horror of God-forsakenness to be experienced by every human being whose right to be counted among God's children is rendered altogether void.[118] My operating premise here is that just as the status of sonship is not something conferred *inalienably* by God, neither should we think that one's identity as image-bearer is inalienable. Given as we have noted before how "sonship" is bound up with "image bearing," it would seem to follow that the judgment of damnation rendering null and void the status of sonship equates at one and the same time to the termination of bearing the image of God. The theological point I am suggesting, therefore, is that the miserific death in relational terms means that every human being who is damned in the final judgment is judicially and relationally stripped of sonship and image-bearing status and dignity. In this way, again, the fittingness of God's retributive justice carries through in how the profound dignity conferred by God on man and woman alike by virtue of being created in his image becomes, for the damned, their being and bearing the utmost indignity.

Insofar as this picture is valid, the damned will not transmogrify from being human to being non-human, but from image-bearer to non-image-bearer. In this way the person who is damned still remains a *human* being, but he or she will no longer be constituted in the image of God. As Meredith Kline likewise states, "Concerning the reprobate, biblical warrant is lacking to ascribe to them in the condition of second death even the status of naked image. This is not to deny that they continue to be human beings, for image of God and humanness, it must be remembered, are not simple equivalents."[119] Kline's point is consistent with the point above that sonship and image bearing are mutually a dignity and a status—take away the status in judgment and no

---

118. In my view, the critical difference to note here is that in Christ's experience of God-forsakenness, his filial relation to the Father was never actually voided, but it seems he did lose all sense of filial consciousness. So in the existential sense of feeling forsaken by the Father, he did experience damnation.

119. Meredith G. Kline, *Images of the Spirit* (Eugene, OR: Wipf & Stock, 1999), 33.

corresponding filial/image-bearing dignity can remain. By extension, the damned will be *aglorious* human beings—that is, human persons no longer constituted to reflect the image-bearing glory of God, hence being *glory-less*. Perhaps a kind of parallel here can be argued between humans and angels. Just like the apostate angels are still angelic beings (of the angel kind), so the damned will still be human beings (of the human kind), with neither group constituted to reflect the glory of God as they once had been.[120]

THE ESCHATON:
THE BEGINNING OF THE ETERNITY OF ALL THINGS

In the age to come the reconciliation of the fractured cosmos that God has accomplished in an "already but not-yet consummate" way through the reign of Christ will be transformed at last into the consummative cosmic kingdom of the new heavens and earth. All that Christ as the exalted king of the universe redeems and brings to its consummative glory is entailed in this. Then will be fully realized God's kingdom come, God's will perfectly done on earth as it is in heaven (Matt 6:10). For the consummation of all things brings the denouement of the new creation, which "shall be filled with the glory of the LORD" (Num 14:21; cf. Isa 11:9).

Stepping back and taking a panoramic view of the principal phases of the theodrama, the beauty of God reflected in the created order is along these lines: at the outset of creation the climax of God's sixfold affirmation in Genesis 1 of the goodness of creation expressed his full delight in a created order altogether imbued with original beauty. But because of the fall of our primal parents, the glory of God is reflected now in a created order and a humanity laboring under the judgment curse of God in Genesis 3. Thus in indeterminable ways the created order itself is tainted/corrupted, and humanity's ability to rightly perceive and experience the beauty of God reflected in it is obscured/

---

120. For true justice to be executed, however, continuity of one's metaphysical identity (i.e., numerically identical) cannot be lost or severed between this age and the age to come. Since the Father has given the Son "authority over all humanity" (John 17:2 NET), continuity of one's metaphysical identity would seem to be preserved sovereignly through the relation of Christ as the eternal Judge of the damned.

distorted. In the age to come, the reconciliation of the fractured cosmos that God has accomplished through Christ will reflect the beauty of God in a glorified new creation when God proclaims at last, "Behold, I am making all things new" (Rev 21:5). The old creation now operating under the effects of God's judgment curse will be recreated in the consummation of the divine plan.

The new creation can be seen as the divine work of consummation in which the whole of reality created by God—both creation and redemption—are consummated as one order in the new heaven and new earth. As Stephens puts it, "The new creation is distinguished by the full and uninhibited presence of God, as the previously opposed realms of heaven and earth become merged into an interpenetrative unity. ... 'This, in the last resort, is what is 'new' about the new creation. It is the old creation filled with God's presence.'"[121] It seems theologically fair to say that the new creation in effect is the coinherence of the orders of nature (creation) and grace (redemption) in which is realized the glorification of all things redeemed—call it the order of glorification. The final goal here, writes Rikki Watts, "is not the destruction of creation but rather the unification of heaven and earth such that the renewed earth itself becomes Yahweh's throne room" (cf. Eph 1:10).[122] In this way the proto-eschaton themes of sacred time and sacred space that the creation account suggested, represented respectively by God's Sabbath rest and the garden of Eden (God's garden of delight), become eschatologically realized in the renewed earth—Yahweh's throne room.[123] The renewed earth as such can be seen as the sacred spacetime where God's image-bearing sons and daughters will experience the pure joy of his presence. As Cornelis Venema rightly notes, "The renewal of the creation is the only context or environment within which the resurrection glory of believers in fellowship with Christ can be appreciated and

---

121. Stephens, *Annihilation or Renewal?*, 257, quoting Richard Bauckham, *The Theology of the Book of Revelation* (Cambridge: Cambridge University Press, 1993), 140.

122. Rikki E. Watts, "The New Exodus/New Creational Restoration of the Image of God" in *What Does It Mean to Be Saved?: Broadening Evangelical Horizons on Salvation*, ed. John G. Stackhouse Jr. (Grand Rapids: Baker Academic, 2002), 36.

123. See Chapter 3 subsections, Sacred Time: The Climactic Sabbath of the Creation Week; and Sacred Space: The Garden of Eden as the Archetypal Temple-Sanctuary.

understood. Without the glorification of the creation, the glorification of the new humanity in Christ would be an isolated and strange event."[124]

Moreover, of consequence here is the principle I stipulated in Chapter 2, namely, that for any given created theater, God's glory must be exercised in such a manner as to display all his communicable attributes.[125] In the present order of creation, this principle is properly extended to God's self-revelation as Redeemer in the person and work of Christ, for it is in and through the Son incarnate that God's glory is manifested so as to display all his communicable perfections (Col 2:9). Apart from the consummation of all things, however, humans could know God in his self-revelation as Creator and Redeemer but would be without a realized eschatological context to know him as *Consummator*. God's new humanity in God's new creation will in this way manifest his glory in his self-revelation as Consummator of his divine plan. In his role as Consummator, God reprises as it were his role as Creator in ultimate fulfillment of his role as Redeemer. In Jonathan Edwards' words,

> when the Creator takes the world in hand the second time, it will be as a Creator, not only bringing to pass some external change of the order and situation of the more gross parts, but will cause a most inward change in the nature of things, and bring all in that respect into a much more perfect state (it being their last and eternal state), more fit to show forth the glory of his perfections.[126]

With the new creation, the eschatologically realized beauty of God in the economy of consummation becomes especially distinguished in its gloriousness against that of the economies of creation and redemption (cf. Eccl 3:11). Struck by this same notion, Bavinck articulates the splendor and vitality of the new creation this way:

> The state of glory (*status gloriae*) will be no mere restoration (*restauratie*) of the state of nature (*status naturae*), but a re-formation that,

124. Cornelis P. Venema, *The Promise of the Future* (Edinburgh: Banner of Truth Trust, 2000), 377–78.

125. I have appropriated this principle from Oliver D. Crisp, *Retrieving Doctrine: Essays in Reformed Theology* (Downers Grove, IL: IVP Academic, 2010), 91. See Chapter 2 subsection, The Fittingness of the Trinity Operating Economically.

126. Jonathan Edwards, "Misc. no. 929," *WJE* 20:172.

thanks to the power of Christ, transforms all matter (ὕλη) into form (εἶδος), all potency into actuality (*potentia, actus*), and presents the entire creation before the face of God, brilliant in unfading splendor and blossoming in a springtime of eternal youth.[127]

In some such marvelous way the beauty of the new creation typifies the perfectly fitting kingdom realm for the beatific life of the saints domiciling in the fellowship of God's presence in glorious Spirit-filled communion.[128]

New Creation:
Creatio Originalis Becomes *Creatio Nova*

The unitive nature of the divine plan is evident in the shape of the Bible's overall story pattern, which we characterized in Chapter 2 as consisting of a fundamental symmetry between creation and re-creation whose pivotal center is God's reconciling all things to himself through Christ in the redemptive-eschatological fulfillment of his original creational purposes.[129] The relation between the original creation (*creatio originalis*) and the new creation (*creatio nova*) seen in the broad outworking of God's plan points up the integral nature of the glorification of the creation with the glorification of the new humanity in Christ. Below, I present a theological interpretation in evidence of this point. The renewal of creation does not entail that the present creational order itself, over which God had expressed his full delight originally (Gen 1:31), is in any real sense implicated as source of the pandemic ramifications of sin and evil. If it otherwise were the case it would perhaps be fitting for God to expunge this creational order altogether, excepting it from the reconciliation (in redemption) of all things to himself. No, the realm of creation *qua* creation is not constituted with moral agency and as such does not stand guilty (nor can it) before God. For it was the

---

127. Herman Bavinck, *RD*, 4:720.

128. Cf. Jonathan Edwards, "Misc. no. 182," *WJE* 13:328: "And in all probability, the abode of the saints after the resurrection will be so contrived by God, that there shall be external beauties and harmonies altogether of another kind from what we perceive here, and probably those beauties will appear chiefly on the bodies of the man Christ Jesus and of the saints."

129. See my discussion in Sublime Comedy: The Theodramatic Form of the Divine Plan.

first Adam who in effect pulled down the whole world with himself to brokenness and futility, but Christ as the last Adam and High King of the universe pulls all that he redeems with him to glory.

It is thus perfectly fitting for the present realm of creation to be incorporated in the reconciliation (in redemption) of all things to God through Christ, thereby renewing creation to be perfectly fit for the beatific life of the saints with God. So when Paul, for example, refers to "the present form (σχῆμα) of this world" as something that is "passing away" (1 Cor 7:31), a fair reading is that the world "in its present, sin-damaged form" (Gestalt) is not preserved in the final apocalypse (cf. 1 John 2:17). "Accordingly, with reference to the passing of the present world," writes Bavinck, "we must no more think of a destruction of substance than [we would] with regard to the passing of the earlier world in the flood."[130] Or to make the point here positively, what will not pass away in the final apocalypse is the substantial nature (Gehalt) of the world.

The apostle Peter describes the passing away of the old order in more graphic terms, but the underlying meaning concerning the world order of the earth is the same. As regards the earth, the fire that "will melt away in a blaze" the heavens is in this case, indeed, *that of a refiner*— purifying and purging so that "the earth and every deed done on it will be laid bare" (2 Pet 3:10; also v. 12 NET).[131] This means that the new creation is not the creation *ex nihilo* of another world, but it speaks rather to the radical nature of the present order of creation's consummative transformation.[132] In this way a kind of analogy holds

---

130. Bavinck, *RD*, 4:717.

131. For a helpful treatment on this passage concerning the various interpretive options proposed for understanding the apostle's graphic apocalyptic language as it applies to the heavens and the earth, see Peter H. Davids, *The Letters of 2 Peter and Jude* (PNTC; Grand Rapids: Eerdmans, 2006), 282–87.

132. Cf. Bavinck, *RD*, 4:720: "Just as the caterpillar becomes a butterfly, as carbon is converted into diamond, as the grain of wheat upon dying in the ground produces other grains of wheat, as all of nature revives in the spring and dresses up in celebrative clothing, as the believing community is formed out of Adam's fallen race, as the resurrection body is raised from the body that is dead and buried in the earth, so too, by the re-creating power of Christ, the new heaven and the new earth will one day emerge from the fire-purged elements of this world, radiant in enduring glory and forever set free from the 'bondage to decay' [Rom. 8:21]."

between the new earth and the resurrection bodies of the saints. With respect to the latter, while there will be radical qualitative discontinuity between the "natural body" (σῶμα ψυχικόν) and the "spiritual body" (σῶμα πνευματικόν), an essential continuity nevertheless maintains in that the resurrection bodies of the saints are still *human* bodies. "We are creatures of time and space," writes Michael Horton, "and we will transcend not our humanity but the bondage of our humanity to the conditions of sin and death."[133] Likewise, while there will be radical qualitative discontinuity between the earth in its present form and the new earth in its consummative form, an essential continuity maintains with respect to the substantial nature of the earth.[134]

That the divine plan maintains an essential continuity between the present order of creation and the new order of creation is corroborated by the Old Testament prophetic visions concerning the restoration and renewal of the judgment-cursed earth. Worth noting in particular are the vision narratives in Isaiah 65:17–25 and Ezekiel 47:1–12.[135] With respect to Isaiah, the preceding context in 64:10–65:7 makes plain that the rebelliousness and corruption of the people have precipitated the devastation of the land ("Zion has become a wilderness, Jerusalem a desolation," 64:10). According to Mark Stephens, the Lord's subsequent declaration in Isaiah 65:17—"For behold, I create new heavens and a new earth"—is best construed not as new creation *ex nihilo*, but as a "transformation which retains some form of continuity with the present." For what God promises here is that "God himself will bring about a new state of affairs for his faithful servants, by exercising his

---

133. Horton, *The Christian Faith: A Systematic Theology for Pilgrims On the Way*, 989.

134. Cf. Stephens, *Annihilation or Renewal?*, 257: "In the same way that Paul could speak of an individual's body dying (1 Cor 15:36), and then that same body being raised to a qualitatively different kind of existence (1 Cor 15:42–49), so [the apostle] John envisages the old creation dying (or ending), only for it to be transformed into a qualitatively different kind of existence. The helpfulness of this metaphor lies in the way it at once affirms both discontinuity and continuity in a single label." See also Anthony A. Hoekema, *The Bible and the Future* (Grand Rapids: Eerdmans, 1979), 280.

135. With debts following here to Stephens, *Annihilation or Renewal?*, specifically, his larger discussion in chapter 2, New Creation in the Hebrew Bible, and chapter 6, New Creation in Revelation (II): The Key Texts.

sovereign creative power to impart order and harmony where there is now presently chaos and discord."[136]

The Ezekiel passage, on the other hand, depicts post-exilic restoration and renewal by showing the curse on the land being reversed by a fructifying river that flows from an eschatological temple. Having been given a visionary tour of the eschatological temple (chapters 40–42), here Ezekiel describes how the effluence of this temple-stream affects with life and healing all the dead and sterile regions it flows to—"everything will live where the river goes" (Ezek 47:9). The fountain and wellspring of all the fecundity and blessing is the sanctuary of the Lord (Ezek 47:12), with the striking Edenic imagery (cf. Gen 2:8–10, 16–17) lending a sense of continuity between the old order and the new in the resultant transformation of the land. Stephens sums it up thus: "Coming as it does before the account of the boundaries and division of the land (Ezek 47:13–48:35), it indicates Yahweh's intent to heal the cursed ground and to remove its defilement."[137]

Similarly, John's vision narrative in Revelation 4 and 5, which inaugurates the "apocalypse proper" at the head of the main theodrama that follows, also corroborates how the creational-re-creational symmetry of the divine plan maintains an essential continuity between the present order of creation and the new order of creation. The throne of God, theologically so central throughout Revelation in magnifying God's majestic sovereignty, predominates in the vision in chapter 4, "climax-[ing] with a hymnic acclamation of God as Creator (Rev 4:11)."[138] Given how the hymn spotlights God as Creator, Stephens argues that hermeneutically this ties in to the creational motifs earlier in the chapter. Of consequence for our purposes is the image of a rainbow "around the throne" (Rev 4:3). If Stephens is correct, the rainbow imagery alludes at least in part to the Noahic covenant. In connection with the accent

---

136. Stephens, *Annihilation or Renewal?*, 27.

137. Stephens, *Annihilation or Renewal?*, 33–34. Stephens adds in closing, "To be sure, the locus for Ezekiel's eschatological restoration is narrowly circumscribed within the confines of the land of Palestine. In Ezekiel we do not detect a universal dimension to the eschatological restoration, such as is hinted at in the work of Isaiah. Nevertheless, Ezekiel provides greater depth to his vision of a transformed world, even to the point of depicting specific places which will experience blessing."

138. Stephens, *Annihilation or Renewal?*, 173.

on God as Creator, this suggests that, in the final analysis, the eschatological drama to come upon the earth in the form of seal, trumpet, and bowl judgments would be tempered with the kind of divine mercy we see ingredient to the Noahic covenant (Gen 8:20–22; 9:9–17).[139]

Revelation 21 gives us another picture of God speaking from his heavenly throne directly to the implied audience. The last time God was pictured as such was in Revelation 4, a point that serves to underscore the significance of the utterance. Just prior John already had announced the debut of "a new heaven and a new earth" (Rev 21:1). Discontinuity is certainly evident with the eradication of the sea (Rev 21:1) and death (Rev 21:4), signifying altogether "the cessation of all God-opposing and life-destroying forces which bring threat to creation."[140] There is discontinuity entailed as well with the appearing of the new order of creation, for the "the first heaven and the first earth had passed away (ἀπῆλθαν)."[141] A distinction in this case, however, is to be made in recognizing both continuity and discontinuity. The present created order in and of itself is not necessarily eradicated, but rather "the provisional, sinful and vulnerable order in which death was at play, and the threat of chaos remained."[142] Thus, however fantastic the transformation will be from the "first heaven and first earth" to the "new heaven and new

---

139. Stephens explains further, "This is important, because if one were to read, in isolation, the cumulative visions of destruction that follow, such visions could potentially be construed as evincing an annihilationist attitude towards creation. But with their being preceded by this opening vision of the heavenly court, John creates an undercurrent of cosmic renewal to the surface imagery of cosmic destruction." Stephens, *Annihilation or Renewal?*, 191.

140. Stephens, *Annihilation or Renewal?*, 242. In a symbolic sense the sea is well known in ancient Near Eastern mythology and throughout the Scripture canon as being a kind of archetype of the forces of chaos, death, and destruction. John's reference to the earthly sea in Revelation 21:1 is to be distinguished from his reference to the empyreal sea in Revelation 15:2.

141. BDAG 102 s.v. ἀπέρχομαι 2: to discontinue as a condition or state. Stephens, *Annihilation or Renewal?*, 230, comments thus: "The verb ἀπέρχομαι (employed in 21:1) can often be used figuratively to mean the cessation of a state or condition. Indeed, John appears to use it in this fashion on two earlier occasions, where ἀπέρχομαι is used to describe the cessation of a state of woe (9:12; 11:14). Therefore, it is legitimate to press beyond a phenomenological interpretation, and instead render ἀπῆλθαν with a phrase like 'passed away,' a translation which implies that something significant about the first heaven and earth has indeed come to an end."

142. Stephens, *Annihilation or Renewal?*, 242.

earth," the "all things" (πάντα) that God makes new in Revelation 21:5 need not be read as the utter annihilation of the present creational order. The "all things" at issue here, moreover, stands in deliberate parallel with the "all things" in Revelation 4:11, which, as we referenced above, involves acclaiming God as Creator. In this way, it is fair to say, God's honor as Creator is shown to be perfectly unimpeachable as *creatio originalis* becomes *creatio nova* not through annihilation of the former but through its redemptive-eschatological transformation to glorified newness. Thus, the greatest love that God could (and did!) show humanity as Redeemer by way of the Son's laying down his life on their behalf, expresses with it the delight he has never lost for his creation and the honor he bestows on it as Consummator in its consummative renewal in consequence of the Son's atoning work. "A new song will be sung in heaven (Rev 5:9, 10), but the original order of creation will remain," explains Bavinck, "at least to the extent that all distinctions of nature and grace will once and for all be done away with. Dualism will cease. Grace does not remain outside or above or beside nature but rather permeates and wholly renews it. And thus nature, reborn by grace, will be brought to its highest revelation."[143]

The theological interpretation given above is compatible as well with Paul's teaching in Romans 8:19-23. Rich in theological import is his remarkable statement in verses 20-21, declaring that the "hope" of a future redemption is already entailed in creation being subjected to futility in the Adamic fall (cf. Isaiah 24-26). For the cosmic ramifications from the judgment curse of God in Genesis 3 will be overturned to realize at last the hope in which God subjected the world to futility. In some mysterious sense the present creation itself has been eagerly awaiting to "be set free from its bondage to corruption and obtain the freedom of the glory of the children of God" (Rom 8:21). The birth pangs metaphor with which Paul describes the whole creation—"groaning together in the pains of childbirth until now" (Rom 8:22)—suggests that the present creation, affected by sin, will become in the eschatological gestation of history, born-again as the glorious new creation. Bavinck captures the point nicely: "Just as anyone in Christ is a new creation in

---

143. Herman Bavinck, "Common Grace," trans. Raymond C. Van Leeuwen, *Calvin Theological Journal* 24 (1988), 59-60.

whom the old has passed away and everything has become new (2 Cor 5:17), so also this world passes away in its present form as well, in order out of its womb, at God's word of power, to give birth and being to a new world."[144] This new world to come involves the "restoration of all things" (Acts 3:21), itself bound up with the participation of the whole creation in the redemption and revelation of glorified sons of God. The picture the apostle Paul paints, then, is that the transformation of creation is its redintegration, and this corresponds directly to the liberation of creation from its present bondage and futility—all of which correlates to the liberation of the children of God. And that liberation of the sons of God is when their adoption will be fully revealed and realized in the redemption of their bodies, which is to say, the glorification of their bodies (cf. Phil 3:21).

The Sublime Comedy:
The Happy-Ever-After Ending Begins

The happy-ever-after ending of the theodrama—that is the beautiful ending for the people of God because most of all they will live and move with Christ *in Deo*, deified by the Spirit, knowing God by way of God.[145] In the age to come the redeemed of all the ages will experience the sublimity of the new creation as the beatific life in the new heavens and new earth, the realization *in concreto* of the eternal realm of the consummated kingdom of God. In this kingdom realm God's creational intention for humanity becomes fully realized in flourishing lives of eternal shalom for the children of God in glorious Spirit-filled communion with God. "Shalom incorporates *delight* in one's relationships," states Nicholas Wolterstorff. "To dwell in shalom is to find delight in living rightly before God, to find delight in living rightly in one's physical surroundings, to find delight in living rightly with one's fellow human beings, and to find delight even in living rightly with oneself."[146] Uniquely characterizing the sublime comedy, the eschatological

---

144. Bavinck, *RD*, 4:717.

145. Farrow, *Ascension Theology*, 150.

146. Nicholas Wolterstorff, *Educating for Shalom: Essays on Christian Higher Education*, ed. Clarence W. Joldersma and Gloria Goris Stronks (Grand Rapids: Eerdmans, 2004), 23.

fulfillment of God's master plan thus brings something incomparably and everlastingly more glorious than its protological beginning.

With the eradication of sin and evil, the new creation and its inhabitants will be characterized not only as "very good" but as "consummately good" because fellowship with God will be consummated. According to our theological aesthetic, moreover, what uniquely characterizes the subjectively experienced aspect of the beauty expressed in God's outward works is its effect of evoking pleasure or delight in the act of perceiving it. God's new humanity in God's new creation will not labor under the judgment curse he pronounced in Genesis 3. Thus, the delight that beauty evokes in the act of perceiving it will be as God intended it because new humanity's ability to rightly perceive and experience God's beauty will be as he intended it. Not least of all, the eternal affect of beholding the beauty of the Lord will be the purest response of worship—an unalloyed reflection of God's own beatitude expressed as doxological delight. For Jonathan Edwards, this translates to God communicating his happiness out of his own fullness of Being: "This happiness consists in enjoying and rejoicing in himself, and so does also the creature's happiness. 'Tis, as has been observed of the other, a participation of what is in God; and God and his glory are the objective ground of it. ... And the communication itself is no other, in the very nature of it, than that wherein the very honor, exaltation and praise of God consists."[147] As those who will be glorified partakers of the divine nature, the capacity of the redeemed to consummately delight in God and in everything that is true, good, and beautiful is thereby also perfected.

Furthermore, the consummation of our salvation involves the fully realized inheritance of all the benefits of our salvation founded on the person and work of Christ. As we saw previously concerning the redemptive work of Christ accomplished on our behalf, those benefits are identified both in negative terms in which the redeemed are liberated *from* something and in positive terms in which they are liberated *for* something. Francis Turretin encapsulates the point in rich dichotomies: "There will be light without darkness, joy without grief, peace

---

147. Edwards, "Concerning the End for Which God Created the World," *WJE* 8:442.

without war, glory without disgrace, tranquility without labor, security without fear, truth without falsehood, happiness without misery, riches without poverty and life without death."[148] The final two chapters of Revelation identify in broad terms a succession of things that speak to what will never more exist in the consummated kingdom of God. As regards those things in which the redeemed are liberated "from" in the eschaton, we have already touched on certain of these, so for our purposes here it will suffice simply to cite portions of the relevant texts in Revelation 21–22 that mention the things in question:

- "the first heaven and the first earth had passed away, and the sea was no more" (Rev 21:1).

- "He will wipe away every tear from their eyes, and death shall be no more, neither shall there be mourning, nor crying, nor pain anymore, for the former things have passed away" (Rev 21:4; cf. Isa 25:8).

- "But as for the cowardly, the faithless, the detestable, as for murderers, the sexually immoral, sorcerers, idolaters, and all liars, their portion will be in the lake that burns with fire and sulfur, which is the second death" (Rev 21:8).

- "and its gates will never be shut by day—and there will be no night there" (Rev 21:25; cf. Rev 22:5).

- "But nothing unclean will ever enter, nor anyone who does what is detestable or false, but only those who are written in the Lamb's book of life" (Rev 21:27).

- "No longer will there be anything accursed" (Rev 22:3).

In all these ways captured in John's vision narrative (and unquestionably in countless and unspoken other ways), Scripture conveys in

---

148. Turretin, *IET*, vol. 3, Topic XII, Quest. VIII, Sec. XVIII (page 613). Edwards, *Charity and Its Fruits*, Sermon 15, *WJE* 8:371, elaborates on this idea in compatible terms: "There shall be no pollution or deformity of any kind seen in any one person or thing. Everyone is perfectly pure, all over lovely; everything shall be perfectly pleasant. That world is perfectly bright without darkness, perfectly clear without spot. There shall be none appearing with any defects, either natural or moral. There is nothing seen there which is sinful, nothing weak or foolish. Nothing shall appear to which nature is averse, nothing which shall offend the most delicate eye. There shall be no string out of tune to cause any jar in the harmony of that world, no unpleasant note to cause any discord."

categorical terms how the cosmic ramifications from the judgment curse of God in Genesis 3 are forever overturned. "The new creation is distinguished from the old [in part] by the *absence* of all forces which would bring corruption, pain, or chaos. Hence, the new creation has no place for sinful moral agents or the chaotic sea, and the thought of death and mourning can no longer be countenanced."[149] To reiterate John's way of gathering it all up in Revelation 22:3, there will no longer be any curse (κατάθεμα).[150]

Now in regard to those things in which the redeemed are liberated "for" in the eschaton, we have discussed certain of these already as well. But before moving on it will be of value to recapitulate the celebrated ones we have addressed. Included are the following aspects:

- Adoptive sonship will be that dearest and most precious privilege the redeemed come to know in a consummative way in filial relationship with the Father through the Son in the Spirit.

- The redeemed will have a body that is biologized pneumatically with the life-giving Spirit of Christ. Our bodily redemption is at the same time our completed spiritual redemption from sin in which our re-created and glorified selves live everlastingly in the freedom of the *non posse peccare* and of the *non posse mori*.

- The ethical-relational dimension of all interpersonal relationship among the redeemed will be reflective of that mutual love and eternal delight the Father, Son, and Holy Spirit in which also is entailed their infinitely deserving regard for one another.

- The official aspect of image-bearing will be eschatologically fulfilled through how the redeemed come to share in the glory and honor of Christ's High Kingship and High Priesthood.

- The redeemed are brought to eschatological perfection in consummative blessedness—their glorification confirmed in beatitude—experiencing in an eternal and fully glorified way the pure enjoyment of God's presence.

- God will dwell with his people so intimately, it is appropriate to describe the communion of the saints as the church deified by the

---

149. Stephens, *Annihilation or Renewal?*, 257.
150. L&N 33.474 s.v. κατάθεμα: "that which has been cursed—'cursed, accursed.'"

Spirit, living and moving with Christ *in Deo* like a Bride made beautiful in her glory, living and moving in covenantal union with her Lord in his glory.

• As those who will be glorified partakers of the divine nature, the capacity of the redeemed to consummately delight in God and in everything that is true, good, and beautiful is thereby also perfected.

Another side of Scripture's eschatological imagery speaks to a constellation of aspects that together highlight the flourishing, vitality, celebration and doxological praise of God's people in a flourishing new creation. Writ large in this constellation of aspects is the creational-re-creational symmetry of the divine plan in connection with the happy-ever-after ending of the theodrama. Included in this is the Edenic imagery in Revelation 22:1-2, which, at the macro level, represents what the garden of Eden in Genesis 2:8-17 meant at the micro level as part of God's creational intention for humanity. In a real sense the new earth in its entirety is God's new-creational garden of delight, unsurpassably more than just creational paradise regained, it is *paradise consummated*, if you will. As the sacred spacetime where God's image-bearing sons and daughters will experience the pure enjoyment of his presence, it is the Edenic paradise consummately realized. Of note is how "the spring of the water of life" described in Revelation 21:6 becomes "the river of the water of life" in Revelation 22:1 (cf. Ps 46:4-5), mirroring in effect the swelling of the temple-stream in Ezekiel 47:1-12. As well, the tree of life in the garden of Eden, alluded to by John first in Revelation 2:7, appears in 22:1 on each side of the river of life and producing twelve varieties of fruit. "Even the leaves of the tree," observes Gundry, "will be used as a poultice for the healing of the nations of redeemed peoples who make up the new Jerusalem. John promises eternal good health for their resurrected bodies—preventative medicine to the utmost."[151] The river of the water of life, the trees of life, the leaves for healing—all of these together bring out a key dimension that characterizes the holism of the Lord's salvation, namely, complete and eternal well-being in all respects of the whole person for all the people of God. Edwards ties it up pneumatically:

---

151. Gundry, "The New Jerusalem: People as Place, Not Place for People," 406.

There the Holy Spirit shall be poured forth with perfect sweetness, as a pure river of water of life, clear as crystal ... a river whose waters are without any manner of pollution. And every member of that glorious society shall be without blemish of sin or imprudence or any kind of failure. ... In that world, wherever the inhabitants turn their eyes they shall see nothing but beauty and glory.[152]

Thus in ever-renewing fashion God will nourish his people with living water and trees of life and healing. And in inseverable union with Christ through his life-giving Spirit, he will be their delight and they will flourish forevermore (cf. Isa 55:1; John 4:10, 14).

One other set of eschatological imagery I will mention that bespeaks fellowship, celebration, and doxological praise in the age to come has to do with reference to "the banquet at the wedding celebration of the Lamb" (Rev 19:9 NET) and portrayals of anthemic praise. From this standpoint, the way the world as we know it ends is with neither a bang nor a whimper, but with the marriage feast of the Lamb. The supreme joy and intimate fellowship between Christ and his church—Bridegroom and Bride—is reflected in the imagery of that feast. Then at last will be realized Jesus' words that "many will come from the east and west to share the banquet with Abraham, Isaac, and Jacob in the kingdom of heaven" (Matt 8:11 NET; cf. Matt 22:1–14). At that time, too, will Jesus make good on his eschatologically-charged announcement to his disciples that he would not eat of his last Passover supper nor drink wine with them "until it is fulfilled in the kingdom of God" (Luke 22:16–18).[153] As regards the aspect of anthemic praise, the messianic fulfillment of universalizing praise and blessing that is represented in the concluding *hallel* of Psalms 146–150 is gloriously portrayed throughout Revelation. From the depths of their very being the saints are in this respect worshiping God and the Lamb as *homo laudatur/homo adorator*,

---

152. Edwards, *Charity and Its Fruits*, Sermon 15, *WJE* 8:371.

153. Cf. Adam Warner Day, "Eating Before the Lord: A Theology of Food according to Deuteronomy," *JETS* 57 no. 1 (March 2014): 95, writes, "Food has an innate celebratory quality, and is one of the ways that human beings experience blessing, joy, and fullness. When the Israelites reflected on the fact that Yahweh was the one who continually providing food for them, it was to bring an experience of joyful worship. ... The feasts were not merely about food, they were about the Israelites' relationship to Yahweh." See, for example, Deuteronomy 16:15; 28:4–5, 11–12.

reflecting back to God in doxological act the praise, honor, and glory due his name (cf. Rev 19:5–7; Isa 12:2–6). "Most pervasive of all is the singing of the saints in heaven over their redemption and glory (Rev 5:6–14; 7:9–12; 14:1–3; 15:2–4)."[154] Here the words of the psalmist for the people of God achieve their highest aesthetic end—"For it is good to sing praises to our God; for it is pleasant, and a song of praise is fitting" (Ps 147:1; cf. Ps 104:33). As that wonderful verse in *Amazing Grace* proclaims, "When we've been there ten thousand years, Bright shining as the sun, We've no less days to sing God's praise Than when we'd first begun."

What life will be like in the age to come for the children of God is one of those wonderful imponderables. In the same way, we can be certain that on this side of the veil what we know and experience of beauty in all its expressions will be transcended beyond what we can even possibly conceive of and imagine. In his book *Edwards the Exegete*, Douglas Sweeney offers a splendid distillation of the Bible's meta-story, reflective of how Jonathan Edwards understood it:

> His rendition of redemption had a tragic-comic plot—heavy with sin, suffering, death, and eternal reprobation. But its Hero saved the day, asking everyone to marry Him. The lovely ones who found it in their hearts to consent would live happily ever after in a city paved with gold. To many late-modern readers, this appears to be a fairy tale, far too good to be true. But to Edwards it was veridical—as true as true could be.[155]

Striking the same fundamental overtone as Edwards, the note we will simply end on here is a happy one. It is the same note we have called the happy-ever-after ending of the theodrama, seen through an aesthetic lens as a sublime comedy. In God's reconciling all things to himself through Christ in the redemptive-eschatological fulfillment of his original creational purposes, the final dramatic movement of the happy-ever-after ending is fully realized. A glorious new order is come for the redeemed of all the ages in the consummated kingdom of God.

---

154. "Music" in *DBI*, 576–78, here 578.

155. Douglas A. Sweeney, *Edwards the Exegete: Biblical Interpretation and Anglo-Protestant Culture on the Edge of the Enlightenment* (New York: Oxford University Press, 2016), 183.

Such an ending should bring a smile to our face, a smile that envisions being utterly content simply to bask in the smile of God's countenance upon us. Therein at last will be fully realized for all of God's sons and daughters the yearning of David's heart—to gaze upon the beauty of the Lord Jesus, the beauty of our Redeemer-King. And on *that* most wonderful of notes, I conclude with a beautiful description by P. T. Forsyth of the heavenly smile upon that which will eternally ever remain God's sublime comedy: "Heaven does not laugh loud but it laughs last—when all the world will laugh in its light. It is a smile more immeasurable than ocean's and more deep; it is an irony gentler and more patient than the bending skies, the irony of a long love and the play of its sure mastery; it is the smile of the holy in its silent omnipotence of mercy."[156]

---

156. P. T. Forsyth, *The Justification of God: Lectures for War-Time on a Christian Theodicy* (New York: C. Scribner's Sons, 1917), 215.

7

Conclusion

The question posed by Hans Urs von Balthasar that I cited in the Introduction is appropriate to reiterate now as before: "May it not be that we have a real and inescapable obligation to probe the possibility of there being a genuine relationship between theological beauty and the beauty of the world."[1] In affirmation of that relationship, this book has demonstrated that the objective beauty of the person of Christ, the beauty of the work of Christ (redemption accomplished), and the beauty of Christ's work ongoing through the Holy Spirit (redemption applied) are the preeminent aspects of God's "beautiful self-showing" according to the redemptive-eschatological fulfillment of his original creational purposes. In all of this the Son's glory is always fittingly manifest in every stage of the theodrama. With respect to the divine economy in general, my argument is that the theodrama (creation, redemption, and consummation) entails a consistent and fitting expression and outworking of God's beauty, displaying in time the eternal beauty and fittingness of the immanent Trinity.

This required, in the first place, putting forward a theological aesthetic model of the doctrine of God since my argument is premised on the properly dogmatic ground of the Son's fittingness being God's beauty. Admittedly, this model will be controversial first and foremost because the claim that beauty is an attribute of God's nature, as I discussed in my Introduction, lacks consensus in systematic theology offered within a broadly evangelical perspective, if it is even considered at all. Two key reasons why people disagree over whether beauty is a divine perfection

---

1. Hans Urs von Balthasar, *GL*, I, 80.

or not would seem related also to beauty's conceptual ambiguity and its deceptive power. I offered biblical evidence and theological warrant in argument that beauty properly should be considered a perfection of the divine nature, but this matter obviously will not be considered closed on this point.[2] The theological aesthetic model of the doctrine of God I proposed is developed on that premise, and is meant to serve as the properly dogmatic ground for the thesis argued in the subsequent chapters. Besides serving that present purpose, it is also put forward as a theological aesthetic consideration of the doctrine of God in the larger interests of inviting additional engagement and discussion in systematic theology from this perspective.

The theological aesthetic I have argued regarding the Son's fitting-ness as incarnate Redeemer is developed in connection with the theme of the *imago Dei*, which has its tie-in to the idea of God's people being conformed to the image of Christ. So our theological aesthetic has its protological moorings in the biblical creation account because God's original creational purposes are ultimately fulfilled in Christ, the central one being the fate of the creature made in God's image. None of that is particularly controversial. But defining what constitutes the *imago Dei* remains a controverted matter. The theological interpretation of the *imago Dei* I offer says that everything constitutive of the image of God is comprehended in three principal aspects—the official (royal priest), constitutional (whole person, i.e., body-soul), and ethical-relational. All three aspects have their fair share of scholarly support, although not necessarily as comprehended together. My argument here rests on a theological concept of the *imago Dei* having its fullest and clearest witness in the New Testament, with Christ himself as the incarnate image of God who embodies the divine purpose for humanity in accordance with which the first Adam was created. Within the structure of my overall argument this sets out the principal aspects of what it means for humans to bear the divine image, that is, to be-like-God in the world, with the Son incarnate being the archetype. I also argue here that the

---

2. Yet neither is the argument that beauty is a divine attribute an outlier claim for the doctrine of God, for my argument is standing on the shoulders of the illustrious theologians I feature from different church traditions and periods of church history (and many others besides) who affirmed the same.

notions of sacred time represented by God's Sabbath rest and sacred space represented by the garden of Eden point to God's creational purposes for humanity, which will also be fulfilled through Christ, and is all part of the beautiful ending for the people of God I describe in the final chapter.

The core point this work has argued concerning the Son's fittingness as incarnate Redeemer takes up in effect the task Kevin Vanhoozer sets out that I had referenced earlier: "The vocation of the theological interpreter of Scripture is to render judgments—ethical, epistemological, and yes, metaphysical—concerning what is 'meet and right' for Christians to affirm of God on the basis of the various modes of divine self-showing, self-giving, and self-saying."[3] The focus of this work has been to shine the spotlight on the self-showing of what God has done/is doing in Christ. The self-showing at issue pertains to the glory of God in Christ in every stage of the theodrama. Beauty, as I have argued it, is a quality of God's glory and thus the display of God's glory is always beautiful, always fitting, always entails an aesthetic dimension to it. A question integral to my thesis is not whether Jesus' glory was perceived by everyone during his earthly career—we know that it was not and that those who did perceive it are identified as having faith in Jesus. However it has remained an open question as to whether the form of Christ's humanity functioned at all to hide his glory during the state of his humiliation in the form of a slave. While not a particularly live topic of scholarly discussion, it seems that expressed opinions when one comes across them are mixed on this. The view I defend agrees with those who say that Christ's humanity did not function to hide his glory. My argument extends this view in defense that the theodramatic fittingness of the Son corresponds to the form of his humanity in the economy of salvation. "Theodramatic" qualifies the person of Christ in the various aspects of his messianic identity that he lives out and fulfills, that is, his being and doing as displayed predominantly in his obedient relationship to the Father demonstrated through the experiences of his earthly life. The eternal beauty/fittingness of the immanent Trinity proposed in my theological aesthetic model of the doctrine of

3. Kevin J. Vanhoozer, *Remythologizing Theology: Divine Action, Passion, and Authorship* (Cambridge: Cambridge University Press, 2010), 198.

God is evinced in, or is at least consistent with, the Son's fittingness as incarnate Redeemer, whose glory is expressed appropriately in and through whichever form of his economic identity is in view.

The theological aesthetic argument for the Son's fittingness as his perfect conformity to the form of his humanity in the undertaking of his messianic mission involves no redefining of the person and work of Christ as traditional orthodoxy accepts. And that is a good thing. The import of my theological aesthetic argument to Christology is that it provides a sound basis to affirm the glory of God in Christ during his earthly career as being a divine self-showing that was always God's unveiled glory expressed most fittingly in and through the form of the Son's humanity. Given the various modes of God's self-revelation in and through the form of Christ's humanity, the theological aesthetic argument is not a reductionist impulse of aesthetics being read into Christology, but stems from reflection on the aesthetic dimension of what God was/is doing in Christ. On that basis, I have argued, the glory of Christ manifest while in the form of a slave was no less his unveiled glory than it was at the event of his transfiguration, nor was he emptied of his glory in his crucified form; it rather magnified it. My argument is not an over-realized theology of glory, however, but an affirmation of a theology of God's grace in his saving work through Christ appreciated through a theological aesthetic lens. In a word, the Son's mission/work is beautiful always and everywhere to everyone who has eyes to see it. An entailment of my thesis is that the Son's fittingness as incarnate Redeemer points up the perfect fittingness—aesthetic and otherwise— within the tapestry of God's plan and purposes that he has realized in Christ Jesus. In this light the event of Jesus' baptism, which he affirms as fitting to fulfill all righteousness, serves to highlight the aspect of fittingness in his whole messianic undertaking to fulfill all righteousness. This is evident as well in how the author of Hebrews takes up the notion of fittingness in direct reference to God's redemptive work through Christ concerning his being perfectly qualified to become our high priestly mediator.

Fundamental to the argument of this work is that the ground of the Son's fittingness is God's beauty, which entails that everything God does is perfectly fitting—and hence beautiful in its God-glorifying nature.

A challenge I address, related to the traditional evangelical view of the penal substitution theory of Christ's atonement, is the form of God's glory pertaining to his judgment upon Christ in the place of sinners. I contend that the retributive justice rendered by the Father upon Christ was perfectly fitting in its due proportionality between the collective "crime" committed against God and the judgment meted out upon Christ. At the same time the beauty of God's glory is seen in the perfect equipoise of God's righteous holy love, where his perfect justice is reconciled with the most condescending mercy. Another aspect I argue is with respect to God's work through Christ in the state of his heavenly exaltation. The Son's fittingness as incarnate Redeemer is not something that served to display his glory only during earthly career but does so in every stage of the theodrama, which obviously includes his heavenly exaltation. In this latter state, Christ's glory is manifest in an already but not-yet order of reality governed under the preeminence of his heavenly rule. Based on Paul's letter to the Ephesians, I argue that God's reconciling operations through the reign of Christ evince the beautiful nature of his work in the form of an already but not-yet unity and harmony operating in the spheres of human-divine relations and human-human relations in the perfecting of his church.

The subject of the perfecting of God's people brings us around to the protological moorings of our theological aesthetic, which began with the spotlight on humanity's identity and destiny as image of God, the essence of which is to be-like-God in the world. In God's master plan, his creational purposes are ultimately fulfilled in Christ such that God's people are ultimately conformed to the image of the Son incarnate, and altogether as one body arrayed in holy splendor. I draw the theological implication that Christian fittingness, understood as God's people living in conformity to their identity in Christ, is both modeled after Christ's theodramatic fittingness during his earthly career as represented in the Scriptures, and based on Christ, as the incarnate image of God, being the full measure of the image in which humans were created and thus the full measure of the image-bearing glory inherent in and expressed through his human form. An appreciation of how Christ's theodramatic fittingness serves to display his glory in every stage of the theodrama not only gives proper acknowledgment to this aspect of

God's own self-witness, but serves what "learning Christ" means for living out fittingly one's identity in Christ.

The denouement of the christological contours of beauty presents the eschatological realization of humanity's identity and destiny as image of God, which means that the redeemed in Christ become in a consummative way—fully realized and glorified—who they already are in Christ. These will be sons and daughters of God who will reflect their consummative transformation into the image of Christ, and altogether as the church who will reflect her form as the glorified Bride of Christ. God's people will be perfectly fitted for sharing eternal life with God and in God on the renewed earth, the sacred spacetime where they will experience the pure joy of the Father's presence through the Son in the Holy Spirit. My theological interpretations concerning the redeemed in their consummative state are within the evangelical mainstream; exceptions will be taken here and there of course. The content of the material at issue here highlights substantive points in keeping with my theological aesthetic regarding the consummation phase of the theodrama. The entailment of our thesis that everything God does is beautiful in whatever ways he displays his glory—I apply that to the judgment of damnation upon unredeemed sinners. The content of this material also highlights substantive points in keeping with my theological aesthetic, but admittedly the theological issues of my concern as they apply to damnation are quite plainly underdetermined by Scripture. With all humble regard for that fact, the theologoumenon I offer is an extrapolation of my theological aesthetic in consideration of what may perhaps be inferable regarding the fate of the creature made in God's image when that fate is one's complete severance from humanity's identity and destiny as image of God. I proposed that every human being who is damned in the final judgment is judicially and relationally stripped of sonship and image-bearing status and dignity. The damned as such will be human persons no longer constituted to reflect the image-bearing glory of God. They will be altogether glory-less.

The christological contours of a biblically based theology of beauty that I have put forward have involved theological consideration of an aspect of God's self-revelation generally overlooked when we speak about the doctrines of creation, fall, incarnation, redemption, and consummation, namely, the aesthetic dimension. While true that in the Introduction we granted the postulation that "righteousness in all the relations of man as a moral being is the key to [the Bible's] inspiration, the guiding light to correct understanding of its utterance. But it is everywhere inspired and writ in an atmosphere of aesthetics,"[4] it is fitting now to give backend theological reflection on beauty in relation to the plan and purposes of God that he has realized in Christ Jesus. In retrospect, the theory of beauty stemming out of the classical tradition that has served to fund the theological aesthetics with which our biblical and systematic theology of beauty as defined by the divine economy of redemption has been developed may now be more properly qualified. The transcendentals of truth, goodness, and beauty in God's work of creation, redemption, and consummation are strongly correlated, I have argued, because these attributes—coordinate with God's knowledge, will, and beatitude—are communicable perfections of God's essential nature and thus are expressed inherently in all his outward works. These transcendentals are mutually reinforcing, for what is true and good is likewise beautiful in form and content, and vice versa. There is therefore perfect correlation and unity between all that is true, good, and beautiful. Given that beauty is integral to God's essential nature, however, that reality in and of itself does not require that God conform his self-revelation to our this-worldly norms and notions of the beautiful. Keeping that in mind, theological aesthetics situates the beautiful as an entailment of whatever ways God displays his glory, that is, whatever is God-glorifying, most especially through the person and work of Christ. How theological aesthetics may or may not conform to our norms and notions of the beautiful or to our conceptualization of fittingness does not drive how we must understand and appreciate it. The plan of God as revealed in the economies of revelation and redemption in which all things are summed up in Christ Jesus drives the form and content of its theological aesthetics.

We see, for example, that in the epoch of this present evil age, the beautiful is not highlighted or weighted as the most pronounced aspect of the glory of God expressed in the economies of revelation

---

4. C. Caverno, "Beauty" in *The International Standard Bible Encyclopaedia*, vol. 1, ed. James Orr (Chicago: The Howard-Severance Company, 1915), 420.

and redemption. More specifically, in the economies of revelation and redemption the most pronounced aspect of God's self-revelation—that is, the cardinal quality with central significance—that highlights the glory of God in his righting all that is disordered and corrupted in this present evil age is not "beauty." Rather, it is the cardinal qualities of his righteousness, holiness and covenant love that are the most pronounced. Bavinck distills the panoramic picture of the divine plan in his own lapidary way: "The essence of the Christian religion consists in the reality that the creation of the Father, ruined by sin, is restored in the death of the Son of God, and re-created by the grace of the Holy Spirit into a kingdom of God."[5] Even in the visionary narrative of Revelation the accent with respect to God's cardinal qualities is on his being holy, true and righteous (e.g., Rev 15:3-4). In this light, one may see the fittingness in how God is revealed as righting for all time all that is wrong as it pertains to the entire order of created reality, and so reveals his holy, true and righteous nature to bear upon all unrighteousness and defilement.[6] As the apostle Peter puts it, "But according to his promise we are waiting for new heavens and a new earth in which righteousness dwells" (2 Pet 3:13). It seems theologically fair to say that the justice established for all eternity for the redeemed in Christ in the new heavens and earth—that realization *in concreto* of the eternal realm of the consummated kingdom of God characterized by its perfect shalom—will be a reflection of the primary justice that characterizes the mutuality within the Godhead. In this respect that perfect shalom will be reflective of that mutual love and eternal delight between the Father, Son, and Holy Spirit in which also is entailed their infinitely deserving regard for one another.

The theory of beauty stemming out of the classical tradition that has served to fund our theological aesthetic needs to be more properly qualified in the biblical key in terms of the "how much more" surplus at the end of the Bible's story, the happy-ever-after ending of the sublime comedy for the redeemed in Christ. Our theological aesthetic

---

5. Bavinck, *RD*, 1:61.

6. For a recommended treatment relevant to this point, see Robert C. Olson, *The Gospel As the Revelation of God's Righteousness: Paul's Use of Isaiah in Romans 1:1–3:26* (WUNT 2/428; Tübingen: Mohr Siebeck, 2016).

thus entails not only recognition of the symmetries, proportion and unity evident in the structure of the divine plan, but also recognition of its *aesthetic asymmetry and disproportion* evident in the surplus of the gloriousness of its consummation ending compared to its creation beginning. In this way a biblical-theological characterization of God's beauty as is reflected economically in the phases of creation, redemption, and consummation—notably in and through God the Son—culminates in surprising asymmetry and disproportion through what we might qualify as an *eschatological symmetry and proportion*. Like the notes in a musical score that sound discordant in isolation but within the larger musical composition sound fully concordant, any seemingly incongruous asymmetries within the form of the divine plan are best appreciated as contextualized within its overall eschatological form. Considering the overall scheme of things, then, why does not our theological aesthetic with its salient concepts of symmetry and fittingness lend itself to the plan of God being redemptively universalistic? It is a fair question, after all, in view of how our theological aesthetic is premised on the belief that everything God does is perfectly fitting—and hence beautiful (i.e., God-glorifying). Nevertheless, in the same way that God's self-revelation need not conform to our this-worldly norms and notions of the beautiful, so it is that God need not conform his overall plan and purposes in the divine economies of redemption and consummation to our this-worldly notions, preconceptions, or expectations of its outworking.

As I mentioned at the outset of this work, theological approaches to the subject of aesthetics are varied and most of the theological scholarship on aesthetics is being done in the way of religious aesthetics or theology of the arts. Within a broadly evangelical perspective, the primary neglect has been in the area of specifically biblical- and systematic-theological treatment. As a consequence, a theological view of beauty plays almost no part in the work and pedagogy of systematic theology and its contribution to Christian doctrine. The theological aesthetic argument of this work has given attention to this area in relation to the doctrine of God, Christology and the related theme of the *imago Dei*. The featured theologians that I positioned in its chapters—Irenaeus of Lyons, Anselm of Canterbury, Thomas Aquinas, Herman Bavinck,

Karl Barth, Hans Urs von Balthasar, and Jonathan Edwards—are the key luminaries across church history and traditions whose views on divine beauty/theological aesthetics have inspired and informed the work of this project. In the argumentation of my theological aesthetic I have recognized and in different ways affirmed key insights of theirs on beauty in the course of my theological interpretation of the biblical text, worked out in conjunction with a classicist theory of beauty. A brief review of some of their key insights is in order.

For all seven featured theologians, the fullness of God's being—that is, the plenitude of his perfections, is the glorious life of God *ad intra* (Irenaeus' work in this regard is nascent of course since the theological heritage from which he is working is very early in church history). The close correspondence of beauty with God's glory that is a critical point within my own argument is explicitly called out in Edwards, Bavinck, Balthasar, and Barth, although the exact nature of the correspondence differs between them. Among those four, Bavinck appears to equate beauty with God's glory, although his treatment is brief so he does not elaborate on that. For both Edwards and Balthasar, beauty is a perfection of God's glory; Edwards even accords it a certain preeminence of what distinguishes God from all other beings. In Barth's case beauty is not a perfection of God's glory but rather is the delight and pleasure for God that is awakened in us by the persuasive force in the form of the glory of his revelation to us. Barth's view of divine beauty, then, corresponds to what I described as the subjectively experienced aspect of beauty as distinguished from its objectively real aspect (for Barth, God's perfections themselves are beauty's ontological ground). Edwards' theological aesthetics as well as Balthasar's also affirm the subjective experience of delight that beauty elicits in beholding it, most especially in perceiving the beauty of God in Christ.[7] As I have also argued, the common denominator concerning such spiritual perception is the necessity for perceiving through "eyes of faith," which come from God.

---

7. In addition to its objectively real aspect, Anselm and Aquinas also affirmed the subjectively experienced aspect of beauty as part of its natural characteristic as a transcendental property of being but did not develop it in their theological aesthetics.

The crucial aspect of my thesis, of course, has to do with "fitting-ness," namely, the Son's fittingness as incarnate Redeemer, the properly dogmatic ground of which is God's beauty. As we saw in Chapter 2, both Anselm and Aquinas argue that it was most fitting for the Son to become incarnate Redeemer rather than the Father or the Holy Spirit based on the order of relations within the Godhead and the Son's role in the economy of redemption. Interestingly, fittingness is not one of Aquinas' three formal criteria of beauty—comprising proportion, integrity, clarity—but it is an important aspect he sees as applying to the roles of the divine persons in the economy. Anselm especially calls attention to the idea of fittingness as a defining characteristic of the aesthetic aspect of redemption, reflected in the evident symmetries entailed in its outworking. In his view the redemptive-eschatological structure of the divine plan demonstrates the aesthetic unity in which all things are governed and brought to their ultimate completion. The recapitulation of all things in Christ that so defines Irenaeus' theology represents another expression of the symmetry and unity entailed in the structure of the divine plan.

The concept of Christian fittingness that derives from the argument of my thesis ties in nicely with Irenaeus' view of the recapitulation of all things in Christ, which has at the heart of it the idea of the totality of human development being summed up and brought to perfection in the person and work of Christ. Irenaeus' concept that human beings must become "habituated" or "accustomed" to the participatory life offered in the incarnate Son likewise pertains to the Pauline idea of growing in conformity toward the full measure of Christ's image. The theological aesthetics of Balthasar and Edwards each emphasize in their own way the aesthetic dynamic involved in this already but not-yet reality. The essence is the same: whatever it fully means to be conformed to the image of Christ includes the dimension of becoming truly beautiful like him in the inner self, which is expressed through the outer, and experiencing the delight in the Lord that is part of that spiritual work.

It is my conviction that beauty is as true a metaphysical reality in the spiritual realm as it is in the material realm, and the Scriptures corrob-orate this. As such, theological approaches to the subject of aesthetics should properly include interdisciplinary engagement of systematic theology and the domain of aesthetics. Moreover, theological aesthetics not only is an area of relatively untapped potential for evangelical dogmatics today, but its value extends to theologically enriching and informing Christian praxis and spiritual formation in their fullest expressions. In other words, to speak, act, and live in ways that bear witness to the truth, goodness, and beauty of Christ Jesus. For God's work in this present age of forming and making beautiful his children and altogether his church involves his people growing in conformity toward the full measure of Christ's image as they live out fittingly their identity in Christ. And in the age to come is the eschatological realization of humanity's identity and destiny as image of God—the sons and daughters of God who will, at that time, reflect their consummative transformation into the image of Christ. In all respects the fittingness of God's people will be complete for sharing eternal life with God and in God because in all respects Christ is the archetype of humanity and for humanity through whom the redeemed are imaged eschatologically. Yet more, the gloriousness of God's plan and purposes comes to its crescendo with the identity and destiny of the church fully transformed as the glorified Bride of Christ, formed and adorned for her nuptial union with Christ, her Bridegroom. Therein at last will be fully realized for all of God's sons and daughters the yearning of David's heart—to gaze upon the beauty of the Lord Jesus, the beauty of our Redeemer-King. "He who testifies to these things says, 'Surely I am coming soon.' Amen. Come, Lord Jesus!" (Rev 22:20).

The General Witness of Scripture to the Aesthetic Dimension

At the lexical level both the Old Testament and the New Testament reveal a rich vocabulary of terms that convey a sense of beauty or aesthetics. Although Scripture's attestation to the aesthetic dimension is not accounted for merely in recognition of these various word groups, an aesthetic sense in the text may bring out a theologically thicker description of the biblical narrative. In her book, *Toward a Theology of Beauty: A Biblical Perspective*, Jo Ann Davidson provides a helpful compilation of terms that, at the lexical level of the Old Testament and New Testament, reveal a rich vocabulary that conveys a sense of beauty or aesthetics.[1] On the next two pages is an abbreviated summary borrowing in part from Davidson's work.[2]

---

1. Jo Ann Davidson, *Toward a Theology of Beauty: A Biblical Perspective* (Lanham, MD: University Press of America, 2008), 151–74.

2. For another recommended Old Testament word study on aesthetics, see William A. Dyrness, "Aesthetics in the Old Testament: Beauty in Context," *JETS* 28 no. 4 (December 1985): 421–32, especially 423–26.

TERMS EXPRESSIVE OF "BEAUTY"
IN THE OLD TESTAMENT

1. אוה—to be beautiful, desirable (*Nifal*).[3]

2. הדר / הָדָר / הֲדָרָה / הֶדֶר—to honor, adorn, make splendid/ornament, splendor/adornment, splendor, glory/ornament, adornment, splendor.[4]

3. הוֹד—splendor, majesty, vigor, glory and honor.

4. חמד—to desire, take pleasure in, be desirable.[5]

5. טוֹב—good, excellent, pleasant, beautiful, agreeable, delightful.[6]

6. יפה / יָפֶה / יֳפִי—to be beautiful/beautiful/beauty.[7]

7. כָּבוֹד—the large constellation of meanings includes the sense of weightiness, glory, power, wealth, honor, dignity, majesty and splendor.[8]

8. נאה / נָאוֶה—to be beautiful or befitting/beautiful, comely, suitable.[9]

9. נוה—to adorn, beautify, glorify.[10]

10. נצם / נָעֵם / נָעִים—to be pleasant, delightful, lovely/delightfulness, pleasantness/pleasant, delightful, lovely, beautiful.

11. פאָ—to beautify or glorify.[11]

12. צְבִי—beauty, ornament, decoration, honor.[12]

---

3. In this word group are several derivative nouns, all meaning "desire." Some lexicographers place the three occurrences of the verb in the *Nifal* under the verb נאה and not אוה.

4. The semantic range includes honor, adorn(ment), ornament, and glory, most often describing kingly majesty.

5. Several nouns and adjectives built on the verbal root also pertain. The semantic range includes pleasantness, preciousness, and desirability.

6. The broad semantic range includes both ethical and aesthetic meanings.

7. The semantic range includes the aspects of outward physical beauty.

8. The noun is frequently used in parallelism with synonyms connoting beauty or splendor.

9. This word family involves the state of being beautiful, as in suitable/befitting, appropriate, or desirable.

10. Occurs only in the Song of Moses, Exodus 15:2, in the *Hifil*.

11. תִּפְאֶרֶת / תִּפְאָרָה is the nominal derivative, frequently as an aesthetic synonym used in parallel relationship. When the subject is God or things precious to God, the meaning of תִּפְאֶרֶת relates either to beauty, glory-splendor, or honor.

12. Common usage is the sense of ornamental or decorative beauty. It also

13. מַרְאֶה—sight, appearance, countenance, beauty.[13]

14. שׁפר / שֶׁפֶר / שִׁפְרָה—to be beautiful, fair, comely/beauty, goodliness/fairness, clearness.

TERMS EXPRESSIVE OF "BEAUTY"
IN THE NEW TESTAMENT

1. ἀστεῖος—beautiful, well-pleasing, of personal grace and charm, well-bred.[14]

2. δόξα—glory, majesty, sublimity, splendor, radiance, brightness.[15]

3. εὐπρέπεια—fine appearance, beauty.[16]

4. καλός—beautiful, fine, morally good, useful, excellent, praiseworthy, ordered.[17]

5. κοσμέω—make beautiful or attractive inwardly/morally, beautify, adorn, do credit to.

6. κόσμος—the world, the (orderly) universe, order, adornment, adorning.

7. προσφιλής—pleasing, agreeable, lovely, amiable.[18]

8. φαίνομαι—to appear as something [beautiful].

9. ὡραῖος—beautiful, fair, lovely, pleasant, coming at the right time, timely.

The general witness of Scripture to the aesthetic dimension briefly described here refers to aesthetically pleasing works or achievements in the context of the culture at large and as pertains to ordinary categories of the arts (e.g., music and song). The aesthetic dimension in this sense is simply being recognized as part of the fabric of life, though life in the

---

appears in conjunction with תִּפְאֶרֶת, conveying a parallel relationship between beauty and glory.

13. From the verb ראה, "to see."

14. Occurs twice, in Acts 7:20 and Hebrews 11:23.

15. Corresponds to the Hebrew term כָּבוֹד.

16. Occurs only in James 1:11.

17. The broad semantic range includes both ethical and aesthetic meanings. The noun follows the adjectival sense, and means that which is ordered or whole or healthy in the sense of "the good," "virtue," and "the beautiful," "beauty."

18. Occurs only in Philippians 4:8, a rich aesthetic statement.

biblical context depicting the relationship of God and his people. The following selection of examples provide a general witness to a strong aesthetic element being part and parcel of the biblical narrative. Gerhard von Rad observes that Israel's regard for the aesthetic was that which is common to every people and culture: "Quite certainly there is no particular significance in many of the statements which ancient Israel made about beauty; and the reason why there is nothing characteristic in them is that they move on the plane of the experience of beauty common to all men."[19] His point is not that aesthetics play an insignificant role in the life and history of Israel. It is quite the contrary. "Her most intensive encounter with beauty was in the religious sphere, in the contemplation of Jahweh's revelation and action."[20] And the monumental artistic achievements that testify to this are reflected in the narrative, poetry and song, and wisdom literature that comprise the Hebrew Scriptures.[21] The witness of Scripture to the aesthetic dimension thus includes its aesthetically intentioned literary forms.

Relevant to this, we see a direct correlation between the artistic nature of Israel's writings and the aesthetic nature of divine action. "All her hymns, all her songs of victory and all her artistically shaped narratives testify to the fact that she perceived a strong aesthetic element as well in the actions wrought by Jahweh."[22] Even the biblical portrayals reflecting God variously as master Artisan and Artist (e.g., "potter," "musician," "poet," and "architect") offer further testimony to

---

19. Von Rad, *Old Testament Theology*, 1:364. Von Rad adds, "For pleasure in artistic imitation was no less strong in her than in any other people of antiquity." See Von Rad, *Old Testament Theology*, 1:364-70, for his overall treatment here.

20. Von Rad, *Old Testament Theology*, 1:365.

21. The following treatments by Robert Alter are recommended: *The Art of Biblical Poetry*, 2nd ed. (New York: Basic Books, 2011), and *The Art of Biblical Narrative*, 2nd ed. (New York: Basic Books, 2011). See also Leland Ryken, *The Literature of the Bible* (Grand Rapids: Zondervan, 1974).

22. Von Rad, *Old Testament Theology* 1:365. For a recommended treatment on the relationship between Scripture's literary forms and communicative content, see Kevin J. Vanhoozer, "Love's Wisdom: The Authority of Scripture's Form and Content for Faith's Understanding and Theological Judgment," *Journal of Reformed Theology* 5 no. 3 (January 2011): 247-75. Cf. Ecclesiastes 12:10: "The Teacher sought to find delightful words, and to write accurately truthful sayings" (NET). Here the translator's note on Ecclesiastes 12:10 states: "In other words, Qoheleth wrote his proverbs so effectively that he was able to take moral and aesthetic delight in his words."

the aesthetic connection made to his character.[23] Theophanies as well are described in language charged with aesthetic overtones. A potential objection here might be that the accounts in Scripture of the theophanies and the Shekinah-presence of the Lord, as well as prophetic visions, are not described as evoking an affective response of aesthetic pleasure or delight. Rather, the most powerful collective sense such manifestations elicit involve various degrees of awe, proskynesis, fear, reverence, terror, praise, or acclamation. Suffice it to say here that beauty is not the only quality of the glory of God that can evoke an affective response (although beauty remains unique *in what way* it affects the percipient). Any and all of these affective responses are befitting before the "splendor of his majesty" (Isa 2:19).

Furthermore, the people of Israel were called to worship the Lord in the "splendor (הֲדָרָה) of holiness" (1 Chr 16:29; cf. Ps 29:2; 96:9). In the biblical accounts of their construction, the OT tabernacle and temple give us superlative examples of artistic and architectural beauty (Exodus 25–30, 35–39; 1 Kings 6–7; 1 Chronicles 22–27; 2 Chronicles 2–4). In reference to the tabernacle, the "divine sanction for this artistry is not only that God gave the plans for the construction; he also inspired the artists who did the work (Exod 31:1–6; 35:30–36:1)."[24] We see as well that the priestly garments of Aaron and his sons were to be made "for glory (כָּבוֹד) and for beauty (תִּפְאֶרֶת)," richly embroidered and ornamentally symbol laden (Exodus 28). With respect to the arts, music and song occupy a special place among the biblical images in the domain of aesthetics, especially at the heart of temple worship in the Old Testament (2 Sam 6:5; 1 Kings 10:12; 1 Chr 15:15–16; 2 Chr 29:25; 35:15; Neh 7:1; 12:27–43). The music performed involved string, wind, and percussion instruments. The role of song, moreover, is given as a basic practice of

---

23. See Davidson, *Toward a Theology of Beauty*, 15-24. I address the ontological relation of beauty to the divine nature in Chapter 2.

24. "Beauty" in *DBI*, 82–85, here 83. In regard to the temple, Edmund Clowney, "Living Art: Christian Experience and the Arts" in *God and Culture: Essays in Honor of Carl F. H. Henry*, ed. D. A. Carson and John D. Woodbridge (Grand Rapids: Eerdmans, 1993), 239, offers the following insight: "At this time, God did not inspire a Bezalel and Oholiab with his Spirit. Rather, since God is the God of all the earth, and since Solomon's reign of peace raised the witness of Israel before the surrounding nations, it was fitting that the holy house of God should be shaped by the hands of gifted Gentiles."

the early church (Acts 16:25; 1 Cor 14:14-15, 26; Eph 5:19; Col 3:16).[25] Of particular note, in John's Apocalypse the twenty-four elders and the host of all those before the throne of the Lamb of God are shown singing the "new song" (Rev 5:9; 14:3; cf. Pss 33:3; 96:1; 98:1). All the faithful saints who have endured to the end are even described as singing the Song of Moses and the Song of the Lamb (Rev 15:3-4; cf. Pss 86:9-10; 111:2; 145:17). As J. Clinton McCann Jr. puts it, "The faithful people of God—from here and there and yonder, from then and now and yet-to-come—will be gathered around the throne of God ... singing a psalm!"[26]

---

25. See "Music" in *DBI*, 576–78.

26. J. Clinton McCann Jr., *A Theological Introduction to the Book of Psalms: The Psalms as Torah* (Nashville: Abingdon Press, 1993), 175.

Bibliography

Alexander, T. Desmond. "Royal Expectations in Genesis to Kings: Their Importance for Biblical Theology." *Tyndale Bulletin* 49, no. 2 (1998): 191–212.

———. *From Eden to the New Jerusalem: An Introduction to Biblical Theology*. Grand Rapids: Kregel, 2008.

Allison, Dale C. *The New Moses. A Matthean Typology*. Minneapolis: Fortress Press, 1993.

Allison, Gregg R. "Toward a Theology of Human Embodiment." *Southern Baptist Journal of Theology* 13, no. 2 (2009): 4–17.

Alter, Robert. *The Art of Biblical Poetry*. 2nd ed. New York: Basic Books, 2011.

———. *The Art of Biblical Narrative*. 2nd ed. New York: Basic Books, 2011.

Anderson, Bernhard W. *From Creation to New Creation: Old Testament Perspectives*. Minneapolis: Fortress Press, 1994.

Anselm. *Basic Writings*. Translated and edited by Thomas Williams. Indianapolis: Hackett, 2007.

Aquinas, Thomas. *Summa Theologica*. 5 vols. Translated by Fathers of the English Dominican Province. Westminster, MD: Christian Classics, 1981.

Aristotle, *The Basic Works of Aristotle*. Edited by Richard McKeon. New York: Modern Library, 2001.

Augustine. *Expositions of the Psalms, 33–50*. Edited by John E. Rotelle. Translated by Maria Boulding. Hyde Park, NY: New City Press, 2000.

———. *Confessions*. Translated by Henry Chadwick. Oxford: Oxford University Press, 2008.

———. *The Trinity*. 2nd ed. Edited by John E. Rotelle. Translated by Edmund Hill. Hyde Park, NY: New City Press, 2012.

Averbeck, Richard E. כָּפַר. *NIDOTTE* 2:681–701.

———. "Leviticus." *NIDOTTE* 4:906–22.

Balthasar, Hans Urs von. *The Glory of the Lord: A Theological Aesthetics*. Vols. I–VII. San Francisco: Ignatius Press, 1982–1991.

———. *Theo-Drama: Theological Dramatic Theory*. Vols. I–V. San Francisco: Ignatius Press, 1988–1998.

———. *My Work: In Retrospect*. San Francisco: Ignatius Press, 1993.

———. *Theo-Logic: Theological Logical Theory*. Vols. I–III. San Francisco: Ignatius Press, 2000–2005.

———. *Epilogue*. Translated by Edward T. Oakes. San Francisco: Ignatius Press, 2004.

———. *Mysterium Paschale: The Mystery of Easter*. Translated by Aidan Nichols. San Francisco: Ignatius Press, 2005.

Barclay, John M. G. "Under Grace: The Christ-Gift and the Construction of a Christian Habitus." In *Apocalyptic Paul: Cosmos and Anthropos in Romans 5–8*, edited by Beverly Roberts Gaventa, 59–76. Waco, TX: Baylor University Press, 2013.

Barth, Karl. *Church Dogmatics*. Translated by Geoffrey W. Bromiley. Edinburgh: T&T Clark, 1956.

Barton, Stephen C. "The Transfiguration of Christ according to Mark and Matthew: Christology and Anthropology." In *Resurrection*, edited by Friedrich Avemarie and Hermann Lichtenberger, 231–46. Wissenschaftliche Untersuchungen zum Neuen Testament 135. Tübingen: Mohr Siebeck, 2001.

Bauckham, Richard. *Jesus and the God of Israel: God Crucified and Other Studies on the New Testament's Christology of Divine Identity*. Grand Rapids: Eerdmans, 2009.

Bavinck, Herman. "Common Grace." Translated by Raymond C. Van Leeuwen. *Calvin Theological Journal* 24 (1988): 35–65.

———. *Reformed Dogmatics*. 4 vols. Edited by John Bolt. Translated by John Vriend. Grand Rapids: Baker Academic, 2003–2008.

Bawulski, Shawn. "Reconciliationism, A Better View of Hell: Reconciliationism and Eternal Punishment." *Journal of the Evangelical Theological Society* 56, no.1 (March 2103): 123–38.

Beale, G. K. *We Become What We Worship: A Biblical Theology of Idolatry*. Downers Grove, IL: IVP Academic, 2008.

———. *A New Testament Biblical Theology: The Unfolding of the Old Testament in the New*. Grand Rapids: Baker Academic, 2011.

Beale, G. K. and Mitchell Kim. *God Dwells among Us: Expanding Eden to the Ends of the Earth*. Downers Grove, IL: InterVarsity Press, 2014.

Beck, James R. and Bruce Demarest, eds. *The Human in Theology and Psychology: A Biblical Anthropology for the Twenty-first Century*. Grand Rapids: Kregel, 2005.

Beetham, Christopher A. "From Creation to New Creation: The Biblical Epic of King, Human Vicegerency, and Kingdom." In *From Creation to New Creation: Biblical Theology and Exegesis*, edited by Daniel M. Gurtner and Benjamin L. Gladd, 237–254. Peabody, MA: Hendrickson Publishers, 2013.

Begbie, Jeremy, ed. *Sounding the Depths: Theology through the Arts*. London: SCM Press, 2002.

Berkhof, Hendrikus. *The Doctrine of the Holy Spirit*. Richmond, VA: John Knox Press, 1964.

Berkhof, Louis. *Systematic Theology*. New ed. Grand Rapids: Eerdmans, 1996.

Berkouwer, G. C. *The Person of Christ*. Studies in Dogmatics. Translated by John Vriend. Grand Rapids: Eerdmans, 1955.

Blocher, Henri. *In the Beginning: The Opening Chapters of Genesis*. Translated by David G. Preston. Downers Grove, IL: InterVarsity Press, 1984.

———. "Everlasting Punishment and the Problem of Evil." In *Universalism and the Doctrine of Hell*, edited by Nigel M. de S. Cameron, 283–312. Grand Rapids: Baker, 1992.

———. "Biblical Metaphors and the Doctrine of the Atonement." *Journal of the Evangelical Theological Society* 47, no. 4 (December 2004): 629–45.

Bray, Gerald. "The Significance of God's Image in Man." *Tyndale Bulletin* 42 (1991): 195–225.

Bremmer, Jan N. "Paradise: From Persia, via Greece, into the Septuagint." In *Paradise Interpreted: Representations of Biblical Paradise in Judaism and Christianity*, edited by Gerard P. Luttikhuizen, 1–20. Leiden: Brill, 1999.

Briggs, Richard S. "Humans in the Image of God and Other Things Genesis Does Not Make Clear." *Journal of Theological Interpretation* 4, no. 1 (Spring 2010): 111–26.

Brown, Frank Burch. "The Beauty of Hell: Anselm on God's Eternal Design." *Journal of Religion* 73 (July 1993): 329–56.

———. *Religious Aesthetics: A Theological Study of Making and Meaning*. New York: Oxford University Press, 1999.

Bruce, F. F. *The Epistle to the Hebrews*. New International Commentary of the New Testament. Grand Rapids: Eerdmans, 1990.

Brueggemann, Walter. *Theology of the Old Testament: Testimony, Dispute, Advocacy*. Minneapolis: Fortress Press, 1997.

Brunner, Emil. *Man in Revolt: A Christian Anthropology*. Translated by Olive Wyon. London: Lutterworth Press, 1939.

Burger, Hans. *Being in Christ: A Biblical and Systematic Investigation in a Reformed Perspective*. Eugene, OR: Wipf & Stock, 2009.

Calvin, John. *Commentary on the Book of the Prophet Isaiah*. Vol. VIII. Translated by William Pringle. Calvin's Commentaries. 22 vols. Grand Rapids: Baker Book House, 1979.

———. *Commentary on a Harmony of the Evangelists, Mark, Mark, and Luke*. Vols. XVI and XVII. Translated by William Pringle. Calvin's Commentaries. 22 vols. Grand Rapids: Baker Book House, 1979.

———. *Commentary on the Gospel according to John*. Vol. XVIII. Translated by William Pringle. Calvin's Commentaries. 22 vols. Grand Rapids: Baker Book House, 1979.

———. *Commentary on the Epistles of Paul the Apostle to the Corinthians*. Vol. XX. Translated by John Pringle. Calvin's Commentaries. 22 vols. Grand Rapids: Baker Book House, 1979.

———. *Institutes of the Christian Religion*. Edited by John T. McNeill. Translated by Ford Lewis Battles. The Library of Christian Classics. Louisville: Westminster John Knox, 2006.

Canlis, Julie. "Living as God's Children." In *Evangelical Calvinism: Essays Resourcing the Continuing Reformation of the Church*, edited by Myk Habets and Bobby Grow, 331–52. Eugene, OR: Pickwick, 2012.

Carroll, Noël. *Art in Three Dimensions*. Oxford: Oxford University Press, 2010.

Carson, D. A. "John and the Johannine Epistles." In *It Is Written: Scripture Citing Scripture: Essays in Honour of Barnabas Lindars, SSF*, edited by D. A. Carson and H. G. M. Williamson, 245–64. Cambridge: Cambridge University Press, 1988.

———. *The Gospel according to John*. Pillar New Testament Commentary. Grand Rapids: Eerdmans, 1991.

———. "Mystery and Fulfillment: Toward a More Comprehensive Paradigm of Paul's Understanding of the Old and the New." In *Justification and Variegated Nomism: The Paradoxes of Paul*. Vol. 2, edited by D. A. Carson, Peter T. O'Brien, and Mark A. Seifrid, 393–436. Grand Rapids: Baker Academic, 2004.

Caverno, C. "Beauty." In *The International Standard Bible Encyclopaedia*. Vol. 1. Edited by James Orr, 420–21. Chicago: The Howard-Severance Company, 1915.

Chisholm Jr., R. B. "Retribution." In *Dictionary of the Old Testament Prophets*, edited by Mark J. Boda and J. Gordon McConville, 671–76. Downers Grove, IL: IVP Academic, 2012.

Ciampa, Roy E. and Brian S. Rosner. *The First Letter to the Corinthians*. Pillar New Testament Commentary. Grand Rapids: Eerdmans, 2010.

Clarke, W. Norris. *The One and the Many: A Contemporary Thomistic Metaphysics*. Notre Dame, IN: University of Notre Dame Press, 2001.

Clines, David J. A. "Humanity as the Image of God." In *On the Way to the Postmodern: Old Testament Essays, 1967–1998*, 447–97. Vol. II. Journal for the Study of the Old Testament: Supplement Series 293. Sheffield, England: Sheffield Academic Press, 1998.

Clowney, Edmund. "Living Art: Christian Experience and the Arts." In *God and Culture: Essays in Honor of Carl F. H. Henry*, edited by D. A. Carson and John D. Woodbridge, 235–53. Grand Rapids: Eerdmans, 1993.

Cole, Graham A. "The Living God: Anthropomorphic or Anthropopathic?" *The Reformed Theological Review* 59, no.1 (April 2000): 16–27.

———. *God the Peacemaker: How Atonement Brings Shalom*. Downers Grove, IL: InterVarsity Press, 2009.

———. *The God Who Became Human: A Biblical Theology of Incarnation*. Downers Grove, IL: InterVarsity Press, 2013.

Collins, C. John. *Genesis 1–4: A Linguistic, Literary, and Theological Commentary*. Philipsburg, NJ: P&R Publishing, 2006.

Collins, Raymond F. *1 and 2 Timothy and Titus: A Commentary*. Louisville: Westminster John Knox, 2002.

Cooke, Gerald. "The Israelite King as Son of God." *Zeitschrift für die alttestamentliche Wissenschaft* 73, no. 2 (1961): 202–25.

Cooper, John W. *Body, Soul, and Life Everlasting: Biblical Anthropology and the Monism-Dualism Debate*. Grand Rapids: Eerdmans, 2000.

Coxon, Paul S. *Exploring the New Exodus in John: A Biblical Theological Investigation of John Chapters 5-10*. Eugene, OR: Resource Publication, 2015.

Crisp, Oliver D. "Divine Retribution: A Defence." *Sophia* 42, no. 2 (October 2005): 35-52.

———. "The Logic of Penal Substitution Revisited." In *The Atonement Debate: Papers from the London Symposium on the Theology of Atonement*, edited by Derek Tidball, David Hilborn, and Justin Thacker, 208-27. Grand Rapids: Zondervan, 2008.

———. *Retrieving Doctrine: Essays in Reformed Theology*. Downers Grove, IL: IVP Academic, 2010.

Crowe, Brandon D. *The Obedient Son: Deuteronomy and Christology in the Gospel of Matthew*. Berlin: De Gruyter, 2012.

———. *The Last Adam: A Theology of the Obedient Life of Jesus in the Gospels*. Grand Rapids: Baker Academic, 2017.

Dabney, Robert Lewis. *Lectures in Systematic Theology*. Grand Rapids: Zondervan, 1972.

Davids, Peter H. *The First Epistle of Peter*. New International Commentary of the New Testament. Grand Rapids: Eerdmans, 1990.

———. *The Letters of 2 Peter and Jude*. Pillar New Testament Commentary. Grand Rapids: Eerdmans, 2006.

Davidson, Jo Ann. *Toward a Theology of Beauty: A Biblical Perspective*. Lanham, MD: University Press of America, 2008.

Davies, W. D. and Dale C. Allison Jr. *Commentary on Matthew VIII-XVIII: A Critical and Exegetical Commentary on the Gospel according to Saint Matthew*. Vol. II. International Critical Commentary. Edinburgh: T&T Clark, 1991.

Day, Adam Warner. "Eating Before the Lord: A Theology of Food according to Deuteronomy." *Journal of Evangelical Theological Society* 57, no. 1 (March 2014): 85-97.

Dearman, J. Andrew. "Theophany, Anthropomorphism, and the *Imago Dei*: Some Observations about the Incarnation in the Light of the Old Testament." In *The Incarnation: An Interdisciplinary Symposium on the Incarnation of the Son of God*, edited by Stephen T. Davis, Daniel Kendall, and Gerald O'Collins, 31-46. Oxford: Oxford University Press, 2004.

De Boer, Willis Peter. *The Imitation of Paul: An Exegetical Study*. Kampen, Netherlands: J. H. Kok, 1962.

Dolezal, James E. *God without Parts: Divine Simplicity and the Metaphysics of God's Absoluteness*. Eugene, OR: Pickwick Publications, 2011.

———. "Trinity, Simplicity and the Status of God's Personal Relations." *International Journal of Systematic Theology* 16 (January 2014): 79-98.

Downey, Patrick. *Serious Comedy: The Philosophical and Theological Significance of Tragic and Comic Writing in the Western Tradition*. Lanham, MD: Lexington Books, 2001.

Dubay, Thomas. *The Evidential Power of Beauty: Science and Theology Meet*. San Francisco: Ignatius Press, 1999.

Dumbrell, William J. *The End of the Beginning: Revelation 21–22 and the Old Testament*. Eugene, OR: Wipf & Stock, 2001.

Dyrness, William A. "Aesthetics in the Old Testament: Beauty in Context." *Journal of the Evangelical Theological Society* 28, no. 4 (December 1985): 421–32.

Eastman, Susan Grove. "Philippians 2:6–11: Incarnation as Mimetic Participation." *Journal for the Study of Paul and his Letters* 1, no. 1 (Spring 2011): 1–22.

Eco, Umberto. *The Aesthetics of Thomas Aquinas*. Translated by Hugh Bredin. Cambridge, MA: Harvard University Press, 1988.

———, ed. *History of Beauty*. Translated by Alistair McEwen. New York: Rizzoli, 2004.

Edgar, William. "Aesthetics: Beauty Avenged, Apologetics Enriched." *WTJ* 63, no. 1 (Spring 2001): 107–22.

Edwards, Jonathan. *The Works of Jonathan Edwards*. 26 vols. New Haven, CT: Yale University Press, 1957–2008.

Ellis, Brannon. *Calvin, Classical Trinitarianism, and the Aseity of the Son*. Oxford: Oxford University Press, 2012.

———. "The Spirit from the Father, of Himself God: A Calvinian Approach to the Filioque Debate." In *Ecumenical Perspectives on the Filioque for the 21st Century*, edited by Myk Habets, 87–106. London and New York: Bloomsbury T&T Clark, 2014.

Emery, Gilles. "Trinity and Creation." In *The Theology of Thomas Aquinas*, edited by Rik Van Nieuwenhove and Joseph Wawrykow, 58–76. Notre Dame, IN: University of Notre Dame Press, 2005.

Enderlein, Steven E. "To Fall Short of Lack the Glory of God? The Translation and Implications of Romans 3:23." *Journal for the Study of Paul and His Letters* 1, no. 2 (Fall 2011): 213–24.

Engberg-Pedersen, Troels. *Paul and the Stoics*. Louisville: Westminster John Knox, 2000.

Erickson, Millard J. *Christian Theology*. 3rd ed. Grand Rapids: Baker Academic, 2013.

Estelle, Bryan D. *Echoes of Exodus: Tracing a Biblical Motif*. Downers Grove, IL: IVP Academic, 2018.

Evans, Craig A. *Mark 8:27–16:20*. Word Biblical Commentary 43B. Waco, TX: Word, 2001.

Fabiny, Tibor. *The Lion and the Lamb: Figuralism and Fulfilment in the Bible, Art, and Literature*. New York: St. Martin's Press, 1992.

Farrow, Douglas. *Ascension Theology*. London: T&T Clark, 2011.

Fee, Gordon D. *The First Epistle to the Corinthians*. New International Commentary of the New Testament. Grand Rapids: Eerdmans, 1987.

———. *Paul's Letter to the Philippians*. New International Commentary of the New Testament. Grand Rapids: Eerdmans, 1995.

———. *Pauline Christology: An Exegetical-Theological Study*. Peabody, MA: Hendrickson Publishers, 2007.

Fisk, Bruce N. "*See My Tears*: A Lament for Jerusalem (Luke 13:31–35; 19:41–44)." In *The Word Leaps the Gap: Essays on Scripture and Theology in Honor of Richard B. Hays*, edited by J. Ross Wagner, C. Kavin Rowe, and A. Katherine Grieb, 147–78. Grand Rapids: Eerdmans, 2008.

Forsyth, P. T. *The Justification of God: Lectures for War-Time on a Christian Theodicy*. New York: C. Scribner's Sons, 1917.

———. *The Person and Place of Jesus Christ*. Eugene, OR: Wipf & Stock, 1996.

———. *The Work of Christ*. Eugene, OR: Wipf & Stock, 1996.

Fowl, Stephen E. *Philippians*. The Two Horizons New Testament Commentary. Grand Rapids: Eerdmans, 2005.

France, R. T. *Jesus and the Old Testament: His Application of Old Testament Passages To Himself and His Mission*. Downers Grove, IL: InterVarsity Press, 1971.

Frye, Northrop. "The Archetypes of Literature." In *The Myth and Ritual Theory: An Anthology*, edited by Robert A. Segal, 218–30. Malden, MA: Blackwell, 1998.

Gaffin Jr., Richard B. "The Usefulness of the Cross." *Westminster Theological Journal* 41, no. 2 (Spring 1979): 228–46.

———. "Speech and the Image of God: Biblical Reflections on Language and Its Uses." In *The Pattern of Sound Doctrine: Systematic Theology at the Westminster Seminaries: Essays in Honor of Robert B. Strimple*, edited by David VanDrunen, 181–93. Phillipsburg, NJ: P&R Publishing, 2004.

Garner, David B. "Adoption in Christ." PhD diss., Westminster Theological Seminary, Philadelphia, PA, 2002.

Garrett, Stephen M. *God's Beauty-in-Act: Participating in God's Suffering Glory*. Eugene, OR: Pickwick Publications, 2013.

Gentry, Peter J. and Stephen J. Wellum. *Kingdom through Covenant: A Biblical-Theological Understanding of the Covenant*. Wheaton, IL: Crossway, 2012.

Gilson, Etienne. *Elements of Christian Philosophy*. Garden City, NY: Doubleday, Catholic Textbook Division, 1960.

Goetz, Stewart and Charles Taliaferro. *A Brief History of the Soul*. Malden, MA: Wiley-Blackwell, 2011.

Goldsworthy, Graeme. *Gospel-Centered Hermeneutics: Foundations and Principles of Evangelical Biblical Interpretation*. Downers Grove, IL: IVP Academic, 2006.

———. *The Son of God and the New Creation*. Wheaton, IL: Crossway, 2015.

Gombis, Timothy G. "Cosmic Lordship and Divine Gift-Giving: Psalm 68 in Ephesians 4:8." *Novum Testamentum* 47, no. 4 (2005): 367–80.

Green, Bradley G. *Covenant and Commandment: Works, Obedience and Faithfulness in the Christian Life*. Downers Grove, IL: InterVarsity Press, 2014.

Grogan, Geoffrey W. *Isaiah*. Vol. 6, edited by Tremper Longman III and David E. Garland. Expositor's Bible Commentary. Grand Rapids: Zondervan, 2008.

Gundry, Robert H. "The New Jerusalem: People as Place, Not Place for People." In *The Old Is Better: New Testament Essays in Support of Traditional Interpretations*, 399–411. Tübingen: Mohr Siebeck, 2005.

Gunton, Colin E. "The Doctrine of Creation." In *The Cambridge Companion to Christian Doctrine*, edited by Colin E. Gunton, 141–57. Cambridge: Cambridge University Press, 1997.

Hamilton Jr., James M. *God's Glory in Salvation through Judgment: A Biblical Theology.* Wheaton, IL: Crossway, 2010.

Hansen, G. Walter. *The Letter to the Philippians.* Pillar New Testament Commentary. Grand Rapids: Eerdmans, 2009.

Hart, David Bentley. *The Beauty of the Infinite: The Aesthetics of Christian Truth.* Grand Rapids: Eerdmans, 2003.

Hart, John-Mark. "Triune Beauty and the Ugly Cross: Towards a Theological Aesthetic." *Tyndale Bulletin* 66, no.2 (2015): 293–312.

Hawthorne, Gerald F. *Philippians.* Rev. ed. Expanded by Ralph P. Martin. Word Biblical Commentary 43. Waco, TX: Word, 2004.

Haykin, Michael A. G. "Defending the Holy Spirit's Deity: Basil of Caesarea, Gregory of Nyssa, and the Pneumatomachian Controversy of the 4th Century." *Southern Baptist Journal of Theology* 7, no.3 (Fall 2003): 74–79.

Healy, Nicholas M. *Thomas Aquinas: Theologian of the Christian Life.* Burlington, VT: Ashgate Publishing, 2003.

Helm, Paul. "The Impossibility of Divine Passibility." In *The Power and Weakness of God: Impassibility and Orthodoxy*, edited by Nigel M. de S. Cameron, 119–40. Edinburgh: Rutherford House, 1990.

Hoekema, Anthony A. *The Bible and the Future.* Grand Rapids: Eerdmans, 1979.

———. *Created in God's Image.* Grand Rapids: Eerdmans, 1986.

Hogg, David S. *Anselm of Canterbury: The Beauty of Theology.* Burlington, VT: Ashgate Publishing Company, 2004.

Holmes, Stephen R. "Image of God." In *Dictionary for Theological Interpretation of the Bible*, edited by Kevin J. Vanhoozer, Craig G. Bartholomew, Daniel J. Treier, and N. T. Wright, 318–19. Grand Rapids: Baker Academic, 2005.

———. "A Simple Salvation? Soteriology and the Perfections of God." In *God of Salvation: Soteriology in Theological Perspective*, edited by Ivor J. Davidson and Murray A. Rae, 35–46. Farnham, Surrey, England: Ashgate, 2011.

Holmes, Christopher R. J. "Disclosure without Reservation: Re-evaluating Divine Hiddenness," *Neue Zeitschrift für systematische Theologie und Religionsphilosophie* 48, no. 3 (2006): 367–80.

———. *Revisiting the Doctrine of the Divine Attributes: In Dialogue with Karl Barth, Eberhard Jüngel and Wolf Krötke.* New York: Peter Lang, 2007.

Horton, Michael S. *People and Place: A Covenant Ecclesiology.* Louisville: Westminster John Knox Press, 2008.

————. *The Christian Faith: A Systematic Theology for Pilgrims On the Way*. Grand Rapids: Zondervan, 2011.

Hughes, Philip Edgcumbe. *The True Image: The Origin and Destiny of Man in Christ*. Grand Rapids: Eerdmans, 1989.

Hunsinger, George. *The Eucharist and Ecumenism: Let Us Keep the Feast*. Cambridge: Cambridge University Press, 2008.

Hurtado, Larry W. *How on Earth Did Jesus Become a God? Historical Questions about Earliest Devotion to Jesus*. Grand Rapids: Eerdmans, 2005.

Irenaeus of Lyons. *Against Heresies*. In *The Ante-Nicene Fathers*. Vol. 1. Edited Alexander Roberts and James Donaldson. Buffalo, NY: Christian Literature, 1885; reprint, South Bend, IN: Ex Fontibus, 2010.

Jenson, Philip Peter. *Graded Holiness: A Key to the Priestly Conception of the World*. Journal for the Study of the Old Testament: Supplement Series 106. Sheffield, England: JSOT Press, 1992.

Johnson, S. Lewis. "The Transfiguration of Christ." *Bibliotheca Sacra* 124 (April-June 1967): 133–43.

Käsemann, Ernst. "A Critical Analysis of Philippians 2:5–11." *Journal for Theology and the Church* 5 (1968): 45–88.

Kennedy, Joel. *The Recapitulation of Israel*. Tübingen: Mohr Siebeck, 2008.

Kline, Meredith G. *Images of the Spirit*. Eugene, OR: Wipf & Stock, 1999.

————. *Kingdom Prologue: Genesis Foundations for a Covenantal Worldview*. Eugene, OR: Wipf & Stock, 2006.

Koester, Craig R. *The Word of Life: A Theology of John's Gospel*. Grand Rapids: Eerdmans, 2008.

Konstan, David. *Beauty: The Fortunes of an Ancient Greek Idea*. Oxford: Oxford University Press, 2015.

Köstenberger, Andreas J. "John." In *Commentary on the New Testament Use of the Old Testament*, edited by G. K. Beale and D. A. Carson, 415–512. Grand Rapids: Baker Academic, 2007.

————. "The Glory of God in John's Gospel and Revelation." In *The Glory of God*, edited by Christopher W. Morgan and Robert A. Peterson, 107–26. Wheaton, IL: Crossway, 2010.

Kovach, Francis J. *Philosophy of Beauty*. Norman, OK: University of Oklahoma Press, 1974.

————. *Scholastic Challenges to Some Medieval and Modern Ideas*. Stillwater, OK: Western Publications, 1987.

————. "Beauty." In *New Catholic Encyclopedia*. Vol. 2, 184–86. 2nd ed. Washington, DC: Gale Group, 2003.

Kynes, William L. *A Christology of Solidarity: Jesus as the Representative of His People in Matthew*. Lanham, MD: University Press of America, 1991.

LaCocque, André. *The Trial of Innocence: Adam, Eve, and the Yahwist*. Eugene, OR: Cascade Books, 2006.

Lane, William L. *The Gospel according to Mark: The English Text with Introduction, Exposition, and Notes*. New International Commentary of the New Testament. Grand Rapids: Eerdmans, 1974.

————. *Hebrews 1–8*. Word Biblical Commentary 47A. Waco, TX: Word, 1991.

Lee, Dorothy. *Transfiguration*. London: Continuum, 2004.

Lee, Simon S. *Jesus' Transfiguration and the Believers' Transformation: A Study of the Transfiguration and Its Development in Early Christian Writings*. Tübingen: Mohr Siebeck, 2009.

Leithart, Peter J. *Deep Comedy: Trinity, Tragedy, and Hope in Western Literature*. Moscow, ID: Canon Press, 2006.

————. *Traces of the Trinity: Signs of God in Creation and Human Experience*. Grand Rapids: Brazos Press, 2015.

Levenson, Jon D. "The Temple and the World." *The Journal of Religion* 64, no. 3 (July 1984): 275–98.

Levering, Matthew. *Scripture and Metaphysics: Aquinas and the Renewal of Trinitarian Theology*. Malden, MA: Blackwell Publishing, 2004.

Levison, John R. "Adam and Eve in Romans 1.18–25 and the Greek *Life of Adam and Eve*." *New Testament Studies* 50, no. 4 (October 2004): 519–34.

Lewis, C. S. *Till We Have Faces: A Myth Retold*. Orlando, FL: Harcourt, 1980.

————. *Perelandra: A Novel*. 1944. Reprint, New York: Scribner, 2003.

Liefeld, W. L. "Transfiguration." In *Dictionary of Jesus and the Gospels*, edited by Joel B. Green and Scot McKnight, 834–41. Downers Grove: InterVarsity Press, 1992.

Lindsey, F. Duane. "Essays Toward a Theology of Beauty." *Bibliotheca Sacra* 131 (April 1974): 120–36.

Link, H.-G. and C. Brown, ἱλάσκομαι, *NIDNTT* 3:148–66.

Lister, Rob. *God Is Impassible and Impassioned: Toward a Theology of Divine Emotion*. Wheaton, IL: Crossway, 2013.

Longhurst, Christopher Evan. "Discovering the Sacred in Secular Art: An Aesthetic Modality That 'Speaks of God.'" *American Theological Inquiry* 4, no. 1 (2011): 13–21.

Longman III, Tremper. *Daniel*. NIV Application Commentary. Grand Rapids: Zondervan, 1999.

————. "The Glory of God in the Old Testament." In *The Glory of God*, edited by Christopher W. Morgan and Robert A. Peterson, 47–78. Wheaton, IL: Crossway, 2010.

MacKenzie, Iain M. *Irenaeus's Demonstration of the Apostolic Preaching: A Theological Commentary and Translation*. Translated by J. Armitage Robinson. Aldershot, Hants, England: Ashgate, 2002.

MacLeod, David J. "Imitating the Incarnation of Christ: An Exposition of Philippians 2:5–8." *Bibliotheca Sacra* 158 (July-September 2001): 308–30.

Macleod, Donald. *Christ Crucified: Understanding the Atonement.* Downers Grove: IVP Academic, 2014.

Malpas, Jeffery Edward. "Putting Space in Place: Relational Geography and Philosophical Topography." *Planning and Environment D: Space and Society* 30 (2012): 226–42.

Martin, Ralph P. *Carmen Christi: Philippians 2:5–11 in Recent Interpretation and in the Setting of Early Christian Worship.* Cambridge: Cambridge University Press, 1967.

Martin, Ralph P., and Brian J. Dodd, ed. *Where Christology Began: Essays on Philippians 2.* Louisville: Westminster John Knox, 1998.

Mathews, Kenneth A. *Genesis 1–11:26.* New American Commentary. Volume 1A. Nashville, TN: Broadman & Holman Publishers, 1996.

Mattson, Brian G. *Restored to Our Destiny: Eschatology and the Image of God in Herman Bavinck's Reformed Dogmatics.* Boston: Brill, 2012.

Mays, James L. *The Lord Reigns: A Theological Handbook to the Psalms.* Louisville: Westminster John Knox Press, 1994.

———. "The Self in the Psalms and the Image of God." In *God and Human Dignity*, edited by R. Kendall Soulen and Linda Woodhead, 27–43. Grand Rapids: Eerdmans, 2006.

McCall, Thomas H. *Which Trinity? Whose Monotheism? Philosophical and Systematic Theologians on the Metaphysics of Trinitarian Theology.* Grand Rapids: Eerdmans, 2010.

———. *Forsaken: The Trinity and the Cross, and Why It Matters.* Downers Grove, IL: IVP Academic, 2012.

———. "Trinity Doctrine, Plain and Simple." In *Advancing Trinitarian Doctrine: Explorations in Constructive Dogmatics*, edited by Oliver D. Crisp and Fred Sanders, 42–59. Grand Rapids: Zondervan, 2014.

McCann Jr., J. Clinton. *A Theological Introduction to the Book of Psalms: The Psalms as Torah.* Nashville: Abingdon Press, 1993.

McConville, J. Gordon. "God's 'Name' and God's 'Glory.'" *Tyndale Bulletin* 30 (1979): 149–63.

McDowell, Catherine L. *The Image of God in the Garden of Eden: The Creation of Humankind in Genesis 2:5–3:24 in Light of the mīs pî pīt pî and wpt-r Rituals of Mesopotamia and Ancient Egypt.* Winona Lake, IN: Eisenbrauns, 2015.

McGrath, Alister E. *The Open Secret: A New Vision for Natural Theology.* Malden, MA: Blackwell Publishing, 2008.

McKnight, Scot. *A Fellowship of Differents: Showing the World God's Design for Life Together.* Grand Rapids: Zondervan, 2014.

Meeks, W. B. "The Man from Heaven in Paul's Letter to the Philippians." In *The Future of Early Christianity: Essays in Honor of Helmut Koester*, edited by Birger A. Pearson, 329–36. Minneapolis: Fortress Press, 1991.

Meilaender, Gilbert. *Neither Beast nor God: The Dignity of the Human Person.* New York: Encounter Books, 2009.

Merrill, Eugene H. *Everlasting Dominion: A Theology of the Old Testament*. Nashville: Broadman & Holman, 2006.

Middleton, J. Richard. *The Liberating Image: The Imago Dei in Genesis 1*. Grand Rapids: Brazos Press, 2005.

Mitchell, Alan C. "The Use of πρέπειν and Rhetorical Propriety in Hebrews 2:10." *The Catholic Biblical Quarterly* 54, no. 4 (October 1992): 681–701.

Mitchell, Louis J. "Jonathan Edwards on the Experience of Beauty." *Theology Matters* 9, no. 6 (November/December 2003): 6–9.

———. "The Theological Aesthetics of Jonathan Edwards." *Theology Today* 64 (2007): 36–46.

Moo, Douglas J. *The Epistle to the Romans*. New International Commentary of the New Testament. Grand Rapids: Eerdmans, 1996.

———. "Paul on Hell." In *Hell Under Fire*, edited by Christopher W. Morgan and Robert A. Peterson, 92–109. Grand Rapids: Zondervan, 2004.

Moreland, J. P. and Scott B. Rae. *Body and Soul: Human Nature and the Crisis in Ethics*. Downers Grove, IL: InterVarsity Press, 2000.

Morgan, Christopher W. "Toward a Theology of the Glory of God." In *The Glory of God*, edited by Christopher W. Morgan and Robert A. Peterson, 153–87. Wheaton, IL: Crossway, 2010.

Morris, Leon. *The Gospel according to John*. Revised Edition. New International Commentary of the New Testament. Grand Rapids: Eerdmans, 1995.

Moses, A. D. A. *Matthew's Transfiguration Story and Jewish-Christian Controversy*. Journal for the Study of the New Testament: Supplement Series 122. Sheffield, England: Sheffield Academic Press, 1996.

Mounce, William D. *Pastoral Epistles*. Word Biblical Commentary 46. Waco, TX: Word, 2000.

Muller, Richard A. *Dictionary of Latin and Greek Theological Terms: Drawn Principally from Protestant Scholastic Theology*. Grand Rapids: Baker Book House, 1985.

———. *Post-Reformation Reformed Dogmatics: The Rise and Development of Reformed Orthodoxy, ca. 1520–1725*. 4 vols. Grand Rapids: Baker Academic, 2003.

Murphy, Francesca Aran. *Christ the Form of Beauty: A Study in Theology and Literature*. Edinburgh: T&T Clark, 1995.

Murray, John. *Redemption Accomplished and Applied*. Grand Rapids: Eerdmans, 1955.

———. *Collected Writings of John Murray*. Vol. 2, *Select Lectures in Systematic Theology*. Edinburgh: Banner of Truth Trust, 1977.

Neusner, Jacob. *The Incarnation of God: The Character of Divinity in Formative Judaism*. Philadelphia: Fortress Press, 1988.

Newbigin, Lesslie. *The Household of God: Lectures on the Nature of the Church*. New York: Friendship Press, 1954.

Nicole, Emile. "Atonement in the Pentateuch." In *The Glory of the Atonement: Biblical, Historical and Practical Perspectives: Essays in Honor of Roger Nicole*, edited by

Charles E. Hill and Frank A. James III, 35–50. Downers Grove, IL: InterVarsity Press, 2004.

Niskanen, Paul. "The Poetics of Adam: The Creation of אדם in the Image of אלהים." *Journal of Biblical Literature* 128, no. 3 (2009): 417–36.

Nouwen, Henri J. M. *The Return of the Prodigal Son: A Story of Homecoming.* New York: Doubleday, 1994.

Oakes, Edward T. *Pattern of Redemption: The Theology of Hans Urs von Balthasar.* New York: Continuum, 1994.

———. "Hans Urs von Balthasar." In *The Oxford Companion to Christian Thought,* edited by Adrian Hastings, Alistair Mason, and Hugh Pyper, 743–45. Oxford: Oxford University Press, 2000.

O'Brien, Peter T. *The Epistle to the Philippians: A Commentary on the Greek Text.* The New International Greek Testament Commentary. Grand Rapids: Eerdmans, 1991.

———. *The Letter to the Ephesians.* Pillar New Testament Commentary. Grand Rapids: Eerdmans, 1999.

———. *The Letter to the Hebrews.* Pillar New Testament Commentary. Grand Rapids: Eerdmans, 2010.

Olson, Robert C. *The Gospel as the Revelation of God's Righteousness: Paul's Use of Isaiah in Romans 1:1–3:26.* Wissenschaftliche Untersuchungen zum Neuen Testament 2/428. Tübingen: Mohr Siebeck, 2016.

Orsi, Francesco. *Value Theory.* New York: Bloomsbury Academic, 2015.

Osborn, Eric. *Irenaeus of Lyons.* Cambridge: Cambridge University Press, 2001.

Oswalt, John N. *The Book of Isaiah, Chapters 1–39.* The New International Commentary on the Old Testament. Grand Rapids: Eerdmans, 1986.

———. *Isaiah.* NIV Application Commentary. Grand Rapids: Zondervan, 2003.

Nichols, Aidan. *Redeeming Beauty: Soundings in Sacral Aesthetics.* Aldershot, Hants, England: Ashgate, 2007.

Noll, Mark. *The Scandal of the Evangelical Mind.* Grand Rapids: Eerdmans, 1994.

Pao, David W. *Acts and the Isaianic New Exodus.* Eugene, OR: Wipf & Stock, 2016.

Pao, David W. and Eckhard J. Schnabel. "Luke." In *Commentary on the New Testament Use of the Old Testament,* edited by G. K. Beale and D. A. Carson, 251–414. Grand Rapids: Baker Academic, 2007.

Pate, C. Marvin. *The Glory of Adam and the Afflictions of the Righteous: Pauline Suffering in Context.* Lewiston, NY: Mellen Biblical Press, 1993.

Pattison, Bonnie. "Splendor and Beauty in Calvin's Ecclesiology: The Aesthetic and Ethical Implications of Calvin's Christology for the Spiritual Worship of the Church." Paper presented at the Sixteenth Century Society Conference, New Orleans, LA, October 16, 2014.

Paul, Shalom M. "Adoption Formulae: A Study of Cuneiform and Biblical Legal Clauses." *Maarav* 2, no. 2 (1979–80): 173–85.

Peters, George W. *A Biblical Theology of Missions*. Chicago: Moody Press, 1972.

Peterson, David. *Possessed by God: A New Testament Theology of Sanctification and Holiness*. Grand Rapids: Eerdmans, 1995.

Postell, Seth D. *Adam and Israel: Genesis 1–3 as the Introduction to the Torah and Tanakh*. Eugene, OR: Pickwick Publications, 2011.

Rad, Gerhard Von. *Old Testament Theology*. Vol. 1, *The Theology of Israel's Historical Traditions*. Translated by D. M. G. Stalker. New York: Harper & Row, 1962.

——. *Genesis: A Commentary*. Rev. ed. Philadelphia: Westminster Press, 1972.

Rae, Murray A. "The Baptism of Christ." In *The Person of Christ*, edited by Stephen R. Holmes and Murray A. Rae, 121–37. London: T&T Clark, 2005.

Ramm, Bernard. "Angels." In *Basic Christian Doctrines*, edited by Carl F. H. Henry, 63–69. New York: Holt, Rinehart and Winston, 1962.

——. *Them He Glorified: A Systematic Study of the Doctrine of Glorification*. Grand Rapids: Eerdmans, 1963.

Ramsey, Arthur Michael. *The Glory of God and the Transfiguration of Christ*. London: Darton, Longman & Todd, 1967.

Reymond, Robert L. *A New Systematic Theology of the Christian Faith*. 2nd ed. Nashville: Thomas Nelson, 1998.

Rogers, Katherin A. *The Anselmian Approach to God and Creation*. Lewiston, NY: Edwin Mellen Press, 1997.

Rosner, B. S. "Biblical Theology." In *New Dictionary of Biblical Theology*, edited by T. D. Alexander and B. S. Rosner, 3–11. Downers Grove, IL: InterVarsity, 2000.

Ross, James. "Religious Language." In *Philosophy of Religion: A Guide to the Subject*, edited by Brian Davies, 106–35. Washington, DC: Georgetown University Press, 1998.

Ryken, Leland. "In the Beginning, God Created." In *The Christian Imagination: Essays on Literature and the Arts*, edited by Leland Ryken, 55–67. Grand Rapids: Baker Book House, 1981.

Sammon, Brendan Thomas. *The God Who Is Beauty: Beauty as a Divine Name in Thomas Aquinas and Dionysius the Areopagite*. Eugene, OR: Pickwick Publications, 2013.

Samra, James G. *Being Conformed to Christ in Community*. London: T&T Clark, 2006.

Schlatter, Adolf. *Romans: The Righteousness of God*. Translated by Siegfried S. Schatzmann. Peabody, MA: Hendrickson Publishers, 1995.

——. *The History of the Christ: The Foundation for New Testament Theology*. Translated by Andreas J. Köstenberger. Grand Rapids: Baker Books, 1997.

Schneider, J. σχῆμα. *TDNT* 7:954–56.

Schüle, Andreas. "Made in the 'Image of God': The Concepts of Divine Images in Gen 1–3." *Zeitschrift für die alttestamentliche Wissenschaft* 117 (2005): 1–20.

Scruton, Roger. *Beauty*. Oxford: Oxford University Press, 2009.

Sklar, Jay. *Sin, Impurity, Sacrifice, Atonement: The Priestly Conceptions*. Sheffield: Sheffield Phoenix Press, 2005.

Smith, Julien. *Christ the Ideal King: Cultural Context, Rhetorical Strategy, and the Power of Divine Monarchy in Ephesians.* Wissenschaftliche Untersuchungen zum Neuen Testament 2/313. Tübingen: Mohr Siebeck, 2011.

Sprinkle, Preston, ed. *Four Views on Hell.* 2nd ed. Grand Rapids: Zondervan, 2016.

Steenberg, Matthew C. "Children in Paradise: Adam and Eve as "Infants" in Irenaeus of Lyons." *Journal of Early Christian Studies* 12, no. 1 (2004): 1–22.

———. "Two-Natured Man: An Anthropology of Transfiguration." *Pro Ecclesia* 14, no. 4 (Fall 2005): 413–32.

———. *Of God and Man: Theology as Anthropology from Irenaeus to Athanasius.* London: T&T Clark, 2009.

Stek, John H. "What Says the Scripture?" In *Portraits of Creation: Biblical and Scientific Perspectives on the World's Formation,* edited by Howard J. Van Till, Robert E. Snow, John H. Stek, and Davis A. Young, 203–65. Grand Rapids: Eerdmans, 1990.

Stephens, Mark B. *Annihilation or Renewal?: The Meaning and Function of New Creation in the Book of Revelation.* Tübingen: Mohr Siebeck, 2011.

Stump, Eleonore. "Dante's Hell, Aquinas's Moral Theory, and the Love of God." *Canadian Journal of Philosophy* 16, no. 2 (June 1986): 181–98.

———. "Simplicity." In *A Companion to Philosophy of Religion,* 2nd ed., edited by Charles Taliaferro, Paul Draper, and Philip L. Quinn, 270–77. Malden, MA: Wiley-Blackwell, 2010.

Sweeney, Douglas A. *Edwards the Exegete: Biblical Interpretation and Anglo-Protestant Culture on the Edge of the Enlightenment.* New York: Oxford University Press, 2016.

Tatarkiewicz, Wladyslaw. *History of Aesthetics.* Vols. 1–3. New York: Continuum, 2005.

Thompson, Thomas R. "Nineteenth-Century Kenotic Christology: The Waxing, Waning, and Weighing of a Quest for a Coherent Orthodoxy." In *Exploring Kenotic Christology: The Self-Emptying of God,* edited by C. Stephen Evans, 74–111. Oxford: Oxford University Press, 2006.

Thompson, James W. *Moral Formation according to Paul: The Context and Coherence of Pauline Ethics.* Grand Rapids: Eerdmans, 2011.

———. *The Church according to Paul: Rediscovering the Community Conformed to Christ.* Grand Rapids: Baker Academic, 2014.

Thompson, Marianne Meye. *Colossians and Philemon.* Grand Rapids: Eerdmans, 2005.

Tipton, Lane G. "Christology in Colossians 1:15–20 and Hebrews 1:1–4: An Exercise in Biblico-Systematic Theology." In *Resurrection and Eschatology: Essays in Honor of Richard B. Gaffin Jr.,* edited by Lane G. Tipton and Jeffrey C. Waddington, 177–202. Phillipsburg, NJ: P&R Publishing, 2008.

Treat, Jeremy R. "Exaltation in and through Humiliation: Rethinking the States of Christ." In *Christology, Ancient and Modern: Explorations in Constructive Dogmatics,* edited by Oliver D. Crisp and Fred Sanders, 96–114. Grand Rapids: Zondervan, 2013.

Turretin, Francis. *Institutes of Elenctic Theology*. 3 Vols. Edited by James T. Dennison Jr. Translated by George Musgrave Giger. Phillipsburg, NJ: P&R Publishing, 1992–1997.

VanDrunen, David. *God's Glory Alone: The Majestic Heart of Christian Faith and Life*. Grand Rapids: Zondervan, 2015.

Vanhoozer, Kevin J. "Human Being, Individual and Social." In *Cambridge Companion to Christian Doctrine*, edited by Colin E. Gunton, 158–88. Cambridge: Cambridge University Press, 1997.

———. *The Drama of Doctrine: A Canonical-Linguistic Approach to Christian Theology*. Louisville: Westminster John Knox Press, 2005.

———. *Remythologizing Theology: Divine Action, Passion, and Authorship*. Cambridge: Cambridge University Press, 2010.

———. "Love's Wisdom: The Authority of Scripture's Form and Content for Faith's Understanding and Theological Judgment." *Journal of Reformed Theology* 5, no. 3 (January 2011): 247–75.

———. "Theological Commentary and 'The Voice from Heaven': Exegesis, Ontology, and the Travail of Biblical Interpretation." In *On the Writing of New Testament Commentaries: Festschrift for Grant R. Osbourne on the Occasion of his 70th Birthday*, edited by Stanley E. Porter and Eckhard J. Schnabel, 269–98. Boston: Brill, 2013.

———. *Faith Speaking Understanding: Performing the Drama of Doctrine*. Louisville: Westminster John Knox Press, 2014.

Vanhoozer, Kevin J. and Owen Strachan. *The Pastor as Public Theologian: Reclaiming a Lost Vision*. Grand Rapids: Baker Academic, 2015.

Van Til, Cornelius. "Nature of Scripture." In *The Infallible Word: A Symposium by the Members of the Faculty of Westminster Theological Seminary*, 3rd rev., edited by N. B. Stonehouse and Paul Woolley, 263–301. Phillipsburg, NJ: P&R Publishing, 2003.

Venema, Cornelis P. *The Promise of the Future*. Edinburgh: Banner of Truth Trust, 2000.

Viladesau, Richard. *Theology and the Arts: Encountering God through Music, Art, and Rhetoric*. New York: Paulist Press, 2000.

Vos, Geerhardus. *Biblical Theology: Old and New Testaments*. Edinburgh: Banner of Truth Trust, 1975.

———. *The Eschatology of the Old Testament*. Edited by James T. Dennison Jr. Phillipsburg, NJ: P&R Publishing, 2001.

Walton, John H. *Genesis 1 as Ancient Cosmology*. Winona Lake, IN: Eisenbrauns, 2011.

Warry, J. G. *Greek Aesthetic Theory: A Study of Callistic and Aesthetic Concepts in the Works of Plato and Aristotle*. New York: Barnes & Noble, 1962.

Watson, Francis. *Text and Truth: Redefining Biblical Theology*. Grand Rapids: Eerdmans, 1997.

Watts, Rikki E. *Isaiah's New Exodus in Mark*. Grand Rapids: Baker Academic, 2000.

———. "On the Edge of the Millennium: Making Sense of Genesis 1." In *Living in the LambLight: Christianity and Contemporary Challenges to the Gospel*, edited by Hans Boersma, 129-51. Vancouver: Regent College Publishing, 2001.

———. "The New Exodus/New Creational Restoration of the Image of God." In *What Does It Mean to Be Saved?: Broadening Evangelical Horizons on Salvation*, edited by John G. Stackhouse Jr., 15-41. Grand Rapids: Baker Academic, 2002.

———. "Mark." In *Commentary on the New Testament Use of the Old Testament*, edited by G. K. Beale and D. A. Carson, 111-249. Grand Rapids: Baker Academic, 2007.

Webb, Stephen H. *The Divine Voice: Christian Proclamation and the Theology of Sound.* Grand Rapids: Brazos Press, 2004.

Webster, John. *Confessing God: Essays in Christian Dogmatics II.* London: T&T Clark, 2005.

———. "God's Perfect Life." In *God's Life in Trinity*, edited by Miroslav Volf and Michael Welker, 143-52. Minneapolis: Fortress Press, 2006.

———. "Theologies of Retrieval." In *The Oxford Handbook of Systematic Theology*, edited by John Webster, Kathryn Tanner, and Iain Torrance, 583-99. Oxford: Oxford University Press, 2009.

———. "Trinity and Creation." *International Journal of Systematic Theology* 12, no. 1 (January 2010): 4-19.

Welke, Michael, ed. *The Depth of the Human Person: A Multidisciplinary Approach.* Grand Rapids: Eerdmans, 2014.

Wellum, Stephen J. *God the Son Incarnate: The Doctrine of Christ.* Wheaton, IL: Crossway, 2016.

Wenham, Gordon J. *Genesis 1-15.* Word Biblical Commentary 1. Waco, TX: Word, 1987.

———. "Sanctuary Symbolism in the Garden of Eden Story." In *"I Studied Inscriptions from Before the Flood": Ancient Near Eastern, Literary, and Linguistic Approaches to Genesis 1-11*, edited by R. S. Hess and D. Tsumura, 399-404. Sources for Biblical and Theological Study 4. Winona Lake, IN: Eisenbrauns, 1994.

Wenham, John. *The Enigma of Evil: Can We Believe in the Goodness of God?* Grand Rapids: Zondervan, 1985.

West, Ryan and Adam C. Pelser. "Perceiving God through Natural Beauty." *Faith and Philosophy* 32, no. 3 (July 2015): 293-312.

Williams, Michael D. "First Calling: The *Imago Dei* and the Order of Creation—Part II." *Presbyterion* 39 (Fall 2013): 75-97.

Wilson, Gerald H. "King, Messiah, and the Reign of God: Revisiting the Royal Psalms and the Shape of the Psalter." In *The Book of Psalms: Composition and Reception*, edited by Peter W. Flint and Patrick D. Miller Jr., 391-406. Boston: Brill Academic, 2005.

Wilson, R. Ward and Craig L. Blomberg. "The Image of God in Humanity: A Biblical Psychological Perspective." *Themelios* 18 (April 1993): 8-15.

Witsius, Herman. *The Economy of the Covenants Between God and Man: Comprehending a Complete Body of Divinity*. 2 vols. Translated by William Crookshank. Escondido, CA: Den Dulk Christian Foundation, 1990.

———. *Sacred Dissertations on What Is Commonly Called the Apostles' Creed*. 2 Volumes. Translated by Donald Fraser. Escondido, CA: The den Dulk Christian Foundation, 1993.

Wolterstorff, Nicholas. *Art in Action: Toward a Christian Aesthetic*. Grand Rapids: Eerdmans, 1980.

———. *Educating for Shalom: Essays on Christian Higher Education*. Edited by Clarence W. Joldersma and Gloria Goris Stronks. Grand Rapids: Eerdmans, 2004.

———. "Is There Justice in the Trinity?" In *God's Life in Trinity*, edited by Miroslav Volf and Michael Welker, 177–87. Minneapolis: Fortress Press, 2006.

Wright, Christopher J. H. *Knowing Jesus through the Old Testament*. Downers Grove, IL: InterVarsity Press, 1992.

———. *Old Testament Ethics for the People of God*. Downers Grove, IL: InterVarsity Press, 2004.

———. *The Mission of God: Unlocking the Bible's Grand Narrative*. Downers Grove, IL: IVP Academic, 2006.

Wright, N. T. *Jesus and the Victory of God*. Minneapolis: Fortress Press, 1996.

———. *The Challenge of Jesus: Rediscovering Who Jesus Was and Is*. Downers Grove, IL: InterVarsity Press, 1999.

———. *The Resurrection of the Son of God*. Minneapolis: Fortress Press, 2003.

———. *Simply Christian: Why Christianity Makes Sense*. San Francisco: HarperSanFrancisco, 2006.

Wright, Stephen John. *Dogmatic Aesthetics: A Theology of Beauty in Dialogue with Robert W. Jenson*. Minneapolis: Fortress Press, 2014.

Wynne, Jeremy J. *Wrath among the Perfections of God's Life*. London: T&T Clark, 2010.

Zachman, Randall C. *Image and Word in the Theology of John Calvin*. Notre Dame, IN: University of Notre Dame Press, 2007.

Zaibert, Leo. "The Fitting, the Deserving, and the Beautiful." *Journal of Moral Philosophy* 3, no. 3 (November 2006): 331–50.

Zaleski, Carol. "In Defense of Immortality." Paper presented at the Harvard Divinity School Ingersoll Lecture, Cambridge, MA, March 16, 2000.

Zemach, Eddy M. *Real Beauty*. University Park, PA: Pennsylvania State University Press, 2004.

Scripture Index

Subject Index